MEN
OF THE
RED
BERET

With best wishes

Max Arthur

MEN
OF THE
RED
BERET

Airborne Forces 1940-1990

MAX ARTHUR

HUTCHINSON
London Sydney Auckland Johannesburg

This book is dedicated
to all who have served
or been involved with
the Airborne Forces

© Max Arthur 1990

The right of Max Arthur to be identified as Author of this
work has been asserted by Max Arthur in accordance with the
Copyright, Designs and Patent Act, 1988

This edition first published in 1990 by Hutchinson

Century Hutchinson Ltd
20 Vauxhall Bridge Road, London SW1V 2SA

Century Hutchinson Australia (Pty) Ltd
20 Alfred Street, Milsons Point, Sydney NSW 2061, Australia

Century Hutchinson New Zealand Limited
PO Box 40–086, Glenfield, Auckland 10, New Zealand

Century Hutchinson South Africa (Pty) Ltd
PO Box 337, Bergvlei, 2012 South Africa

British Library Cataloguing in Publication Data
Arthur, Max, *1939–*
Men of the red beret.
1. Great Britain. Army. Parachute Regiment, history
I. Title
356.1660 941

ISBN 0–09–173931–4

Photoset by Speedset Ltd, Ellesmere Port

Printed and bound in Great Britain by
Butler & Tanner Ltd, Frome and London

Contents

Epigraph

When an enthusiastic horseman said that there was no delight on earth like that which is to be found on horseback there were neither aircraft nor parachutes. If a canter on a good horse is a wonderful sensation, it is one that cannot be compared with that of soaring into the air with the terrific but controlled power of an aircraft.

Greater than either, however, is the almost superhuman sensation of the parachute jump. It alone compresses into the space of seconds feelings of concentrated energy, tenseness and abandon; it alone demands a continual and unconditional readiness to risk one's life. Therefore the parachutist experiences the most exalted feelings of which human beings are capable, namely that of victory over one's self. For us parachutists, the words of the poet, who said that unless you stake your life you will never win it, is no empty phrase.

General-Leutnant Bruno Brauer
German Parachute Regiment

Men of the Red Beret has been written to coincide with the fiftieth anniversary of Airborne Forces and is the result of extensive interviews with the men who served during this period. The major operations since 1940 are recalled in their own words and provide a unique record of Airborne Forces in action.

Through their personal accounts, be it of North Africa, Normandy, Arnhem, Aden, Northern Ireland or the Falklands Campaign, we see how their spirit remains indomitable and their humour irrepressible.

I am also delighted to see that Max Arthur has chosen to include accounts of those who were closely involved with Airborne Forces, not least the RAF, the WAAF parachute packers, the FANYs and Kate ter Horst who, along with so many of the Dutch, sacrificed so much for those who fought at Arnhem. They are all an integral part of the Airborne family and rightly have their place in this very fine book.

Colonel-in-Chief The Parachute Regiment
HRH The Prince of Wales

List of Illustrations

MAPS

PLATES

Section One: Jumping from a Whitley bomber; showing off a new cushioned boot; adjusting a Corporal's harness. Aerial photograph of Bruneval; discussing a successful mission. 1st Parachute Battalion 1942; at Kowshock farm in Tunis. Luftwaffe admire Lt Rendell's shooting; Airlanding Brigade's artwork on a glider.

Section Two: Crash-landed gliders by Caen Canal; Dutch civilians welcome army of Liberation. Men of 1st Airborne Division; Major Bruce Dawson, wounded; a Sturmgeshütz III; two of the Arnhem fatalities. RAF photograph of Arnhem bridge; 'a damn good run for their money'. Fighting in Oosterbeek; 'anyone who could walk had to walk'; gliders ready for the Rhine Crossing.

Section Three: October 1944 campaign against ELAS troops; occupying the Acropolis; street fighting in Athens. De-crating a jeep, El Gamil; departing for Borneo. Terrorist suspects, Palestine; arresting a priest in Cyprus; in the Malayan jungle. 3rd Battalion under fire in the Radfan.

Section Four: Comforting a student after bomb blast; Catholic tea ladies; 2nd Battalion patrolling; Warrenpoint. Leaving for the Falklands; disembarking HMS *Intrepid*, San Carlos. Tending the wounded; advance to Furze Bush Pass. Celebrating the Argentinian surrender; the next generation.

Preface

MEN OF THE RED BERET is based on interviews with those who have served or are at present serving with the Airborne Forces. The majority of the accounts are from members of The Parachute Regiment. However men of the Airlanding Brigades, the 1st Polish Parachute Brigade, the 1st Canadian Parachute Battalion, the RAF, women from the WAAF, the FANYs and that fine Dutch lady, Kate ter Horst, tell of their involvement with the Airborne Forces.

I did not set out to write the history of the Airborne Forces; rather I sought to capture something of the spirit of these men and those who have worked with them both in the early days and in action.

The majority of accounts have been taken from taped interviews. These interviews were transcribed, typed and edited. A typed account was then sent to the person interviewed who was asked to correct any errors that might have crept in and also to add more material if they wished. Wherever possible the historical accuracy of these accounts has been checked, but errors of time, places and names may still be present. Apart from the occasional interlinking sentence, these accounts are entirely in their own words. The rank given at the start of each account is that held at the time.

After a brief account of the early days of parachuting and the formation of No. 2 Commando I have given an outline of the training and the operations undergone until the 1st Parachute Brigade Group embarked for North Africa. From then on the book is solely based on first-person accounts and though it concludes with the Falklands Campaign, the Northern Ireland section continues up to the present day.

Each account is a chapter in itself, a chapter in the life of the person who related it. I have arranged these accounts within the context of the operation in which he or she was involved and because these are personal experiences, not cold histories, the order will undoubtedly be imperfect. Many of these accounts start in the United Kingdom and go on until they return. Others begin in the aircraft, glider or at the start line – some select the most affecting moments. This is particularly the case in the accounts of

Northern Ireland, where I have also for reasons of security excluded the names of the men involved.

Throughout the writing of this book it has been my privilege to meet so many fine men and women. I believe their words not only provide a unique chronicle of the many facets of the Airborne Forces in action, and in particular The Parachute Regiment, but also illustrate their inimitable and indomitable character. These are their words – I have been but a catalyst.

Max Arthur
London
March 1990

In the Beginning

One and a half centuries separate the first successful parachute drop and the founding of the Parachute Regiment. In 1784 Jean-Pierre Blanchard jumped successfully from a hot air balloon in France. It was certainly not the British who first led the field; our earliest memorable pioneer was the aeronautical enthusiast Robert Cocking, who, in 1837, persuaded the balloonist Charles Green to drop him from a balloon at a height of 5,000 feet over Vauxhall Gardens in London. Cocking's home-made parachute disintegrated immediately and the intrepid pioneer was killed. Nevertheless, experimental parachuting had begun.

It was with the invention of aeroplanes that the potential of parachuting as a means of rescue in emergency as well as a sporting stunt was first seriously considered. Before long, military applications became conceivable. At Saint Louis in 1912 Captain Albert Berry of the United States Army made the first successful jump from an aeroplane. In 1914 the first British aeroplane parachutist, William Newell, dropped from a biplane at Hendon. In 1916 it was possible to deliver supplies by parachute to General Townshend's beleaguered force at Kut-al-Amara in Mesopotamia, and in 1919 Sylvia Boyden, the first British female parachutist, made a successful descent at Cricklewood. However, despite these advances, parachutes were not issued to air crew in World War I. It was feared that this would encourage the men to jump as soon as the going got rough and that battles would be lost as a result.

The spectacular developments in the early years of parachuting were the fruit of careful design, painstaking production, and skilful manufacture of the parachute itself, in the United States, in Britain and in Italy. In 1910 a railway engineer named Everard Calvert devised the 'Guardian Angel' parachute, and in 1915 a firm in the Edgware Road in London entered into production. Meanwhile, a team of Americans were conducting experiments in manufacture and operation at McCook flying field in Ohio; among them Leslie Leroy Irvin, who jumped in 1919 from a biplane at 1,500 feet (and broke his leg). His 'Irvin' parachute superseded the 'Angel' in 1925, and he set up a production line at Letchworth in Hertfordshire in 1926. In 1934

Raymond Quilter and James Gregory established the GQ Parachute Company in an old skating rink at Woking in Surrey. Between them Irvins and GQ designed the 'X type', only about 25lb, with a silk or rayon canopy of 28-foot diameter, 28 rigging lines, a twelve-and-a-half foot static line and a 22-inch hole at the top. By 1936 the Italian air force, who had been trying out an alternative 'Salvatore' parachute, also opened by static line, were ready to drop supplies to forward troops in their Abyssinian campaign.

But it was back in 1918 that Colonel William Mitchell of the American Expeditionary Force in Europe put a remarkable plan to the General Staff, namely to drop a division of troops by parachute behind the German front; an operation which, in his view, if it was feasible, could have overcome the immovable confrontation of four years of trench warfare. There was no way of implementing such a plan at the time. But it was a seminal strategic idea, and in due course the Russian, Italian and German military authorities took to it.

In 1936 the Soviet Red Army surprised observers by parachuting 1,500 troops near Minsk. 'If I had not witnessed the descents,' the British General Wavell reported to the War Office, 'I could not have believed such an operation possible.' The Russians repeated the exercise a couple of years later, dropping 1,200 men, 150 machine-guns and 18 light field-guns, a substantial force of infantry and artillery, ready for battle in eight minutes.

The Germans were on the warpath too. An air-landing training school was opened in 1936 at Stendal, and in 1937 a company of Fallschirmjaeger was dropped in the Fuehrer's presence. General Kurt Student was appointed to the command of a new airlanding corps, and in July 1939 a battalion, 1,000 strong, landed by parachute on a single dropping zone. The 7th Fliegerdivision, comprising nine airborne and two parachute battalions, was ready for World War II.

In April 1940, after the first quiet months of that war, German parachute detachments were committed to action in Denmark and Norway. In May, in the Blitzkrieg into the Low Countries and France, a parachute and glider descent on top of the Belgian fortress of Eban Emael on the Lower Rhine immediately overwhelmed the defence: 4,000 parachute troops were deployed in Holland, backed by 12,000 airborne infantry: very soon Hitler was in Paris.

Only a year later, in May 1941, the Fliegerdivision invaded Crete in the biggest airborne operation ever undertaken with an army of some 22,000 men transported in 500 Junkers Ju 52s and 75 gliders. They defeated a British force of 30,000 troops but lost 4,000 lives and 170 transport aircraft in the process. The heavy casualties sustained in Crete led Hitler to suspend further major airborne operations.

In June 1940, when the Germans had overrun Poland, Denmark, Norway, Holland, Belgium and France and chased the British out of Europe, there were no airborne forces in Britain. A year later, when the Germans landed that massive airborne force in Crete, there was a single unit of some 400 parachute soldiers. That was No. 2 (Parachute) Commando, located in Knutsford and Congleton.

On 22 June 1940 Winston Churchill, newly appointed Prime Minister, addressed a minute to General Sir Hastings Ismay of the Cabinet War Secretariat. 'We ought to have a corps,' he wrote 'of at least 5,000 parachute troops. I hear something is being done already to form such a corps, but only, I believe, on a very small scale.'

The irregular, colourful and eccentric bunch of volunteers so hastily assembled in June were a modest British answer to the German Air Army. Ground training began on 8 July. Parachuting started on 13 July, when the first descent was made by the 'pull off' method, jumping from the rear of the plane. Major Peter Cleasby-Thompson, who began parachuting at Ringway that August, describes the experience. 'My God, that first jump. We crawled into the fuselage of a Whitley named "the Elephant", and so to the rear turret, where the victim squatted in prayer and trepidation gripping a cross-bar. You pulled the ripcord and the silk and rigging lines niggled at your back. Like the crack of a hunting whip, you were yanked from the perch, and saw the aircraft tail departing below as you started the pendulum swing towards terra firma. It usually worked.'

A new technique was, meanwhile, being tested by the Central Landing Establishment. The Whitley had a hole in its under-belly. It was now possible in ten seconds to despatch from a bomber flying at about 100 mph a 'stick' of eight parachutists, dropping one by one through a three-foot circular aperture in the floor of the fuselage which formerly housed the ventral turret. At wind speeds of up to 15 knots, eight soldiers, each armed with a carbine or sub-machine-gun, 120 rounds of ammunition and a couple of hand grenades, could be landed within a stretch of about 400 yards, heavier equipment being dropped in separate containers. Each man's parachute pack was attached by 'static line' to a cable fixed in the fuselage. When a man jumped the twelve-foot line became taut and tore the cover from the packed canopy, which was automatically shaken open. Despite these developments, jumping was not a comfortable business. Major Miles Whitelock describes his first jump from the redesigned Whitley.

I had never been in an aeroplane, let alone jumped out of one, so it was with a sense of awe, bewilderment and apprehension that I climbed into the fuselage of a long, dark, noisy smelly Whitley bomber. This lumbering aircraft had been nicknamed the coffin bomber and to us novitiates, it felt like it. It took off for a seven-minute flight to Tatton Park and circled while we looked down through the round hole in the bottom of the aircraft at the scenery below. The first to go was ordered to swing his legs over the hole and sat with his bottom on the side and his eyes averted to watch the red and green light and the compelling hand of the instructor raised aloft. At this stage the light was red, and one waited tensely for a few seconds, which seemed an eternity. Suddenly the light went green, the instructor's hand went down with a yell of 'Go' and through the hole went our first intrepid trainee volunteer. Soon it was my turn. I was mesmerized by the light and by my instructor's hand. The noise of the aircraft was deafening, the fumes from its engines almost overpowering. The plane slowly circled the dropping zone. I threw my legs over the hole and watched – green light, down the hand 'Go' and through the hole I jumped into space and possible oblivion. Almost before I could draw breath, I felt a jerk on my back, and, as if by magic, I saw above me the reassuring canopy of silk opened out and I began to float gently to earth. The relief was great, not only to be safe, but to be free from the noise, the fumes and the general rigours of the coffin-shaped aeroplane that I just saw disappearing above me. In fact, one of my first sensations was one of peace. I was just beginning to enjoy myself, looking at the view when I realized to my concern that I was fast approaching earth. I could discern a number of figures on the dropping zone, including the reassuring figures of the battalion's doctor and the attractive FANY ambulance driver and her ambulance. Someone shouted up at me 'Keep your feet together – feet together, you clot.' I did so and bumped the ground without injury. The first jump was over.

Within two months of those beginnings 21 officers and 132 other ranks of the Commando completed the course of instruction. Thirty had jibbed at this novel adventure and were returned to their parent units. On the one hundred and thirty-sixth jump at Ringway the parachute of Driver Evans (RASC) failed to open – a 'Roman candle'. That was the first fatal casualty. Something had gone wrong. The two troops under training at the airfield at the time were transferred for a month to Torcastle, a Highland hide near Fort William, for instruction in fieldcraft, explosives and unarmed combat.

Training was strenuous, and the rain merciless. In the meantime parachute design and in particular the strength of the static line were checked and modified. In the middle of August parachuting was resumed at Ringway.

On 3 December, in the presence of a prestigious gathering of the 'top brass', 32 men of the battalion were dropped on Salisbury Plain from two Whitley bombers, flying from Old Sarum. To demonstrate progress and potential Peter Cleasby-Thompson's B Troop carried out a surprise attack on the village of Shrewton, which was heavily defended by troops of Southern Command. It was, as he described the occasion, 'a cold dawn, pale fuselage lights and green faces, joy, pride, conceit, anxiety. On, on to the objective. Guerrilla tactics, seize an unguarded car, away. Bang, bang, blank cartridges, thunderflashes. The bridge is ours. What to do with the bloody car? Whose is it anyway? A suitcase in the back. "Olav, Crown Prince of Norway". Bowler hat? Court martial?' Happily it was not so, for Prince Olav knew good soldiers when he saw them. When the Commando's flag was flying from the church tower and the Prince, together with the Commander-in-Chief Home Forces, repaired to base at the Shrewton pub, His Royal Highness sent the landlady with a tray of beer and his Norwegian compliments to Harry Pexton and his mates on post outside. The exercise ended at Cleasby-Thompson's club in Pall Mall at a party attended by Prince Olav, by the Crown Prince of the Netherlands and, as he records 'by the officers of B Troop clean and slightly oiled'.

By the end of 1940 about 500 soldiers had done their qualifying jumps. Initial parachute training at that stage entailed five jumps, the first at 800 feet, two more individual jumps at about 500 feet and two jumps in 'stick' at the same height. When trainees had achieved this, 'Wings' badges were issued to them, as well as parachute pay or 'danger money' at four shillings a day for officers and two shillings for other ranks.

At Ringway the Central Landing Establishment was devoted to the development of equipment, parachutes, aircraft, experimental techniques and training apparatus. At its disposal by 1941 were half a dozen obsolescent Armstrong-Whitworth Whitley bombers, some Heath-Robinson-like gymnastic appliances in a hangar, and the park at Tatton Hall, a country house five miles from Ringway outside Knutsford, used as a 'dropping zone'. There was also a dedicated contingent of parachute packers of the Women's Auxiliary Air Force, and an ambulance van, driven by the actress Cicily Paget-Bowman of the First-Aid Nursing Yeomanry.

Recruits were first billeted at Benchhill and Gatley, Manchester suburbs close to the airport. Thereafter they joined the battalion quartered at Knutsford and Congleton, where the unit was reorganized into Headquarters and three companies R, S and T. There were of course not nearly enough Whitley aircraft to train the few hundred paratroops now being assembled, to say nothing of the thousands required, and the Bombay bomber, equally suitable for military parachuting, could not be spared by Bomber or Transport Command of the Royal Air Force. Since November, in response to this need, the staff at Ringway had been experimenting with an anti-aircraft barrage balloon, dropping from a basket suspended below it. The balloon, anchored in Tatton Park, a 'bulbous abomination' in Cleasby-Thompson's words, was now brought into service for training, and balloon jumping by men of the battalion, by day and by night, started in April. Descent from a basket quietly swaying in thin air at 600 or 700 feet above the park was found a bit disconcerting, and at first balloon jumps were not keenly sought after. As he swung his legs over the hole in the bottom of the basket, one parachutist padre was overheard saying, 'All my life I have put my faith in God, but, I'm ashamed to say, now I put more faith in the young lady who packed my parachute.'

However, the arrival of that old balloon in Tatton Park made it possible to arrange much more frequent practice jumping, weather only permitting. During the following dreary months of tactical exercises, close-order drill, musketry, field-firing, route-marching and PT, the familiar routine of 'square-bashing' and 'bullshit', parachuting became for many a rather coveted thrill. After first fears were overcome, most officers and men began to vie with one another in getting more and more jumps, and some had soon scored 20 or more. Flying Officer Charles Agate of the training staff at Ringway, credited with 16 jumps in a day and in the end with no less than 1,400 in four years, was the envy and admiration of all.

By the month of June 1941 the Central Landing Establishment had registered 7,000 parachute descents during the first year at Ringway. That achievement was a small beginning towards an eventual grand total of 400,000 jumps by 1945, and 60,000 men (and women) trained to parachute.

In December the battalion, now under Lieutenant Colonel Eric Down, moved to Derbyshire, away from the 'cushy' billets with the kind Knutsford ladies, into the austere world of Nissen huts at Hardwick Hall. There they joined the 2nd and 3rd Battalions of the newly formed 1st Parachute Brigade. Infantry training resumed at once in that grim muddy scene and continued there through a snowy winter. The new battle-drill was introduced: assault courses were constructed, pistol and submachine-gun shooting took place in a quarry in the park, field-firing on Midhope Moor, street-fighting practice in Sheffield, route-marching through the countryside around Shirebrook and Bolsover, and tactical exercise at Heath, Glapwell and other mining villages in the neighbourhood.

At the end of March the battalion moved into smart new brigade barracks at Bulford Camp, on Salisbury Plain, along with the 2nd and 3rd Battalions. Training continued there through the summer of 1942, with platoon and company exercises and battalion manoeuvres across the plain by day and night. A battle course was rigged up in 'Terror Wood' on Beacon Hill above the camp, enlivened by explosive traps, pop-up targets, smoke bombs and thunderflashes.

At about that time, the winged horse Pegasus, ridden by Bellerophon, in the design of the painter Edward Seago, became the badge of Airborne Forces. The now famous maroon berets were chosen by Daphne du Maurier, wife of the divisional commander, Major General Frederick Browning and issued to all ranks of the new Parachute Regiment, who had hitherto worn the miscellaneous caps and badges of their parent units. The 1st Battalion were now distinguished also by green lanyards, and the 2nd and 3rd Battalions by yellow and red respectively.

Meanwhile, by way of recreation during those spring and summer months, whilst Rommel's Afrika Korps were pushing back towards Alamein in Egypt, the battalion took to football, boxing and cross-country running at Bulford, swimming in the river Avon, and a hockey match played in the nude by the 3rd Battalion! Not to mention the occasional carousal in Salisbury and Amesbury. It was in the yard of the Red Lion Hotel in Salisbury that an impromptu rugby match developed one evening, with a lady's hat for a ball. The lady turned out to be the wife of the commanding officer of that same 3rd Battalion. The officers concerned scored ten days' Confined to Barracks.

On 12 July, Lieutenant Colonel Down was transferred to command the 2nd Brigade now in formation, consisting of a new 4th Parachute Battalion of volunteers and of the 7th Cameron Highlanders and 19th Welch Fusiliers converted into parachute units. Airborne Forces were growing fast. Lieutenant Colonel Hill succeeded Lieutenant Colonel Down in command of the 1st Battalion, and Alistair Pearson become second-in-command in his place. The CO decided the men would benefit from a month's realistic field training on Exmoor. After an action-packed month, the battalion's fitness was tested to the limit when they were ordered to march the 110 miles back to Bulford in three very hot days. The implacable Lieutenant Colonel Hill, always in the lead, joined each company in turn, plying his tall thumbstick with grim resolution. 'March you buggers, march.' Someone was heard to mutter in the ranks: 'Here comes that bloody shepherd with his fucking crook.' Even Bulford Camp was a joy to see that afternoon.

Back on Salisbury Plain the next excitement was the introduction of Dakota aircraft to the role of transportation of parachute troops. It was necessary to get used to this new aircraft – and there were casualties while they were relearning – and adapt procedures to jump from the port-side doorway instead of the uncomfortable aperture in the floor of the fuselage. So jumping practice began again at Netheravon, where the battalion met their new American pilots. The gum-chewing, cigar-smoking style was unfamiliar, but delivery on the dropping zone turned out to be accurate and punctual none the less. The new system was clearly an important improvement, for it was now possible to land 18 men, complete with equipment containers, in a single short stick.

One afternoon in early October the whole battalion was paraded on the football pitch at Bulford, fully kitted out, scrubbed and creased and attended by a brass band. Everyone was filled with a sense of expectancy. The commanding officer conducted the drill in person, led officers and sergeants on a last cross-country run and a frenzy of physical jerks on the summit of Beacon Hill. On 16 October the sergeants shaved their heads: as ever, they seemed to know that some new venture was in prospect. On 23 October the divisional commander announced a move overseas at last, destination unspecified. Speculation ranged from Archangel to Africa.

On 30 October 1942 the 1st Parachute Brigade (less 3rd Parachute Battalion, which flew to North Africa) embarked at Glasgow on the liner *Arundel Castle* as part of a mixed force of the First Army. Far out in the Atlantic on 5 November the radio news reported the Eighth Army in pursuit of the Germans from Alamein, and by 8 November it was revealed that the destination of the First Army was North Africa: Operation 'Torch'. The 1st Brigade's training days were over.

CHAPTER ONE
EARLY DAYS

MAJOR TONY HIBBERT, No. 2 Commando

We waded out into the phosphorescent waters of Dunkirk where I and most of my half battery were picked up by a flotilla of launches which ferried us out to a Thames tug. We had been defeated, but they gave us a hero's welcome in Ramsgate. In due course, we reformed at Aberystwyth but since we had no weapons, there was little to do except march up and down the sea front. The only real compensation during this period was the arrival of the Chelsea School of Physical Training for Young Women which had been evacuated to Aberystwyth. These beautiful, healthy girls really kept us on our toes and sometimes even on our knees. But some of us were getting very fed up with being inactive and we started applying to join any unit that looked as if it might have some weapons, and might get us back into the fight again.

I volunteered for No. 2 (Parachute) Commando, and joined it in October 1940. After completing my initial five parachute jumps at Ringway and Tatton Park and getting my wings, I was sent up to Scotland to recruit officers and other ranks for my troop. On the day I got back, in December, they changed the name to 11th Special Air Service Battalion (Parachute Wing). This made little difference to us, and we proceeded with our training, such as it was.

Training was largely based on night attack exercises, weapon training and unarmed combat – sticking knives into the backs of sentries, that sort of thing. We found it exciting, but it probably wasn't very realistic; our commanding officer, Colonel Jackson, was a Tank Corps man. There were very few of us with any experience of commando or special force fighting, and we really weren't sure what we were supposed to be doing. We enjoyed the training, except that nobody was terribly keen on marching. So the fact that you couldn't march far in our specially designed 'shock-absorbing' rubber-soled boots suited us well. I suppose we imagined that marching wouldn't come into our operations – we'd just drop behind the lines and,

1

duty done, we'd be spirited out by some unknown means. We were disabused of these fantasies later.

In those early days nobody knew anything much about parachuting or the use of parachute troops – we had to learn as we went along. Initially the prospect of the parachute jump inspired a certain degree of awe and I suppose fear; the novelty value made it seem more important than it was. If anything went wrong, it could affect morale. So we had to try and find a way of making parachuting seem of less significance. A few of us stirred up a competitive spirit by clocking up as many jumps as we could; one night I did a balloon jump in my mess kit, complete with spurs – I was going to a mess night dinner and had to fit this balloon jump in. It wasn't bravado, but it raised a laugh and perhaps helped make parachuting seem a bit less intimidating.

Morale was pretty unpredictable, though; one week, when Brigadier Gale was in command, there were three or four 'Roman candles' (parachutes which failed to open). The Brigadier decided that to 'restore morale' he would parade the whole brigade in Tatton Park. So he marched us all out there on a Saturday afternoon. As you can imagine, a parade on a Saturday afternoon wasn't exactly conducive to raising morale. When we got there, he sat us down in a huge semi-circle, while he explained that the accidents had been almost entirely due to faults which he personally would put right. But he believed our jumping techniques left a lot to be desired, and to show us how, he'd arranged for seven planeloads of instructors (in Whitleys) to fly over and demonstrate how easy jumping was if you followed the correct drill.

Well, to start off with there was a hell of a delay with the usual singing of 'Why are we waiting?' which cheered everyone except the top brass. Eventually, instead of seven Whitleys, just two of the old dears lolloped overhead and we watched expectantly as the dropping started. Now I've seen some bad dropping in my time but this was absolutely catastrophic – people coming out upside down, legs apart, somersaulting and swinging. Up to this moment the troops had been really rather browned off, but the moment they saw this shambles they cheered up enormously because these were the instructors, the people who were always bullying them and telling them how bloody awful they were. As the instructors came down there were roars of 'Get your legs together!' – the men were yelling out all the orders the instructors used to shout at them. The noise was tremendous. Eventually all 16 demonstrators landed, but only ten got up: they had the stretcher-bearers and ambulances going at full stretch!

Meanwhile, of course, old 'Windy' Gale was tearing his hair – he thought he'd lashed the whole thing and morale would go right down. But it was quite the reverse; the troops roared with laughter – they thought it was the funniest thing ever – they'd got their own back on their instructors. Singing their heads off, they marched back happy as sandboys; they really were a super crowd.

Our first operation was in early 1941 when X Troop was formed from volunteers in our unit for the attack on the Tragino Aqueduct in Italy. We didn't hear of the special training that they had been up to, but the word got round that there was a special operation on and that Major 'Tag' Pritchard would be commanding it. We couldn't get to Tag because he and the troop had been isolated, but all of us, by fair means or foul, managed to get little chits to him pointing out that the operation would be a total and utter waste of time unless we, personally, were included in the party. As you can imagine, our approaches weren't very productive.

Everyone was terribly disappointed that they hadn't been included, even when we heard that the troop hadn't come back. We were all very fit and immensely keen and proud to belong to this special unit; we were quite sure that there were no other troops in the whole British Army in the same league until, in June 1941, Colonel Jackson left and we had a new commanding officer, Major Eric Down. He was a formidable personality, and immediately acquired the nickname of 'Dracula' because he looked like death warmed up. He was absolutely appalled by us; he thought we were totally incompetent and thoroughly undisciplined. Up to now we had planned and trained only on the basis of individual hit-and-run commando raids, but Eric Down came straight from the War Office where he had been working out the forward policy for parachute troops. So he was well aware that instead of always being just one small commando, we would eventually grow to a whole airborne corps made up of two British divisions supported by American airborne forces. He envisaged us as highly disciplined, superbly trained, attacking infantry, the only difference being that we would be delivered to the battle by air instead of by sea or by road. This meant that we'd need a totally different course of training and also a different type of recruit: so, sadly, quite a few of those wonderful first chaps who'd been with us for over a year were returned to unit within weeks of Down's arrival. The new intake were rather more regular, infantry-minded people. Training became very intense; he marched us clean off our feet, hour after hour, day after day, on the cobbles, all round the streets of Manchester. This was absolute torture, as of course we hadn't been used to marching, especially with much heavier equipment than infantry would normally carry, since paratroopers have no means of transport except their own backs. He really bore down on us; discipline was severe and we were given endless weapon training, firing, platoon tactics, company exercises, and on live manoeuvres he insisted the leading platoons follow right up into the creeping artillery barrage. In battle this saves casualties but in training it means accepting casualties and is unpopular with the troops. The men loathed him initially; he had got rid of so many of our friends whom we thought the world of and he'd broken up the unit that we loved and believed to be efficient and effective. We officers were seriously worried that if we went into action some disgruntled chap might even shoot him in the back, he was so detested. And yet, by the time he left the battalion 18 months later I should think he was the most loved, the most revered, the most respected commander I have ever served under. The troops would do anything for him, go anywhere for him; he was confident that he was sending the most highly trained fighting unit in the British Army out to North Africa, and he was right – the performance of the battalion there proved that.

He had created a team the likes of which I had never come across before or since; he picked only the best. The new intake brought in people like Alistair Pearson who ended up as the most highly-decorated officer in the British Army and James Hill who commanded a parachute brigade from D-Day to VE-Day, most of the time in continuous action. Also Vic Coxen who was an outstanding leader and who greatly distinguished himself in fighting in North Africa, Italy and Greece. Of the original stalwarts of 2 Commando who remained with 1st Battalion, there were characters such as Jock Turnbull, who never slept indoors in his life. I shared a billet with him in Knutsford and even with feet of snow on the ground, he would always go outside with his sleeping bag and roll up on the lawn. You'd go out in the morning and all you would see was a little hump of snow. Tough as old boots and brave as a lion, he was. And Philip Mellor, he had only one eye, and died a death which I think everyone in a way envied; he stood there with a leg blown off, only one eye, wounded about seventeen times, and still went on firing his gun to cover his comrades.

Looking back you wonder how some of us ever got accepted into the elite Parachute Regiment; Vic Coxen had most of his stomach missing when he joined us; Philip Mellor had only one eye and I had both my eardrums ruptured at Dunkirk – I practically had to go round with an ear trumpet. And there were many others who would not have passed a medical, if we had had one, but we all had enough enthusiasm and determination to keep us going. Another character was Jock Gammon: he invented the Gammon anti-tank grenade which saved our bacon on many occasions – a brilliant invention. Apparently part of his research involved saving up his girlfriends' discarded stockings! And Dinty Moore – well there was only one Dinty Moore – very short, totally self-confident and without fear. A walking disaster area, he was always in trouble. He had a beautiful sense of humour and was a wonderful raconteur; he made us laugh till we cried. We used to break after parade at eleven o'clock every morning and go to the coffee house in Knutsford; we'd sit in the bay window and drink coffee while Dinty would relate in a loud voice the most hair-raising stories of his adventures in the brothels of Paris. The old ladies of Knutsford seemed to enjoy this tremendously and the coffee house did a roaring trade. Dinty was killed when his carrier blew up on a landmine in North Africa. I'm sure his driver was laughing when it happened.

What none of us had foreseen was the frustration of constantly being ready and eager to go into action and not being called. Or even worse, getting poised for operations which were then cancelled, time and time again. Many of us in 1st Parachute Battalion had joined 2 Commando in 1940 to get into action and here we were, well into 1942, by which time everyone else was getting back into the fight while we were still frigging around in the UK. We'd seen X Troop disappear into Italy, and we'd been green with envy when 2nd Parachute Battalion were given the Bruneval raid.

At last we were briefed for the Dieppe raid in June 1942 – we were going to take out the battery east of Dieppe and then come out by sea – which looked a pretty straightforward and simple operation. On the great day we were taken out to the airfields. Take off was to be at 4 am and we sat in the planes and waited until the engines started up and thought, 'At bloody last, this is it!' But after a bit the engines slowed down and the second pilot came back and told us there'd been a delay. Then a soldier banged on the door and said, 'Heavy winds on the French coast, one hour's delay.' Most of us went to sleep and at the end of an hour there was more banging on the door – 'Another hour's delay.' We were pretty fed-up by this time, but about ten minutes later there was a hell of a thumping on the door so we opened it up, and there at the bottom of the steps was one of our officers, purple in the face, with steam coming out of his ears, and eyes popping out of his head; his batman had forgotten to wake him. So he came roaring into the plane and immediately put his batman on a charge. There was a great deal of laughter, but it wouldn't have been funny for the officer if we'd taken off on time and left him behind. Half an hour later brought the news 'Operation cancelled.' As you can imagine, morale was not high by this stage. Back at base Eric Down had a chat to us and said, 'You've just got to face it – this sort of thing is bound to happen.' My God, how right he was.

SERGEANT ERNIE CHINNERY, No. 2 Commando

When word got about that volunteers were required for special service, I was a corporal with 54th Armoured Training Regiment at Perham Down. I'd been in the Army for twelve years, so I wasn't prepared to spend the next few years in a training unit. So I went and put my name down. Interviews were at Cambrai Barracks, Perham Down, and they asked lots of questions about athletic prowess. I was very fit, so they said, 'Are you ready for a fight?' and I said, 'Any time'. Then they told me I'd have to jump from an aeroplane. I'd never even been in one before, but my thoughts at the time were that I'd sooner go and fight overseas than let those buggers come over here. This was after Dunkirk of course.

I was selected, but I stayed in the same barracks, as that was where the unit formed up, about 60 men and five officers. We were separated into two troops, C and D, commanded by Captain Bailey and Captain Park-Smith (RM). The two subalterns were George Patterson and Ivor Davies, and to my surprise, our own Major Jackson was commanding officer. He addressed us on our first gathering on 22 June 1940, and was very keen about the whole thing. He was a firm man, but not harsh, then aged about 37 who had been trained by the RAF as a pilot.

We were there for about ten days, doing all sorts of training, mostly map reading and going out in twos and threes on initiative tests, getting to rendezvous points all over Salisbury Plain. Towards the end of the month we left Perham Down and went to a place called Benchill which is a suburb within Wythenshawe, where we were put into billets on a large housing estate. We were told that our parade ground would be the Sharston Hotel, a big pub with a large car park. The following day, after the parade, we marched from there up to Ringway, which was about two or three miles away. It was a historic moment for us; we were the very first parachute unit, although we hadn't jumped yet. All the time we were wondering what the jumping was going to be like, but we didn't do any for a few days, just bags of PT. Then we were split up into groups of about six each. They took us over to an aeroplane and said, 'We're going to give you some flights to get you used to flying.'

After two or three flights they fitted up a mock-up hole of the Whitley bomber which was merely a platform with a hole in the middle. You sat on the edge with a parachute pack on your back, and practised jumping through this hole without hitting yourself on the other side. When we weren't doing that, we were taken outside in the grounds in the airport and given different heights to jump from, six feet, seven feet, to get used to shock, and to show us how to fall properly. The motto of the instructors was, 'Knowledge Dispels Fear', which is certainly true. They were a nice bunch, very helpful, and their experience rubbed off onto us.

After this, the officers and the senior NCOs were separated from us to go up in the aircraft to start jumping. I was a corporal so I wasn't amongst them. They were the ones who jumped out of the rear of the aircraft, from the gun turret. I didn't see them jump, but I talked to Sergeant 'Digger' Witts who said, 'Oh, it's very good. You shit yourself before you jump, but it's all right, it's lovely afterwards.' This was the general feeling, so I was quite keen to do my first jump.

The day before our first jump they took us up into the hangar and kitted us up. Strangely we were issued with Sorbo pads to stick on every part of our body including a 'jock strap' to protect our 'wedding tackle', but sod all to protect our head – just aircrew helmets. At this stage there were no packing sheds; you just picked up an unpacked chute and then walked over to a table, lined up and then, in turn, you had to watch while the packer was packing your chute. This took a bit under ten minutes, and all the time the chaps were showing us and telling us what they were doing. This gave you a bit more confidence; you knew what was going to happen when you jumped. Then when they had packed it, they said, 'Feel all right about it?' and gave you your chute. You'd stick with that like shit to a blanket; you'd seen it done so if anything was wrong, it was your own bloody fault.

The first three jumps were fine. On the fourth there was a chap called Driver Evans in our aircraft. Two or three men dropped with no problems and then Evans, who was in front of me, left the aircraft and we circled round while I got into position. But before I could jump, the aircrew said we'd got a red light from the ground; the last chap had been injured and we were going back to Ringway.

Back on the ground Squadron Leader Strange, who was the RAF officer in charge of us, assembled us and said, 'I'm afraid I've got some bad news; the last man, Driver Evans, was killed.' We weren't happy about this at all – it was very sad. Then he told us that jumping would be suspended until the problem had been solved. The following morning we were told that we were going up to Scotland, to a place called Torcastle, which is about three miles north-east of Fort William. We were put under canvas by a hunting lodge and it pissed down with rain for about three weeks. I went on a close combat course up in Lochailort. We were taught by some Shanghai policemen who were bloody smashing blokes and they taught us a few tricks of the trade. They used to say, 'You don't need a weapon, all you need is your hands and your feet.' Then Lord Lovat took us out into the blue, up to our necks in heather, and taught us the art of stalking. He had half a dozen instructors with him and he'd say, 'See if you can spot them.' After about ten minutes they'd walk straight into your bloody face. We learnt the art of fishing, too; we'd lob a hand grenade into a stream, it'd go off and all the fish would float to the surface. We'd spear them out with bayonets and feast on fish for a couple of days.

On about 2 or 3 September, we moved down to Knutsford, again into civvy billets, and when we got back there we heard that A and B troops had been formed. So now numbers were up to about 120. We completed our eight jumps from the Whitley and when the weather wasn't good for jumping we used to go in Tatton Park doing a bit of ground training. The canopy opening procedure had been reversed – the rigging lines now came out of the pack first, followed by the canopy. There was a really smashing spirit among the lads, and we did a lot of drinking at our 'headquarters' – the White Bear at Knutsford. We thought we'd be sent over the other side and sabotage Germany, especially when C Troop went to a place called Horwich, where they gave us explosives training and even taught us how to drive trains. One stupid sod flung a squib into a box of explosives – you've never seen such a quick dispersal in all your life.

We qualified on 1 October, but no wings or parachute pay were issued until 4 December. Before wings were issued, the makers (Irvins and Quilters) gave us a little badge and you stuck that on your chest, which expanded about ten times its normal size. Then we carried on with normal military training, and by February 1941 we had eleven troops – about 350 men. It was then that X Troop, a composite troop, was formed from among our ranks. It wasn't a question of us all volunteering and then being selected; each man was picked individually and the troop was segregated from us, doing their training in Tatton Park. We all wanted to be involved, but a lot of the men were chosen for their experience in demolition. That was when we lost two officers from our troop, Patterson and Davies. We had no idea where they had gone or what they were doing until we read the newspaper reports. Thank Christ I didn't go with them. The only action the rest of us saw at that time was the odd fight at the Conservative Club. In those days I used to drink a lot, so did the others, so if ever there was a fight around, we were looking for it. But life changed drastically when Colonel Down took over as commanding officer in June of that year. Jackson had been a very popular sort of bloke. Now we had got an entirely different character. He assembled the whole lot of us in a hall in Knutsford, introduced himself and said, 'Your bloody civvy days are over; I'm going to make soldiers out of you.' Before he came, the atmosphere was pretty 'Ça ne fait rien', but that soon changed. Towards the end of September the 2nd and 3rd Battalions were being formed. About 20 of us from 1st Battalion went over to Hardwick, and took these chaps in pre-parachute ground training. Eventually the rest of our battalion joined us at Hardwick, until we moved to Bulford the following February.

In June and July of 1942 we did extensive training for the Dieppe operation which was aborted only after we'd boarded the aircraft at Hurn Airport. We used to do these exercises at night and have the day off. One night, part of the exercise was to locate the Headquarters wireless operator. There we all were crawling about trying to find this bloke with the adjutant calling his codeword, 'Mary, Mary, where are you, Mary?' No answer. This seemed to go on for ever. Then in the quiet of the night we heard Sergeant McBain, 'Mary, Mary, for fuck's sake, Mary, give yourself up so we can all get some sleep!'

LIEUTENANT JOHN AWDRY, 6th Parachute Battalion

On our first day at Ringway we were taken out to watch balloon jumping. The very first chap we saw come out of a balloon was a Roman candle and went straight into the ground. The instructor shouted, 'All right, about turn, and we'll watch the other balloon.' Next-door to me was a Jewish boy from Manchester – his name was Ashton, later to win the MM in Sicily – small and dark with a very Jewish, expressive face. He looked at me and I looked at him, and he said, 'Faaaahkin 'ell!!' I've heard those words many times since but never with such feeling!

The real heroines however were the WVS ladies on the DZ who served our char and wads. As soon as we'd done our first jump we'd rush up to their wagon to tell our story. 'And there I was, you see. I'd got the twists. I looked down and I saw the ground coming up at me, but I did this and I did that. . . .' 'Yes, dear, very good,' they'd say, smiling and listening as if they'd never heard a story like it. There we were, pale minutes before, and now bursting with pride at having got safely to the ground. If they'd heard the story once, they'd heard it ten thousand times. 'Very good, dear. Well done. Cup of tea?'

LEADING AIRCRAFTWOMAN OLIVE SNOW, WAAF

When I left home to join the WAAF there was a paratrooper from Ringway billeted in our house in Knutsford. I'd got quite fond of him, but when I came home on leave, he had gone off on the Tragino raid. I never saw him again.

9

Then I started work as a parachute packer at Ringway. Every morning I would cycle in from Halebank in time for breakfast and then work from eight until four or five in the afternoon. It was quite a concentrated job; you'd only pack about 20 parachutes each day. Even when you'd been there a while and you might have thought you could do it with your eyes closed, you didn't; a man's life depended on each and every parachute. But it was a very worthwhile job, and we enjoyed it.

We were supervised by a warrant officer, Joe Sunderland – he was great. He always looked after us girls and wouldn't let anyone say anything against us. 'If my girls packed a blanket and four pieces of string, it would open.' That was him. Of course he could be very stern at times if we got chatting to the paratroops who used to come in and watch us; if you saw Joe walking down the packing room with his hands behind his back, you knew he was on the warpath.

There were a few deaths when I was there, but only one was a packer's fault. She hadn't packed the rigging right, so the parachute didn't open – it was a Roman candle. Of course they moved her from the camp straight-away, but it was a terrible thing for all of us; it could have been any of us who made that mistake. That death cast a gloom over the place for a while, and it really made us think more about the work. But you had to carry on.

We saw a lot of the paratroops of course, especially at teatime in the YMCA where all the motherly volunteers were serving tea to the boys after they'd done their jumps. There'd be a few with bumped heads and bumped noses from the jump, but they were always cockahoop when they got their wings at the end of the fortnight's training. That evening they'd buy us a drink at the airport pub and we'd sew their wings on for them. Then the process started all over again with new trainees coming in.

We had a lot of foreign paratroopers: French, Polish, Canadian and American, and some of them were pretty cheeky. I got friendly with one Frenchman and chatted to him at teatimes for about a week. One day he came up and said, 'There's a little church up the road. Can we go down there and get married?' He was quite serious about it! But I said, 'Oh no, I couldn't do anything like that.' Things like that happen in wartime. A lot of the girls did get married to paratroopers and PJI (Parachute Jump Instructors), but I never got close to any of them, because actually we had it drilled into us: 'Don't get too involved with the paratroopers; they're only here for a fortnight and then they're off and might well get killed.'

All the men who trained for Arnhem were at Ringway. That was a fiasco if ever there was one; very few of them came back. They made a very big impact on us; we were terribly upset as quite a few girls were fond of the paratroopers who were lost in that dreadful battle. So it was a sad time and a happy time, but it's the happy memories you hold on to. You've got to keep going, haven't you?

CICILY PAGET-BOWMAN, FANY

I was acting in a repertory company in Glasgow when France fell in 1940. The only response from my colleagues was, 'Oh dear, how very awkward, what's going to happen to the company?' and it suddenly hit me that I couldn't carry on with this any more. I must do something for the war effort – join the forces – but what could a useless actress do? Then I realized that the one thing I could do was drive, so I left the company and applied to the WRENS (Women's Royal Naval Service). They didn't want anyone for another two years, but then I heard that the FANYs were reforming in Western Command and wanted drivers. So I went to see a Mrs Bentley in London, and when I told her I knew nothing about car maintenance or First Aid she said, 'Oh, that's all right – you'll be taught all that when you get there.' So off I went to Moston Hall, a rather bleak hut hospital outside Chester where I was taught absolutely nothing.

I'd been there a couple of months when this summons came for somebody to go to a place called Knutsford. They must be tough – able to stand nights in the Welsh mountains on manoeuvres, that sort of thing. The others all quailed at this, and since I was the new girl, they said, 'You go.' So I did, although I had no idea what I was going into – I wasn't told anything. What I found when I got to Knutsford was the newly-formed parachute commando, the first 40 troops who'd come from various regiments. This was their training ground. The men were marvellous – I was the only female there – and they were wonderfully friendly. I saw a lot of them because I spent most of my time on the jumping field at Tatton Park, driving the ambulance for the medical officer. It was all very exciting; I'd never seen a parachutist jump before – I was absolutely dazed at the whole thing – it was all so new.

It wasn't long before they started calling me their mascot: 'Miss Bowman and her blood tub.' As I was the only one doing the job I was on call 24 hours a day, seven days a week, and the boys used to say that when they went overseas they were going to take my ambulance and have four parachutes attached to it so the ambulance could come down with them. Oh, they were a wonderful lot. Everything from dons to gaol-birds – an incredible crowd. We used to meet every night at the George and play endless games of darts and drink a lot of beer – we had an enormous amount

11

of fun. Then we had the first tragedy. It was a routine drop of a stick of men from one of the Whitleys. The last man came out and I thought, 'Oh, they've dropped the overcoats', because they did sometimes drop them separately. Suddenly I saw two hands coming out to feel for the rigging but it wasn't there – the parachute had failed to open. Everyone, absolutely everyone, was shocked; it was the first bad accident they'd had and all that had gone wrong was that the bar to which the parachutes were attached had broken. And all they had to do was to put an ordinary dog leash clip on that bar from then on. It was dreadful. Although the troops were pretty shaken, they were so young and keen that they managed to throw it off. They were so different from ordinary soldiers; they had to be special to get in, and they trained very hard, but they still retained their great individuality. That was the lovely thing about them, because they were allowed to come out of uniform and wear civvies, so they didn't become a mass of trained automatons. Oh no, they had a lot of fun.

They had a balloon in Tatton Park which was used for jumping. One evening, after a rather good dinner, Tony Hibbert decided to jump out of that balloon, wearing his blues, and with his spurs on. Then they were dragging me along saying, 'Now, come on, you're going to jump', but I said, 'No, I'm not – I should break myself up.' Most of them were five or six years younger than me – but I don't regret refusing to jump – I would have broken both my legs.

Although I was only with them for 18 months, I saw many of them maturing into soldiers. They found their first jumps very frightening, of course, but they said the second jump was the worst; for the first one you were so frightened that you weren't even conscious of what you were doing, but by the second one you knew more about it and you'd thought more about it. But then they'd describe the exhilaration of coming down – they said there was nothing like it in the world. Landing wasn't easy, though; we treated lots of scrapes and bangs and broken limbs. One afternoon we had to get the fire brigade in, one poor little chap got stuck up in a fir tree. He could have got down, but he was paralyzed with fright and we had to treat him for shock!

By 1941 the battalion had grown to 500 and they put on a big display at Ringway which Churchill attended. His response was, 'Yes, yes, very fine, very splendid, but where are the rest of them?' Of course, there were no others, and it was then that everything started to change. Colonel Jackson was replaced and they started recruiting a lot more people. Very soon Knutsford became too small to hold them – as it was, they were billeted all over the place. So it was decided they should move to Hardwick. All the men wanted me to go with them, but I couldn't, because the powers that be wouldn't allow my transfer. I was absolutely heart-broken.

When one cockney chap heard I was having to leave, he came up to me and said, ''ere, you know the ol' Germans are comin' over 'ere, you know that, don' you?' So I said, 'Yes, they probably will, but never mind.' And he said, 'Now, I want you to 'ave somethin' – I want you to 'ave this.' And he gave me an enormous commando knife. I asked him what I should do with it, and he said, 'Well, say you're drivin' along and they stop you – they will, they'll stop you – and they put their ruddy 'ands on your truck door, so you just take out the knife and chop 'em off!'

Can you imagine? – cutting someone's hands off! But this was just like them; they gave me such wonderful affection and protection. I never fell in love with any one of them, but I loved them all. We all shared a fine sense of comradeship. In those early days we really had a marvellous time; we laughed an enormous amount at a time when there wasn't all that much to laugh about.

CHAPTER TWO

TRAGINO
Operation Colossus
1941

O PERATION COLOSSUS, THE FIRST BRITISH AIRBORNE operation, was carried out by seven officers and 31 men from X Troop, 11th Special Air Service Battalion on the night of 10 February 1941. The objective was the demolition of the Tragino aqueduct in southern Italy (*see* map of Italy, p. 90), which carried the water pipeline that supplied the ports of Taranto, Brindisi and Bari. The force, in Whitley bombers, flew across occupied France to Malta from where the operation was mounted. After blowing part of the aqueduct, the men made their way to the coast to be picked up by submarine. Unfortunately they were all captured.

LIEUTENANT TONY DEANE-DRUMMOND, 11th Special Air Service Battalion

After selection for No. 2 Commando we trained hard through the summer of 1940. When we had finished our jumps we were sent up to Scotland for further training. Two people in particular stand out from that time, they were ex-Shanghai policemen who looked like benign businessmen. Their task was to teach us unarmed combat. I remember one of them standing in front of us saying, 'In unarmed combat, gentlemen, there is only one thing to remember, balls, ears and eyes – go for them!' All good stuff. We were also trained to blow up anything and how to use a sextant in case we were dropped miles from the target. When I asked what was the use of knowing where you were, if you were miles away, there was no answer.

Around Christmas 1940 we were told to prepare ourselves for an operation in about a month's time. Six officers and 31 men had been selected to make up X Troop, under the command of Major T. A. G. Pritchard.

We all trained hard in that cold month of January 1941. We left our very comfortable billets in Knutsford, and moved to Ringway for the final rehearsals. In the months to come, we were to look back nostalgically on how well we'd been fed and looked after in Knutsford.

Ringway was hard. Three-mile runs followed by 30 minutes PT before breakfast and usually a 12–15-mile march after it. With full parachute marching order we were expected to do 5–6 miles an hour. For the final rehearsal we used two or three old Whitleys – not really a suitable aircraft for parachuting. It was originally designed to carry a gunner half way down the fuselage in a dustbin-shaped protuberance. When this was removed it left a hole about four feet across. The fuselage itself was only four feet high so half the stick would sit either aft or forward of the hole. When the pilot warned us over the intercom that there was 15 minutes to the target there was always frantic activity as we checked our equipment and parachute static lines. Then with five minutes to go, we opened the exit door. When the red light came on, indicating five seconds to the drop, the nearest two sat on the edge facing each other and the remaining six edged up close to each other. On the green light we dropped as quickly as possible so that in 15 seconds the stick of eight were out. Speed was essential, so that you all arrived close together on the ground. But you bashed your face if you pushed too hard and hit the far edge or if you moved too gingerly, the parachute bounced you off your side so your face then hit the far side. There were many walking around Knutsford with the 'Whitley kiss'. We suffered one fatality when Lance Sergeant Dennis was blown by the wind into an ice-covered pond and was stuck deep in the mud and drowned under the ice.

In spite of every precaution our final rehearsals did not go to plan. The night was cloudy, the wind was strong. Half the aircraft dropped their sticks in the wrong place so that many landed in trees and had to face the ignominy of being helped down by the local fire brigade.

A month later I flew ahead to our advanced base in Malta, in a Sunderland, from Plymouth during an air raid. Shortly before the flight I was told our objective was the aqueduct at Tragino which was used to supply the Italian army; we were to blow it up. The operation had been cynically code-named 'Colossus'.

At dawn on 9 February all eight Whitleys under the command of Wing Commander Tate arrived after a 1,400-mile journey from England. Thirty-six hours later we took off on a gin-clear night. Like the rest, I was a bit concerned, that after blowing up the aqueduct, we were to split up into three parties and rendezvous five days later on the coast, to be picked up by the submarine, HMS *Triumph*. However, we were all asleep when the intercom told us there was '15 minutes to target'. We prepared ourselves and waited. Then suddenly the rear gunner came through – 'Get cracking, you're due to drop in one minute.' The intercom had failed. Pandemonium broke out as we wrestled with the door. With no more time to think, I found myself sitting watching the red light over my head thinking this is unreal; what am I doing sitting over a hole looking down on Italy? Through that hole I could see houses and a river. Then the green light. 'No. 1, No. 2, No. 3, "Containers"'; a wait to let them get away, 'No. 4', then me.

Immediately I noticed the silence away from the aircraft. We'd dropped at 500 feet and were down in about 15 seconds. I made my best ever landing into a ploughed field about 100 yards above the aqueduct. It was so still. I could hardly believe I was in enemy territory. We waited for the others to drop and I had a funny feeling inside that the other planes had lost their way and that we were on our own.

The aqueduct was similar to the one we had practised on but it was made of reinforced concrete, not masonry as we'd expected. The sapper officer arrived half an hour later, a bit weary as he and his stick had been dropped a mile from the bridge. They'd found some friendly Italians who were only too willing to carry the heavy boxes of explosives. They told us that it would give them something to talk about for the rest of their lives. One old wizened chap who'd worked as a bell-hop in New York said, 'Are you guys English?' One of our cockneys replied, 'No, chum, we are Abyssinians on the way to Sunday School!' We heard later that these most helpful civilians were awarded medals for their brave conduct in the face of the enemy.

Corporal Watson, RE in my stick, set the charges on the tiny bridge that led up to the aqueduct. The explosion of one box of gun cotton was the signal that the aqueduct was about to blow. When we heard that we moved to a safe position. George Patterson, in the absence of the senior Royal Engineer officer, who had been dropped in the wrong valley about five miles away, had decided to put all the explosives, half a ton of gun cotton, on one pier of the aqueduct instead of on three.

Watson lit the fuse and we withdrew. With an almighty blast the bridge went up, clouds of flying concrete, iron rails – bits of masonry showered everywhere. Our bridge had been cut. Thirty seconds later, up went the second enormous explosion from the aqueduct.

We now waited higher up for 'Tag' Pritchard to tell us the results of the explosion. Tag came back with a smile on his face and stopped us talking.

'Listen', he said. What we heard was the sound of a great waterfall – we'd done it. We cheered and cheered. Not the best thing to do in enemy country, because we would have been heard a long way away. But after all our weeks of preparation and training it was a great relief. Now we had to make it to the coastal rendezvous.

As arranged we split up. Tag gave the order to lighten our loads so we were left with just our personal weapons, because we were relying on reaching our RV (rendezvous) unseen. Right from the start we were in knee-deep mud, in impassable ravines and every farmhouse had a barking dog. Going roughly on compass course we must have covered 15 miles that first night, but had only done about six out of the 60 to the coast. We sheltered in a little ravine and got a few hours' sleep before the cold woke us. We boiled water on our primus stove and brewed tea or made porridge of pemmican and biscuits which tasted like concentrated greasy Bovril!

The countryside around us was beautiful but the feeling of being hunted prevented us from really appreciating it. Tag had spotted a shepherd and his goats coming down a path in the cliff that we were going to have to climb. So that night we sweated and heaved our way up 300 feet of mud and shingle and when we got to the top we were panting and exhausted. It really took every ounce of energy to get up there and we felt it later. We covered some 20 miles that night; everyone was exhausted. We only kept going by the fear of being discovered. At last, through the mist, we saw some trees, but as we dragged ourselves there we saw they sheltered a farmhouse. That was too much – we just collapsed on the ground as one man. Our sweat-soaked clothes became ice-cold and we sat and shivered. Tag and I somehow managed to scramble up 50 more yards where we found some rocks. Tag went back and brought up the men. It wasn't the perfect hiding place but we just dropped where we were among the rocks, curled up and slept.

At dawn I woke with my teeth chattering and every bone in my body aching, to see a peasant standing not 100 yards away.

Tag sent Private Pichi, our Italian, who'd volunteered for this operation, to talk with him. He did his best, but I knew in my heart that the game was up. Tag decided it was useless trying to move off as we would attract more attention.

Soon some half-naked and filthy Italian children and old peasant women, dressed in black, came up to see us. Then a peasant with a couple of dogs and a shotgun came up and babbled away about us dropping our personal weapons. I realized I couldn't kill these people for a few hours' more freedom. As we put our arms to the ground the peasants and children ran forward and took them and our equipment. I have never felt so ashamed before or since.

We learned later that one of the two Whitleys which had gone off to bomb Foggia had developed engine trouble and had ironically ditched, after the aircrew had baled out, in the sandy mouth of the River Sele, where two days later HMS *Triumph* was to have arrived to pick us up. None of our other parties made the rendezvous. It wouldn't have mattered if they had, because with all the activity in the area, it was deemed wise that no submarine should be sent.

We found out later that the Italian authorities were very angry that we'd been able to slip in undetected and blow the aqueduct. I don't think blowing the aqueduct cut off water for more than about a month, but it had a profound psychological effect upon the Italians. It was a slap in the face for Italian pride. It meant that troops were brought from the front to be on guard duty all over Italy protecting bridges and other vital installations.

We were all made prisoners-of-war and interrogated, but revealed nothing. Sadly Pichi was handed over to the Fascist militia, tortured, court-martialled and shot. I am quite sure that he remained silent.

CHAPTER THREE

BRUNEVAL
Operation Biting
1 9 4 2

THE 2ND PARACHUTE BATTALION BEGAN TO FORM IN THE autumn of 1941, with the aim of reaching operational readiness in the summer of 1942. However, it had barely completed parachute training when in January 1942 C Company, led by Major John Frost, was chosen for a special mission proposed by Admiral Lord Mountbatten, Chief of Combined Operations.

The target was a Wurzburg precision radar dish, one of a series of early-warning installations on the north coast of France. This particular radar dish was situated close to an isolated clifftop chateau near the French coastal village of Bruneval, north of Le Havre. The objective was not to destroy the dish but to dismantle it and return to England with as many of its vital parts as possible. It was a task which could be accomplished only by airborne troops, as Bruneval's steep cliffs and a string of machine-gun posts ruled out a direct beach assault. Operation Biting was mounted on the night of 27 February. The raid achieved complete surprise. However, the sappers of 1st Parachute Field Engineers under Captain Dennis Vernon, with Flight Sergeant Cox, a radar specialist, had very little time to dismantle, photograph and sketch the Wurzburg radar before Major Frost ordered a withdrawal to the beach. After an alarming delay, they were taken off by landing craft of the Royal Navy. The operation was a complete success.

MAJOR JOHN FROST, 2nd Parachute Battalion
In 1936 I was serving with the Cameronians in Aldershot Command. One afternoon General Archie Wavell was talking to us in Aldershot about a film he'd seen in which the Russian Army had parachuted 1,500 men from

BRUNEVAL 27/8 FEBRUARY 1942

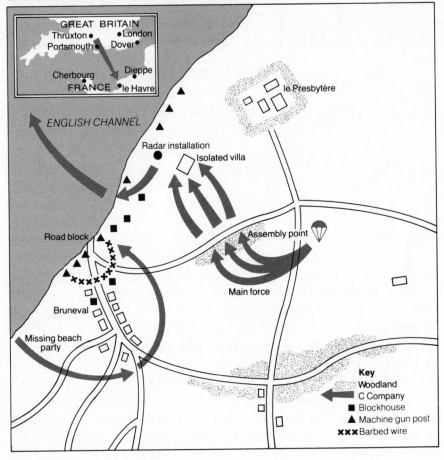

aircraft. In summing up, he said he thought it was a funny way to go to war and advised us to go home and forget all about it.

In 1940 I was with the Cameronians on beach defence in Suffolk. It was a boring period and the 15th Scottish Division, to which we belonged, was not earmarked for any great and glorious venture. One evening after returning from a solitary walk the company office clerk handed me a letter marked 'Secret'. The War Office were looking for volunteers for Special Air Service battalions. I had little idea what they were about, but presumed it would be something to do with commandos, and therefore action.

I went up to London and did really badly in the interview. I couldn't remember the name of my divisional commander or any other important detail. So I thought I'd failed and was quite glad to be back in Suffolk again. However! Ten days later I was posted to Hardwick Hall in Chesterfield. It was a terrible place, hideous countryside, horrible camp, only half-built and bitterly cold, with mud everywhere. The whole atmosphere was very strange. I wasn't at all sure I'd done the right thing or could possibly compete on the physical side. Then I got caught for the adjutant's job. With all the paperwork I had little chance to get fit or train. I thought I could get away without all the training. Came the day and I did my first jump successfully and went up immediately for the next. This time I landed awkwardly and badly damaged my knee. Ten days later, after I'd got out of hospital, I really started to get fit by going for long runs.

I returned from a Scottish New Year to relinquish the adjutancy and take over C Company, who were all Scots, from Philip Teichman. Two weeks later I was told that C Company were to move to Salisbury for special training. However, as I was not qualified, I would have to do all my jumps in one week. Philip took the company down to Salisbury, and if I failed he would resume command.

By the grace of God and a hell of a lot of good luck, I managed, despite the Manchester weather, to get my five jumps done in three days. I took over C Company from poor Philip who was very disappointed to lose it. A few days later we were told that we had to practise landing by night behind imaginary enemy lines and that we would be evacuated by the Navy. We were to demonstrate this to the War Office. A liaison officer came to see me with a bloody awful plan which meant reorganizing the company. So I complained bitterly. He then told me it was an operation that we were practising for and that the War Office knew more about the enemy's positions than I did. So that was that. I was also told the raid was to be made on Bruneval, on the French coast, where we were to dismantle a radar unit. I organized the company into four parties, each named after a famous sailor.

We practised our roles thoroughly on the ground, then went up to Loch Fyne to train with the landing-craft, and subsequently back to Tilshead for practice drops. We never had a successful combined rehearsal throughout the preparation period! Either the weather was too bad to fly or the Navy would come to the wrong part of the beach. It was a shambles. However, we were quite certain that we could play our part, the Navy said they would find us and the RAF were convinced they could put us in the right place, so I was prepared to go without having had a successful practice.

We then had the unpleasantness of postponements. There were only four days up until 27 February when the tides would be right and we would have enough moonlight to carry out our task. We went on the 27th. The day was perfect except at the last moment they told us there was snow on the ground in France. When the time came for us to depart we marched out in our parties to the waiting aircraft. Piper Ewing played our regimental marches which raised our spirits and we cheered him. As we presented ourselves to our aircrew they seemed of a different breed. They were used to night sorties and were at ease in what they wore. We were a very strange-looking new bomb load.

I had been very busy prior to take-off absorbing all the fresh intelligence that was coming to us each day. We knew the exact defensive position of the enemy, their weapons and even some of their names.

At last our twelve aircraft, carrying ten men in each, were off. We sat on our sleeping bags, but it was bloody hard to find a comfortable position. The noise inside the aircraft was considerable, but some played cards and we sang songs like 'Annie Laurie', 'Lulu' and 'Come sit by my side if you love me'. Flight Sergeant Cox, who had volunteered to dismantle the radar apparatus, gave a sentimental rendering of 'Rose of Tralee'.

I had a large water bottle filled with tea and laced with rum which I passed around so most of us were dying for a pee which we did the moment we landed! There was no wind and landing in snow was perfect. I would normally have travelled with Wing Commander Pickard (star of *Target for Tonight*), who took the first two sticks, to make sure they were dropped in the right place. But he was the only one who dropped his sticks in the wrong place!

The plan was that we should basically drop in three parties. The first, under John Ross and Ewen Charteris, would take the beach defences to the rear. The second lot, mine, were to capture the villa and radar equipment, while the senior sapper, Dennis Vernon, and Cox dismantled all the parts that were needed and photographed the rest. The third party, under John Timothy, were to act as reserve and interpose themselves between the radar station and the German-held village.

After we'd had our pee we went straight for the radar. We could see the aircraft dropping our reserve party, so we knew we would have at least three-quarters of the force on the ground.

We had this very complicated plan which I didn't like because there wasn't proper control. For example, I had been ordered to lead the assault on the villa, when I should have been free to command the situation. Instead, there I was with this bloody awful Sten gun, a most inaccurate and unreliable weapon, leading a charge on this villa. Fortunately there was only one German in there, who was quickly dealt with.

After that I could start to assume command, but I had no proper headquarters staff or proper signals set-up. However, up to now all had gone well. Then the enemy opened fire on the villa from 'Le Presbytère', a wooded enclosure, 300 yards away. They continued firing while Vernon and Cox began to dismantle the radar and take photographs.

With more firing and sounds of vehicles approaching I ordered my party to take what they had of the radar and make their way to the beach. The sappers loaded the equipment onto canvas trolleys and off we went. Because I had no communications I had no idea if John Ross was in control of the beach. As we made our way down to the hill in the snow the Germans opened up with machine-gun fire from a pillbox. Sergeant Major Strachen was badly wounded in the stomach. We got some morphine into him and slipped and slithered him down on his bottom. As we got closer to the beach we heard someone call out that everything was clear. Then more firing started and John Ross called out, 'Don't come down. The beach defences have not been taken.' I went to sort out the problem and found Ewen Charteris, who had been dropped by Pickard about a mile and a half short of the correct place. On their way to us they had fought a tricky little battle with a German patrol. He had dealt with the machine-gun that had hit Strachen and with great aplomb dispatched any defender who tried to stop us reaching the beach. He was a brilliant young chap who had arrived at the *moment critique*.

It was 0215 and all we wanted now was the Navy. The signallers couldn't make contact with the Navy. We tried with the lamp, but there was a slight mist and we couldn't see more than half a mile. We had arranged a last-ditch communication, which was a Very light. We fired several of these, but there was no recognition. I'd almost given up hope now and was going to take up defensive positions and go on fighting for as long as we could.

We had just finished tidying up the perimeter when the signaller cried out, 'The boats are here, sir! The boats are here! God bless the bloody Navy, sir!' Unfortunately, instead of coming in two at a time so that we could make an orderly withdrawal in three phases, all six landing-craft came in at the same time. It was a bit of a shambles, and we were not able to check everyone in. On board the gunboat we heard the sad message from two signallers that they'd been left behind. There was no way we could go back for them.

We learnt the reason for the Navy's delay. A German destroyer and two E-boats had passed within a mile of them, but thankfully had not seen them. It was little wonder they hadn't answered our signals. At a very early stage, the scientist who was on the motor gunboat with the radar was able to shout across, 'You've got practically every single thing we'd hoped to see.'

As we entered Portsmouth our flotilla escort of six destroyers passed us with 'Rule Britannia' blaring out from their loudspeakers. We also had Spitfires diving overhead, signalling success with their wings. It was a moment to feel great pride. We had suffered casualties, with two dead and five wounded and those we'd left behind. But we'd carried out a most successful airborne operation.

The raid had been carried out when our country's fortunes were at a low ebb. Singapore had recently fallen and the beleaguered German battle-ships had escaped from Brest up the Channel. The success of our venture, although a mere fleabite, did have the effect of making people feel we could succeed after all. We'd left our barracks, which we shared with the glider pilots, on the Friday and when we got back on the Sunday their quartermaster was reading the Sunday papers with the news of our raid splashed all over the front. 'Good God,' he said, 'I wonder who they could have been.'

CHAPTER FOUR

NORTH AFRICA
Operation Torch
1 9 4 2 – 3

I N NOVEMBER 1942 THE FIRST ARMY, WHICH INCLUDED THE 1ST
Parachute Brigade, landed near Algiers with the aim of advancing and
capturing Tunis and Bizerta 500 miles to the east. The 3rd Parachute
Battalion, which had flown to Algiers via Gibraltar, spearheaded this
advance; they seized the vital Bone airfield on 12 November by parachute
assault, anticipating by minutes a German force with the same task, which
it then abandoned. On 16 November the 1st Battalion dropped near Souk el
Arba airfield and occupied a key road junction at Beja, only 90 miles from
Tunis, from which they actively patrolled. Both these operations were
successful and the airborne troops were quickly relieved by the advancing
main force.

The 2nd Parachute Battalion, initially held in reserve, was dropped at
Depienne on 29 November to destroy enemy aircraft at Oudna. The
airfield, however, was found to be abandoned while unexpectedly heavy
enemy opposition halted the advance of the First Army, leaving the
battalion isolated 56 miles behind enemy lines. Lightly equipped and
continuously attacked by air and ground forces, the battalion successfully
conducted an arduous fighting withdrawal back to the nearest Allied
positions, losing 16 officers and 250 men en route.

The campaign now entered a new phase that developed over the winter
into a bitter slogging match. For the next five months until April 1943, the
Parachute Brigade Group was required to fight in the normal infantry role.
Taking part in more battles than any other formation in the First Army,
they inflicted over 5,000 casualties with a loss to the brigade of 1,700 men.
The brigade's actions in this operation earned them the name of *Rote
Teufel*, or the Red Devils, from the German forces.

TUNISIA 1942-3

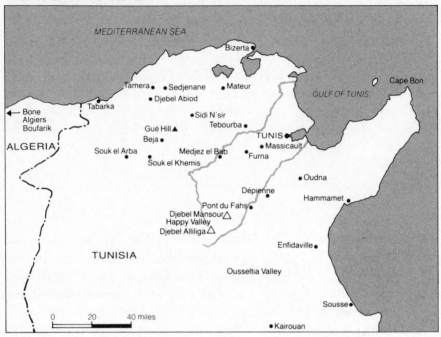

LIEUTENANT COLONEL JAMES HILL, 1st Parachute Battalion

As an officer and a gentleman you have one perk in the army and that's having a good batman. I had a good Royal Fusilier batman whom I had kept through the battle of France and Dunkirk in the early part of the war. When Churchill called for volunteers for parachute troops this wretched fellow came to me and said he'd like to go and try. I decided my duty to my country was to let him go. I was then looked after for six weeks by a Pioneer, which was an uncomfortable experience, so I had absolutely no alternative but to volunteer for parachuting in order to get my batman back! I was very lucky because Eric Down, who was commanding the 1st Parachute Battalion, wanted a second-in-command. I was interviewed by him at Bulford and he gave me the job.

Eric Down was the most marvellous battalion commander, but luck ran against him throughout the war, as he was always promoted before any battle took place. He was moved on to form the 2nd Parachute Brigade and on 17 July 1942, I was fortunate and became CO of the 1st Parachute Battalion.

In those days, to maintain morale and momentum, various raids were always being thought up. The first one I was involved in, which was to take the island of Alderney for 24 hours, wasn't really considered of sufficient importance to justify the effort. The next one was far more interesting. We were to drop in Dieppe with the Canadians and silence the coastal defence batteries. The great day arrived. We had got into the aeroplanes and the operation was cancelled. Apparently a front had come down which meant the aircraft could not have seen their DZs. This upset Lord Mountbatten, the Chief of Combined Operations, who decided to eliminate the air drop. A month later the operation took place and we were replaced by the commandos. We nearly had a mutiny on our hands from our fellows who had been waiting and training, some of them since 1940, and were now denied their battle. It was lucky for us in many ways that we didn't take part, because it appeared a costly failure. However, from the lessons learned very many lives were undoubtedly saved on D-Day and other seaborne operations.

Some time later I was sent for by Lord Louis. I and my adjutant presented ourselves at Richmond Terrace in Whitehall and were received in the hallway by a gorgeous, smart-looking MTC (Motor Transport Corps) driver who was slapping her boots with her stick. She escorted us upstairs where we were given a most secret woman, whose task was to type our operation orders for us. Then I met the great man who told me my task was to capture the island of Ushant and to hold it for 48 hours and then be taken off by Hunter-class destroyers. Ushant was heavily held and an important gun station in the Germans' coastal defences: it would be a very hard nut to crack.

I went back again to train the battalion vigorously for about a month and then we all went down to Hurn airport where I was allowed to brief the chaps. They were thrilled because it was just up their street.

We all got into the aeroplanes, taxied to the end of the runway and prepared for take-off. Then the operation was scrubbed, again due to a front which scattered the Flying Fortresses which had taken off to bomb the relevant German airfields. The Fortresses were tailed by our latest high-altitude Spitfires, and came down over France and Spain. Quite understandably I had another near mutiny on my hands.

I decided we must do something fairly drastic to keep the chaps quiet, and so we went down to Exmoor to do some rather dangerous field firing exercises with live ammunition. I thought I was going to lose my commission there and then because some of the overs were going into Exford. After ten days of this I decided we would march back to Bulford which was about 112 miles. Every man had to carry about 60 pounds plus, and they were told that anybody who didn't make the grade would not go on the next operation. We did the march in about two and a half days. About 30 per cent, including one company commander, didn't make it. They paid the price. Others were hobbling and in much pain, but nothing would induce them to give up.

Shortly after the march I was told that we were going to sail to North Africa. We prepared for this and on 29 October 1942 set off from the Clyde in the *Arundel Castle*.

Our task was to capture Tunis airport at El Alouina. We had the most marvellous briefing arrangements for this which included wonderful models and maps, so we spent two or three hours every day on the ship, briefing all the way down to section level. When we got into the Mediterranean a very unwelcome message came through to say that 10,000 German parachute troops had been airlanded in Bizerta. So our beautiful planning went by the board.

We arrived in Algiers and spent the night in the Botanical Gardens. The next day I was told to take my battalion to the local airport at Maison Blanche. I was sent for and given my new orders by General Anderson. I thought he was probably a good general, but he was a crusty old boy who didn't know anything about parachute troops and didn't like what he had heard about them. I think he was pleased to get rid of us. He gave me very clear orders. The first one was to seize the key road junctions at Beja in Tunisia some 400 miles to the east of where the British Army was forming up near Algiers. The second was to harry the enemy wherever we could find them; and third, and most important of all, was to bring the French Army in on our side. I thought to myself, fancy being paid for doing this. It was too good to be true. We also had to see if Souk el Arba, which was 30 miles from Beja, was suitable as an air-landing strip for fighter aircraft.

Off we went in Dakota aircraft commanded by a splendid American colonel. He and his men had never dropped parachutists before. They also had no intercom between their aeroplanes and no intercom within the aircraft itself. The only map I could get hold of was a one-quarter-inch-to-the-mile French motoring map, which included Beja!

We hadn't got enough aircraft to take the whole battalion so I had to leave some behind. As we were taxi-ing off the next morning I looked out of the pilot's window and was horrified to see about 20 chaps, borrowed parachute in one hand and weapon in other, running to the doors and being pulled in by their mates. We had to abort the mission because cloud came down and we couldn't see a thing, but next morning we had a wonderful flight. The plan was that as soon as everyone saw me jump the other sticks were to follow, which they all did.

As soon as we got on the ground we commandeered (we were very good at this sort of thing) transport, some of which was fuelled by charcoal. I left Alistair Pearson with some men to pick up the precious parachutes. While the equipment was being salvaged arrangements were made for the funeral of Private Webster who had been killed on the drop. The whole town turned out for the funeral.

I left orders for the battalion to stop at the top of the hill overlooking Beja and I went down into the town with Major des Voeux, our liaison officer, to interview General Barre, the French area commander. The French had a great inferiority complex about German armour and so I was cross-examined as to what weapons we had to deal with German tanks. I told him in the most glowing terms of the armoured divisions that were rushing to our aid and of our very latest, secret type of anti-tank mortars! After more discussion in our best French, he agreed to let us take over. I asked how many men he had holding the junctions. He told me he had a regiment of 2,500 men. Quite obviously we could not take over in broad daylight otherwise our numbers (525) would be exposed.

At dusk the next day I sent the first lot in with red berets and large gaps between the men and as soon as they cleared the town they doubled up the hill and joined on behind the next group who were all wearing steel helmets. We dressed up medical trolleys to look like our secret weapons and marched through the town twice – which completely fooled them. We took over from the French regiment and neither they, nor the enemy, had any idea of our weakness in numbers.

We wanted desperately to bring the French in on our side and demonstrate to the local population that the Germans were not infallible. We had learnt that each morning a column of German armoured vehicles would come up to the French lines on the road to Mateur and exchange cigarettes and food at 11 am. I got permission from the French to send Major Cleasby-Thompson's S Company through their lines and minefield to carry out an ambush on this convoy.

The next morning the column consisting of three heavy eight-wheeled armoured cars and three armoured recce vehicles passed as expected. While they were fraternizing with the French, S Company laid two belts of '75' grenades across the road approximately 20 yards apart. Two further mine belts were laid some hundreds of yards down the road after the tail of the column had passed. The company then took up ambush positions along the road. The recce vehicles had led the column down so the armoured vehicles would lead it back. The excitement among the men was intense. They had been waiting and training for this for two years. At eleven o'clock the leading armoured vehicle approached and a groan could be heard as it passed straight over the first belt of mines. Everyone reckoned it would blow up on the second belt, but it appeared to have a charmed life and passed over it to the utter dismay of S Company. The second armoured car however, made no mistake and blew itself up good and proper on the first row of mines. The armoured car that had got through must have thought his mate had got a puncture and slowly backed all the way down the road onto the second string of mines and blew itself up. There was a short and furious scrap and all the Germans who were left were taken prisoner. A great success.

I know under the Geneva Convention I shouldn't have done this, but I put the prisoners into two captured recce vehicles and, with our drivers, drove them through Beja to show the French how we dealt with German armour. It happens once in a lifetime. It was marvellous. The French were delighted and they appeared to regard our men as mysterious wizards who could deal with the German armour of which they were so afraid.

The Germans retaliated the next day by Stuka-ing Beja. Within minutes of this the Arabs started looting. The French then shot the looters and peace prevailed. This German attack incensed the French and made them better disposed to our cause.

We were now well on the way to carrying out two of the tasks, namely, harrying the enemy and holding the town of Beja, but we still had to bring the French Army in on our side. On 19 November a meeting took place between the French divisional commander at Medjez el Bab and the German Minister to the Bey of Tunis, who demanded that the Germans be allowed to man the bridge at Medjez at 11 am the next morning. We had made it clear to the French that if the Germans attempted to cross the bridge at Medjez we would fight them, no matter if the French took part. The French general got exasperated with the German minister and told him they would fight. The news reached us at 3 am. It meant our remaining task was on the way to being accomplished.

The next day the Germans attacked in force at 11 am. The French backed by R Company under Major Conron fought magnificently. The French casualties were particularly high. But the Germans were beaten back, so our third task was successfully completed. Later that day we heard that a mixed American gunner battery (which came from the south across the mountains) would arrive to support us in the Medjez el Bab sector. We saw them approaching at a furious speed. Much to our consternation, the column advanced and swept straight on to the forward slope covered by the German positions. A furious battle started. When we had extricated them their commanding officer was asked the reason for this unusual manoeuvre. He explained that some 14 miles back his gun teams had worked it out that one of them could be the first American to fire a shot against the Germans in World War II.

On the morning of 22 November I visited the French at Sidi N'sir. A French sailor who had been discharged after being wounded by the British at Oran told us that an Italian force of about 300 men, plus tanks, were harboured, each night, about nine miles north east of Sidi N'sir. I decided that we would attack that night. The French gave us a company of Goums (Moroccan troops) who carried our extra mortar ammunition. I thought this was marvellous – the French really were on our side.

Our immediate objective was a small hill called Gué. It was a moonlit night and you could see the stars. We were endeavouring to keep as quiet as possible, but every farmhouse we came to had a bloody dog that barked. However, we got to the foot of the hill undetected. I sent our excellent Royal Engineer troops, under Captain Geary, round to the back of the hill to mine the road leading to it, so if any armour tried to escape they would be blown up.

As we got ready to attack three loud explosions shook the air. The sappers had been carrying their Hawkins anti-tank mines in sandbags ready to lay them. Somehow, one of them had accidentally exploded and set off the rest. Three officers and 24 men were killed.

The Germans opened up at once. Heavy machine-gun fire was coming from a conical hill with a gradient of one in three. The assault went straight in and the two platoons swarmed the stone wall to finish off the enemy with bayonets. Sitting where I was I could see three tanks which were firing rather ad lib down the hill. I thought this was too good to be true, we must do something about it. So I got hold of two or three chaps and went up the side of the hill where we could see the first of these tanks which was blazing away. It was rather a small tank, but it was dug-in. Most armoured vehicles have a little round hole which they can open up to peep through. I put my revolver into the hole and pulled the trigger and of course the bullet went whee-e-e-e! all the way round the inside of the tank. Up went the hatch of the tank and out came a chap shouting 'Italiano, Italiano!' This was too good to be true. That was the first tank dealt with. We went up to the next tank, I put the revolver in and again the same thing – 'Italiano, Italiano!' This seemed much too good. We went up to the third tank and tried the same thing again. Everything looked as if it was working all right, but instead of an Italian, out came a great big German. He was a much tougher chap. He came out with his hands up, and I saw that he had a revolver in his right hand. As he jumped down, he shot at me. One bullet hit me in the middle of the chest and two others hit me in the neck and arm and I went down.

Eventually I was collected and taken down to the foot of the hill to Headquarters. They sent a message for Alistair Pearson. As I lay there an extraordinary flash came to me – you are not going to die! So I was very pleased to accept that one. After that it never occurred to me that I would die, and I handed over to Alistair. Miles Whitelock, my adjutant, was brought in. Poor fellow, he had been shot in the head and lost part of his nose, which is an extremely unpleasant thing to happen.

Both Miles and myself were put in the side-car of a motorcycle which had been captured in the battle, and driven down a railway track, bumping all the way over the sleepers for five miles or so, to Sidi N'sir. When we got there we were taken to Beja where my parachuting surgical team had set up. I was taken into a cottage room and operated on by Captain Robb, who undoubtedly saved my life.

I had three weeks in the Casualty Clearing Station at Souk el Arba before evacuation to the General Hospital in Algiers. Whilst there, one morning the matron and cleaners came in. I was 'spruced up' and to my amazement General Giroux, who had taken over from Admiral Darlan as C-in-C in North Africa, a magnificent 6ft 3in, covered in a big moustache and medals, swept in, kissed me on both cheeks, removed the Legion of Honour from his aide, Capitaine Bajaine, and pinned it on my pyjamas.

I had french windows to my room so I was able to do some illicit training by night. When I judged myself sufficiently fit, I made an unofficial exit from the hospital and returned to 1 Para Brigade. It was immediately obvious to me, as it was to Brigadier Flavell, the brigade commander, that Alistair Pearson had done such a splendid job commanding the battalion in my absence that there could be no question of removing him. In order to resolve his problem, and save me from the ire of the hospital authorities, he arranged an immediate flight for me, via Gibraltar, to the UK and home.

LIEUTENANT COLONEL ALISTAIR PEARSON, 1st Parachute Battalion

On 12 November 1942 the 1st Para Battalion landed at Algiers and bivouacked in the Jardin d'Essai. As 2 i/c I remained on the docks to supervise the unloading of stores and parachutes. The parachutes were in sealed waterproof containers, which was a good thing as a number fell into the dock and had to be rescued by a diver at 500 francs a go. I thought this was a good bargain and money well spent, but unfortunately for me, Allied Forces HQ thought differently and refused to pay because I had no authority to employ a diver. We'd always been taught initiative was to be encouraged!

The battalion moved to billets at Maison Blanche Airfield and was briefed to take off for Souk el Arba airfield at 0630 hours on 15 November. As 2 i/c I was responsible for the packing and loading of containers on aircraft. This was not completed till 0500 hours on the 15th. The commanding officer, James Hill, decided that we should not go on first lift. This was disappointing but sensible. The battalion took off at 0710 hours and I went for a sleep. I was no sooner asleep when I was wakened to be told the battalion was returning. Bad weather over Bone had made the mission impossible. I and my loading party were included in the next day's flight manifest. We dropped on Souk el Arba airfield not knowing whether the French garrison was friendly or not. Fortunately they were as they had some armoured vehicles which would have made mincemeat of us on landing.

We had very few casualties but Private Webster was unfortunately cremated when he hit the power lines. The battalion moved off in buses in the afternoon to Beja. I was left behind to collect parachutes from the dropping zone and return them to Algiers by train.

Next day I attended Private Webster's funeral. This was an endurance test as the whole population of Souk el Arba attended and we had a walk of about three miles in blazing heat carrying all our equipment to the graveyard outside the town. I shook hands afterwards with about 500 mourners, climbed into the hearse and rode back in state. I then requisitioned a railway engine and two trucks, loaded all the stores and caught up with the battalion at Beja Station. I was welcomed with much joy as I had the rations and cigarettes. The Battalion HQ was situated in an abattoir.

The battalion group had spent the previous night miserable and cold on the hills above Beja without cover. The CO visited the French HQ who were not particularly helpful as they had not decided which side to back. Beja was a centre of communication with roads going in all directions. The CO decided that the best form of defence was offence. This was done by sending out fighting patrols to harass the enemy wherever they could be found – information about which was scarce.

On 17/18 November Major Cleasby-Thompson, with a strong patrol, had considerable success on the Sidi N'sir/Mateur road, ambushing a German column consisting of three heavy eight-wheeled armoured cars and three light recce cars. The next day the situation started to deteriorate and the battalion was put on immediate notice to move to Medjez. Blade Force

HQ arrived commanded by Colonel Hull. We decided to move the battalion to Medjez but it was too late as Germans had crossed the river and the French had started withdrawal. A defensive line was taken up on the hills around Beja supported by two platoons under Captain Coxen and Lieutenant Perrin-Brown to try and persuade the French to fight. They were not keen as they said British forces in the area were not strong enough. They wanted to see some British aircraft in action. We were told that Medjez was going to be bombed the following morning by the RAF at 8.00 am. The French took up position on a hill for a grandstand view. It was a misty morning and at eight o'clock there was no sign of aircraft. As the minutes ticked by the French were fast losing interest. About 8.15 interest was revived by the sound of aircraft approaching. All eyes on Medjez. Then 18 Stukas came through the clouds and knocked hell out of the spectators. Allied prestige reached a new low. We heard that the RAF had failed to take off due to bad weather!

The next main event was Gué Hill. Information was received that an Italian force of some 300, with 17 to 20 tanks, harboured every night some nine miles down the railway line from Sidi N'sir. James Hill got permission to attack the positions with the battalion, less R Company, during the night of 24/25 November. The plan was to attack the positions simultaneously from the south and east.

The battalion was guided by a French sailor who appeared to know the way. I was with the mortar platoon and the Moroccans who were in reserve. It was as black as hell and walking up a railway line in the darkness was not fun. At Z minus 4 I gave the mortars the order to fire. The Moroccans disappeared into the darkness and were never seen again. There was a lot of enemy fire and the action went on for about an hour and three-quarters. At about 0430 hours I made my way to Battalion HQ. There I found James Hill had been badly wounded, the adjutant, Captain Whitelock, had been shot through his rather large nose and also in the back of the neck, and three other ranks were wounded and three killed. We'd heard an explosion just after Z hour, which had been a major disaster for the REs. They were carrying anti-tank mines with the detonators in them in sandbags; one man slipped and his mines went up and the rest followed, by sympathetic detonation, killing three officers and 24 men.

As the CO was seriously wounded I took over command of the battalion and made the necessary plans for withdrawal. We put James Hill and Miles Whitelock into a box on a motorbike. It must have been a very rough ride for them, being bumped by going over the railway sleepers but it was the quickest way back. We were lucky in that we had a Para surgical team operating in Beja Hospital. Their presence probably saved James Hill's life.

The battalion arrived back at Beja and I reported to Colonel Hull at Blade Force HQ. I appointed Major Cleasby-Thompson as 2 i/c and we then got orders to protect the 17th/21st Lancers' tank harbour on the Sidi N'sir/Mateur road. The battalion was to move by day with air-cover and be in position by sunset. The only air-cover we got was German and we lost eight killed and 13 wounded. The battalion next took up position in Kowshok Farm. Captain Coxen went out and recce'd a farm, afterwards known as Coxen's Farm, about three miles to our front and reported it was unoccupied except by animals which were all staggering around drunk! The farm had been machine-gunned and the vats punctured so the place was swimming in red wine. There was a great drunken bull so I released it in the direction of the enemy. We patrolled out from there, inflicting heavy casualties on the enemy with minimum loss to ourselves.

On 28 November the 2nd Battalion Lancashire Fusiliers arrived and I came to a friendly agreement with their CO. They would work by day and we would work by night.

We were having considerable trouble from two Messerschmitts, known as Mutt and Jeff, who visited us daily, sometimes twice. The RAF were conspicuous by their absence. However on 4 December we witnessed a most frightening air battle above our Battalion HQ when 13 Blenheims and four Spitfires were shot down by Mutt and Jeff.

We left Coxen's Farm and life continued in hellish weather, wet and cold. We were continuously on the move and in close contact with the enemy every day. The battalion withdrew to Sidi N'sir. We had been in action fighting continuously for 26 days and it was now time for a rest and to take a look at ourselves. Having survived 21 days as acting CO I was now entitled to become a temporary lieutenant colonel so I got myself a couple of pips – the only advantage of rank is that it gives you more power to negotiate – instead of dealing with the monkey it is now the organ grinder.

We moved to a rest area at Souk el Khemis where we battled for billets against all and sundry and being 1 Para we won in the end. Our doctor, Captain Haggie, organized wine from the nearest monastery and we got a substantial NAAFI ration of booze and cigarettes. A bathhouse was found which was enjoyed by all. Oeufs and oranges were plentiful and cheap thanks to the Controle Civile de Beja. We also received some pay. We reorganized and re-equipped and began to look less like tinkers and more like soldiers.

We moved back to the Beja area on 21 December. Morale was

extremely high and the battalion was briefed for an attack on Longstop Hill, which to our relief was cancelled.

The padre was promoted and to celebrate his advancement to major went into Beja, joined a queue for what he thought was a shop and found himself in the local brothel. Much to his irritation this bit of intelligence spread round the battalion like wildfire.

Christmas Eve was a very cold night and our sand-fire was going down in the officers' mess. I decided to put some life into it with petrol. It exploded and I caught fire. By the time I was extinguished I found that some bugger had nicked my watch.

On Christmas Day it was raining as usual – no presents except for the 2 i/c who discovered he had tapeworms. The post arrived with a parcel for him with 300 green lanyards – it was not his day. The padre visited the NAAFI and got half a bottle of beer per man to go with their roast pig and mutton. Two days later we took over from the 3rd Battalion in Beja Gap. It was a wet bare-arsed hillside but the local sheik was bribed with cigarettes to provide accommodation for Battalion HQ.

On 7 January a train was laid on to move the battalion from Souk el Khemis to Boufarik, a three-day journey. The conditions on board were desperate. The officers were all right but the men travelled in cattle trucks. The train was a glorious sight: cooking tins and pots suspended from every truck. The last man on was Monsieur Borg who arrived with this live goose on a string, a present from the Doctor. Monsieur Borg was a French Maltese who had 'volunteered' to join us as an interpreter. The journey was pretty slow with frequent stops – a good thing as there were no washing or other conveniences on board. Every time the train stopped the men were out like a flash to answer the call of nature or to get hot water for shaving from the engine driver. Then on we'd go with hordes of Arab beggars chasing after us.

When we arrived at Boufarik a half-colonel came up to me and said, 'I've just come to take over 1st Parachute Battalion.' I told him to get lost. I was the CO till somebody senior to me told me otherwise or until I got it in writing. He went off in a huff.

James Hill appeared back from hospital so there were now three lieutenant colonels all hoping to command 1 Para. A book was opened: I was 10–1 on, James Hill evens and Gofton-Salmond 5–1 against. Doc Haggie sorted it all out by declaring Gofton-Salmond medically unfit and James Hill was sent back to hospital which left some officers poorer and others richer, but I was back in the chair I'd never really left.

On 24 January we got on HMS *Beatrix* at Algiers, which was very comfortable: cabins for all the officers, a well-stocked bar and white bread for breakfast for the first time since leaving England. We docked at Bone and made our way by road in the pouring rain to Souk el Arba. The town major was a very unpleasant chap who refused to let us through; I had a flaming row with him and said I was going through his bloody town whether he liked it or not. He threatened me with court-martials – the lot – but on we went and arrived at Ghardimady in the early hours. There was no food and everybody crawled into bed exhausted, wet and hungry. Next day the battalion arrived at El Aroussa after a hellish night drive to our lying-up area – a wet orange grove.

The next day I was ordered to take and hold Djebel Mansour. With Chris Perrin-Brown I visited Captain Favreau of the Foreign Legion. A fine man. He promised to provide a guide and assistance with a fighting patrol. Vic Coxen was in charge of the patrol, but I went along because I wanted to see the best place for the start line and also work out the enemy's fixed lines. It was a long walk and we had to climb down and up this bloody great dry wadi about 30 feet deep. The Germans were very good at firing on fixed lines at night, but you could get underneath if you were careful. The patrol was a success and we captured three Germans from their Mountain Division who occupied Djebel.

Unfortunately Lieutenant Norton was hit badly in the thigh, but he was conscious. I asked the RAMC Corporal Morton who was with us what we should do with him. He was a clever man. He said, 'If we carry him back down the wadi it will take eight hours. The doctor will see him and then we'll have to put him in a jeep to the Field Ambulance Station, which is going to take another four hours and he'll be dead.' So I asked him the best solution. He said, 'Well sir, you know who's up there, they'll probably come down and collect him.' I went and broke the news to Norton. It was a most unpleasant decision to have to make but he took it well. I left a sergeant under cover to watch him and to see if the Germans came down. Sure enough after five minutes Norton fired his Very light pistol. Within half an hour he was picked up by a patrol.

We finally agreed on a plan of attack with the French. Two thousand yards of white tape normally used for marking minefields was used to mark the route to the start line. I had a theory that if we were going to get lost then let us all get lost together. The captain with his French guides would run out the tape and we would all walk along it till we reached the start line. Even with this elementary precaution S Company got lost. We crossed the start line at 0500 hours and began to climb the Djebel through the scrub. It was a hard climb of 500 yards, being machine-gunned and mortared the whole way. We reached our first objective according to plan just before first light. The Germans withdrew and brought down a devastating mortar concentration on our positions and followed this by an immediate counter-attack which we managed to defeat. S Company arrived having suffered heavy casualties on the way from a German machine-gun. So Djebel Mansour was captured and we then tried to get on to El Alliliga but we had too few men to exploit the situation. I decided to consolidate on the centre of the position. An urgent message was sent for the Guards to come and assist as promised. The day was spent in digging in and evacuation of the wounded. Some 105 casualties were evacuated and 35 PoWs. We had captured a German medical orderly who told us they had picked up Lt Norton and while he was in a bad way they had got him to hospital in Tunis in three hours and he was certain that Norton would survive, minus a leg (which he did).

Major Cleasby-Thomson arrived with a mule train bringing rations and ammunition and also the good news that the Guards Brigade were mounting a large-scale attack through the El Alliliga position to the Pont de Fah road. During the night Captain Favreau's company of the French Foreign Legion arrived and were put on the left flank. A Guards company also arrived and the company commander, Major Tufnell, said he was in reserve and was to move on to El Alliliga as soon as it was taken.

I sent the IO, Perrin-Brown, at first light to see what was happening on El Alliliga. The Guards reserve company had moved during the night – where to nobody knew. Perrin-Brown returned in a filthy temper saying that the Guards had not attacked and the only contact he had made was with an enemy machine-gun.

The Guards were found later, down the bottom of the hill. They'd not been told to attack. I then learned that they were to attack later that afternoon. To cover this we laid down smoke. Their attack did not dislodge the machine-gun on the eastern side of El Alliga because that continued to cause us difficulties. I sent a number of calls to the Guards Brigade, but to no avail. At dawn on 1 February the French were overrun in a German counter-attack and their positions occupied. It was no mean feat by the Germans as the French fought well – all their officers were wounded. They had a brave company sergeant major who fixed bayonets and led his men in a counter-attack; but it wasn't successful.

By now we were in big trouble; we needed reinforcements PDQ as we'd suffered a lot of casualties and our mortars had run out of ammunition. But I decided to hang on as long as possible. At 1000 hours S Company were completely out, but remained brandishing grenades. R and T Companies had about 100 rounds between them. Major Conron had been killed and no officers were left in R Company.

I tried to get permission to withdraw at 1010 hours, but they wouldn't give it. At 1030 hours the German mortars stopped which meant they were going to close in any minute. At 1045 hours I asked again for permission to withdraw as the enemy were about 40 yards away. S and R Companies were calling for the Germans to come closer so that they could throw their grenades at them! But I was told to hang on for five minutes and I'd get an answer. I told them that if I hung on for two more minutes there would be no one here to take their bloody answer. I got permission and told the companies to withdraw, leaving the seriously wounded behind.

It was difficult to get the wounded down. We carried them on mules and stretchers – but we were under continuous fire. But once the Germans realized we were withdrawing they lifted their fire. They were very good like that – very professional. It was very difficult. We'd worked hard and were desperately tired, but morale was good. We had heavy losses – 35 dead, 132 wounded and 16 missing – nearly 50 per cent of our strength and we were back where we started.

To this day I have never been able to discover the importance of Djebel Mansour or El Alliliga. For the overall battle all we did was to occupy about a regiment of a crack German division for about four days which may have helped the general situation, but I always ask myself: was it worth the cost?

For the next few days we moved from one orange grove to the next trying to reorganize. We finally finished up in Tontla where I found my chest giving me hell. The MO thought I had pneumonia so I was put to bed in a byre with a donkey and a cow for bedmates. I slept for about 24 hours and woke as good as new.

Nine officers and 144 men from the 5th Camerons and the 6th Royal Welch Fusiliers plus some old hands from hospital came to us as reinforcements. We were soon back to war again on a bare-arsed hillside called Argoub where we were mortared and shelled. It was difficult to dig in but we had tank support which cheered us up. We remained there till the beginning of March which gave me the opportunity of resting companies and training the new boys. It also gave me an opportunity of co-operating with other arms, something we had not done up to that date because we had always been on our own.

Our next big task was Tamera. We got there in the evening on 6 March, took over from a Guards battalion and lay in the bushes in the rain all night. We knew where the Germans were but we did not know their strengths. Fortunately they had no idea how weak or spread out we were. We didn't really dig in but each company took up an area. Vic Coxen took the front company and remained in one place while the others were prepared to move. We were all within shouting distance of each other. The first attack came down the road as we expected at 0730 hours. It was about two companies strong. They hadn't expected anything other than Vic Coxen's company and they didn't spot the other two. We let the enemy advance to within 300 yards of our main position where they were enfiladed by S Company, commanded by a wild Welshman, Major 'Taffy' Lloyd Jones. We then brought down artillery and mortar fire and the enemy was pinned down in some dead ground and 40 prisoners were captured. The main attack was on S Company. I ordered T Company to make a sweep to clear up the front. While this was going on Brigadier Down who was determined to see the fight arrived at the command post.

I was sitting there in this hole in the ground and I wanted to get a written message to Vic Coxen. I was busy, so without looking up I shouted for a runner. 'Take this to the OC R Company – urgent', and thrust it into a hand. When I looked up Brigadier Down, or 'Charlie Orange' as he was affectionately called, was streaking across the country clutching my message. I thought I might have to do a bit of explaining if he got killed! But he got through. The troops loved it and it was a great morale booster to see a bare-headed brigadier acting as a runner. T Company's sweep was 100 per cent successful, returning with 100 prisoners including Witzig's para-troops.

That afternoon battle commenced again with an attack on S Company and 'Taffy' Lloyd Jones called for reinforcements. I ordered R Company to move to the right of S Company. Two hours later S Company reported that they had been completely overrun. I had anticipated this and moved T Company in, ready to counter-attack. They retook the position but not without heavy casualties. By 1800 hours the situation was under control and so ended a day of very hard fighting where 1 Para came out on top, but with the loss of four officers.

The following day Lieutenant Mayhew attacked a village and killed 13 of the enemy and took prisoners without casualties. This was a brilliant bit of initiative on his part.

Brigade asked me to take six tanks and make a recce down the road to Sedjenane. I told them it was a waste of time as they could not deploy off the road. I was summoned to HQ and told to make the recce. At 1230 hours battle began when the tanks and R Company, who were supporting them, came under attack. Half an hour later they withdrew – cost two tanks, three killed and five wounded on our side – we captured 17 prisoners.

We confirmed what we already knew about the enemy at a cost I doubt was worth it; tanks were scarce. The day ended with the DLIs attacking 2 Para, much to Colonel Frost's annoyance.

The following morning started as usual with sporadic shelling. We had a bit of a shock when the enemy got within 50 yards of the Battalion HQ. Jock Clements initiated a counter-attack with about 30 men, cooks and clerks. They all went at them screaming like banshees. 'Wahoo Mahomet!' It was very tough hand-to-hand fighting. S and T Companies made an attack which completed the destruction of the enemy. That night we had a friendly exchange of wounded PoWs.

By 16 March we'd been fighting for eight days on the trot and had had little sleep. We had been continuously attacked, at times overrun, suffered severe casualties particularly among the officers but in the end had yielded no ground. We handed over to 3 Para and withdrew to Tabarka. There I had time to think and analyse our situation.

There was no doubt in my mind that any form of defence must be offensive and must be flexible. I therefore coined the phrase 'an offensive mobile defence'. But you have to have the terrain on your side; for example at Tamera we had the cork forest. The other factor was the absolute dependence on your junior leaders, be they lance corporals or sergeants, and the determination of the soldier to fight. I was never let down.

Our peaceful existence at Tabarka did not last long for the battalion moved to Djebel Abion to cover withdrawal of the Leicesters. As we withdrew later enemy patrols followed, there were some short sharp encounters and we were also shelled by our own guns. During this Lance Corporal Hewitt of the RAMC carried out one of the bravest acts I've ever seen. He was helping one of the walking wounded when we were shelled. Everybody ran for cover but Hewitt pulled his wounded soldier into a hollow and lay on top of him. He was unfortunately killed by a shell splinter. Everyone agreed he would be commended for a Victoria Cross. It was turned down as Hewitt, unbeknownst to us, was a conscientious objector and as such could neither be promoted nor awarded a decoration.

On 19 March we moved to Truila, dug in and got little sleep. We then had some problems with the Leicesters who had to withdraw from a feature in front of us which resembled a bowler hat.

The next day Lieutenant General Allfrey came to tell me that the 3rd Battalion had failed that night to take Bowler Hat. He said to me, 'It's got to be taken.' I told him my men were very tired. Then I said to Allfrey, 'I'll make a bargain with you, sir. I'll take it, but I'll not hold it, because I've no intention of sitting up there and getting mortared.' 'Right, you take it,' he said, 'and the 3rd Battalion will hold it.'

He arranged for the engineers to put a bridge across the river. I was expecting heavy casualties. I sent two companies up and one round the back. At the bottom of the hill I met the commanding officer of 3 Para, Pine-Coffin. He said, 'Alistair, you must be mad to try to take that hill.' I said, 'Not half as mad as you, 'cos you're going to hold it.'

Three-quarters of the way up the hill it was just beginning to get light when we found slit trenches with men in, still asleep – no sentries up. We captured the feature and took a lot of prisoners by 0300 hours! After that we had three glorious days off in a farm where we could have a bath and catch up on some sleep and lie in the sun.

On 26 March we were told there was to be a big push on Tamera to recapture it. They'd beaten off two previous attacks – I don't think they were expecting another. As far as we were concerned we were to put in our attack with the rest of the brigade and a Thabour of Goums – about 1,000 charming black gentlemen from the Atlas Mountains of Morocco. They were great soldiers, very well led by good French officers. They'd done a recce earlier but our brigadier wasn't too sure how far they'd got. One of the Goums opened a sack and out came five heads. He didn't need much convincing after that. The Goums loved boots; it didn't matter much if the feet were still in them. They used to tie the boots round their necks with the laces.

At 2300 hours on 27 March we crossed the start line. On the way I knew there was a mosque and a farm. I wanted to know the best way to get there so I called Monsieur Borg and told him to get hold of an Arab who knew the area. He brought me an Arab so I tore a 500-franc note in half and told him he'd get the other half when he got us to the farm. It was pitch dark. We had this big French mule called Peter the Great (he could open tins with his mouth!) with a bloody great wireless set on it, and this Arab being poked by Borgy's Sten gun, showing us the way. It was about 2300 hours. We had just got into the wadi when all of a sudden the guns started up from the 70th and 71st Field Regiment, Royal Artillery. I don't know what they were firing at, but they were bloody close to us. Of course the mule went berserk, ditched the radio and it needed four men to hang on to him. The Arab took off, so there I was shouting at Borgy for letting him go.

We reached the objective and it was obvious we were between the Italians and Germans. The Goums were slaughtering the Italians on our left. We then had a very heavy day's fighting mainly in support of 2 Para but we kept pressing on. I personally had very little control of the situation but I knew we were heading in the right direction. Then the plan changed and I was ordered to attack the old 2 Para positions. I couldn't understand this as it was supposed to be the objective of the other nine infantry battalions on our right. We then had a good battle with Witzig's parachutists and were very unfortunate not to capture Colonel Witzig in person. He only escaped our clutches by minutes.

It was a beautiful sunny morning so I sent someone down the road to the Recce Regiment to get as many armoured cars as he could so that we could climb on and chase the Bosch, but he came back disappointed. The next person to come down the road was General Allfrey, immaculately dressed, as always, brown boots, pressed trousers and Sam Browne, sitting on the back of a military policeman's motorbike. I told him I'd sent for armoured cars to support my move. He said he would deal with that: then I said that I understood from my headquarters that there was supposed to be an infantry division in the area. He looked at me and said, 'I'm afraid there has been the biggest cock-up in history. They never even crossed the start line.' And away he went and I heard later that he sacked the CO of the Recce Regiment for not providing support when I wanted it. But we had had a good battle and had been in action, with little sleep, for 56 hours.

We then went up to Sedjenane and we held a long front with the Germans about seven miles away. General Allfrey turned up again and said the Americans were going to relieve us in the next few days. Then he said, 'They also want a prisoner!' My heart sank in my boots. I knew getting a prisoner would cost us the lives of many of my men. I was not best pleased. I had Captain 'Andy' Anderson, who was a radio officer, out on daylight recce patrol. So I said, as soon as he comes in and gives me the latest form we'll go out and I'll lead it myself. As it was getting dark I saw Andy's patrol come in and he was heading in with a German officer from the 256 Mountain Regiment. I could have hugged him. I said, 'How the hell did you do that?' He said he'd taken off that morning and had just been watching a working party. This German officer had come out and set his men some wiring work. Then he'd walked a bit away from them, taken off his jacket, put it under his head and gone to sleep in the sunshine. Andy went down and nicked him. There wasn't even a shot fired. Brilliant.

I sent this German officer straight back to Brigade Headquarters. General Allfrey got straight on to me and he swore blind that I had the German with me all the time he'd been talking to me. 'How the hell,' he said, 'did you get him back before I arrived?' 'Sheer luck, sir,' I said, 'Sheer luck.'

When I'm talking leadership I always think of Andy Anderson. It would have been easy for him lying there to say, 'Bugger it, I'm here and he's there and we're going back next week', but he didn't. He earned the grateful thanks of about 200 chaps and saved us a number of casualties. Andy got the immediate award of an MC. We never did dig defensive positions for the Americans. I went down to see the American colonel. I was 27 at the time and when I met him he seemed an old man. I explained to the colonel the situation as I saw it from where we were positioned. He gathered all his officers and said: 'Say, boys, this is war.' As we were in virtually a rest area I asked if it was really necessary for them to be wearing their steel helmets. The CO looked at me and said, 'If George S. Patton says you wear your steel helmet, you wear it. If George S. Patton says attack, we attack, and that's where the goddamn fuck-up begins.' I was inclined to agree with him.

On 15 April 900 Americans, still in their steel helmets, took over our positions as if a rodeo had come to town. Our battalion, 200 strong, withdrew and made its way through streams of American transport to Viaduct Farm outside Beja, where we had spent Christmas. We had mobile baths laid on and the next day I sent out a party to bury some of our dead in the Tamera area.

General Allfrey arrived to have a look round. We paraded in a hollow square. He was very generous in his praise and he kindly told me I'd got a bar to my DSO. He asked his ADC for a knife and being a good ADC he had one. He then cut the rosette from his MC (he had an MC and bar) and handed it to me saying it would be much easier to replace his than for me to get one. The battalion had done well in their five months in North Africa: four DSOs, eleven MCs, three DCMs, sixteen MMs, one Croix de Guerre and a Legion d'Honneur for James Hill. On 19 April I received orders to move to Boufarik. That was the end of our fighting in North Africa. I think we learned a hell of a lot there. We learned to like to fight, the value of being mobile and not to waste ammunition. We also realized the value of physical fitness, of being very, very quick, and keeping yourself clean. I also learned the best way of communicating was to send a chap running; the wirelesses were no good in wooded areas. You also had to get used to losses, you became hardened to them. It was no use worrying about it. I had a very nice young regular officer who came to me before Tamera and gave me his grandfather's watch to look after. He was convinced he was going to be killed. I told him that if he talked like that he would be killed. Twenty-four hours later he was carried past me on a stretcher. I asked the stretcher-bearer if he'd be all right. He said he would, as he was not badly wounded. I thought, thank God for that. On the road going back to the RAP the ambulance was hit by a German plane and they were all killed.

One of the high points was when we were on a train to Algiers. We passed a prison camp with hundreds of Germans and Italians. They ran to the wire shouting out, 'Red Devils, Red Devils!' – We all waved back. That was a very moving moment.

MAJOR VIC COXEN, 1st Parachute Battalion

We marched ten miles after we landed at Maison Blanche and pulled into some place for the night. In the morning I woke, threw off my groundsheet, looked up and there hanging over my head was a great bunch of bananas. I thought, 'I can stand this, this is all right, it's going to be a nice place to live.' Of course we'd spent the night in the Botanical Gardens, so it was the only fucking bunch of bananas in North Africa!

The next day we parachuted in Souk el Arba and found ourselves 400 miles ahead of Blade Force for the next few weeks. The French hadn't quite decided whose side they were on. We made it difficult because we went and sat in the middle of them. The moment the Germans appeared we went for them. The Germans would then shell the French, so they put their helmets on and said they were in the war.

One of our early contacts with French soldiers was when we dug in on some hills and found when dawn broke that we had dug in about 30 yards in front of the French positions. There behind us stood these huge seven-foot men with black faces and the old Le Bel rifles. They were a regiment of Tirailleurs – the native levies of the French Colonial Army – we didn't stay long.

On the Gué battle I was leading my two platoons up towards my objective which was a rented camp. When we got there, it was a field stacked with corn! Of course it was pitch dark and I was creeping forward on my stomach towards what had been said to be an ack-ack gun position; again there was nothing there, But at night you can't take chances.

On our way up we'd captured a bunch of Italians. One of them put his hands up but he still had a pistol in one hand. I pointed to it with a little stick I carried (we all have our affectations), and he said, 'Oh!' and dropped it as if it would burn him – he was terrified, poor little chap. When I looked at it later it was a .22 Beretta which was as rusty as buggery.

After Gué we were ordered to a farm where a tank battle had taken place. It was at the end of a long valley. I was going to make the move with my company, but one platoon suffered badly from an attack by a Messer-schmitt, then Alistair needed the other platoon, so I set out with ten men. It was a moonlit night so I decided that we would go beyond the farm and come in the back way in case anyone was there. It was slightly eerie with all these smoking tanks around. In the yard was an Italian tank with two blackened corpses. One of my soldiers stuck cigarettes in their mouths. The closer we got to the farm the more my chaps began to cough. I stopped them and said, 'Look, is there any one of you bastards that isn't dying of pneumonia?!' I gave them each an acid drop and they shut up.

We were right up against the side of the house when I thought I heard some noise inside, so I said we'd do the normal drill. As I was a bit bigger than the others, I took a run at the door and wham – over it went with 'Titch' Stanley and the other men firing their Stens over my head. I shouted to them to hold their fire because I landed on the top of three dead Germans. There were seven of them laid out. This place had been a casualty clearing station, and these chaps had all been killed, or shot and died there. They cushioned my fall a bit, but it was a little eerie really. So Coxen's Farm, as it was called from then on, was taken by only ten men, nine of whom were asthmatic! I got on the blower and Alistair sent up the rest of my company. We held the farm for some time, long enough to recover several tanks and blow up those that were beyond repair.

We had been going for some time – about six weeks or so – and I had run out of pants; they had literally worn to bits. I was rummaging around a few drawers in the farmhouse and found some clothes. I had a little boy's jersey which I cut the arms off and opened it so I could pull my head through; it was rather like a bust-bodice. Then I found this magnificent silk chemise and some bloomers which were absolute heaven and I wore them until Blade Force brought up supplies. I was very grateful to that woman, whoever she was, but of course I was frightened to wash and hang them out in case anyone pinched them!

While we were out on patrol Monsieur Borg found a goose, which he presented to Doc Haggie. Borg was a railway employee, who had done military service, and who accompanied a number of patrols – he was very useful to us. The first week in January we moved by train to Boufarik and of course Oswald the goose had to come with us, hidden in the one lavatory in the officers' compartment. One night a senior officer, noted for being rather keen on his appearance, was seen entering the lavatory. A junior officer whipped out a piece of wire and twisted it round the door handle so that it could not be opened from inside. There were no lights on the train, so when the gentleman concerned sat down he disturbed the goose which flapped around, making a hell of a noise. The latrine discipline of geese leaves much to be desired, so the floor was extremely slippery. Cries came from this gentleman, but he was left there for some time until someone took pity on him and opened the door and said, 'What is it, old chap?' The poor man had no clothes to change into, so no one would sit near him.

The train stopped and started with great irregularity so people would jump off, lower their trousers and, just as they were about to do what they had to do, the bloody train would start up again; but it was slow-moving and easy to catch. Of course they were steam trains so we had plenty of hot water to shave in. We took too much once and there was no water to run the train; so they changed it to an electric train, which was rather dull, but it went a little faster. When it stopped everybody leapt off the train, but being electric it would start again without warning and move off quickly so everybody was grabbing their trousers and rushing back like maniacs to clamber on to the last three carriages. They then had to find their way by any means back into their trucks. It was terribly funny to watch, but that was the joy of it all.

We spent about a week in Boufarik where we sorted out COs and Alistair Pearson was allowed to continue. Colonel Gofton-Salmond was the DAQ, and he gave us an absolute guarantee that we would not be moved. So Alistair granted leave to everybody to go into Algiers, which was 10–15 miles away. Needless to say after they had all been despatched, it came through that we were going to be leaving at sparrow-fart the next morning. We had to send out people to search the brothels and bars, to the fury of everyone. But there it was, that was the fun of it. Eventually, we did all manage to get onto this boat at Algiers; some optimists thought we might be sailing for England.

We landed at Bone and travelled by truck to Souk el Arba. The convoy consisted of 1st and 3rd Battalions and was some 20 miles long. Our rations had been skilfully packed at the rear of the convoy. We were getting very hungry. We noticed trucks which were loaded with rations passing by and thought it was too good to miss. So men were supported at the side of their trucks by their friends, and swung at these boxes with pickaxes, hooking them off into their own trucks as we went by. We stayed the night at Ghardimaou and moved the next day to El Aroussa prior to our attack on Djebel Mansour.

The idea of the attack was to shorten the line in and around Djebel Mansour. The line was shaped like a horseshoe, with Djebel Mansour in the centre. If we took Djebel Mansour it would not only shorten the line, but would put us in better control of the two roads that converged on the far side of it, which were in the Germans' hands.

It was decided that I should lead a patrolling force out on 31 January to see how heavily Djebel Mansour was held. Captain Favreau, who commanded a detachment of the Foreign Legion, gave me one of his officers who had patrolled the area, as a guide. This officer showed us to the bottom of this very deep wadi and then left. We crossed this difficult area and eventually got onto the smoother, but steeper ground on the far side of the wadi. We found out later that had we gone farther to the left we would have run into the enemy's defensive position all the way down the side of the hill. It is possible that they thought the approach from the side we had come from was too steep for anyone to attempt. The fact that we didn't hit it was to prove a little costly the next day.

When we got up near the top the scrub became slightly more open, and with the moonlight you could see how far you could go. The hill was slightly convex and therefore the top always appeared to be 20 or 30 yards in front of you, so there was no great field of fire. As we had not come across any barbed wire and I wanted to be fairly close when we did, I moved up to be with the leading section. When we were almost to the top, I was challenged by a German sentry. He was not satisfied with my answer and threw a grenade, which bounced and exploded behind myself and my batman. We were both hit; I had bits of grenade in my back and he had it in one arm, but it was not enough to incommode us. I began firing at the general position of the sentry, to keep his head down, while the section was fanning out and going in. We overran the position completely and took about 14 prisoners. I consolidated the area but it was starting to get light by that time.

I sent Lieutenant Norton along the ridge to have a look at the defences, with instructions not to go farther than the dip, if he met any resistance. We had picked up several machine-guns. Fire started to come not only from the other high point on Mansour, but from Alliliga, which was quite strongly held. I had overrun, probably, the first two platoons of a company. The rest of the ground was strongly held beyond, and it was not a place that one could have held oneself during the day because Alliliga, which was about 500–700 yards away, commanded all the approaches. Frankly the only thing we could do was to get the hell out of there. There was a fair amount of cover going down the slope but once we got into the wadi we were in range of their mortars and there was no place to hide. But we got support fire from the French 75-mm, and smoke, which enabled us to work our way back up across the open ground.

Following that patrol a night assault by the battalion with follow-up by the Guards and a company of the French Foreign Legion was decided. I took out 'Panzer' Manser and the Provo Section and got up there and laid the tape to the start-line. We arrived more quickly than the first time and had about an hour to wait before the battalion came. I spread my people out a little in the hope of spotting patrols. While I was doing this one of my men was coughing a great deal. I put my hand on his mouth, gave him a boiled sweet and told him that if he coughed again I would beat him on the head with my pistol. R and T Companies followed the tape, came up and were put on their start-line with a difficult, but straight, climb. However, S Company lost the tape and didn't turn up at the start-line. Unfortunately they had slipped too far to the left, and had encountered enemy defensive positions near the foot of the hill. They ran into intense machine-gun fire and mines and took quite a lot of casualties, but fought their way past the defence and up and onto their objective. But people like Philip Mellor were killed, a splendid chap. He'd already lost one eye and now he had his leg blown off, but he was last seen sitting up, one eye, one leg off, still shooting at the Germans. When we recovered his body he had 17 bullets in him. S Company's move to the left was a very costly error.

The rest of the battle went on throughout the day and R and T Companies took the smaller hill and S Company continued over and took the other hill. S and T companies occupied part of Alliliga for some time. It was hoped that the Foreign Legion, which we had under command, and the Guards, would have been able to come through and consolidate on Alliliga as well, but the amount of fire brought down on them prevented this. The main advantage the Germans had was the terrain. Behind hills with razor-like tops they were able to bring up reserves to counter-attack. Firing ordinary field guns, or 25-pounders, you couldn't get the crest clearance in to hit the area where their reserves were. The enemy on the forward slopes you could deal with, but you could not stop the build-up of the forces behind, because you couldn't hit them. What one wanted was howitzers or mortar fire, and we were lacking these. Peter Cleasby-Thompson brought up a column of mules loaded with mortars and we used these, with those we'd already captured. During the battle, which took place all the next day and night, we ran out of ammunition, and even to take a casualty back was a four-hour hump.

If Alliliga could have been taken, then there would have been an open way to transport stuff. But as it wasn't going to be taken it was almost inevitable that we couldn't stay there. When Lieutenant Jessop came over the crest and said that we should withdraw, we carried all our casualties with us, but the bullets were starting to push around as we clambered down. Alistair as usual was the last man off. Enemy artillery fire was coming down across the escape route up the far side. Had it been British guns firing they would have done so individually, boom, boom, boom. But with the Germans they were so regimented it was kroom, whee-e-e, boom, then a pause. So, with bat-wing ears you could hear the kroom go and you ran ten yards and went down, said swear words, got up and ran again, waiting for the next kroom. It is helpful when you are tuned in to artillery.

I picked up one man who had been hit earlier and had a morphia tag hanging from his neck. His hip to his knee was very nearly open, and he had also been shot through the body, and one arm. I told him to hang on and help himself as much as possible, and he did. We struggled about 30 yards until we got to the cover; then we did a bit more, until we got to the Guards who were there with their carriers. I think he made those last few yards on willpower alone. As they put him on a carrier I thought to myself, 'Christ, have you got room for me?' I had a note from him about five weeks later to say he was all right. Our Field Ambulance used to operate so close behind, that he would have been sewn up almost right away. Because of the general strength and fitness of these men they did not die of pneumonia or shock.

Had we had better weapons, even as little as the pack mountain howitzers that we had up at Tamera later, we might have been more successful, because we could have impeded the enemy from doing all the things they wanted.

I came across similar situations in a number of places during the war – for example before Cassino. There were a number of knife-ridged crests where a German OP (observation post) could sit forever, unless you actually hit him bonk on target. Anything that missed him exploded 200 yards away and anything that was short merely went into the side of a granite hill. At that stage of the war the Americans had an eight-inch howitzer, which fired a monstrous shell a long way and extremely accurately. If you can fire a nine-iron shot from some distance, accurately, ridge clearance doesn't become quite the same problem.

After Mansour, morale was all right. Certainly people were sorry that their chums had gone, but there was never any dejection about it. Soldiers on the whole don't criticize higher tactics; they don't really care much about them. They simply ask, 'Are we going to fight today? Who are we going to fight? Where is he?' It's the job on hand: let's get on with that – and then deal with the next thing.

Food was important too. The 'oeuf' patrols would often penetrate further into enemy lines than the official ones. Trooper Brown would go out on Alistair's one-eyed stallion and ride for miles with all the battalion's money in search of eggs. You lived off the land to supplement your rations. It was not terribly safe for a sheep to get too near! We used to save up things like sugar and tea, then we'd have a good brew-up – that was a morale-raiser. Soldiers will go a long time without food, but without a cup of tea morale drops a bit.

We moved next to the Argoub where we were reinforced with nine officers and 144 other ranks from the 5th Camerons and the 6th Royal Welch Regiment (later 5 Para Battalion and 6 Para Battalion), who had only been in North Africa two weeks. The Germans were on the other side of the valley, but their OPs were watching, and if anything moved they had bugger-all else to do but to shell it. One shell hit the trench next to mine and my batman, 'Titch' Stanley, was buried. The man on top of him had a piece of shell stuck in his back, about the size of a milk bottle. So we carefully removed him and pulled out 5ft 2in. Stanley who was underneath him. My signaller, Scott, wasn't hit, but he was suffering from shell-shock and his arms and legs were going like a wild dervish. He was in spasm. I sent him to the doctor who came to me the next day and told me that Scott wanted to come back. He thought he'd be all right, but he really couldn't tell. A few days later when shelled Scott suddenly got up, shouting, 'Five men to a tin of duff', and ran out into the middle of the bombardment, throwing his kit up into the air. Thankfully, he wasn't killed. Alistair sent him back to B Echelon and he became an officers' mess steward.

We moved up to Tamera and took up two positions on the Sedjenane road which the Guards had vacated. We had not been there long when S Company reported that the Germans were advancing down the road, about two companies in strength. We just waited and waited until the first company came over the rise and down towards us, and as their second company had just got over the top of the rise, we opened fire. I couldn't fire at the second company from my position but S Company, under Taffy Lloyd Jones, could and did. The gunners and mortars opened up as well. By eleven o'clock that morning we had everything under control and had over 100 prisoners. The prisoners were lined up and marched off with about a dozen or so chaps to guard them.

Two hours later a second attack came in and engaged S Company. Taffy asked for reinforcements so the reserve platoon from R Company moved round to him. T Company were ordered into reserve, ready to counter-attack. S Company were still in position but had suffered a lot of casualties, including Taffy. Alistair ordered T Company in and the position was restored – but it had been a very costly six-hour battle with four officers killed and many wounded. I spoke to Taffy, who'd been shot in the chest, and asked him what had happened. He said, 'It was old 55' (55 Jones was his batman, he himself was 78 Jones). 'I was just about to shoot at this chap and he told me not to because he was one of ours! But he was a German para in an identical smock, so he shot me.' I said, 'You're fucking lucky because a couple of inches more and he'd have got you through the heart!' He replied wryly, 'No, a couple of inches the other way and he'd have missed!'

On 16 March I was told to go up and visit the Leicesters, who were a little uneasy. I went back and picked up a couple of platoons, and just as we got back to the Leicesters small arms fire could be heard. I was asked to go and see what the problem was, and went off with my batman towards the shooting to find out what the hell was going on. I found some 6 Commando people coming back, fighting a rearguard action. I sent them back behind our positions and told my men to hold their fire. The Germans were not expecting to be ambushed and we knocked the shit out of them.

I then got a wireless message through to tell me to withdraw back to 1st Battalion, but I decided I would stay with the Leicesters until they had stabilized their position. Later on I was making a routine check back with them and I got no reply. So I sent Platt, my signaller, back to their HQ. Now Platt was noted for his ability to say fuck as often as possible. He phoned me and said, 'That you, sir?' 'Yes,' I said. 'They've fucked off.' 'Who have?' 'Those fuckers; they've all fucked off.' I thought I might as well get back to my battalion; as I did so the forward company of the Leicesters came through. Their commander said he had been ordered to withdraw to the road. I told Bill Anderson, my 2 i/c, to take them down and put them on the track down to the road, and that we'd follow. A little while later the CO of the Leicesters came up and was apologetic when I told him that no one had told me that he was withdrawing. I got in touch with my battalion and they told me to report to the 2nd Battalion, who told me to take up position on the left-hand side of the road, forming up with them. It was a quiet night but in the morning I heard Johnny Frost give orders for his battalion to withdraw. I had to come up on the radio and say, 'What about me?' He told me to go back down the road. I told him in no uncertain terms that I would not go back that way because the Germans were shelling it and that I would make my way back through the woods. That was the second time in two days that I had been attached to another battalion with my company and been left out of their withdrawal plan.

Three days later, on 22 March, we were ordered to take Sidi Bou Delaa which were two small hills on the far side of a river which divided us from the Germans. The 3rd Battalion had failed to take them the previous evening. It was to be a full battalion attack. The Royal Engineers laid a bridge across the river and as soon as it was dark we moved off. As we approached the feature looked like two sugar loaves.

We shelled them for five minutes, at five minutes to the hour, for five hours. Being good Germans they kept their heads down at five minutes to the next hour and that's when we put our attack in. All went according to plan. I told the Irish to attack one particular section. But the moment the shooting started they went clean through everybody, you know, 'Is this a private fight – or can anybody join in?' R Company went straight up and cleared the feature and we only had one man hurt. When we got to the Germans they were all sleeping or had their heads down and they were killed in those positions. Their reserve company must have heard out 'Wahoo Mahomet', because they ran off like bucks in the moonlight.

One of the Irish fell over, 15 feet below me. I said, 'What's the matter?' 'I've broke my ankle, sir.' So I replied, 'Well, get up and bloody hop down.' Which he did, and he had!

As we were coming back down one of my men thought we were being stalked. I looked back in the moonlight, and there were five figures crouching behind us. I took a chance and said, 'Who's that there?' A voice said, 'Glory be to God, sir, I was just about to throw a grenade at you!' It was Sergeant Birmingham of the Irish platoon. At the bottom of the hill Birmingham said, 'What shall I do with the grenade, sir?' I said, 'What grenade?' 'The one I was going to throw at you.' I said, 'Well, what about it?' 'Well, I pulled the pin out.' I said, 'Well, throw the fucking thing away somewhere – don't bother me with it.' So he turned round, in the middle of this little field, and threw it. I screamed, 'Down!' and we were covered in rock and shit and dust. It really was, 'The man said throw it, so I threw it.' I could have beaten his head in.

On 26 March we got the news that we were to push forward and capture the Tamera position. It was a large attack with about nine battalions. At eleven that evening the artillery barrage went in as were were fording the river. Our first attack was fierce, but we captured the feature. It was dark in the woods and I didn't know where the hell we were. I told Alistair the best thing would be to withdraw with the other companies and I would be the forward echelon for the advance in the morning. He agreed.

The next morning I started forward and I hadn't gone 25 yards before I hit the Germans. This was a dawn attack and they were frightened – they gave in with just a couple of bursts of fire. We then started to move forward through the woods where we were fighting Italians; we captured about 400 of them. The 2nd Battalion were having a hard time of it, they were fighting Germans. We continued to move through the woods till we came down to where the old Battalion HQ was, and there we swung in. The 2nd Battalion had come through and were up on our right. As we were coming through there we missed Witzig, the German para commander, by about five minutes. Our push went right through Tamera and beyond Sedjenane, where we dug in. Eventually an American battalion came out to relieve us.

They'd marched out from Sedjenane and their feet were sore. We had to dig them a battalion position – we were only about 300 strong, and they were about 900. They didn't really understand our way of doing things. I said, 'You see that hill ahead, well, we've got a platoon dug in on the side there and the rest of us are in reserve here. Now, if the German attacks us, the moment he gets close enough we say "Wahooo Mohamet!" and we go for the bugger! You see he hates being attacked when he is attacking – puts him off like anything.' They continued to look rather puzzled. I stayed another day to see they were all right and that was the end of Tamera.

Taffy Lloyd Jones came back to us after his injuries in the first battle for Tamera, where he'd seen about 20 Germans going into a hut. He always carried a walking stick and so he banged on the door and told them to come out in Welsh, because he didn't think they would understand English. He took all their weapons off them and was stuffing them into his smock and down his trousers when one went off and made a hole in his thigh.

He was sent back for repairs. After the Americans took over I was going to a company commanders' meeting with him in a jeep and I asked him how he was. He said in his slow Welsh, 'I went back to the Aid Post and they asked if I was walking wounded and I said, "Yes", so they said get in the truck which took me to another Aid Post. When I got there they asked the same question, and I said, "Yes", so I was put on another truck. When I finally got to where I thought I'd get treatment, there was a lot going on and nobody looked at my wound at all, so I thought I might as well come back, so I did.' The way he told this story made me roar with laughter – 'Great story, Taffy, great story,' I said, slapping him on the thigh, only to realize it was the damaged one. He nearly dropped out of the jeep!

I held on to one German major we'd captured at Tamera, a nice little man who spoke good English. We were talking about the war and he said, 'We are rather in the same boat as you, you have the Americans and we have the Italians.' That night we were bloody tired, but we didn't know what to do with Fritz. There was an old bed so Peter Cleasby-Thompson and I lay on this, with Fritz in between us. When we woke in the morning, he'd gone. Just as I said, 'Well what shall we do?' he came in with two cups of tea and shaving water! One minute you are knocking shit out of each other and the next you are showing each other photographs of your family. It's as if someone has blown the whistle and the game is over.

My soldier servant died at Tamera. A bit of shell had hit his backside, so I carried him over to a tank and he was taken to the hospital about ten miles back and operated on immediately. After we were relieved I went to the hospital to see him. I was amazed when the doctor told me he had died. I said, 'Why, he was a very strong fellow. What happened?' He said a shell had clipped his rectum and bowel, which was not terribly dangerous, but the trouble was he turned his face to the wall and gave up. This was quite out of character. He was a great curse to me in some ways because he was constantly saying, 'Let's do something spectacular, sir!' But he would never turn his face to the wall. It wasn't until later when I went through his kit and found his diary that I realized what had happened. He'd always talked a lot about his wife and child. His diary was full of, 'Haven't heard from home'; 'She's complaining about something'; 'She says she is going off with an American with my daughter.' The final entry said, 'Had our wedding ring for Christmas.' I always feel guilty about it. I only wish he'd talked to me. You're very close to your batman and you rely on him enormously – he was my eyes. When we were doing a reconnaissance I used to say, 'Watch over me and see nobody kills me.' He was very good. I wrote to his wife to tell her of his death, but never had a reply.

COLOUR SERGEANT SEAL, 1st Parachute Battalion

For our move from Souk el Arba we were to use some old French producer-gas-burning charabancs, operating on charcoal, to take us to Beja. In our company we had two brothers, both sergeants, Ted and Tony Baxter. As we lined up for our move Tony put his Sten gun between his knees to adjust his pack, but it fell to the ground and discharged a number of rounds into the legs of the nearest soldiers. Not a great start.

On the morning of 17 November my platoon and another, both of S Company, and a few REs, and one three-inch mortar group embussed and headed for Sidi N'sir, the last French outpost towards Tunis. Our orders were to take German prisoners. When we arrived it appeared to be well-guarded by native troops and French Officers. We then pushed forward, I say 'pushed' because, of the three buses, two broke down, and we had to do a lot of pushing! After an uphill struggle we arrived at a farm, and after a cup of tea we rested.

In the early hours of the morning I woke to the sound of Sten-gun-fire, looked over a wall and there, 150 yards away, on the Sidi N'sir road, were six German armoured cars moving towards the French positions. We let them pass. It was a good thing the buses had broken down because the farm we had stopped in was an ideal position for an ambush. Our plan was for the sappers to string out their Hawkins grenades across the road; a number of men would go under a viaduct with Gammon bombs and we would hide among the rocks with Sergeant Tucker on his mortar. I thought Major

Cleasby-Thompson was in rather a vulnerable spot behind a small haystack in the open ground.

It was a nail-biting few hours' wait for the return of the Germans, then they suddenly burst into view, heading towards our position. The REs were magnificent; the Hawkins grenades were pulled along across the road and the first heavy armoured car went up with a bang. The Germans tried to get out and were shot down by the REs. All hell let loose as we opened up with machine-guns and rifles. The Gammon bombers now sallied forth and started to chuck their bombs. The armoured cars seemed to be blowing up left, right and centre, but the two last ones proved to be very, very dangerous, especially the larger armoured one. It suddenly ventured onto the open ground which we had realized was our most vulnerable point, and really opened up on us. Our area made it doubly dangerous with splinters of rock flying everywhere, one of which I got smack in the face. As it got close towards our position Sergeant Tucker opened up with his mortar which brought it to a halt. After a short, but exciting battle, we finished up with three heavy armoured cars and two light scout cars out of action, one captured intact, and a number of prisoners. We also captured, from these vehicles, the order of battle for the German forces in Tunis.

From Beja we did a lot of patrolling. Some of these patrols were tough and costly. We were called out to help one patrol, but were driven back by fierce opposition. In this attack Company Sergeant Major Bill Cook was captured. But we didn't think he'd stay that way long. He eventually got out via the Vatican.

Our next attack at Gué was tough; a lot of killing went on and a lot of prisoners were taken. The adrenaline was going and I had to stop one of my chaps who was trying to bayonet a poor little Italian who wanted to surrender. We then moved back along the railway line where we saw some tents. In case there were Germans I shouted, 'Hande hoch!' but there was no reply so I ordered shots to be fired through the tents. Out came a few screaming Arabs who had been doing a bit of looting! During this period a number of wounded were being brought along the railway line, including the CO and the adjutant. They looked rather a mess at this time and were unconscious. I then followed on helping to push along some of the lads who were wounded, and at Sidi N'sir we got a welcome cup of black coffee and some vinegar bread.

After this battle the battalion was taken over by Major Alistair Pearson, 'Jock' as we affectionately called him. By now things were getting a bit better organized and towards the end of November we became part of Blade Force, which consisted of 1st Para Battalion and 2nd Battalion Lancashire

Fusiliers, later to be joined by a unit from the 17th/21st Lancers, and moved into new positions in Happy Valley.

In a battalion that spawned so many fantastic officers and men, such as 'Jock', Perrin-Brown, Vic Coxen, Wandless, Gammon, one outstanding man was Captain Philip Mellor. The Germans had brought 88-mm guns into the area and Captain Mellor was given the job of attacking and destroying one or more of these guns. He asked me to be his 2 i/c for this patrol. About 15 of us set off on a dark night. After we had marched for about an hour towards the enemy they heard us and opened up with machine-guns. Our eyes, now accustomed to the dark, could make out the outline of a German 88-mm gun. We moved in a half-circle attack towards it and got within 20 yards of the enemy, when we were forced to take cover because of the heavy firing. I waited till there was a slight pause, stood up to give the order to charge, then realized that Captain Mellor was missing, so shouted, 'Hold your fire!' – which needless to say drew a lot of fire towards me. However, I knew that Captain Mellor was up to something when we heard a huge bang from one of his Gammon bombs. We went straight in and the Germans surrendered. We marched back with ten prisoners, having put the gun out of action. There were a number of casualties on our side, but also missing was Sergeant Tony Baxter, who had dropped his Sten at Souk el Arba.

After this attack Captain Mellor visited me and told me he had recommended me for an award. I did not get one, but felt that if someone like Captain Mellor believed you to be worthy of an award, that in itself was an award. After this, Blade Force was disbanded and the 1st Battalion moved to Souk el Kemis, for a clean-up and a rest – and we needed it – and then to Algiers.

For our next attack, which was on Djebel Mansour, I did a recce fighting patrol with Major Coxen. After climbing for what seemed to be ages we reached the enemy defensive positions, and the battle began. I don't know who took the prisoners, but Major Coxen finally gave orders to withdraw. I did not rush my lads too much, trying to appear unconcerned with Major Coxen around. He soon showed me his concern, because the area was like a disturbed beehive, with Spandaus and rifles blazing away. He shouted, 'Get a bloody move on Sergeant Seal!' Orders are orders, so we got a bloody move on! As we approached the deep wadi which led back towards the French Foreign Legion lines I could swear we were running through streams of bullets kicking the sand up as we ran. We were very thankful to reach the Foreign Legion lines, who were glad to see us. It appeared that the Germans taken prisoner were from the same areas as some of the Saxon and Bavarian legionnaires.

In the main battle for Djebel Mansour, S Company suffered very heavy casualties including Captain Mellor who was killed attacking a machine-gun post, which was typical of the man; thus died an irreplaceable soldier. After the enemy had been killed or driven off the high ground we consolidated our position to await daylight. It was a night filled with bullets and bombs and our battle cry, 'Wahooo Mahomet!' In the early hours of the morning R and T Companies attacked El Alliliga, but failed to consolidate the position and had to withdraw. We finished up holding Djebel. A few of us went down with Major Coxen to check on the enemy ambush area where S Company had been, and to bury our dead. Until then I did not realize what damage the Spandaus could do. There were bodies everywhere, some with arms and hands cut off, still holding weapons; I forget the exact figure, but over 25 dead, plus of course the wounded.

With the Germans overlooking us on El Alliliga we were very exposed and subjected to heavy mortar and shell fire, so we took heavy casualties. The French Foreign Legion took over the left flank of our position, and the Guards tried to take El Alliliga that night, without luck, The 1st Battalion, or what was left of us, were really in the mire. Talk about cannon to left of us, cannon to right of us – we also had them in front and above us. At this stage we had little to fight with, although I did have a few rounds left, but no sensible target to make use of them; we all knew we could not last much longer; we had to withdraw.

After the battle we spent a couple of days sorting ourselves out. Reinforcements started arriving about 12 February, from 2nd Brigade. I took over a full platoon from the 5th Scottish, complete with new platoon officer Lieutenant Sinclair, and took with me the remains of the old 5 Platoon, who had survived Djebel. Mr Sinclair told me he had never been in action before and asked me to run the platoon. I told him that we would run the platoon together. We were both 22 years old, and we got on well together.

S Company was put onto a mobile company role at this time, and was moved to assist the 3rd Battalion whose positions at the Argoub had come under fairly heavy attack. Under cover of darkness the Germans had moved up to within 100 yards of the 3rd Battalion position, cut the wire and dug in. At dawn they attacked and threw back our troops, but the 3rd Battalion and some RE paras counter-attacked and Jerry moved back. We were given orders to attack a German-held farm called Frenchman's Farm. We moved down the wadis towards the farm, and attacked. After quite a heated little battle we captured it and took many prisoners. We also recaptured a British two-pounder anti-tank gun and a Yankee jeep from them, which they had taken earlier from our troops. After this action we handed over our positions to American troops.

In early March we were transported north in lorries that were full of fumes, so by the time we got to Tamera we were as sick as dogs. Little did I realize as we sat in those trucks that within a couple of weeks most of my platoon would be dead, wounded or prisoners.

My platoon, 5 Platoon, S Company, were on the point jutting out from the high ground which was later known as Shell Shock Ridge. At 0700 hours on 8 March we saw German patrols coming down the road from Sedjenane, followed by hundreds of Germans, with machine-guns and light artillery. It was what was to be, for me, one of the hardest days of almost continual fighting I engaged in; I was manning one of the Spandaus we had on loan from the Germans. During the next half an hour the Germans were pushing us very hard and we were getting short of ammunition, so I borrowed the Thompson sub-machine-gun from the observation post officer. Our Vickers machine-gun had been put completely out of action and shells were falling thick and fast. We had killed and wounded on the forward slopes, but it was difficult for the medics to get to them because there were snipers picking off anyone who approached. There were also snipers at our back area to stop reinforcements coming up, and on top of this there was dive-bombing. We lost our company commander, Major Ball, wounded in the chest, as the Germans advanced. Lieutenant Sinclair and I stood side by side firing pistols at almost point-blank range. Then Mr Sinclair fell shot in the chest, I lifted his head, but he was dead. Most of my men by this time were killed, wounded or captured but there was no chance to check them because there were too many Germans around. I moved over to the edge of the wood to report the death of Mr Sinclair to Major Ball, who gave me orders to get my men back. I told what few men were left to withdraw. We moved off quickly, with the German fire cutting the branches around our heads.

Over the next two days S Company was put into reserve company position. There were now only about 35 to 40 men left, and I finished up as OC the company. During this period of commanding S Company, Sergeant Ted Baxter had got himself attached to me, and at every opportunity he asked me about his brother. He'd say, 'Did you see Tony's body? Do you think he could still be alive?' I didn't know, but I was now Ted's contact with Tony and he stuck with me like glue.

In a number of counter-attacks through the woods we used our war cry, 'Wahoo Mahomet!' to keep contact and demoralize the enemy. On one such attack we caught a group of Germans, killed a number and took prisoners. Another time the Germans were around the 3rd Battalion HQ and almost every man who could grab a weapon helped in the charge. Then we moved on and we came to a small clearing that I had never seen before. In it was a sandbagged machine-gun nest with a Spandau poking up out of it and a brown-looking helmet showing over the top. In circumstances like this you have to make up your mind quickly and shoot quickly – or die. I charged, screaming our war cry, and firing from the hip. Some of the men in the sandbagged machine-gun nest fell wounded; unfortunately they were 3rd Battalion men who had come to help us. They'd been in a red sand quarry which had probably rubbed off onto their helmets, and they were using captured Spandaus. Luckily they were not badly wounded.

We had a few day's rest but we were called back because the Sherwood Foresters were losing the position that our battalion had fought and died for. They were not very popular with us that day. By the time we moved back the position was out of control, with some of the infantry coming back towards us as we moved up. Our 2nd and 3rd Battalions were also having a rough time. The 2nd Battalion had to withdraw down a river.

A few days later we successfully took Bowler Hat and handed it over to the 3rd Battalion. We then had a rest period for cleaning up and preparing for further attacks. I found I had scabies and dysentery and I spent much of my time scratching or sitting on a ladder over the toilet trenches. On the move back up to the front I had to rush almost every time we stopped, but these problems disappeared when we were back in action.

The job of 1st Brigade was to clear the road towards Sedjenane, back towards our old positions. On 27 March we moved forward once more to the front; we were to start the attack towards Sedjenane with the 2nd Battalion and the Goums. We were to capture the wooded country to the left of Bowler Hat, the same ground we had covered in our withdrawal from Tamera. The first objective was a French farm. Ninety guns laid down a barrage. We came under fire, but by early morning our company had pushed forwards and taken the Italian and German positions.

We now moved forward to attack the high wooded area which was one of our main objectives; the 2nd Battalion in the meantime had been having a rough time and some of our troops were sent over there to assist. It was a very bad area to attack – high, rocky ground and very heavily wooded. A number of our men were killed on the approach but we gradually pushed the enemy back and managed to establish ourselves on the outer perimeter of the wood. A lot of the troops here were German, and well dug in. There were also a number of snipers about. We were moving from tree to tree. Sammy Steadman was shot through the arm and one officer was killed. Ted

Baxter poked his head out from behind his tree and shouted, 'Be careful Eric, there's a sniper over there!' and bang! – Ted was shot through the eye. Very sad – Tony first, and now Ted.

We then pushed on towards Sedjenane where we spent a considerable time, digging positions and doing patrols. On 14/15 April we were relieved by troops from the 9th American Division, but in reality, for us, the war in North Africa was over.

LIEUTENANT COLONEL JOHN FROST, 2nd Parachute Battalion

I was second-in-command to the 3rd Battalion throughout the summer of 1942, when we were training on Salisbury Plain. In October the 1st Parachute Brigade were given notice that they were off by ship from the Clyde. I moved back to the 2nd Battalion as second-in-command to Gofton-Salmond who had been ill with piles. As soon as he came on board he was forced to take to his bunk. The brigadier thought this a bit unsatisfactory and gave orders for him to be put ashore and for me to assume command.

While we were at sea we were told we would be landed at Algiers as part of the British Army which was to thrust eastwards to occupy Tunis and Bizerta. After landing we spent a few days at Maison Carrée, where we had an awkward time, waiting for some sort of role. The 3rd Battalion had been dropped at Bone and the 1st Battalion at Souk el Arba. My fear was that we would only be used in an infantry role. Eventually it was thought we might drop part of the battalion at Kairouan and the remainder at Sousse. I was sent on a recce of the area in a Bisley bomber and told to liaise with the Americans at a place called Tebessa. On my way back as we came in to land, the Americans opened up with small arms and punctured our tyres so we had a most dicey landing and could not take off again. The only American officer I met had never heard of the 1st Para Brigade. Fortunately there was a Dakota there and I persuaded the pilot that I was needed to lead the attack next day that would bring an early finish to fighting in North Africa. He obviously felt that he might get to the USA faster if he took me back.

When I got back I didn't have a chance to relate my adventure because I was told we were now going to drop on Enfidaville. I carried out a recce of that area the next day, only to be told that was of too!

I was very relieved when they found us a task at last. I was briefed to take my battalion to Pont du Fahs in Tunisia and destroy the enemy aircraft there; likewise on an airstrip at Depienne, twelve miles further on; repeat the dose at Oudna and finally link up with the First Army. We were to find our own transport when we landed. On 29 November I went to the pilots' briefing and needless to say there were changes. Enemy aircraft had left both Pont du Fahs and Depienne so we were now to land at the latter and take up the remainder of our task.

I had to choose a DZ (dropping zone) at Depienne from the leading aircraft but fortunately there was a great big open space nearby and we all came down there. I made my way to a mound and sounded my hunting-horn; slowly the men assembled. We had a certain amount of trouble from local Arabs who always wanted to pilfer the parachutes. As a consequence of this we were told to collect all our parachutes and leave an escort with them, which meant one of the companies was only two platoons strong.

We made contact with a troop of our own armoured cars who said that they would be up with us the next day. After resting in the early part of that night, we moved off across the hills for Oudna and at eleven that morning we were overlooking the airstrip there. It didn't seem as though there were any aircraft on it at all. However, we'd been told that there were. In the event, instead of German aircraft, we found six heavy German tanks who weren't inclined to be polite. At the same time we were attacked by German aircraft. We now had no option but to get up into the high ground and lie up for the night. The optimistic mood which we had when we set out was now dispelled. My worries now increased apace. In addition to the platoon left at Depienne I'd lost a number of men in our short battle and we were already running low on ammunition. Some men were now feeling pretty tired because in the day it was bloody hot and you were pouring with sweat, whilst at night it was so cold it was hard to sleep at all. The soldiers lay huddled together like new-born puppies. I lay back to back with Philip Teichman and we covered ourselves with maps for warmth.

I was sure the enemy would come and find us the next day so I laid an ambush down by a well at the bottom of the hill. Unfortunately, the enemy arrived just as a party went down to fill their water bottles. However, it didn't turn out too badly, and we fought a fairly successful little battle. I then received a report of armour coming up from the rear displaying yellow triangles which were the First Army recognition signs. We all heaved a sigh of relief; we'd not been forgotten. Then John Ross, the C Company commander came to me with a grave face and said, 'Don't be taken in by the yellow triangles, these are German tanks and we are completely surrounded.' This was a terrible shock. I told him that we must get into a stronger position, from which it would be possible to move north the next night. Unfortunately in the move we had to leave our wounded behind with

Doc McGavin. As we moved, the Germans shelled us, sending splinters from the rocks. One man I passed had his face almost sliced from his head, which he held together with his hands. Among the causalities was a mule who scampered off towards the enemy with the battalion's bagpipes. We put the battalion into a reasonable defensive position on Siji Bou Hadjeba Hills about ten miles south of Oudna.

Then the enemy came with infantry, supported by armour and artillery. They assaulted, and a spectacular fire-fight took place. I was horrified to see how much quicker on the draw they were than we were. Time and time again they would get their machine-gun cracking with really accurate bursts of fire pouring into us before we got down to it. As the day wore on I was beginning to wonder how much longer we could hang on. I saw our medical officer, Ronnie Gordon, covered in blood from the wounded men he was attending, but he had nothing to staunch the wounds. Just when things were at their worst along came the Luftwaffe who circled menacingly around. Then down they came and every single bloody bomb landed slap on the Germans, which saved our bacon. They missed us completely. It was a bit of irony really because the German air force must have seen the yellow triangles and thought it was us. Shortly after that it got dark; I decided we'd move to Massicault. We weren't able to collect the wounded at the height of the battle and now we would have to leave without them. I arranged for a platoon to stay behind to find them; this of course meant that they would become prisoners. But I could not leave the wounded exposed to the mercies of the local Arabs and the cold.

I blew my horn and we all set off. It was a terrible march, a lot of it over very heavy ground, with enormous great big clods of earth – dreadful things to walk over. The first time we had a chance of replenishing our water bottles was in a very brackish river. It was just drinkable. We rested ten minutes in every hour. The men would just drop where they were and some violent methods had to be used to get them on the move again. Some were lost in the darkness and were not seen again. Just as it was getting light we found what looked like a reasonable defensive position, a little Arab settlement, with cactus bushes all round, which did as well as a barbed wire fence.

We now consisted of HQ, Support and A Companies with our Sapper Troop. B and C Companies were elsewhere. Suddenly all the Arabs in the area disappeared and we realized that the cause was German figures on the skyline. Slowly, without taking risks, in they came. We kept pretty quiet and I think they began to wonder whether we were there at all. When they came very close we opened fire at the last minute, with excellent results.

As it began to grow dark it was time to withdraw so I blew my hunting horn and we withdrew up into the hills. This went very successfully; we got practically everybody away, including quite a few of the wounded, who were able to hobble along. When we were settled I blew on my horn to bring in any stragglers. I thought I was doing quite well until someone shouted, 'For God's sake stop making that bloody noise, sir, we don't want to tell "them" where we are!' I then held an O Group which must have been riveting, because in the middle of it we all went to sleep!

By now I had decided to make towards Medjez which was further west. We stopped at a big French farm, run by a charming French lady. She had, among other things, two very beautiful daughters who gave the officers amongst us a lovely breakfast of eggs and bacon and champagne. All this at five o'clock in the morning, in the middle of enemy territory, made it quite an occasion! Nothing has ever tasted better. We had just finished when we were warned by one of her employees that a German armoured column was making its way towards us. We moved off hastily and eluded them.

About half-way through that day, we contacted a small American group of lightly armoured vehicles who took me with our wounded back to Medjez. My one thought was to try and arrange means to find the rest of our battalion. We still hadn't managed to get hold of C Company and B Company. I met General Allfrey, the corps commander, and General Everleigh of 78 Division, who said there was nothing anyone could do until the morning when they'd send a force of Americans with us to scour the country. That night we put our heads down in readiness for the morning search, but in the early hours we were roused to hear that a German parachute battalion was about to attack and that we must defend what they thought would be the most likely dropping zone. That was the end of our attempt to pick up the rest of the battalion.

The Americans did go out with some lorries, but without us being with them there was no way they could find our men. Although already less one platoon, C Company had borne the brunt of the battle of Sidi Bou Hadjeba and so, when they withdrew, there was not much more than a handful of them. B Company had gone further right than we did and had been completely surrounded and scuppered, on ground much less defensible than we had managed to find. So there was really nothing much else to be found of the battalion, and we found ourselves now with about 160 men. The only thing that the High Command could say to me was, 'Well, you drew off a lot of the enemy troops and armour, and made it much more possible for our people to hold on to Tebourba.' But that was hardly what we were in the business for; especially as we had no anti-tank weapons. It really was a sad and sorry story.

We were then ordered back after one night off duty to man an airfield in front of Medjez. A flight of Spitfires arrived to exert air superiority and were promptly shot down the next day – it was absolutely crazy. We dug positions near the railway station at Medjez where we stayed about a week. We were in a pretty poor state by this time. We'd had to drink all sorts of filthy water on the way and this had caused many stomach upsets. We'd only been issued with two 48-hour ration packs and had had to find food where we could. Now we found a French army depot near this railway station, so we made ourselves warm by wearing the baggy trousers of the Zouaves and the blue jackets of the Spahis, much to the annoyance of the Military Authority.

Elements of the 10th Panzer Division attacked the outskirts of Medjez just as we were handing over to the Coldstream Guards. We went to Souk el Arba to reform, and I now had time to rest and think about the month we'd been in North Africa. I'd lost several good officers, among them my second-in-command, Philip Teichman, my adjutant, Jock Short, and my intelligence officer, the very fine Ewen Charteris who had gone off from Cactus Farm to try to make contact and explain our desperate position. He'd done so well at Bruneval; I thought he had a charmed life. We had been completely isolated and given bogus objectives and there had been not the slightest attempt to support us. Just one RAF aircraft could have flown out to see where we were. I found it very difficult to be polite to those responsible when I met them.

It was perhaps the most disgracefully mounted operation of the whole war. There seemed to be rather a lack of sympathy for my battalion and this hurt especially as there was so little understanding from Brigade Head-quarters. The only person with any sympathy at all was Alistair Pearson, who was enough of a soldier to realize what had happened. The chief engineer of the corps, who'd done a lot of soldiering, was one of the few who was really appreciative and on looking back I think that getting any of 2 Para out of that pickle was possibly the best thing I ever did.

The corps commander still seemed to think we were expendable because at very short notice we were sent down to a crossroads on the extreme right flank of the British Army. We couldn't get there normally because all the routes had been mined so we had an awful move over hills, which meant we couldn't bring any heavy equipment. On the way I reported to Brigadier Howlett, who told us to hold a crossroads in the Ousseltia valley. It was considered vitally important that we hold it and that we must be prepared to accept heavy casualties. I said, 'Oh, what does the enemy consist of?' He said, 'Well, we know that there are 100 tanks.' So I said, 'I have no anti-tank guns, can you let us have some tanks?' He said, 'I can let you have six light tanks from the cavalry.' 'Thank you, sir, that's a great help.' Then he said, 'Well, they are no use against German tanks.' So I said, 'What about enemy infantry?' He replied, 'Well, there are ten battalions up the road.' I left, shaking my head.

The next day I made a recce with three Bren carriers. As we approached our assembly point I noticed the road had been recently disturbed. I immediately shouted to the two Bren carriers behind, but it was too late. There was a tremendous explosion and one vehicle turned over catapulting out its occupants. It was tragic. Dinty Moore, my battalion headquarters commander, and Dick Ashcroft, the A Company commander, were killed and all the rest were very badly injured. Both the officers were great characters and would be sadly missed. Needless to say the 100 tanks and the ten battalions went somewhere else.

On 8 February 1943 we returned to the fold of the 1st Parachute Brigade south of Bou Arada, which was lovely country and soon became known as 'Happy Valley'. Here we took it fairly leisurely; we had three companies stretched over three miles and only sporadic shelling interrupted our peace. All this changed when the corps commander arrived, absolutely furious. Without looking into the reason, he said to me, 'You've got your battalion spread out all over the place, you haven't bothered to dig in properly, bloody disgrace, I've a damn good mind to send you home,' which wasn't very nice. Charles Keightly, the Divisional Commander of the Armoured Division in that sector, came the next day and took a completely different view and then I went back to Algiers with John Ross on leave. When I returned after ten days' leave I found my battalion in excellent shape and the weather much better. Hill partridges abounded and I regretted not having brought my shotgun with me.

On 26 February we heard intensive gunfire and found out that the 3rd Battalion was being hard pressed. A few hours later our own forward positions came under fire and a large number of enemy infantry could be seen advancing. However, I knew for the first time in North Africa that we had plenty of ammunition, a defensive fire plan worked out, wireless communication between companies and that my men were well-fed and fit. The enemy initially came up against C Company, failed there and began to work their way round the flanks. Our artillery were brought in and pinned them down. I then moved the Spahis forward on foot, which made certain our left flank was secure throughout the battle.

The enemy's next push was from high ground against B Company. Although we were well spread out the gaps were covered by mortar and machine-gun, so the enemy could be dealt with. Towards the end of the day our French anti-tank gunners, tired of waiting, fed up with waiting for enemy tanks, opened up on the enemy infantry. The French observation officer who was standing on a hill, had no communications with his battery other than a megaphone through which he would shout directions and corrections. Two squadrons of the Chasseurs d'Afrique on our right had been particularly good when patrolling so I thought, as the enemy could not withdraw because of our machine-guns, nor come forward, that I would use them in a combined strong right hook that night. But to my amazement their commander said that he couldn't move without higher French authority. As a result I gave Captain Ronnie Stark a couple of platoons and told him to go out through A Company, sweep across our front and them come in through C Company. Off he went and we heard his progress through the night as he moved across no-man's-land, making full use of grenades and Stens. He was back at dawn, large grin on his face, with 78 Italian prisoners.

Elsewhere on the front, the 3rd Battalion and the Irish were having difficulties and in some places the Germans had almost broken through. Brigade had little knowledge of what we'd been doing and after the battle even said, 'What! Were you fighting as well?' That's exactly what we were doing, performing a model infantry battle where the fighting is being done by machine-gun and mortars and where in some cases the infantry don't use their weapons unless they are actually being assaulted. In our previous battles our losses had been grievous; now we'd lost only one killed and two wounded, whereas the enemy, mainly Italian and Austrian, had lost 150 killed and wounded. This estimate was from observations and prisoners' reports. The mortar men, under 'Bombs' Panter, had been trained so well, and in cooperation with the machine-gunners, had put down such accurate and sustained weight of fire that they had won the day for us. The next day we got our orders to move and we handed over to the Americans. As we drove out of Happy Valley morale was sky high.

My next move was to 139 Infantry Brigade where I was briefed by Brigadier Howlett. He looked at me very sadly, and told me that he had a very unpleasant job for me; we were to clear the enemy, consisting of four German battalions, out of a village called Sedjenane. Divisional HQ, however, stopped the battalion on the way to me, without even asking the corps commander, to clear some Germans off a hill called Spion Kop which had been threatening them. I wasn't at all happy about this move, but was assured that divisional artillery would support us. We got up to the hill which was facing Spion Kop relatively easily and then we started going down towards Spion Kop. The Germans exposed their position because we drew their fire. I called on the divisional gunners, but we never succeeded in getting a single round of gunfire from them and now a company of infantry with a troop of tanks on our left ran away. I was so angry I called the whole thing off and went back to Divisional HQ where I found the GSO and said, 'We were promised the whole of your divisional artillery but we haven't had a single round.' He said that the situation had changed since the promise was made. While I was there I met Brigadier Chichester-Constable, who had a couple of DSOs, and had just been sacked. He had been commanding a brigade in the northern sector at Sedjenane and he knew the Germans were going to attempt a big break-through and had quite rightly asked if he could move his defensive position. Not only did they say no, but took one of his battalions away. The Germans attacked and completely overwhelmed him. He lost his guns, his men and his career. They had made him a scapegoat. I took careful note.

We went back to the northern sector to take over a different job, because, thank goodness, the Sedjenane project was no longer on. The day before we arrived the Germans had sent a strong patrol onto a hill in a cork wood, held by the Lincolnshire Regiment, and had taken several prisoners. I was told to take over during the night, because it was likely the Germans would attack in the morning. Sure enough, as we arrived at dawn on 8 March, the Germans attacked. They had been told they were going to meet the Lincolns on top of the hill, and when they found paras they were rather upset!

It couldn't be helped but I'd got my HQ in a position from where I couldn't see very much. News coming back from the companies was sparse, but it nearly all concerned their lack of ammunition. At ten o'clock Johnny Lane, commanding A Company, got through to tell me that he was surrounded – but he was confident. The enemy had begun to infiltrate. Willoughby Radcliffe, the adjutant, frustrated at having to remain below at HQ, decided to organize a mule train loaded with ammunition for A Company. As he was climbing up he was killed by one of the enemy parties who had got between Headquarters and A Company. At the same time Geoff Rotheray, who commanded HQ Company, was killed during a machine-gun duel. He was one of the original parachutists. These were sad losses. Fearing further infiltration between ourselves and the 1st Battalion, the brigadier called for A Company of the 3rd Battalion to link up with part of our C Company. This was a highly successful counter-attack and they captured over 60 prisoners. However, the enemy had not finished, as just before dark a flight of Stukas dived on A Company and dropped their bombs among them. This brought our casualties up to nine killed and 35 wounded.

John Timothy gained us some revenge, when he set upon a small party of machine-gunners and killed six of them and brought back two brand new MG34s. During the next day I saw a number of machine-gun duels. Our own guns were very well sited and, although 2,000 yards from the enemy, were inflicting heavy casualties.

The enemy's next attack came in the rain, which made it difficult for both sides. They were again trying to reach the road between us and the 1st Battalion. We were having a hard time of it, but the latter bore the brunt. The enemy overran T Company and went rapidly towards Battalion Headquarters. What they hadn't taken into consideration was Alistair Pearson. He organized the cooks and clerks and charged into them as they were attacking. This was a quite remarkable and inspired counter-attack. As the day continued the Germans who were brought in were beaten up and bewildered; we captured over 200 of them. They were a tangible harvest and much easier to count than bodies. By this time in North Africa most of us had realized that we did not hate Germans. They had the same needs, habits, strengths and weaknesses as ourselves. The one thing, however, we could never get over was their smell. A sort of combination of untanned leather, soap and food of some kind. We found the smell in their dugouts so strong we could not use them. Yet it was a clean, efficient smell. It may have been that we were so keyed-up to kill each other that nature had given us a special power to detect our own potential enemies.

There were still gaps in our defences, but it was rather like fiddling with a curtain which does not adequately cover a window. However, we were strengthened by our staunch old friends the Parachute Engineer Squadron. Their position on the left was called the Citadel, while the soldiers had christened our feature Cork Wood. During our time in Cork Wood we evolved a drill that made maximum use of a bowl of hot water. We would wash our face, neck, armpits and shave; then our feet where we would pay particular attention to the area between the toes: off then with our pants, squat over the bowl and deal with that region. It was a bit undignified, but we certainly kept pretty free of skin troubles.

One afternoon General Allfrey was to visit us. I had unhappy memories of his visit at Happy Valley and so said John Marshall should see him. He had in fact come to congratulate the battalion on their achievements. He went round the soldiers and he asked them how they were. In true para fashion they said, 'Piece of cake, sir.'

On the morning of 14 March the Germans started to shell us

intensively again; we expected an attack but none came. Then through binoculars we saw a Fieseler-Storch land. This aircraft was capable of incredible feats of landing and taking off. We assumed that it had brought a senior officer to see how all was going. The shelling continued all day and in the evening really intensified. Amidst all this shelling and rain our concentration was not all it should have been, because suddenly a wave of Germans charged, LMGs (light machine-guns) and rifles firing from the hip, grenades being hurled everywhere and all accompanied by Teutonic shouts. They seemed very fresh, but they did not know the ground and although they penetrated some areas they moved off to reorganize, but not before C Company captured a few and rang to tell me they were the formidable 10th Panzer Grenadiers. This was disturbing news. It was imperative that they did not dig in during the night, otherwise they would be all over us at dawn, but I had no reserve to move against them. My front-line companies were now being heavily shelled and our own guns could not clear the crest, though our mortars worked unceasingly. This was not a good situation.

We then heard the inimitable drone of a squadron of Stukas, escorted by Focke-Wulfs. The Germans sent up coloured flares for them as they circled. But not to be outdone, our own NCOs replied with every flare cartridge they possessed. The Stukas circled once more and dived, one behind the other, dropping their bombs absolutely smack bang on top of the Panzer Grenadiers and blowing them literally to bits. A few minutes after this raid our patrols reported our positions were clear of the enemy and that they had found arms and legs and bits of torsos of the Grenadiers high among the trees. This aerial bombardment had been an amazing stroke of good fortune for us. It was ironic that the Grenadiers' motto was 'God with us'.

We had a couple of days' respite while the enemy reorganized. They then began shelling our rear area with very accurate fire. They always seemed to find our companies just when they sat down for a meal. One evening I was hit in the thigh by a small fragment. Ronnie Gordon gouged out the piece with his grubby thumbnail and told me I'd live!

On St Patrick's Day the enemy launched a fierce attack which was mainly aimed at the infantry in front, up the road, and the French who were to the left. They didn't trouble us. However, it soon became apparent that unless those battalions under fire were withdrawn, they wouldn't be there in the morning. I got permission for Dennis Vernon, our sapper, to blow the road. There was an almighty roar as a slice of the road fell into the valley. At our prepared rendezvous I found most of my battalion who by now looked several years older. These last ten days we had lost more than 150, killed or wounded.

70

For our withdrawal I decided to use the river bed. This proved to be very difficult because the river was fast and deep and the bed slippery. As we half swam and struggled shells fell upon us. We were pleased to note that over half the shells didn't explode and assumed the Germans were buying cheaply in Czechoslovakia!

Richard Spender, one of C Company's platoon commanders, and a fine poet, wrote his last poem here:

> Thud,
> In the Mud.
> Thank Gud,
> Another dud.

Trying to carry our wounded proved to be a nightmare. The front ones moved off far too slowly for those in the rear who were being attacked. Dennis Vernon's demolition proved to be a life-saver because we were pursued by a half-track full of Panzer Grenadiers who had hurtled round the corner into the debris. The follow-up party could only fire at us from a distance. But it was still very hard going and we were often up to our necks. We clambered out up to a railway line where John Marshall had brought transport for the wounded, very tired now, but trying to keep our step on to every railway sleeper. We were making our way towards three rocky hillocks, which we called the Pimples. However, we were now withdrawn to the rear for a rest and we made our home in a rather splendid tin mine. After what we'd had before this was sheer luxury; we even had a mobile bath unit with unlimited hot water. Great bottles of wine were available at the NAAFI (Navy, Army and Air Force Institute). We could also catch up with the rest of the world and their war, in the newspapers. It was also a time of healing and coming to terms with loss.

What I wanted more than anything else was to now be deployed in the role we had been trained for, but I was not at all surprised when I heard we would be doing a full-scale infantry attack in the next few days. I went up the Pimples to make a detailed plan of our attack. These had changed hands several times, but had finally been recaptured by the redoubtable Alistair Pearson. His 1st Battalion had great technique, through experience, but as often as not it was the uncanny instinct of Alistair that had brought them their success. He had handed the Pimples over to the 3rd Battalion, who reckoned that the Tunisian Regiment were in front of them.

While I was with the 3rd Battalion, just behind the foremost Pimple, known as 'Bowler Hat', the enemy gave us some indication of the strength and accuracy of their artillery. It all seemed to be aimed at me as I sought cover. What it also showed was how well they had covered all the approaches I'd wanted to use.

That evening we held a service in the big machine shed. We sang hymns to the accompaniment of a rather haunting harmonium. At the end I talked to the men about what we'd been through and I remember saying finally, 'I don't know what you think of us, but I know I speak for all my officers, when I say we have nothing but the highest regard for every single one of you.' You see I was very proud of them, they were extraordinary people.

At precisely ten o'clock on the night of 27 March the divisional artillery opened up. We had never heard an artillery barrage of such intensity before and we felt urged onwards in a strange and mystic way. It was a beautiful warm night and the noise of the shells above us was orchestral in its infinite variation. My two forward companies went up unopposed. I followed behind with a small party laying the tape and following the shell bursts to keep our bearings. Ahead of us we could hear the companies fighting. The enemy's reaction to the end of the artillery fire was to fire a series of light signals. Every time one went up we froze as the glare lit up our surroundings. As it faded we went forward. Somehow we found ourselves on a plateau in the middle of an enemy defensive position. Around us we could hear German voices. One of them blundered into our group and was seized by Sergeant Cloves, the signal sergeant. We were only a party of ten and not equipped for this situation, so I called up C Company to deal with it. In the meantime, as we slithered down the hill, Sergeant Cloves was twisting this chap's arm and he was making rather a lot of fuss. I said, 'Put that man down will you, Sergeant.' He came back with, 'Oh, I can't do that sir, I've never had one before!' C Company came up and cleared up the situation.

I got the impression that the plateau we were on was very near the top and therefore would make a good fire base. The ground fell away on three sides and it now seemed that the crest of the hill, our first objective, was straight ahead and not very far. I decided that we'd attack as a battalion at first light. As soon as it came it was plain that we were still a long way from the top. I had been taken in by a false crest and had failed dismally to take our first objective. Thank God this depressing moment was lightened by us finding, as we moved forward, that despite all the shelling of the previous night, many of the Germans were fast asleep in their trenches – these were not the brightest of men. A Company remained now to hold a firm base, while C Company, under John Ross, and B Company pushed forward. For a time they made good progress, but C Company came up against heavy machine-gun fire. The enemy then counter-attacked. Closely packed groups of well-drilled men advanced through the trees firing from the hip as they came down. At one point they almost enveloped C Company's right flank. Dick Spender charged to push them back and although he killed four of the enemy, this fine and much-loved poet was shot down. John Ross had little option but to pull pack to the ridge, with heavy casualties. The situation was now critical. I informed Brigade who told me, 'Hang on at all costs; things are rosy elsewhere.' To support this message Brigade sent David Dobie with B Company of the 3rd Battalion to our aid. As he arrived Witzig's men moved in closer. I ordered fixed bayonets and we were to charge on the signal of my hunting horn. Somehow the fixing of bayonets always strikes a remarkable note among soldiers and morale reaches a peak. With the usual black humour some comedian was handing out grenades in a box, calling out like an usherette, 'Cigarettes, chocolates, ice cream'; all this while shells were passing overhead.

Our own guns now got their range and our mortars caught the Germans as they closed in on us. This was greeted with shouts of 'Wahoo Mahomet!' by everyone. But the enemy kept up a fierce volume of fire, of which A Company bore the brunt. So I brought a gunner OP to them, who was kept very busy. B Company were making excellent progress and had made contact with part of the 1st Battalion near the top. They struck in on the right and rear of Witzig's men, which had an immediate effect on their counter-attack on us. Unfortunately the 1st Battalion were called upon to switch their axis just when there was an opportunity to overwhelm Witzig. The remnants of B Company, now on their own, called for artillery support and although this was forthcoming, many of the shells fell among them and the casualties sustained left them too dazed and weak to do more. But Witzig's men had had enough as well and pulled back up the hill.

It was tempting to chase them but we now desperately needed to reorganize. We had a number of prisoners, and wounded from both sides who needed attention. I was delighted to see Mickey Wardle carried off by four Germans, for he had seemed so depressed before this battle. I felt now he was safe. Sadly, I was to learn later that he and the four Germans were all killed when a shell landed on them while they were sheltering.

The remnants of B Company came back to the main battalion position. At this time we could muster no more than 160 men. Our patrols had found that although the enemy's counter-attack had failed they were still firmly holding positions further up the hill. To attack with the present strength in daylight would have cost us dearly. Fortunately the brigadier realized this, and sent us a company from the 3rd Battalion. Out of what we now had I formed one rifle company and called it No. 1 Company, and put John Ross in command. The two companies of the 3rd Battalion became Nos 2 and 3. As we moved forward it was pouring with rain and pitch black. The enemy let loose a considerable weight of fire and with this and the extremely difficult climb I was beginning to be concerned. But I need not have worried because the Germans had used the barrage to cover their withdrawal. Apart from several soldiers from the Tunisian Regiment and others who had lost their way, we met no opposition.

At 11.45 on 29 March we arrived on our objective. The battle for Tamera was over. We had been in action, as a brigade, since 7 March. Throughout, nobody but the enemy knew we were fighting. Our presence in the forefront of the battle was not divulged and no reporters were allowed. We had had a very sticky and expensive battle and we had lost many friends, but now it all seemed so well worthwhile. It was time to relax.

The road leading to us had been heavily mined so I was rather amazed to see General Allfrey arrive on the back of a motor cycle. He was a bit upset about my demolition of the bridge, but I explained that I had got Brigade's permission. He then said some very nice things about the 2nd Battalion. He had learnt from prisoners they'd captured that Witzig himself had led the counter-attack against us. He left us in high spirits. I thought that if the general could get through, so could our rum ration, which it did! We were waiting and winding down on the side of the road when a squadron of the Goums went by, looked at our prisoners, and made the most bloodthirsty noise and drew their fingers across their throats. The poor old prisoners were in a terrible state and so we fortified them with some rum.

That evening we had fun – we all joined in together in an impromptu concert. The Germans and Italians sang magnificently, probably delighted to be out of the war, and the paras sang appallingly and were delighted to still be in it. A German feldwebel who'd hardly stopped drinking, was taken the following morning to be interrogated. He was asked where he had spent the previous evening. To the disbelief of his interrogators he replied, 'Singing and drinking with my comrades of the English Fallschirmjaeger.' After the party we were relieved by the Americans. On the train journey back to Algiers we had time to count the cost of North Africa; it had indeed been high. The brigade had suffered 1,700 casualties during our four months.

We received splendid messages from the generals under whom we had served and we felt very proud, especially when General Alexander informed us that we had earned the name 'Red Devils' from the enemy. 'Boy'

Browning's message told us, 'Such distinctions are seldom given in war and then only to the finest fighting troops.' On the way back to Algiers the railway passed the biggest prisoner-of-war camp in North Africa. As the train approached the prisoners recognized our red berets and ran towards the wire, throwing their hats in the air, and cheered and cheered, calling out, 'Red Devils, Red Devils!' I turned to Alistair Pearson and said, 'Is this really happening?' It was our nicest tribute.

COMPANY SERGEANT MAJOR BILL COOK, 1st Parachute Battalion

I was shot on a fighting patrol near Coxen's Farm and captured by the Germans who treated my wounds. The surgeon said that I was in a bad way and had lost my balls. Fortunately I had five children. I was operated on and when I'd recovered I was taken to Camp 54 which was 40 miles from Rome. I was determined I wasn't going to spend the rest of the war there, so with Eddie Mullins, an Australian lad, I dug a tunnel which began in a lavatory used by three doctors. We got out but were recaptured and I was really beaten up which left me speechless and paralysed. I was put into hospital and one day when I awoke Eddie was on his knees praying for me, that I wouldn't die. He gave me the strength to recover. When I got better I got hold of a copy of *Romanus Immortalis* (Immortal Rome), by a British author, in which there was a map. It also said that Rome had changed very little in 1,000 years, so I thought, I've got the map, so I'm off. I was looking for a way out of the hospital, when this little RAF gunner asked me what I was looking for. I told him about my escape plan and he asked if he could go with me. I told him I'd rather go on my own, and in any case, if I was caught I'd be shot and so would he. But he still wanted to come, so I agreed. Then he asked if we could take the skipper of his aircraft – I was even more reluctant, but agreed. That was a mistake.

Straight away this squadron leader started to lay the law down to me, so I said, 'If you know all the answers, you can go on your own.' He then tried to pull his bloody rank on me. I told him that I didn't care if he was a bloody general because this was my idea and we'd go my way.

I'd got everything planned for getting out. We took a couple of screws out of the window of the officer's ward, and got onto the wall, only to find there was a 28-foot drop the other side! Back we had to come. I spoke to a lieutenant commander in the Navy who said that he'd organize getting a rope. He somehow plaited together all the string from the Red Cross parcels. The following night he threw the rope over and only had a four-foot drop at the end.

I'd got the rough directions from my map but there had been a lot of building since my map was drawn! We moved off across the bridge on which there were a couple of little places where you could sit down; we did this to catch our breath. I hadn't seen this Italian soldier who came up and demanded our papers. I stood up and rebuked him, in German – 'You dare speak to me? Who are you talking to? I'm one of the Fuehrer's own police.' There I was, telling him off, standing there in this hospital uniform on which I'd sewn epaulettes and fixed two silver paper stripes. On my head I had a German Afrika Korps cap, with a British button as a cap badge. The other two just had hospital uniforms, which had been rejigged. He saluted and said, 'Oh, I'm very sorry sir, but three Britishers have escaped.' I said 'Do I look like one?' He said, 'Oh no, one of the ones who have escaped has a long beard.' So much for Italian Intelligence.

After that we carried on and got near to the Vatican. I wasn't sure how to get in so I left the other two in the doorway and walked up the road where I saw the main entrance, which was very heavily guarded. I bumped into a kid and said, in German, 'That's the Vatican, is it?' He said, 'You're German?' Now I'd been in the Foreign Legion before the war and spoke German so I said, 'Jawohl, ich bin ein Deutscher.' He said, with a wry smile, 'Ich spreche Englisch and Deutsch.' With an even wryer smile, I replied, 'Gut, sehr gut, junge' and then said, 'Surely ordinary people don't go in the way the Pope goes in!' 'Oh no,' he said, 'they go in at the Porta Sant' Anna.' I thanked him and gave him what coins I had in my pocket.

As we got inside we bumped into an Italian sentry who was smoking. Before he could say anything I said, 'Put that cigarette out and put your rifle on your shoulder properly. Right, now tell me where the other sentries are.' He pointed them out. I told him to get into a corner and finish his cigarette where no one could see him. With some skilful moves we got ourselves to a courtyard where we were stopped by a Swiss guard. 'Are you General de Wiart and Air Marshal Boyd?' I said, 'No, I'm another general altogether, General Cook, and this is General Nightingale and General Macauley.' He showed us the way to the British Embassy. We found out later that General Carton de Wiart and Air Marshal Boyd and another had escaped, but had been recaptured while we were in the Vatican. We were lucky.

When we got to the gate of the Embassy it was still very early. There were three bells, so I rang all of them and an assistant attaché came to the door in his dressing gown and a bit cynically said, 'To whom am I indebted for a visit at this hour of the morning?' Fortunately the butler, who was something to do with Intelligence, said that he'd look after us. He took us into a room and explained that we could stay there, but that the Embassy couldn't be seen to be helping us escape. He though that he might be able to work out an exchange. For this, of all people, Mussolini's son-in-law came to see us. He was a bit pompous and after listening to our chap, he said, 'For the squadron leader, I want three flying majors; for him, three flying gunners; and for him (that's me!), I want three parachutists.' So I started to laugh, I couldn't help it. The Italian was not too pleased and asked me why I was laughing. I said, 'I'm glad you recognize that I'm worth three Italians!' This really pissed him off, so he stormed off, saying there would be no exchange. The squadron leader started to play bloody hell with me, so I told him that he was a pain in the arse and that if it wasn't for me he wouldn't be where he was. The squadron leader went ranting on about reporting me – but I took no notice.

I was then signalled to by a little priest. I went over to him and he asked me in a quiet, Irish voice if I wanted to get out. I didn't realize it then, but he was the man who was eventually to be known as the Pimpernel of the Vatican. He told me that getting us out was a very risky business, but he had successfully got a sailor out so was prepared to do it again; this time he would go with us. He then spoke to the other two and they said they wanted to go as well. He explained that they would be given a pastoral suit each – the sort that priests wear off duty. He then told me that one of his cardinals was away in England so he was going to pinch his robes for me. So there I was, dressed up in these red cardinal's robes. 'That's perfect,' he said, 'now all I've got to do is teach you how to be a cardinal.' So he taught me all I had to know and how to bless people. A couple of days later he and I went round the Vatican giving everyone blessings! Along come this pair of German soldiers who were visiting the Vatican, so I blessed them.

When he felt I had finished my training we were put into a car with the blinds down and driven to Rome airport where we were passed off as a cardinal and three priests going to Madrid. At the airport we were doing well when this plain-clothes bloke, who was on duty, came over. As he opened his mouth to speak I thought now we're for it – but quick as a flash I put my hand on his head and said, 'Kneel down, my son.' When he did, I gave him the blessing, in the approved style and asked him how many children he had. 'I've three children, Father.' 'Then God bless them, my son,' I said, and patted him on the shoulder. Then I walked straight ahead. How I avoided picking up those robes and running for it I'll never know because that walk to the plane was the hardest I've ever done in my life. When I got there I turned around and he was getting off his knees, so I waved to him and he waved back. As soon as we got on the plane for Madrid the priest said, 'It was well done, Sergeant Cook, but it was blasphemy you know – it was blasphemy, blasphemy.' But he had a great smile on his face.

The next day I changed into a suit and flew to Portugal, where we waited five days because the previous Sunderland flying boat, with the actor Leslie Howard on board, had been shot down. We flew first to Ireland and then to Poole in Dorset.

CHAPTER FIVE
SICILY
Operation Fustian
1943

S ICILY WAS TO BE TAKEN BY A RAPID PINCER ATTACK. THE Americans, after landing in the south, were to advance across the island in a wide sweep from the west while Montgomery's Eighth Army, which had landed on the east coast, were to block the enemies' escape route across the straits of Messina. Airborne troops were required to capture the key points of the Ponte Grande, over the canal at the entrance to the port of Syracuse, and the main coastal bridge on the approach to Catania, called Ponte di Primosole. On 9 July the 1st Airlanding Brigade group encountered high winds, so half the force was released too early and landed in the sea and the rest were scattered inland over many miles. A platoon of the 2nd Battalion The Staffordshire Regiment captured the Ponte Grande and held it until the morning when they were forced to withdraw. However, they had gained valuable time for the Eighth Army, which arrived that afternoon by sea and secured Syracuse.

On the night of 13 July, the 1st Parachute Brigade had a very dispersed drop due to receiving heavy fire from our own ships, which forced the inexperienced American aircrews to take excessive evasive action. Only about 300 officers and men dropped accurately enough to seize the Ponte di Primosole which they held long enough, despite German attacks in strength, to ensure the bridge was intact when the Eighth Army arrived.

LIEUTENANT COLONEL ALISTAIR PEARSON, 1st Parachute Battalion
We joined the remainder of the 1st Airborne Division at Matmore in Algeria which was a bare-arsed hillside and on one side was a deep wadi. I know because I fell into it making my way back from the officers' mess one

SICILY 13/18 JULY 1943

Key
British troops
German troops

Catania

Primosole Bridge
Mount Etna▲
SICILY

Syracuse
Avola

*1st Airlanding Brigade lands
9/10 July at Ponte Grande*

**Group Stangenberg
Counter-attack 14 July, noon**

R. Dittaino

Primosole Bridge

*1st Parachute Brigade
Air drop and glider landings
13-14 July, evening*

50 Division, evening 14 July

R. Gornalunga

Malati Bridge

*3 Commando
Landing from sea 13-14 July,
evening*

R. Lentini

Lentini
Carlentini

XIII Corps (Dempsey)

Augusta, 13 July

5 Division
(Bucknall)

50 Division
(Kirkman)

0   5   10 miles

night. We had an airfield just below, housing 62 Group – Americans with Dakotas. Every time they took off we got the benefit; the dust they threw up took about two hours to clear – everything got covered, with the result that our 24-seat back-to-back latrine was in constant use. There was a theory that if the latrines were dug deep enough they wouldn't need emptying – ours was twelve feet deep. The Yanks worked differently. Every day we watched with interest as a petrol lorry drew up and poured high octane petrol into their loo. A fuse was lit and the shit was blown to the four winds of heaven!

By the first week in August we moved on to another tented location between Sousse and Kairouan and started training again. While we were there somebody in another battalion thought the best way to clear a cactus hedge was to set fire to it. The wind caught the flames which ignited the divisional ammunition dump and produced a major firework display. It was completely destroyed – the Germans couldn't have done better. It took tremendous work to replace it before Sicily.

The battalion ran a most successful and profitable eggs and chips and wine canteen. The hotter the weather the more the boys enjoyed their chips. We had a very successful dance in the officers' mess, inviting the nurses from the Sousse hospital. Walking around before I saw the PMC was mixing the drink in a bath. He had about ten gallons of it. I thought I'd better taste it, but before doing so I poured some onto the Mess table and put a match to it, which resulted in a minor explosion! I told the PMC to pour five gallons of orange juice in and saved a potential disaster!

The outline plan for Sicily was that the Airlanding Brigade would capture the Ponte Grande Bridge outside Syracuse on D-Day. 2nd Para Brigade would secure a bridge north of Augusta on D+1 and 1st Para Brigade would seize and hold the Ponte di Primosole some ten miles south of Catania on D+3, or any subsequent date. My task as CO of 1 Para was to capture and hold the bridge. The code word was 'Manston Tonight'.

The 2nd Para Brigade operation was cancelled due to the speed of the advancing Eighth Army. On D+3 our operation was postponed for 24 hours. The next day we went to an airstrip outside Kairouan. They told us the operation was on but they didn't tell us the time of it – that depended on how well the army was doing.

The airfield was a sandy strip in the desert. We got there at midday and the only shade was under the wings of the Dakotas. We lay underneath and waited and slowly baked. By the time we got the code word the problems of the Airlanding Brigade had filtered back. The fact that a large number of our aircraft had been shot down by friendly naval vessels did not help our morale. We were assured, however, that this would not happen again. At dusk we set off. Inside the Dakota I was reading my book and the rest of the soldiers were chattering away. Then all of a sudden there was the clatter of machine-gun fire. I could see all these ships below belching fire at us. They thought we were Italian torpedo bombers. Eventually we settled down, then one of my signallers told me we were over Mount Etna, which was nowhere near where we should have been. I struggled out of my parachute in order to get to the cockpit to see what was happening. As I passed one of our soldiers who'd been an RAF officer I said jocularly, 'Can you fly one of these things?' and he said he could. I got up to the cabin and realized that we were heading back again. I said to the pilot, 'The DZ's down there, what are we doing?' His co-pilot was sitting with his hands over his face crying, 'We can't, we can't.' 'Can't do what?' I said. 'We can't go in there.' I could see quite clearly blobs of fire. I knew what was going through his mind, it was going through mine as well, because on the ground were what I thought were burning Dakotas. I said to the pilot, 'There's nothing for it boy, we've got to do it. If your co-pilot's no good I've no hesitation in shooting him.' I pulled out my revolver. The pilot continued with his protests. So I said, 'I could shoot you as well.' 'You can't do that, who'd fly the aeroplane?' I said, 'Don't worry about that, I've got a bloke in the back who can fly this.' 'Yeah, but he won't know how to land it!' 'No-one has asked him to land the bloody thing – you don't think he's going to hang about to land it do you? He'll be stepping out very sharp!' He decided very reluctantly to go in. I got back into my parachute, the bell rang and we all stood up. I thought we were going in too fast. We seemed to be going downhill as well. Out I went over the DZ and I didn't think my chute had opened, because I was down on the deck as soon as I'd jumped. I'd gone out number ten, my knees hurt, but I was all right; my batman at number eleven was all right but the remainder of the stick all suffered serious injuries or were killed. I was very angry. We all got to our RV and soon discovered the burning Dakotas were no more than haystacks alight.

With only about 200 men including a couple of platoons of 3 Para I formed a defensive position around the approaches to the bridge. The Germans put in a series of attacks in the afternoon. We weren't in any danger of being overrun but we were suffering casualties and were running short of ammunition. But I considered we could hold out until dark.

However at 1830 hours I was ordered to withdraw by Brigadier Lathbury, with which I disagreed. But in the end I had to do as I was told and withdrew my battalion up to the hills. Before I withdrew I took my provost sergeant 'Panzer' Manser and my batman, Jock Clements and made a recce of the river bank because I had a gut feeling I was coming back again. It was stinking and the mosquitoes were there in their millions. About 500 yards along I found a ford where we crossed and made our way back to battalion lines. The following morning I had a grandstand view as the 9th Battalion of the Durham Light Infantry, who were the leading element of the Eighth Army, put in a full-scale infantry attack on the bridge. It was unsuccessful and they suffered very heavy casualties.

I was called up to Durham's Brigade HQ to see what the next move was. I listened in amazement as the brigade commander put forward the idea of another attack that afternoon. I said, in a voice louder than I should have done, 'If you want to lose another battalion, you're going the right way about it.' There was deathly silence as the two brigadiers gave me a long look. But Brigadier Lathbury, who was also at the meeting, saved my bacon and persuaded them to listen to what I had to say. I told them that I would take the 8th DLIs across the river that evening by the route I'd recce'd. The brigadier just looked at me and said, 'All right, Pearson, what do you want?' In other words, how many tanks, what artillery; so I said, '2,000 yards of white tape!' 'What's that for?' he said. 'If we're going to get lost we'll all get lost together,' I said. He agreed. I then said that it was to be a silent attack with two companies and I wanted the remainder of the Durham Light Infantry with its armoured support to be in a position on the road, ready to move as soon as they saw the success signal, a green Very light. At midnight I asked the CO of the DLI and his two company commanders to come with me while the remainder moved down the tape. The CO was a bit anxious and said to me, 'What's out in front?' I said, 'My bloody batman, I hope!' Panzer Manser was leading with the tape. One of my soldiers who was two behind me had one up the spout. For some reason he pulled the trigger and the bloke in front of him dropped dead, shot straight through the back of his head. The noise was unreal – a single shot at night. I really thought we'd passed the line of no return. But the Germans made no response.

Jock Clements, my batman, was standing there. So I said, 'Away across the river Jock.' 'What me, sir?' 'Aye, you, yes. Here's my torch. If you see anything give it a wee wave.' 'If there's anyone on the other side you'll soon know about it.' The Durham's CO was with me, and he couldn't believe that batmen talked to their COs like that. I told Clements to make it towards the bridge with the tape. We crossed over the river and got onto the bridge. It was about 0400 hours. I told the Durham's CO that the Germans would probably attack at first light and he was to get his two companies out to the edge of the orchard because if the Germans got in he was in trouble. He did not agree. By this time it was beginning to get light and the remainder of his battalion should have been joining him as the success signal had been fired. I had done my job and the three of us left and made our way up the road. I expected to see the Durhams go into action – streams of jeeps and tanks – the only person I met was a War Office observer on his bike. I told him the form and he pedalled off – but it was dawn before they crossed the bridge. By then it was too late. Later that day the remains of Para Brigade were moved by transport to Syracuse. I was fast asleep in the front of the truck when I was awakened by Clements to be told that the Commander-in-Chief, Monty, was behind. Just at that moment the familiar khaki Humber passed with its pennant flying and signalled for us to stop. I thought a rocket was impending for being asleep but not so. He greeted me by name like a long-lost friend and congratulated us on our efforts and then said he'd like to talk to the men.

My RSM who was right behind me was pretty quick-witted and moved off to wake them. But he was a clever bugger, old Monty. He got his ADC to throw some packets of cigarettes into the trucks where the men were. Then he said, 'Walk with me, Pearson.' So we went about 200 yards down the road while he told me that although our casualties had been high, the cost was well worth it. He then walked slowly back again. When we got to the trucks he was greeted by cheering men all smoking Monty's fags and saying, 'How's Alamein, sir?' There he was, lapping this all up – all the cheers. It was very, very clever how he knew where I was and a great morale raiser.

Back in Sousse I got a bad dose of malaria and had to go into hospital. After I recovered I was to return to England to take up my new appointment as G1 Air 1st Airborne Division. I managed to get to Gibraltar where I met up with a squadron of Albemarles from our own group. Their wing commander offered me a lift home. There were only three of us on the flight. I sat in the co-pilot's seat. Before we took off the navigator gave me a lemonade bottle of water and told me to pour it down the pilot's neck every time he nodded off. The bottle was empty when we arrived at Hurn airport, UK.

LIEUTENANT PETER STAINFORTH, 1st Parachute Squadron RE

As I floated down the whole dropping zone seemed to be on fire – tracer bullets had set the tinder-dry stubble alight. There was no time to get my bearings before I landed with a hell of a thwack on my back in a deep ditch. I felt something warm trickling down my leg. 'Oh my God!' I thought, 'I've been hit!' I pulled my hand away and it was water. My water bottle had burst and was crushed flat. When I had got my breath back I picked myself up and set about gathering up the rest of my chaps and finding our weapon containers. Fortunately, we were all complete, but two of our weapon containers were missing.

The Germans had put barbed wire road blocks at both ends of the bridge, but opened them up to allow a truck towing a field gun to pass through just as our assault party charged in. In the fire fight that followed Brigadier Lathbury was on the receiving end of a grenade and got several splinters in him. So when I came up there was the brigadier, trousers around his ankles, bent over having shell dressings applied to his backside. As mine was the only sapper section to arrive the brigadier told me to get the demolition charges off the bridge as quickly as possible. The charges were obvious enough, but it was difficult to distinguish detonating cable from the masses of field telephone cables that they had laid. But it didn't matter. It all went the same way. We climbed up the girders at both ends and set about the cabling with machetes and chucked the whole lot in the river, explosives and all! Then we examined the piers and found that they, like a lot of the continental bridges at the time, had been built with chambers to take sacks of powder explosives. So all we had to do was to pull out the sacks and dump them in the river as well. Within half an hour the job was done.

It was now daylight and Alistair Pearson's 1st Battalion was being shelled. We got some shell burst over us. The ground was rock-hard and almost impossible to dig in with an entrenching tool. Fortunately one of my sappers found an air raid trench, a good eight feet deep with steps down and so we got down into this and awaited developments. We were the brigade's reserve on the south side and could do nothing useful for the moment. Pearson was holding off the Germans on the north side and there was quite a lot of firing going on up in the hills where John Frost was. He had an artillery officer with him who eventually made contact with a Royal Navy cruiser, the *Arethusa*. Things apparently had got pretty desperate until she began sending over seven-inch shells, which made a hell of a difference. Colonel Hunter, thinking that the Germans might cross the river and take us in the rear, asked me to go with our Bren-gunner onto the right flank where there was a Vickers machine-gun. By this time the 1st Battalion, almost out of ammunition, had withdrawn to the south side of the bridge, so the Germans, having reinforced from Catania, turned their full fury on us. Lathbury had no alternative but to abandon the bridge. The brigade major, who crawled along to our position, gave me the impression it was every man for himself. I must have been one of the last to leave because there was hardly anyone about.

We lay up in some scrub land until it was dark and then decided, by making a big loop to the west, to by-pass the enemy position to our south. The rightness of my decision seemed to be confirmed when we passed over ground covered with German parachutes and abandoned weapon containers bearing the words FJR IV – Fourth German Parachute Regiment! There were also some tents lit with hurricane lamps, which were skirted as quickly as we could! We lay up again the whole of the next day, and the following night turned south to join up with our ground forces just north of Lentini – actually with a unit of the RAF Regiment who were hoping to put Catania airfield to Allied use! From there we hitched a lift back to Syracuse where the remnants of the brigade were collecting, and thence back to North Africa on board an assault craft. As we were riding at anchor in these open craft, the Germans decided to bomb the harbour. The Royal Navy ordered smoke-screens to be laid and let off volumes of acrid black smoke to cover us. So what with being bombed and shot at by the Germans, and being choked to death by the bloody Navy, we were not sorry to leave Sicily!

STAFF SERGEANT T. N. MOORE, Glider Pilot Regiment

About 6 pm on 9 July 1943, Ivan Garrett and I took off in our Waco glider from Tunisia, bound for Sicily. We carried twelve infantrymen, four handcarts of ammunition and a Bangalore torpedo. It was Ivan's twenty-ninth birthday. Shortly after take-off a Perspex panel in the front of the cockpit blew out. The intake of cold air caused great discomfort to the troops and the noise made it extremely difficult to maintain telephonic communication with the towing Dakotas. We turned south and flew down the coast towards the landing zone near Syracuse and were caught in a searchlight beam. Our tug pilot dived and we followed him down almost to sea level.

We cast off at about 2,300 feet, a mile and a half from the coast. The wheels were smashed on landing and the glider came to an abrupt stop as the nose hit a large rock. This penetrated the nose of the machine, broke my ankle and pinned my legs under the cockpit seat. Garrett was unhurt and he kicked his way through the side of the cockpit.

Within a few seconds of landing the fabric top of the fuselage was in flames caused by grenades thrown by the Italians. Flaming patches of fabric fell into the handcarts of ammunition in the centre of the glider and before all the troops could escape there was a series of explosions, caused by the ignition of phosphorus grenades and mortar bombs. Six of the airborne infantry managed to get out but the remainder perished. Those who did escape took cover among the rocks and shrubs, but the explosions were so violent that one man was killed well over 100 yards away. I saw Garrett help one injured man from the burning machine and then stumble. A piece of flying grenade or bomb struck his left arm and tore away practically the whole of the elbow joint. I was unable to move and the cushion on my seat was beginning to burn. Garrett struggled to the nose of the glider and with his right arm lifted it a little. I knew this was my only chance. I threw myself forward and wrenched my leg free. As I did so I felt the bone break. Once free, Garrett and I tried, but without success, to pull another man from the wreckage. He was unconscious and already burnt. We scrambled about 30 yards away and took cover in the rocks as protection from the explosions. They continued for about two hours until one particularly violent one scattered the blazing skeleton of the glider far and wide. Later we learned that the fire had acted as a landmark for many of our unfortunate comrades who were down in the sea.

During the night Garrett lost a lot of blood (he was given a total of seven pints when he reached hospital in Tripoli) and he suffered from the intense cold. I used a puttee as a tourniquet to control the bleeding, but by morning his forearm was completely black. As the sun got up our hopes rose, for as the sea mist cleared we could see the invasion fleet landing barges nosing into Avola about five miles away to the south and we hoped our position would soon be overrun by the invading forces.

We heard a cry from some 50 yards away and saw someone propelling himself towards us on his back by the use of his elbows. We recognized him as the corporal from our glider; he had been struck between the knees by an exploding grenade. I ripped the legs off his trousers and tried to dress his wounds but it was almost hopeless, for the hole in each knee was larger than a field dressing. By noon I had given up hope of aid from Avola reaching us.

I decided that, to avoid having to spend another night in the open, I must reach either the landing base at Avola or the shipping. I dragged myself towards the wreck of our Waco and came across a dead Italian. I took his carbine and bayonet and found that together they would serve as a crutch. On reaching the beach I lay there for some time half-submerged in the sea. I dozed for a time and when I awoke found a large fish nosing around my legs. It had been attracted by the blood oozing from my trousers into the water. I thought of tickling trout in the Cumbrian hills, but without the finesse that I had been taught there I scooped it out of the sea on to the beach. I ate it raw with great gusto. I swallowed two Benzedrine tablets and set out to swim to the shipping. About a quarter of a mile out I saw the corporal had reached the first apron fence and got himself a couple of wooden sticks. He began to hobble along in a southerly direction towards Avola. I could see a farmhouse about three-quarters of a mile ahead of the corporal, and near the beach, and I decided to swim along the beach and contact him there. I scrambled ashore near the farm and hauled myself towards it along a wire fence. It proved to be completely deserted. The corporal followed slowly and was obviously in great pain as he pushed himself along with his sticks. By the time he reached the farm he was obviously at the end of his strength. He lay down in front of a smouldering charcoal fire and proceeded to fortify himself with an enormous piece of cheese. We discussed means of getting Garrett under cover. The corporal had found a path which led quite near the glider and we made plans to use a couple of donkeys from the stable. I had made myself a splint for my injured leg and found that with a stick I could get along. These plans, however, were upset by an action of the corporal.

He wanted some water from the well in the courtyard and on his way out poked the smouldering charcoal fire. It immediately burst into flame and the glow must have been plainly visible for quite a distance, for the door was open. In a few moments I heard voices so I hid under a friendly pile of beans. I heard the sound of approaching footsteps and someone stood in the doorway silhouetted against the evening sky. For a few anxious moments there was silence and then I realised that the visitor was wearing a British steel helmet. A medical officer and a stretcher party from an Indian division having spent all day searching for us had given up and were returning to Avola when they were attracted by the light at the farm.

They found Garrett and brought him in an hour later. He was conscious but suffering from gangrene, loss of blood and exposure. The Indians sent for additional stretcher bearers and we were carried to Avola. The cross-country journey was most arduous because of the rocky terrain, innumerable stone walls and Italian cross-fire. On the journey to the field dressing station in Avola we saw the farm where we had taken refuge completely destroyed by naval gun fire.

Later we were evacuated to Tripoli, and the three of us spent four months in hospital there. Garrett lost his arm and the corporal found he would never bend his knees again. Garrett, by his bravery and self-sacrifice, had undoubtedly saved my life.

CHAPTER SIX
ITALY
1 9 4 3 – 4

BY 17 AUGUST THE FIGHTING IN SICILY ENDED AS THE ALLIED armies converged on Messina. The Eighth Army crossed the straits of Messina to land on the toe of Italy on 3 September, followed a few days later by the first American landings at Salerno. After the arrest of Mussolini in July, secret negotiations had been in progress with the new Italian government and their surrender was imminent. The 1st Airborne Division was ordered to sail in Royal Navy and American warships to capture and open up the port of Taranto and to operate in advance of the main force soon to be landed there. On 9 September, the 4th Parachute Brigade aboard HMS *Penelope* and the USS *Boise*, passing the Italian fleet on its way to surrender in Malta, sailed into Taranto and scrambled ashore to secure the port, followed by the 2nd Independent Parachute Brigade. Unfortunately HMS *Abdiel*, a minelayer, with 6th Parachute Battalion aboard struck a mine. It detonated the mines aboard the ship which sank in two minutes with the loss of 58 lives.

156th and 10th Parachute Battalions advanced swiftly on two axes against strong rearguard action from the 1st German Parachute Division and in a few days captured the airfield at Gioia Dell Colle, which was urgently needed for the RAF to provide air support for the Salerno landings. The divisional commander, Major General Hopkinson was killed watching an attack by the 10th Battalion.

1st Parachute Brigade and 1st Airlanding Brigade landed and took over the advance, pushing on to Foggia 125 miles inland where the division outran its meagre supply and transport system. Main elements of the Eighth Army took over the advance up the east coast. In October the 1st Airborne Division was withdrawn to Taranto and in the following month returned to the UK. The 2nd Independent Parachute Brigade remained in Italy as General Alexander's airborne assault force, but the Germans had formed a

ITALY 1943

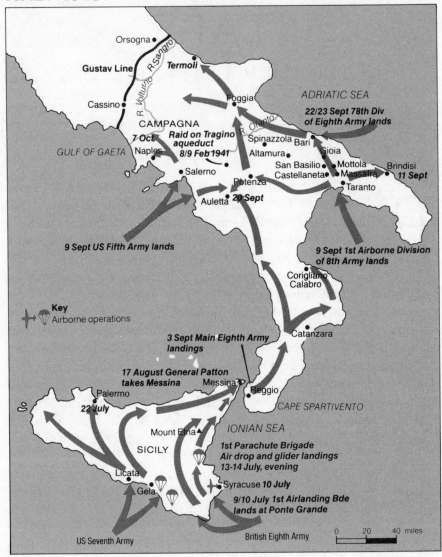

Orsogna
Gustav Line
R. Sangro
Termoli
R. Volturno
Cassino
Foggia
ADRIATIC SEA
22/23 Sept 78th Div
of Eighth Army lands
CAMPAGNA
R. Ofanto
7 Oct
Raid on Tragino
aqueduct
8/9 Feb 1941
Spinazzola
Bari
GULF OF GAETA
Naples
Altamura
Gioia
Salerno
San Basilio
Mottola
Brindisi
Castellaneta
Massafra
11 Sept
Potenza
Taranto
20 Sept
Auletta
9 Sept 1st Airborne Division
of 8th Army lands
9 Sept US Fifth Army lands
Corigliano
Calabro
Key
Airborne operations
Catanzara
3 Sept Main Eighth Army
landings
17 August General Patton
takes Messina
Messina
Reggio
CAPE SPARTIVENTO
Palermo
IONIAN SEA
22 July
Mount Etna
1st Parachute Brigade
Air drop and glider landings
13-14 July, evening
SICILY
Licata
Syracuse 10 July
Gela
9/10 July 1st Airlanding Bde
lands at Ponte Grande
US Seventh Army
British Eighth Army
0   20   40 miles

strong defensive line in the hills and the campaign had already become
static with little scope for airborne action. The brigade therefore fought as
infantry from November to March, 1944 in the Adriatic sector where they
were attached to the New Zealand Division. Here they carried out
aggressive patrolling and suffered many casualties during the bitter winter

fighting. In April the brigade was moved west to the Cassino Sector where they continued patrolling before being withdrawn to Salerno in May 1944.

MAJOR TONY HIBBERT, HQ, 2 Parachute Brigade

By the summer of 1943 the whole of the Airborne Division was in Sousse in North Africa. By August the resistance of the enemy in Sicily had ended and the Eighth Army was at the foot of Italy. On 8 September, the 1st Airborne Division, under Major General Hopkinson, was transported by cruisers and a minelayer to invade Italy.

As we approached Taranto harbour we saw the Italian fleet leaving the harbour to surrender at Malta. It was a quite magnificent sight, all the battleships and cruisers. We crept into the harbour just as it was getting dusk and everything was very, very silent. On an airfield about a mile inland you could hear a plane starting up. It then came lumbering towards us at about 250 feet. It was an old Junkers transport plane and it was unarmed. We could see the pilot and the people in the cabin peering down at us in disbelief. But the entire British Navy unfortunately was thinking of other things and apart from one gunner on a destroyer, no one thought of shooting it down. By this time we were just coming up to the jetty with about 600 troops standing on the deck. This gunner chap got behind his Bofors gun and traversed along following the plane. Unfortunately the chap who elevated the gun didn't get there so the gunner just opened up and raked the entire side of our ship. Now a Bofors gun is fast-firing and lethal. Fortunately all the shells hit about 18 inches below the level of the deck, but it was a rather tense moment for those standing on top! Luckily all was well. When we docked, the jetty was about twelve feet above our bows and there was no visible means of getting up from the deck onto the jetty. I saw two rather venerable people peering right at me, one an Italian admiral in full dress and what looked to me to be a cardinal, neither of whom could speak English. When I yelled to them to throw a rope down the cardinal spoke to me in fluent Latin, which made me feel guilty about not working harder at school! However, we soon got some ropes down and then launched the 2nd Brigade into the northern outskirts of the town to produce a perimeter defence against any attack. The Italians, who had capitulated by now, were all very co-operative and glad to see us.

As we were just digging in we heard this enormous explosion behind us. HMS Abdiel had swung across a mine which had detonated the mines on board. The 6th Battalion suffered very heavy casualties. The whole sky was lit up and we could hear what sounded to us like thousands and thousands of voices crying out.

Compared with North Africa, the next few months were for us an interesting, gentlemanly little campaign. It was the British Airborne Division against the First German Parachute Division. Sometimes there were battalion or full company attacks, but mostly it was just really vigorous patrolling on both sides, with the occasional bump. There was a great deal of hanging around which made people impatient, especially the unit commanders. When this happens they tend to go out in front themselves instead of sending patrols. In very quick order we lost our divisional commander, General Hopkinson, and then Tony Deane, commanding the 4th Battalion, ran into a German ambush. Even Brigadier Down, who was commanding the 2nd Brigade, went sculling off on a long range patrol where he bumped into a German patrol, but he was more fortunate.

One of the things we had to watch for was the ambivalence of the Italians. Although most of them were pleased to see the back of the Germans, there were still quite a few ardent Fascists. One day we were roaring down a road and there, leaning against an olive tree, was a reasonably well-dressed peasant with both hands behind his back. I was a bit nervous because I thought he might have a grenade, so I got my gun ready. As we got closer he must have thought we were German because he whipped one hand out from behind his back and started to wave a little Nazi flag as hard as he could. He then suddenly realized his mistake, put that behind his back and started waving a Union Jack!

FUSILIER GUS PLATTS, 6th Parachute Battalion

We left from Bizerta in Tunisia. The whole of the 6th Battalion, less A Company, went aboard HMS *Abdiel*, a fast mine-laying cruiser. The mine decks were piled with 1st Airborne Divisional stores and about 400 troops in all. We were in the illustrious company of HMS *King George V*, HMS *Howe*, the USS *Boise* with the 12th Cruiser Squadron and the 14th Destroyer Flotilla. Seemingly nothing could go wrong as we arrived at Taranto late in the evening of 9 September. We were due to land some time after midnight and were already inside the harbour wall, at anchor, in a balmy, evening breeze. I was on deck with the mortar platoon, and we had our mortar bombs and equipment on our backs, waiting to go ashore, just lying down to take the weight off our feet, with our belts unfastened. Then, all of a sudden, there was this unholy bang, immediately followed by what I thought were tracer bullets, but were actually sparks shooting out of the funnel. It looked like we had been attacked – been bombed. After the explosion the ship trimmed by the stern and listed to port. About 30 seconds later she righted herself partially for a few seconds and then went rapidly over to port, sinking by the stern. In actual fact she had broken in two and burst in many places from stem to stern.

I was thrown upwards and hit the bottom of the lifeboat I was under. As I got to my feet the ship was already listing badly. A naval officer appeared in front of me in his whites saying, 'Get over the side.' I didn't need telling. I had to climb up the deck to get to the rail, and could actually sit on the ship's side as she was turning over. At that moment Bill Dillerstone, one of my mates, was having trouble blowing up his inflatable life-jacket. I blew it up for him – he couldn't swim. Into the water we went, and then we became separated. I struck out away from the vessel as fast as I could – I was dressed in denim trousers, shirt, one boot and one gaiter. I must have swum about 100 yards in the dark, in water full of thick fuel oil and shoals and shoals of jellyfish. I came across another mate of mine, from the machine-gun platoon, struggling in the water. We ended up with a barrel between us, holding ourselves up. You could see in the distance only the bow of the *Abdiel*, still sticking up out of the water, and there were men sitting on it, smoking cigarettes. It was only for a second, and then she went completely.

A large rowing boat picked us up. There was a rat clinging to my shoulders – I threw it off, but it came back again. The damned rat stayed with us until I was pulled out into this boat, and I slung it away in the water. There were eight or nine guys in the boat, one of them was very seriously wounded, with a leg coming off. It took us only a short distance and we got picked up by a little Italian tug flying a Red Cross flag. We got aboard – we were a bit shell-shocked, wet and smelly, and covered in black oil – and we were taken ashore. There were probably about 20 of us and we were put in a cinema near the docks. It was there that I came across Bill, as black as I was, and with a big grin on his face. I thought he'd gone under because he couldn't swim, but he had swum all the way in – a hell of a way. He pulled a tin of cigarettes out of his pocket, a 50-tin of Players; he opened them up and they were perfect. He gave me a fag and we handed them around – they went very quickly. The only thing I had that wasn't contaminated with oil was my beret, which I had rolled up and put inside my shirt.

We thought we were going to be in the cinema for a long time, but when it got light a navy launch took us aboard the *Howe*. The first thing we did was go into the showers, scrub down and get all the oil out of our hair. Then someone gave me a packet of fags and a pair of blue naval overalls, and we got our heads down on the floor and on the tables. We were given big mugs full of what the Navy called 'kia' – like cocoa. It was very tasty. The next thing we knew the bugle was blowing for reveille. We gathered on deck trying to sort out who was who.

Brigadier C. H. V. Pritchard from our old battalion – 'Charlie Orange' to us – came aboard from a launch. He told us we were going ashore and carrying on the fight. There were three big cheers, but none of us had anything to fight with. Things got going on the *Howe* somehow, and we were supplied with gear. We were given the Marines' equipment, all pre-war stuff, and for many many years afterwards you used to find ex-6th Battalion men still walking about with distinctive white waistbelts, which immediately identified them as coming from the *Abdiel* sinking.

There were less than 100 of us on the *Howe*. The CO, Lieutenant Colonel J. A. Goodwin, and the RSM, WOI F.T. Langford, were lost; the senior man was the PTI Sergeant Major, John Reid, who called the roll that morning. We were shipped out with all our strange gear. I got a pair of white Navy plimsolls, blue Navy overalls – no shirts or anything else – and white webbing equipment with a pack and some pouches. I was given a Lanchester sub-machine gun, a typical Navy weapon, like a Browning. It fired 9-mm and they believed we would find plenty of ammo in Italy – we had none ourselves.

The next day, after a night ashore, we sorted ourselves out into something like a fighting unit, though we looked more like a band of guerrillas. I discarded my Lanchester at this stage for an Italian Breda. For a while I found myself a machine-gunner in an infantry section because at first we had no mortars with us.

Part of the brigade went up to Foggia, then Bari along the Adriatic coast to Manfredonia. All our kit had come into Bari docks from Africa, and the whole lot went up in the big bang when the Germans raided Bari and hit an ammunition ship. So going into Italy I hadn't got a single piece of equipment except my beret – I lost everything else.

Along the eastern side of Italy every few miles there was a river, and in winter they were raging torrents. Jerry had dug himself in on the Sangro River. When we got there it was in flood – it was very, very strong. The REs built a bridge that was swept away in a night. The Indian sappers eventually rebuilt it and we got across and some tanks followed. It was a fairly rotten time – the weather was bleak and it was one big mud hole. We were in the same gear we'd got from the *Howe* – I was still wearing my Navy overalls. It was cold. You could find yourself a coat or the odd thing, but for a few weeks it was pretty grim. We didn't wait and let stuff come through to us – we just got on with it.

After the Sangro we joined up with the 2nd New Zealand Division – we had been everybody's poor relations until then. We went on to Lanciano, a little up the coast. By December 1943 the 1st Airborne Division had gone home. We stayed on as the 2nd Independent Brigade Group – it was a fairly big unit, spanning the three infantry battalions, the 4th, 5th (Scottish) and 6th (Royal Welch), with a squadron of engineers, a battery of gunners and even a glider pilot section.

Just before Christmas we had taken a place called Casoli, a village on top of a hill, seemingly a favourite place for villages in that part of Italy. We set up our position on a day when it was snowing. We dug our mortar pits four or five feet down, did one or two shoots during the day, and then at night the snow really came down. We were just below a ridge about ten feet high. I went into my slit trench, put my groundsheet on top of me and in next to no time I was asleep, sitting on my steel helmet to keep out of the wet trench. I was found absolutely snowed under and had to be dug out. If they hadn't found me I would still have been there now, frozen solid. My sergeant gave me a tot of rum to thaw me out.

Throughout this time our casualties were coming from shell and mortar fire. At Arielle, in front of Chieti, the route coming up to our position from rear echelon was under such constant shell fire that it became known as the 'mad mile'. You were more likely to get killed going back to base there than staying in the line. We used to go down it like a bat out of hell – yet every day a supply truck would get blown up.

Every time the Germans stopped they got into a prepared position which they defended. Our brigade never ever went back – always forward – but the Germans had mountains, rivers or prepared defences to pull back to. While they were holding one defensive line, they were getting another ready. We were constantly having to find our way in – they could call the tune. The only time they couldn't was when things like Anzio happened, when we got behind them and interfered with their plans.

Eventually we moved over from the Eighth Army front to the Fifth Army front, for the fourth battle of Cassino. We hadn't really known what was going on on the other side, and Cassino was just another place, another name to us. We came out of the line, loaded our mortar platoon windscreen-less jeeps and trailers, and just went straight across the country in one night. It was early May, but pretty nasty. We got there late at night, off the trucks and a long carry. We took all our equipment through, but not the mortars because we were going to take over the Welsh Guards' mortars in their positions. We got to our positions and we made ourselves familiar with the fire plan. Then the Welsh Guards left and all of a sudden there was

95

a lot of noise behind us – they were going off in their Bren carriers or whatever – and Jerry didn't want to lose a moment, he had been alerted and started stonking us. We were also under sniper fire, and one we called 'Schmeisser Joe' paid us a visit almost every night across the Rapido. We were in on the final attack on Cassino, on 11 May. For this we moved over into the mountains, a steady climb of two or three hours, into a new position for the attack. We brought the ammunition up over two or three nights using mules. We had Italian animals – very good beasts really. They were very sure-footed and you never had to help them the way you did the little Indian mules.

About eleven o'clock at night the balloon went up. Something like 1,600 guns went off at the same moment. That's forgetting all the mortars – we were just small fry, firing on targets already selected. It was like the earth opening – a tremendous noise – and the whole mountain lit up. And we had a hell of a shoot ourselves. We ranged on a target – a crossroads or an area where there were German positions and fired continuously until the barrels were red-hot. We had to urinate on them to get them cool. All night we were firing. We pulled out at dawn the following morning, when the attack had gone through, and the Germans were moving back to their next defensive line. Cassino had been broken at last!

CHAPTER SEVEN
SANGSHAK
Assam, India
·1944

ARLY IN MARCH 1944 THE SPEARHEAD TROOPS OF THE Japanese 15th and 31st Divisions put in an unexpected 'backdoor' flanking attack from the east, stealthily crossing the River Chindwin, and moving through dense jungle-clad mountainous ranges, to capture Imphal and Kohima, taking the 14th Army completely by surprise. The Indian, Gurkha and British troops of the 50th Indian Parachute Brigade happened to be on a widely deployed patrolling exercise at that time and were the first to be attacked in strength. Suffering casualties, they were hastily ordered to concentrate, whilst still under fire, at the key-point Naga village of Sangshak, which is perched on a steep hillside between Imphal and the Chindwin, and to delay the Japanese onslaught at all costs. From this position, isolated and unsupported from either flank or from the rear, the Indian Parachute Brigade group held up the Japanese advance on India for six days under the most appalling conditions, inflicting heavy Japanese casualties, at great loss to themselves.

At one stage the Japanese gained a foothold right inside their position. Fierce hand-to-hand fighting took place in the Sangshak church area but the brigade held on desperately.

As the battle raged on neither evacuation of the wounded nor reinforcements were possible at Sangshak but the delay they imposed allowed the garrisons at Kohima and Imphal to be strengthened. Finally the brigade was ordered to fight their way out and return to Imphal. Their mission had been completed successfully but at great cost. Imphal, with its vital airfield and its Corps and Divisional Headquarters nearby, had thereby been saved from disaster and from being overrun and captured in accordance with Japanese plans.

SANGSHAK MARCH 1944

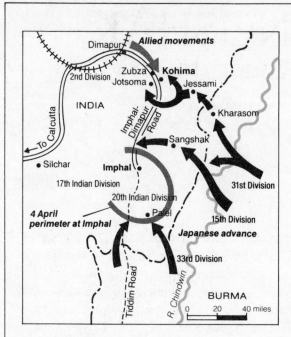

Dimapur
Allied movements
Zubza **Kohima**
2nd Division Jotsoma Jessami
INDIA
Kharasom
Imphal-Dimapur Road
Sangshak
To Calcutta
• Silchar
Imphal
17th Indian Division
20th Indian Division 31st Division
4 April perimeter at Imphal • Palel
15th Division
Japanese advance
33rd Division
Tiddim Road
R. Chindwin
BURMA
0   20   40 miles

50TH INDIAN PARACHUTE BRIGADE'S BATTLE POSITIONS 26 MARCH 1944

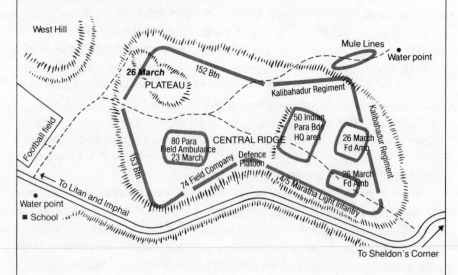

West Hill

Mule Lines
Water point

26 March 152 Btn
PLATEAU Kalibahadur Regiment

Kalibahadur Regiment

50 Indian Para Bde HQ area 26 March Fd Amb

80 Para Field Ambulance 23 March CENTRAL RIDGE

153 Btn 74 Field Company Defence Platoon 26 March Fd Amb

Football field

To Litan and Imphal 4/5 Maratha Light Infantry

Water point
■ School

To Sheldon's Corner

CAPTAIN L. F. 'DICKY' RICHARDS, HQ, 50th Indian Parachute Brigade

At Delhi in October 1941, the original composition of our 50th Indian Parachute Brigade embraced 151 British, 152 Indian and 153 Gurkha Para Battalions, together with its complement of Engineer, Signals and Medical units. Volunteers came from almost every regiment and corps, in both the British and Indian Armies, practically regardless of caste or creed. Many were professionals, and others were wartime soldiers, from many different walks of life, but with one thing in common: an urgent desire to get to grips with the enemy. We were all fairly rugged, hardened and carefree and set about the training of our men in the arts of killing and survival with a vengeance. Danger didn't seem to have much meaning at that time; everyone at home in UK was facing up to it, so why not us. Even jumping itself with a single parachute, in those early days, was a hazardous business, particularly in India during the first year or two when for every 100 jumps there would be one fatality. We had to make light of the problem; fatalities became casually referred to as 'bouncers'. Some of us even subscribed to what was called the 'Bouncers Club', each putting a rupee or two into the kitty, with the proceeds going to the next-of-kin of the 'winners'.

We worked hard and played hard and the men usually turned in at night completely exhausted. The system got us over the 'ditch periods' and by the time experts had sorted out our parachuting problems, the common danger had strengthened the bonds of comradeship which enabled us to face up to the absolute hell which broke loose at Sangshak, only months later. I did not see any signs of fear in anyone of any rank when their friends' parachutes failed to open, nor during the six-day carnage on the battlefield, either in our own men or the Japanese. Far from it; acts of bravery and courage on both sides were frequently almost suicidal.

By November 1942, 151 British Para Battalion had been urgently moved to the Middle East and replaced by 154 Gurkha Para Battalion who were still Para training. 152 Indian and 153 Gurkha Para Battalions were fit and fully prepared, waiting to set off on a parachute operation against the Japanese-held island of Akyab. As planning neared completion, we had to call off the operation because the enemy had moved elsewhere. It was a morale-shattering blow which led to some unrestrained drinking for a day or two to 'drown our sorrows'. Our commander, Brigadier M. R. J. 'Tim' Hope Thomson – an imaginative planner – persuaded GHQ India to send us on a 'jungle warfare exercise in a threatened area' which meant the Assam–Burma border to the east of Kohima and Imphal, down to the line of the river Chindwin; it sounded challenging and our spirits rose.

A few weeks later we set up camp near Kohima and were briefed by GOC 23rd Division, Major General Ouvry Roberts. He emphasized that it was thought that the expected main Japanese thrust against India could only develop from well south of Imphal and this made sense to us, since it seemed highly improbable that a major attack could be mounted from the east. There were several thickly jungle-clad mountain ridges, rising up to 3,000 or 4,000 feet, which ran north to south, and also the Chindwin which an attacker would have to cross. Certainly the terrain looked almost impenetrable by a force of any size. He then gave us a vast area of this mountainous jungle, on the east side of Kohima and Imphal measuring about 80 by 50 miles, down to the line of the Chindwin, which we were to patrol on foot with animal transport only. Our orders were to keep the area clear of Japanese patrols and infiltrating agents. It was an exciting challenge and since we were expected to 'live off the country', if needs be, some of us had even brought fishing rods and shotguns. The first to move south was 152 Indian Para Battalion, to set up patrol bases some 20 miles east of Sangshak. It was breathtaking country but progress anywhere was slow because of the narrow muletracks and footpaths (almost vertical in places) which had to be followed much of the time. One false move by man or mule could result in a 1,000-foot plunge down the 'khudside'. At the beginning of March, at Brigade HQ, reports of small, one- or two-man Japanese patrols, stealthily moving between clumps of bamboo, began to filter in. It was what we had been warned to expect. But on the 14th a small intelligence post reported that they were being heavily fired on. They did the best they could, and retired. This was only the beginning.

At 8 am on 20 March, a message came from 152 Battalion saying that C Company, under Major Fuller, was under attack from two Japanese battalions beyond Sheldon's Corner near the Chindwin. They had no wire or other defence stores so would soon be in grave difficulties. The other three companies of 152 Battalion were deployed too far apart to give mutual support, so C Company were on their own. By 10.35 am they were overrun and had heavy casualties; other companies were ordered to give support and an appeal was made for supplies of Dannert wire to be dropped by air; without barbed wire they hadn't a hope in hell of keeping the massive attack at bay. But none arrived, and despite gallant attempts to relieve them, all but a few of C Company were killed that day.

Only the day before the deputy commander of 23rd Division Head-quarters had put out a signal to all brigade and 'box' commanders, telling them that 'the Japs have embarked on a foolhardy ambitious plan for the capture of Imphal, and may be expected to "infiltrate" any day.' Infiltrate my foot! This was the start of a major offensive by two divisions of Japanese who had got safely across the Chindwin and were heading our way, with only our para brigade between them and Imphal with its Headquarters, airfields and massive store dumps practically undefended; and we were widely dispersed as it was, completely without defence stores.

Corps Headquarters and the Headquarters of 23rd Division between them had decided that we should form what had come to be known as a 'strong box', a self-contained base, in the village of Sangshak. This was a small Naga village on a piece of high ground, tactically very well-sited; with artillery and mortar batteries one could prevent, or at least delay, the Japanese advance on Imphal and even Kohima. We moved up from the Sheldon's Corner area whilst still under fire from the enemy. The men of 152 Battalion marched a wearisome ten miles on their flat feet, carrying as much as 70 or 80 pounds of equipment per man through the mountainous terrain to Sangshak. At the head of the column marched Lieutenant Colonel Paul 'Hoppy' Hopkinson and Lieutenant Alan Cowell. Hoppy refused my offer of a lift although he was tired; he would continue marching with the rest of his men to the end of the road, he said.

Led by Captain Ray Steele, D Company of the 4th/5th Marathas occupied a hill west of Sangshak and they covered the rest of us as we got into position. This hill was an obvious position to hold on to, but we simply couldn't do it; the ground was solid rock so you couldn't dig down without explosives, there was no time to build walls and no barbed wire to slow down enemy advance. We had to pull the 4th/5th Maratha Company back off West Hill and bring them down into the main positions. As the last men withdrew, heavy Jap mortar fire crashed down on the hill; it was soon overrun and occupied in strength. They opened up with machine-guns which swept the length and breadth of our position, causing casualties. Then, and only then, did we all realize that the battle had started in earnest. We'd wanted some action, and now we were going to get it. Again we signalled to Imphal for defence stores, but to no avail.

At Brigade Headquarters we took stock of our forces. It didn't take a great tactical genius to deploy the troops in the most effective manner; 152 Indian Battalion and 153 Gurkha Battalion held the major northerly and south-westerly flanks of what came to be known as the Church area, and whoever held that ruled the situation in Sangshak. The Field Ambulance we had down in a hollow, next to Brigade Headquarters, and the Defence Platoon and the 4th/5th Maratha Light Infantry looked after the least threatened southern flank. The Kalibahadur Regiment (a native state battalion) we positioned on the quiet easterly flank, as they were more used to facing civil disturbances than vicious attacks by the Japanese.

In the early hours of 23 March the Japanese were busy probing our perimeter and drew our fire; we couldn't afford to take any risks, being without wire. At first light the perimeter was littered with bodies of three Japanese officers and 86 men, and orders went out to recover the officers and senior ranks, in case they were carrying anything important. Major John Ball, the brigade Machine-Gun Company commander asked me to help pull in some bodies which were just below the church, on the enemy side, and exposed to their fire. I made a grappling hook out of a decapitated wireless aerial and some line, hoping that with any luck the corpses could be hooked in from a distance even under fire. We got up to the eastern edge of the church without attracting any fire, but whilst we were scanning the dead through binoculars, a Japanese machine-gun opened up and started traversing. Bullet holes started to appear in a line from the far end of the whitewashed mud and wattle wall, about 18 inches from ground level. For a moment I froze, then John shrieked 'Down!', the spell broke, and we flung ourselves face downwards, flat on the ground. The fire passed over us with only an inch or two to spare, going to and fro for some minutes. John called for some mortar fire which shut them up long enough for us to pull in a few bodies and get clear. It was a worthwhile expedition; one of the Japanese officers had some very interesting maps showing the plan and intended routes for the attacks by the Japanese 15th and 31st Divisions on Imphal and Kohima, a priceless find, which was taken back to Headquarters at Imphal by two brave men.

From the maps it was quite obvious that our position at Sangshak would have to be eliminated if the Japanese were to carry on according to plan. And we were inspired by a message from the corps commander based on the captured maps saying that the holding of Sangshak was vital to the main plan, and that plans for the reinforcement of the brigade were in progress, but that it could not be carried out for some time. This caused much optimism all round, despite the fact that we were almost on our knees from lack of sleep alone, as well as shortage of food and water.

Supply drops were a serious problem. The mountainous nature of the ground and the low-lying cloud made air supply hazardous, even if you could identify the target upon which to drop it. Naturally, at base, if supplies were dispatched they assumed that they had arrived, but communications were so bad that at times they had no idea that two-thirds of them had got into Japanese hands, or fallen elsewhere.

Cooking what little food we had was very difficult indeed, but we had one tremendous character, a Madrassi cook, nicknamed Swamy, who had an enormous, filthy, smoke-grimed brass pot. Everything, but everything, went into Swamy's pot, and Swamy fed everybody; he was the focal point for anyone who needed a morsel of food of any sort. Whatever went into it we shall never know, but it was never empty.

So we continued to fight by day and night. The position became utterly gruesome and macabre. The perimeter was littered with corpses which could not be buried and there were mule carcasses everywhere. Some went into the cooking pot, but others very quickly rotted in that climate, and there were Japanese bodies, our own bodies, and excreta everywhere: it was impossible to construct properly dug-down trenches. Dysentery became rife and the situation was almost intolerable.

We were getting weaker by the hour; our men were getting killed off one after the other, we were running out of ammunition and food and some men were almost delirious after many days without sleep. Some of us would drop off for a few minutes in mid-conversation, but it seemed to be just enough to revive mind and body. The situation was desperate, and by about the 25th I don't think any of us expected to get out alive. But somehow that didn't seem to mean anything, either – we just went on, relentlessly. I never heard a single man complain.

Shortly before dawn on the 26th the Japanese actually penetrated our position in the Church area, and set up machine-guns in the trenches which had been occupied by the brave men of 152 and 153 Battalions. Things got incredibly intense – they were now only 100 yards from Brigade Headquarters and we'd run out of grenades. But our men became even more ferocious and daring. Every man was fighting for his life and there seemed no limit to their endurance; everyone, everywhere, was pleading for more ammunition and grenades. By 0730 hours the situation was desperate, but the brigadier was determined to regain complete control of the Church area. He sent a party from the Brigade Defence Platoon on a frontal counter-attack. This was led by young Lieutenant Robin de la Haye, nicknamed the 'Red Shadow' by the men because of his habit of doing the rounds at night when the 'exercise' first started wearing exquisite Jermyn Street red silk pyjamas under his webbing equipment. Robin and his men made a spirited attack but were cut to pieces by enemy fire from West Hill. Again and again we counter-attacked, now led by Lieutenant Colonel Hopkinson, later by Colonel Abbott, but each time we were beaten back. At last, at 0930 hours, Major Jimmy Roberts with his A Company of 153 Battalion was successful and restored the situation, accompanied by deafening blasts from our own howitzers firing over open sights.

Just before six that evening there was a shout from one of the Brigade

HQ signallers for everyone to keep quiet: a message was coming through from Major General Ouvry Roberts. His shout was so urgent and excited that everyone fell silent. The signaller listened hard to the crackling set and scribbled on his pad, talking into his handset. It seemed to go on for ever. Then he suddenly shouted into the microphone, 'You can stuff your thoughts, General; what about the bleedin' reinforcements?' He was beside himself with rage as he handed over the message. It read: 'FIGHT YOUR WAY OUT; GO SOUTH THEN WEST. AIR AND TRANSPORT ON THE LOOKOUT' and ended with the words, 'GOOD LUCK; OUR THOUGHTS ARE WITH YOU.' It was this last comment which had prompted the signaller's reply! Our reactions resembled a 'Bateman' cartoon. For a moment we were horrified by his audacity, but seconds later broke the tension with spontaneous laughter, a sound not heard at Sangshak for quite some long time.

A conference of unit commanders was called and as night was about to close in, we heard the familiar sound of the air-supply Dakotas in the distance. Our initial euphoria at this last-minute chance of survival was soon dampened by the enormous problems of evacuating the seriously injured, who would have to be carried, and the walking wounded, bearing in mind the sheer mountainous jungle slopes between us and Imphal. I cursed when I found that the bulk of our supply drop had fallen straight into the hands of the Japanese; as the night darkened they lit fires and sounded overjoyed at this unexpected bonus.

Brigade Commander Tim Hope Thomson decided that there should not be any movement before 2230 hours that night. Units were to give top priority to pairing off walking wounded with their comrades, using every able-bodied man to help carry and protect the stretcher cases. Our greatest concern was the plight of the wounded; many were within an hour or two of death and others so serious that death would occur if they were moved. It was the worst dilemma to face any man and we were stunned by the selfless courage of our Indian Medical Services senior officer, Lieutenant Colonel 'Bobby' Davis, who almost pleaded to be allowed to remain behind, after the evacuation, to tend to the dying men who could not be moved, and anyone else who might not have been found in the utter shambles we were to leave behind.

Tim Hope Thomson and his Deputy, 'Abbo', gave it much deep thought but they both knew that on past records of the Japanese neither the gallant doctor, nor his patients, would have any chance of survival. We should try and take those who were considered to be mortally wounded, no matter how slim their chances of survival appeared to be. At Brigade HQ our cook, Swamy, excelled himself, keeping his cauldron on the boil well into the evening. We were amused to see him adopting the role of a Brahmin high priest, which was hardly his status, giving dispensation to the Hindu to accept the possibility of corned beef within the cauldron, and the Muslim not to reject the infamous American made 'soya link' sausage and gallons of rum included in the pot!

As the 2230 hours start-time approached, tension mounted. That evening Japanese fire had been limited to sporadic shots and a few bursts, but we wondered whether they would strike – if they did, our chances for survival would have been slim – but they didn't. Colonel Abbott ordered me to channel the few remaining exhausted men of 152 Indian Para Battalion through the 4th/5th Maratha Light Infantry position which was the safest of the lot. The former had taken a terrible hammering with casualties amounting to 23 officers, with 18 dead or dying, 7 VCOs (Viceroy's Commissioned Officers) and 328 NCOs and sepoys. Few had properly eaten or rested for well over a week and they were now practically without ammunition or grenades, or senior ranks to guide them, with a tortuous journey facing them, through the Jap-infested jungle to Imphal.

As the break-out got under way I felt surprised at the quietness and orderliness as parties with makeshift bamboo stretchers and walking wounded vanished from sight into the jungle below. It was a painful and heart-rending experience, particularly for the medical men whom I saw patching up and attending to anyone showing any signs of life.

Nearly a week later I arrived back at HQ 23rd Indian Division in Imphal, with Colonel Abbott, Lieutenant Colonel Paul Hopkinson with a foot in plaster, and a small group. We had survived walking into an armed Japanese supply column heading for Sangshak by throwing ourselves or rolling into the thick elephant grass and lying 'doggo', whilst they passed within feet of some of us; we had no grenades and hardly a round between us. Days later whilst intelligence officers were debriefing us I had a quiet cup of tea with the GOC, Ouvry Roberts, whom I knew well, having served with him in the Middle East. He left me in no doubt about the value of the stand which we had made. He said that the brigade, with its attached units, fighting under what must have developed into most appalling conditions, had undoubtedly saved both Imphal and Kohima from the danger of being immediately overrun by the Japanese spearhead troops, later to be confirmed in a Special Order of the Day by General 'Bill' Slim himself.

As we were taking our leave, I asked him off the record whether he had heard the British signaller's comments on his personal message – 'You can stuff your thoughts, General. . . .' His reply was just an enigmatic smile.

LIEUTENANT COLONEL PAUL HOPKINSON, 152 Indian Parachute Battalion

The question which must always come to mind is why Sangshak was selected as the 50th Brigade position that March. The answer, I suppose, must be that we were not expecting to have to put up a prolonged defence against a large Japanese force. When the need came to oppose and delay the progress of a large Japanese force heading for Imphal and Kohima, Sangshak was the obvious choice. At first glance the village seemed ideal, commanding as it did several important track junctions on the routes the Japanese would take to Kohima and Imphal. The position was already occupied by two companies of the Kalibahadur Regiment who had dug a two-company position on the eastern edge of the Sangshak plateau, which could be incorporated into a brigade position, thus saving vital time. Other characteristics of the position were not in our favour, however; it was a barren hill-top some half a mile long by a quarter wide, and the jungle came right up to the perimeter. There were no water points within the position; the Kalibahadurs were using small, exposed springs well outside the perimeter. Overlooking the whole position at the highest point was a small church belonging to an American Baptist Mission. This was in the very north-west corner of the site, and was surrounded by large stacks of firewood which were to prove all too good cover for the enemy.

The 50th Brigade only just beat the Japanese to Sangshak; by 22 March the latter were converging on the village from the directions of both Pushing and Ukhrah, at the same time as we were occupying the position, so we had very little time to organize ourselves or dig in before the Japanese were upon us. It was mayhem: 15th Battery of the 9th Mountain Regiment Indian Army was in action shelling enemy columns coming down the track from Ukhnil, 4th/5th Marathas were covering the concentration of the brigade from a ridge about 500 yards west of the perimeter (West Hill). The Medium Machine-Gun Company were digging in as fast as possible. 153 Battalion had arrived the night before and were occupying part of the western perimeter. We (152) had been allotted the northern and part of the western face including the vital church area, but there was too little daylight left when we arrived on the 22nd to do more than occupy the Kalibahadur slit trenches and weapon pits. A proper appraisal of our position would have to wait until the next morning.

As soon as it was really dark the Japanese started to attack and kept these attacks up continuously throughout the night regardless of their heavy casualties. As daylight came they withdrew into the jungle and firing ceased temporarily. Examination of our position showed very shallow slit trenches, no communication or crawl trenches dug to connect up the various posts, no barbed wire and very few picks and shovels. The forward posts being on the edge of the jungle, fields of fire were poor and restricted and the Japanese were able to approach them concealed by the thick jungle. Any movement in the open attracted fire from snipers, and also from medium and light machine-guns sited to sweep the plateau with fire. We lost a number of officers, VCOs and NCOs from this fire whilst visiting their platoon and section posts. This lack of cover within the perimeter also made the distribution of ammunition and rations in daylight very difficult.

It was the same, of course, with other units in the brigade but 152 and 153 Battalions were on the most exposed part of the perimeter and because of the rock near the surface, it was impossible either to dig down sufficiently or to find materials for building up our defences. The brigade Medium Machine-Gun Company suffered especially heavily through this inability to dig their gun pits deep enough – the number ones firing the guns were very exposed and many were killed including Major Ball, the company commander, and Captain Gaydon, both shot through the head whilst keeping the guns firing after the original number ones had been killed.

During the morning of the 24th our patrols reported large enemy columns with motor transport and elephants moving up towards Sangshak from the east. About midday the Japanese started shelling our positions, having brought up artillery, and they also attacked in considerable strength. It took fierce hand-to-hand fighting to push them back. We called for air support and a number of our fighters came over and engaged the enemy but as the jungle targets were very difficult to locate, some of our own positions were accidentally shot up as well. As I was watching the fighters from the Battalion Command Post, one came straight at us. We just had sufficient time to lie flat on the floor before the post was riddled with machine-gun fire from our own side.

We soon began to feel the shortage of water but we were lucky that evening – there was heavy rain which we managed to collect in our mess tins and other containers. It was apparent that Brigade Headquarters would have to consider urgently what to do about the large number of mules we had with us which had carried ammunition for the jungle mortar and mountain batteries. It was obvious that there was insufficient water for them and that their rations would not last long. On the other hand, once the mules had gone the mountain and mortar batteries would be immobile.

The night of the 24th was similar to the previous one with almost continuous attacks, each of which was driven off. Everyone was now beginning to feel the effects of lack of sleep, and ammunition and water were running low. Casualties were mounting and the Field Ambulance was crowded with wounded and dying. The doctors and the surgical team were having to work without sleep or a break to cope with the numbers.

During the morning we were heartened by the sound of transport aircraft and a supply drop took place. In desperation we watched our urgently needed supplies drift away over the jungle to be collected by the Japanese. One aircraft, however, came over very low and made a number of runs over us dropping only two parachute loads each run so that we were able to collect the entire aircraft load. The pilot was magnificent – each time he made his run he was so low that the Japanese opened up intense small arms fire on him from the jungle whilst we waved and shouted encouragement. He was so low that we could see him waving to us and the despatchers in the doorway. The same thing happened on subsequent days – out of all the supply aircraft that flew over we could only rely on being able to collect this one carefully dropped load. It was only later that I found out the reason for this pilot's bravery; he and his crew had taken part in the brigade's air training and when they heard that 50 Brigade was cut off and having to rely entirely on air supply they were determined that whatever happened, regardless of risk to themselves, we should at least get their entire aircraft load.

This failure to keep us supplied by air meant that our stock of essential supplies dwindled very fast and we became very short of ammunition including shells for the guns and mortar bombs. In 152 Battalion we ran out of grenades completely; ironically these were the most useful weapon for breaking up night attacks at close quarters. Rations were down to a bare minimum and what little water there was had to go to the Field Ambulance for the wounded. In the battalion we had enough for one small mug of tea per man each day. So I suppose it wasn't surprising that there was a general rumour throughout the brigade that a relief column was being sent out from Imphal – the men believed that the explosions and firing which they heard coming from the direction of Litan was the column fighting its way towards us. Those of us who had talked to other officers on our way through Dimapur, Kohima and Imphal knew that 17th and 20th divisions were having to withdraw fast on Imphal to avoid being cut off and that 23rd Division had been sent to cover the withdrawal. Some felt that any possibility of relief was a vain hope. There were just not enough troops in Imphal to enable an attempt to be made. The failure of the air supply and the large number of wounded in the position who could not be evacuated inevitably led one to the conclusion that the only course open to us was to fight it out where we stood.

We had very little scope for offensive action – all we could do was send fighting patrols to disrupt the Japanese attacks. In 152 Battalion we were stretched to the limit manning our sector of the perimeter. We now had only two rifle companies and these were depleted by casualties, and we had to keep our forward positions fully manned as, without any barbed wire and with the jungle coming up to the edge of the perimeter, they were very vulnerable to sudden attack. The area of high ground by the Church was subjected to almost continuous attack and the fiercest fighting of the battle took place here; it was the key to the whole position and the Japanese seemed to realize this only too well. From there they would have been able to sweep the whole plateau with fire and could have made the mortar and mountain battery positions untenable. Early on Lieutenant Cowell had gone out and burned all the piles of brushwood near it to improve our field of fire and to prevent the enemy using them as cover. Despite this, several times the enemy got up to the Church and even into one end of it but each time we drove them out. Lieutenant Cowell was involved in nearly all this fighting and he it was who carried Captain Gaydon back under fire when the latter had been hit. No praise is enough for the manner in which the IORs (Indian Other Ranks) stuck it out although exhausted by lack of sleep, food, water and ammunition.

On the evening of the 25th as I reached the Battalion Command Post a savage attack was made on 152 Battalion's sector of the perimeter. The enemy gained a footing in some of our forward positions but were eventually driven out with heavy casualties. This concentration of heavy attacks on the Church position was serious for us: not only were we depleted by casualties but everyone was physically exhausted by the continuous fighting on this sector.

At 4 am on the 26th the Japanese made a further large-scale attack against the Church position preceded by very heavy artillery, mortar and small arms fire. Eventually they gained this dominating point after the garrison had all been killed or wounded and we were unable to retake it. By this stage, all the company commanders in my battalion had been killed or badly wounded, and most of the junior officers and many of the VCOs and NCOs were also casualties. In Battalion Headquarters, both the signal and intelligence officers had been killed. Our weapon pits were a shambles of dead and dying, both our own and Japanese. The brigade commander tried to restore the situation by using his only reserve, the Brigade Headquarters Defence Platoon. The platoon was overwhelmed and Lieutenant de la Haye killed.

I decided to make another attempt to restore the position and together with Major Steward, the second-in-command, collected every man I could find from amongst Headquarters personnel – runners, signallers and orderlies – and counter-attacked. After fierce fighting we got back into some of our old positions, but were caught by a counter-attack from the flank and, largely owing to our lack of grenades, could not hold them. I was badly wounded and pulled out by the quartermaster and taken to the Field Ambulance.

After this failure A Company of 153 Battalion, under the command of Major Roberts, made a very dashing and gallant attack which stabilized the situation for the time being. The Church position, however, was still firmly in Japanese hands, which meant that our remaining guns, mortars and the Field Ambulance were now exposed to fire from the Church position and had to be moved back towards the centre of the perimeter where there was a little cover. After this there was a lull in the fighting whilst the enemy reorganized and prepared for fresh attacks.

The message to withdraw came as a complete surprise to us all because it had seemed that there was really only one course open to us and that was to fight to the bitter end. As Major Steward had taken over command of 152 Battalion, he had the difficult and heart-breaking task of arranging for the evacuation of the battalion's large number of wounded. This was done by detailing certain men to be responsible for those individual wounded whom it was considered had a chance of surviving the march back to Imphal. Parties were also detailed to look after and carry any stretcher cases who might survive. Owing to the large number of casualties amongst sub-unit commanders and the physical exhaustion of the troops, it was difficult to ensure that, when the time came for the break-out, everyone had actually received the order to go. There were cases where the order never reached individuals or else they were too worn out to realize that the time had come. The fact that the battalion was holding the northern face of the perimeter, the opposite side to that on which the break was made, did not help. From documents captured afterwards, it was discovered that the Japanese were planning to make a heavy attack at 0300 hours and this may well have been the reason why there was so little opposition at the time.

So ended the battle of Sangshak, and the survivors, many of them wounded, exhausted and without food, made the long journey back on foot through the dense jungle and over the mountainous ranges to Imphal. Our achievement had been significant; by seriously disrupting Japanese forces when speed was vital to them, we gained the time necessary for defences to be built up in Kohima and non-combatant units to be evacuated. We also inflicted very heavy casualties on the Japanese which they could not afford

Top: Jumping from a circular aperture in the floor of a Whitley bomber somewhere over Tatton Park, circa 1940

Left: Lieutenant C.I.A. Jackson, the commanding officer of 11 SAS Battalion, showing a new cushioned boot to General Sir John Dill, later the first Colonel Commandant of The Parachute Regiment

Above: Making adjustments to a Corporal's harness prior to boarding the Whitley at Ringway. The container in the front is an anti-gas respirator

An oblique aerial photograph taken prior to the raid on Bruneval. It shows the isolated villa with the radar disc in the foreground. La Presbytère is in the clump of trees (top left)

On board a gunboat Flight Sergeant E.W.F. Cox, RAF and a Corporal of C Company, 2nd Parachute Battalion recount their successful recovery of the radar disc to Group Captain Sir Nigel Norman, who had been in charge of air operations

Above: 1st Parachute Battalion, Bulford 1942. (Left to right) top row: Lt Jessop, Lt Coxon, Lt Fogarty, Lt Perrin-Brown, Lt Beevers, Lt Kellas, Lt Haggie, Lt Qm Rees. Centre row: Lt Disney, Lt Stewart, Lt Sheriffs, Lt Wandless, Lt Turnbull, Lt Mellor, Lt Hibbert, Lt Maude, Lt Lloyd, Lt Gammon. Bottom row: Capt. Spiller, Capt. Whitelock, Maj. Hood, Maj. A. Pearson, Maj. Hill, Lt Col Down, Maj. Martin, Maj. Conron, Capt. Ince, Capt. Bull

Below: Captain Vic Coxen with some of his company at Kowshock Farm in Tunis after their attack on the tank harbour at Gué

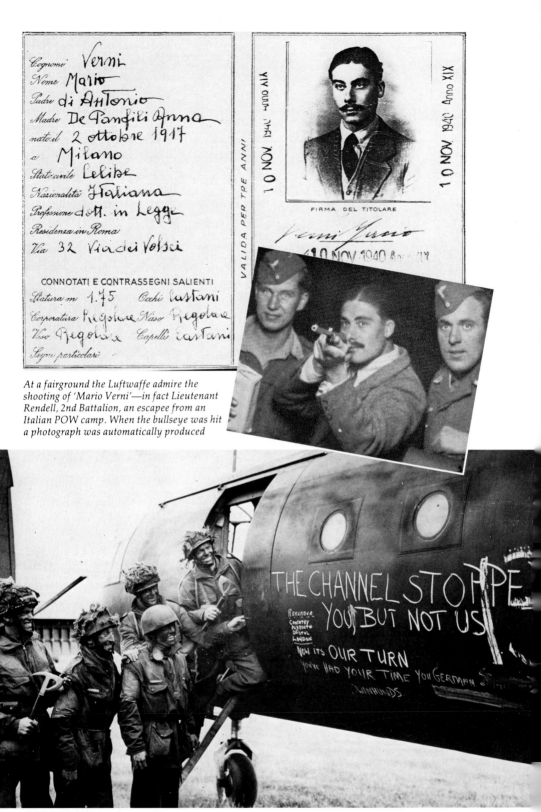

At a fairground the Luftwaffe admire the shooting of 'Mario Verni'—in fact Lieutenant Rendell, 2nd Battalion, an escapee from an Italian POW camp. When the bullseye was hit a photograph was automatically produced

Airlanding Brigade troops enjoying their artwork on a glider prior to emplaning to reinforce those already in Normandy so early in their campaign and were not able to replace; 2,000 enemy troops died in Sangshak. However, on our side, the only parachute brigade in India had suffered severe casualties fighting in an infantry role, and it would take a long time to replace these trained men. The position in 152 Battalion was especially serious; we were reduced to about half our strength, and a very high percentage of the casualties was among the more experienced officers. Many of them had served with the battalion since its formation.

CAPTAIN F. G. NIELD, 153 Gurkha Parachute Battalion

The day after we arrived in Sangshak (22 March) we started to dig in in earnest; 152 Battalion were expected in that evening. To speed our actions, we watched the Japanese appearing from over the hill down the road from Ukhrul. It was unbelievable – we might have been watching a play from the dress circle. We had the 15th Battery of the 9th Indian Mountain Regiment with us, commanded by Major J. P. Lock, a typical mountain gunner if ever there was one. He was a large burly fellow, with the appearance of a rugger player, wearing the most ridiculous little fore and aft forage cap and puffing contentedly at a pipe. He was in no hurry and waited until the whole length of the road was full of Japs before he let them have it. We saw the little white puffs bursting all along that road. Lock beamed – his only regret was that the guns had no shrapnel. He said that it was the best day's shoot of his life. It was to be almost his last, as he was killed a few days later.

All night long the attacks came in, and all night long the wounded passed through the regimental post where I was medical officer. There was little that we could do except stop any bleeding, give morphia and then evacuate them during lulls to the 80th Para Field Ambulance in a little dip about 200 yards away in the centre of the perimeter. Here, long hours were worked by Lieutenant Colonel Bobby Davis, the SMO (Senior Medical Officer) and many operations done by the surgical team of Jack Hyslop, with Harry Pozner giving the anaesthetics.

During the day we began to realize the seriousness of our position as the total reports of the casualties came in. The machine-gun company had suffered very heavily. John Ball and his second-in-command, redheaded Max Gaydon, had both been killed, besides many of their machine-gun number ones all shot through the head while sitting up firing from their exposed positions. We were only partially heartened by finding a large number of Japanese dead in front of our positions. What funny little men they looked – in the bright light of day it was more as if we were taking part in some strange Wellsian fantasy than fighting for our lives against these yellow hordes.

On the afternoon of the 24th something was obviously afoot – the Hurricanes were diving on the road some miles to the east and the rumour spread that the Japs were bringing up artillery by elephants. It was not long before we were able to test the truth of the rumour. Just after dusk the Jap whizzbangs began to open up, directed on the mountain battery, exposed just above our heads. Their four guns were stationed around the crest of the hill and could not be moved, while the whizzbangs were fired from the depths of the jungle and could only be spotted by their flashes. Even so our own gunners succeeded in knocking out one Jap 75-mm, but themselves losing one 3.7. One Jap shell unfortunately landed in one of our mortar-pits, killing Harry Butchard's second-in-command outright and cutting the barrel of the mortar as cleanly in two as a sharp knife divides cheese.

All next day, the 25th, sporadic enemy attacks and shelling took place, but in the early hours of the 26th the Japs came in with a savage attack on the parts of the perimeter held by 152. The position was now critical. To relieve the situation counter-attack after counter-attack was thrown against them. Troops from other sectors of the perimeter were drawn in, and it was only after several hours of savage hand-to-hand fighting that the Japs were thrown out, A Company having the final distinction of clearing the perimeter.

Things were now desperate – of 25 British officers in 152 who had gone jungle training to Ukhrul about a fortnight before only two were not wounded, 18 had been killed. Among them were many of our earliest volunteers of Delhi days. That night it rained with all the sadistic violence of a tropical storm. Water seeped everywhere, the wounded slid into the mud and the floor of the operating dug-out became a treacherous maw into which precious surgical instruments and dressings were washed and finally disappeared. In the rain-lashed dark the wounded shivered in sodden blankets, and a few silently died. Every available piece of dry clothing was heaped upon them and all who could be spared from the defences, from the brigadier to the sweeper, worked unceasingly under the supervision of the senior medical officer to provide a modicum of comfort for the wounded.

MAJOR HARRY BUTCHARD, 153 Gurkha Parachute Battalion

The 153 Battalion left Kohima early one morning and spent a day travelling towards Imphal – no food. On the second day we got there and dug in – no food. The third day we arrived at Sangshak and were told to dig in and still there was no food. On top of this we had minimum ammunition, only 100 rounds per rifle, 18 rounds per mortar, ten magazines per Bren, ten grenades a man. No barbed wire and no decent digging tools. So we couldn't have been worse equipped for a prolonged defensive battle – since we had been briefed and prepared for long-range patrolling only. There seemed to us to be no organization from above – it was total chaos and indecision. All very much the responsibility of 4 Corps Headquarters.

The first night at Sangshak was pretty frightening – despite intensive training most of us had never been in action before, and we weren't used to the dangers of moving about the position at night; more than one man was accidentally shot because he failed to hear the whispered challenge – he was taken for an infiltrating Jap. The Japs were doing their best to undermine our confidence – in front of the Gurkha trenches they spoke Gurkhali, outside the Indian position, Urdu, and during lulls in the firing and general pandemonium you'd even hear the enemy addressing you by name and rank. It was all rather eerie. By day, conditions on the plateau soon became pretty grim – bodies lying about, human and animal, decomposing rapidly. Snipers were a constant nightmare – one morning I was speaking to two officers of 152 Battalion, and when I returned that way a few minutes later I found them lying dead, in exactly the same place – shot through the head. The Field Ambulance area, packed with wounded, dead and dying men, was very vulnerable to small arms fire, but the senior medical officer was convinced that the bullets were coming from this vast thickly-leaved tree above the hospital. You could easily picture a slant-eyed Jap strapped to a branch up there, aiming at us as we walked about below. There was sort of grim humour about this situation, which was finally resolved by a Gurkha with a kukri in his teeth who climbed up the tree, covered by two or three riflemen and the intelligence officer. Nothing was found up the tree, but that feeling of being watched remained.

Day by day the toll of friends killed or wounded grew; every morning you'd wonder who else would be missing. What turned out to be our last day in the position started very badly – the Japs got a foothold in 152 Battalion's sector and overran a gun position. Several officers were killed or mortally wounded leading desperate counter-attacks, but rumours that reinforcements were on their way from Imphal kept the men fighting relentlessly; the British three-inch mortar battery sergeant major kept telling his troops that he could hear the pipes of the Seaforths in 1st Brigade coming up the Litan road! But things were getting really desperate; you wouldn't believe it, but a large number of grenades were found to be completely useless. By that evening I had both my remaining three-inch mortars in 'Suicide Alley' and my command post just above them: my third detachment received a direct hit from a shell and they all blew up together with the mortar and the bombs.

That evening we stood to, to await what horrors the night would bring, when a runner arrived calling me to a COs' conference. There the news was broken that we were to break off the action and retire to Imphal bringing our wounded with us. At this stage the senior medical officer, Lieutenant Colonel Davis, asked for 100 men from each battalion for the huge job of collecting up the wounded. This was impossible – even if the men had been available, we couldn't have assembled them on a hilltop under fire to look after badly wounded men whose present location wasn't known; this confusion had been caused when the Field Hospital had to be moved and the wounded were pushed into holes in the ground wherever some cover could be found. When he realized the hopelessness of the task, Lieutenant Colonel Davis offered to stay with the wounded who couldn't be moved so he could look after them while the Japanese moved in. But the brigadier turned this down – he knew the doctor would have little chance of survival, let alone of being allowed to care for the wounded.

As the time to leave got closer everyone tended to group together and there was a lot of movement as men tried to find wounded friends or were sent by the medical officers to search different areas. I suppose it was inevitable that, when the time came to go, we had still not found all the wounded, and some had proved impossible to move . . . so in the end some of them were left behind. Those that managed to leave didn't exactly have an easy time of it – the majority of the 'stretcher cases' became 'walking wounded' in spite of incredible injuries as we simply didn't have many proper stretchers. Those who could get away unaided filtered off into the darkness in complete silence without a shot being fired.

Our descent from Sangshak was a slow, laborious process, with many single-file snakes heading south, often halted by obstacles or the agony of the wounded. One halt was so long that I moved up the column to find out why, only to discover that the men waiting to cross a ditch had fallen into a deep sleep – I had to kick them into action, they were so exhausted. We'd just got going again when, over to our left, there was a huge stampede as of several elephants, and a crashing of bodies. We froze to the ground, until we realized that two of our columns had met each other in the dark, each convinced that the other was Japanese. Confusion reigned for a few minutes, but no shots were fired.

Shortly after dawn I came into a clearing with a rocky stream and grassy banks. There I was astonished to see four fellow-officers including Pat Paterson who was a 'walking wounded' – it was good to see him. We had our first drink of decent water for a week and then exhaustion overtook us and we slept until midday when luckily we awoke and realized we still had a long way to go. That evening we came upon Colonel Abbott the brigade deputy commander, a large, heavily built officer with a ruddy complexion who, the day before, while the battle was raging in Sangshak, had said to me, 'Harry, I am determined I am going to die of an excess of port in my old age.' He was half-carrying Hoppy Hopkinson, CO of 152 Battalion, who had been wounded in the foot and, with his arms round Abbo's neck, was hopping up the hill. We added this party to our strength and settled down for the night in a wood. Nobody had more than a biscuit or two, so after a drink of water and a cigarette we retired hungry and exhausted to sleep. Cigarettes were few and far between but I smoked a pipe and had been lucky enough to get a one-ounce tin of 'Ogdens Coolly Cut Tobacco' from a British mortar sergeant the day before we left Sangshak, so I was happy enough.

At dawn after a wash and a drink of water we set off in groups at intervals. There was a long climb ahead, following the dangerously blazoned trail of those who had gone before us. We crept up to the ridge and two recently dead bodies at the side of the track warned us to watch out for an ambush. When the going looked clear, we sprinted across the track and down the other side until we got into thick cover by a rocky stream – it was about 2 pm and our first sight of water since before dawn. We needed a rest after this exertion so we sat down for a brief spell, while one of the Assam Rifles' Gurkhas produced a cigarette tin half full of rock salt and raisins which we shared out. Much refreshed, we carried on down the watercourse led by the Gurkhas. Going round a bend in the nullah the Gurkhas suddenly stopped and pointed ahead to two figures, one leaning against a tree and another on guard over him.

It was the brigadier, Tim Hope Thomson who had been injured and had a blood-stained bandage round his head, guarded by his Pathan orderly. They were entirely alone so they joined our growing party. As it was nearing nightfall we selected a convenient spot near water and were settling down to sleep when suddenly a noise of boots and movement caused some alarm. Eventually a party of about 30 soldiers led by two Indian doctors appeared from a branch nullah. Many of them were badly wounded, one hopping on home-made crutches and another with the lower part of his jaw shot away. You could smell the wounds yards away – gangrene had set in.

Two days later we stumbled across a party of British officers and men brewing up tea in a mess tin. No-one had any news of anyone and they were completely in the dark as to the military situation. We assumed Litan had fallen but we had no idea whether we were in front of or behind Japanese lines. But the main talk between officers that night was about Sangshak: how and why did we get so overwhelmed, what were our mistakes, how could we have done it better, had certain high-up officers at Divisional and Corps HQs let us down? And what was going to happen now? Would we get back to Imphal – and what were we going to find anyway?

Not surprisingly, the atmosphere the next morning was tense and apprehensive – morale was very low. That afternoon the brigadier asked me to try to get some food as a number of people were becoming pretty weak. We were obviously getting close to Imphal as there were semi-wild cattle around; he suggested I should shoot one of these, but I felt it would be too time-consuming a job. So I got everyone together (we were about 50, all told) and we emptied out our haversacks and shared whatever food we had left. I saw that no-one would approach the Indian with the terrible face wound so I told him to put his head back and gently dribbled some tea through the hole in the front of his face – one could hardly call it his mouth. That night we came within sight of Imphal, and realized that, for better or worse, we would know the answers to our questions tomorrow. The next day we entered a village and asked for food; the villagers were delighted to give us an enormous meal of curried fish and rice, and they refused any offers to pay. I will always remember that meal.

We were now ready for our contact with Imphal, and we still didn't know whether the Japanese held it or not. I went ahead with a small party and to my relief saw the familiar khaki of an Indian sentry. So we halted to close up our band of scarecrows and made a bold effort to march in as though we were soldiers. It was with huge relief that we loaded our incredibly stoical wounded onto waiting ambulances. Many of them lived to fight again.

CHAPTER EIGHT
NORMANDY
Operation Overlord
- 1 9 4 4 -

THE 6TH AIRBORNE DIVISION'S TASK ON AND AFTER 'D' DAY, 6 June was to secure the left flank of the Allied landings which were to take place on the beaches of Normandy. This flank had to be held as it would eventually be the hinge on which the Allied armies would pivot as they broke out of the bridgehead to sweep on to Paris, Brussels and the Rhine.

The objectives for the 6th Airborne Division were the high ground east of the River Orne which overlooked the beach-head and the seizure, intact, of the bridges of the Caen Canal and the River Orne, the destruction of the five bridges in the flooded valley of the River Dives some seven kilometers beyond the high ground, and finally the silencing of the strongly fortified, major coastal defence battery at Franceville Plage – the Merville Battery.

Although the night drop was accomplished in less than ideal conditions and the troops were widely scattered, all the divisional objectives were achieved. The Germans quickly mounted counter-attacks against the entire beach-head, in particular, on the vital ground held by the 6th Airborne Division. Heavy fighting continued for some weeks. When the counter-attacks were finally stopped the airborne troops held their positions by vigorous patrolling actions. On 17 August the 6th Airborne Division advanced eastwards, overcoming German resistance at Cabourg, Dozule, Putot-en-Ange and Pont L'Évêque and on 26 August they reached the Seine. In this hard-fought but successful operation, the 6th Airborne Division suffered the loss of 1,166 men, either killed or missing.

NORMANDY JUNE 1944

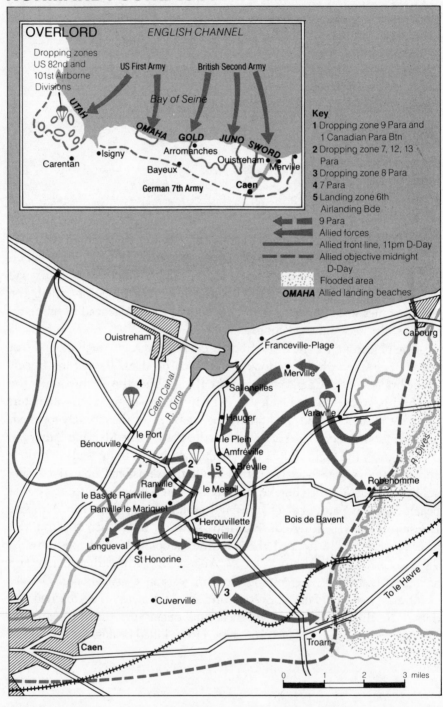

OVERLORD

ENGLISH CHANNEL

Dropping zones
US 82nd and
101st Airborne
Divisions

US First Army

British Second Army

Bay of Seine

UTAH

OMAHA

GOLD

JUNO

SWORD

Arromanches

Ouistreham

Merville

Isigny

Carentan

Bayeux

Caen

German 7th Army

Key

1 Dropping zone 9 Para and 1 Canadian Para Btn
2 Dropping zone 7, 12, 13 Para
3 Dropping zone 8 Para
4 7 Para
5 Landing zone 6th Airlanding Bde
 9 Para
 Allied forces
 Allied front line, 11pm D-Day
 Allied objective midnight D-Day
 Flooded area
OMAHA Allied landing beaches

Ouistreham

Franceville-Plage

Cabourg

Merville

4

Salenelles

1

Caen Canal

R. Orne

Hauger

Varaville

le Port

R. Dives

Bénouville

le Plein

Amfréville

2

5

Bréville

Robehomme

Ranville

le Mesnil

le Bas de Ranville

Ranville le Mariquet

Herouvillette

Bois de Bavent

Longueval

Escoville

St Honorine

To le Havre

3

Cuverville

Troarn

Caen

0   1   2   3 miles

FLIGHT LIEUTENANT ALEC BLYTHE, RAF

I had recently married and was living in Ashton Keynes, a tiny Gloucester village. A week before D-Day, I rode my bicycle at a leisurely pace through the quiet and peaceful countryside past little places like Cerney Wick, to the airfield at Down Ampney. There I was to prepare for what, I suppose, was to be the largest military operation that had ever taken place.

I had met the Royal Engineers, whom I was to drop on D-Day, and they seemed jolly nice chaps. However, when they came up to the Dakota on the night of the operation with blackened faces they looked a fearsome lot. One pulled out his dagger and said that it was going to find a German that night. I was rather glad they were on our side.

Pathfinders were supposed to set up a piece of radar beacon, called Eureka, which would guide us to the dropping zones. Unfortunately very few Pathfinders were dropped accurately, so most of us found there was no Eureka beacon to track to and we had to fall back on our own navigational equipment. My DZ was one and a half minutes flying from crossing the French coast to dropping. The briefing therefore had to be tremendously detailed. Accurate models of the Normandy coast and hinterland were constructed. From these models cine films were made of the tracks to each of the dropping zones. So we were prepared with a mental picture of what we could expect to see as we flew in. The films were made in daylight, whereas we would be dropping at night.

As we crossed the coast, my navigator reported two large houses which we expected to see before a line of trees came out of the murk. I was getting ready to drop my troops south of the road to Caen. There was a fair amount of moonlight and I could see that the Germans had flooded the area south of the road where we were supposed to drop. I didn't have much time to think, but decided I had better drop to the north of the road rather than in the water. The red light was on and the Engineers were standing ready. There was some flak but I hadn't had to take evasive action. I was intent on making as steady a run as possible when suddenly the aircraft banked almost 45 degrees. In a flash of light from the ground I saw a Stirling bomber passing in front of us. Clearly we had been caught in his slip-stream which threw us off course. I had therefore to bring the wings level and regain heading as quickly as possible. The paratroops in the back no doubt were hurled about and were probably cursing me for taking violent evasive action. I never saw them again to explain the reason for their discomfort. Unfortunately the accuracy of the drops on D-Day wasn't as high as one would have hoped. I would like to think that my Engineers were accurately dropped especially as the two bridges assigned to them were blown up.

The following evening we resupplied the 6th Airborne Division in the same area. The Royal Navy apparently hadn't been told about this because a couple of ships started to shoot at us. I could see the tracer criss-crossing in the evening sky. Fortunately they were not very good shots and we were not hit. When I got back to Down Ampney and had been de-briefed, I quietly cycled home.

STAFF SERGEANT ROY HOWARD, Glider Pilot Regiment

In 1942 I was with the Royal Signals and volunteered for the Glider Pilot Regiment. We trained extremely hard; in fact I'd been training and doing exercises for 21 months before D-Day. We had practised a number of precise night landings although we didn't know why. We were only told three days before D-Day what our final destination would be. My objective was a small corner of a particularly tiny field of rough pasture close to the Orne bridge. If I overshot I would crush us all against a 14-foot high embankment; if I undershot I would destroy my seven tons of powerless aircraft and its human cargo on a belt of 50-foot high trees. There was simply no room for error. The significance of the two bridges to be attacked by a *coup de main* force was emphasized to us. With the 6th Airborne Division landing to the east of the river, and the whole invasion coming ashore to the west of the canal, it was vital that they should be able to cross the two bridges over the Orne and the canal. These two bridges were the only ones where you could do this between Caen and the sea. So it was absolutely vital that we had the maximum surprise element, and the only way to do this was for us to carry out our operation before the rest of the invasion started. So we were going to sneak in just after midnight, and some six and a half hours before the seaborne invasion came ashore.

Someone had made a most marvellous sand-table, a perfect model of what was on the ground in Normandy – even down to the last tree and ditch. The chap who'd made it had put some wires above the area, and slid a cine camera down these wires, filming all the way, and therefore had simulated what a glider pilot would see on his approach. It was incredibly clever, and impressed us all very much indeed. So we were very confident.

Each Horsa glider with its 88-foot wingspan was going to carry 28 troops, a mixture of Oxford and Buckinghamshire Light Infantry, plus two or three Engineers; we were also going to carry an assault boat, and numerous other bits of equipment, because it was thought that the bridges might be blown before we got there. We got out onto the airfield about 9.30 pm on 5 June. I think everyone knew on the airfield what was happening except one of the ground staff from the Air Force, who came up to me and said, 'Are you bringing this one back tonight, Staff?' I said, 'No. I don't think so.' He walked away looking dazed.

We'd met the Oxf and Bucks lads a few days before and they were a very good bunch. However, on the night they arrived all blacked up, loaded with arms and ammunition they looked a right bunch of cut-throats; I think I was more afraid of them than I was of the Germans! We loaded up, drank a cup of tea, chatted and at about twenty to eleven, when it was nearly dark – we had double summertime in those days – we mounted up and when somebody fired the green flare, the engines started and one by one we got underway.

When gliders Nos 1, 2, and 3 cast off they were going to fly straight ahead for about four or five miles, then do a big 180-degree turn to the right and come in and land by the canal bridge, which is now called Pegasus Bridge. Gliders Nos 4, 5, and 6 – and I was No. 6 – were set for the Orne River bridge, now called Horsa Bridge. We were to make the turn slightly to the right, and then fly three different compass courses for varying amounts of time, the whole while descending as steeply as possible, because we hadn't got nearly so far to go. Ours was a straight-in approach so by the time we had finished flying this third course, we were going to be pointing due south, and hopefully straight into our field.

We took off, rumbling along on our wheels at the end of a 275-foot towrope, climbed round and left the British coast over Worthing. Paddy O'Shea, the tug navigator came up on the intercom, which ran down the towrope, and told me what to set my gyro compass on. He gave me 'three minutes to cast-off'. I kept the craft steady then got the OK to go. We began to descend at a very steep angle to get rid of all the height which I didn't really want. I was somewhat disturbed to find that we were grossly overloaded, and the trim wasn't right. I was nose-heavy, with the control column right back up against my chest, and we were going down at 90 mph like a streamlined brick! I turned round and shouted to Lieutenant Fox in the fuselage for two men from the front to go to the back, which sorted out the trim. The nose came up and I was able to put the control column forward. We were now back on our planned descent rate of 1,500 feet per minute. We held our course of 212 degrees for 90 seconds, then 268, then 212 again, my second pilot, Freddie Baacke, guiding us by stop-watch lit by the tiniest of hand-held lights. We did see a little bit of flak coming from the 20-mm on top of the Merville battery, firing away at the tugs who were flying on in the decoy mission up towards Caen but we carried on and eventually turned onto the last course. When we got to about 1,200 feet I looked out of the glider for the first time – previously I hadn't taken my eyes off the instruments – and I could see the ground and it looked exactly like the model, which was quite fantastic – I felt I had been there before. The only trouble was that the field was a little bit further away than it should have been; I had been too successful in losing my height. I ripped the flaps off very quickly and stretched the glide, flattened the glide path and brought her down. There we were, at nineteen minutes past midnight just six yards from our allotted spot and 100 yards from the bridge. There was the briefest moment of total silence. I turned and called, 'Mr Fox, you are in the right place, sir' – because they had no way of knowing – 'Off you go!' They went out with a stampede of boots and very quickly captured the bridge.

I realized that instead of being No. 3 glider into the field, I was the only one there, which shook me a little. No. 5 had undershot a bit, and was actually about 400 yards behind me, but No. 4 had been taken by his tug to the wrong bridge on the wrong river, nine miles further east. They had captured it and, realizing their error, had fought their way back through enemy-held territory and arrived 24 hours later. It was a stupendous effort.

Once the chaps had rushed out this was a dodgy moment for a glider pilot. I leapt out of the glider and crawled to the nearest ditch. There I threw off my flying helmet and equipment and proceeded to kit myself out as a soldier. It was a strange transition. We were trained soldiers, but we were also trained pilots, so our objective was a quick return to the UK for further flying, not to be involved with the fighting for longer than necessary. By 8 June we were back at Tarrant Rushton having been released by the operation commander at 2100 hours on D-Day.

MAJOR JOHN HOWARD, 2nd Battalion, Oxford and Buckinghamshire Light Infantry

Central to the 6th Airborne Division's plan to seize the left flank of the area north-east of Caen, was the capture of two bridges over the Caen Canal and the River Orne which we knew the enemy had prepared for demolition. Any German attack against the Allied flank would have come along the coastal road between Benouville and Ranville and cross both these bridges. It was therefore decided that these bridges should be captured intact by a glider-borne *coup de main* party.

My company, D Company, 2nd Battalion Oxfordshire and Buckingham-shire Light Infantry, was selected for this task. We were supplemented by two platoons from another of our companies and 30 Royal Engineers, making a total force of 180 to be carried in six gliders. After my top secret

PEGASUS BRIDGE 5/6 JUNE 1944

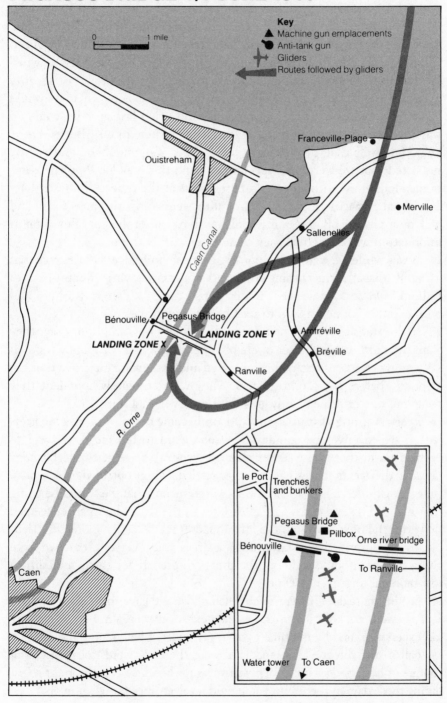

Key
▲ Machine gun emplacements
● Anti-tank gun
✛ Gliders
Routes followed by gliders

0   1 mile

Franceville-Plage

Ouistreham

Merville

Caen Canal

Sallenelles

Bénouville
Pegasus Bridge
LANDING ZONE Y
LANDING ZONE X
Amfréville

Bréville

Ranville

R. Orne

Caen

Inset:

le Port
Trenches and bunkers

Pegasus Bridge ▲
▲ ■ Pillbox
Orne river bridge

Bénouville
▲ ●
To Ranville →

Water tower   To Caen

briefing at the end of April, we had about a month's training. It was very boring initially because for three or four days we just attacked mock bridges, as a battle drill. We exercised every possible permutation of landing and made sure that every platoon could do any one of the six tasks that had been allocated. They went over and over this until everyone was very browned off, but they all knew that complete flexibility was essential. For security reasons, I could not breathe a word to anyone about exactly where we would be landing, not even my second-in-command Brian Priday. All I could do was imply that it was for a special exercise somewhere in UK. But everyone knew full well that the invasion, or D-Day, was imminent and rightly suspected that we were on a special task, and this blew up esprit de corps tremendously. As with all 6th Airborne units at the time, ATS (Auxiliary Territorial Service) girls, dressed in mufti, were going into pubs to try and pick up if anyone off duty was letting anything out of the bag. But as far as information was concerned they came away with nothing.

It was while we were doing our last exercise on bridges near Exeter that a Don R (dispatch rider) came down with a message saying, 'Report back to Bulford.' On 26 May we went to our transit camp at Tarrant Rushton and on the 28th I got permission to start briefing everyone.

In the transit camp we met our twelve glider pilots and I must say, they were the most wonderful set of chaps I met during the war. They were all fully trained soldiers who had volunteered and undergone intensive training as pilots, before going onto gliders. They were absolutely confident they could put one of those bloody great Horsas down on a sixpence!

Every morning at transit camp a Don R came down from Headquarters with a sealed envelope containing a code word to tell me if we were to prepare to go that night. After about a week we were getting a bit edgy because the weather was becoming unsettled. Then out of the blue on 4 June I got the code word 'Cromwell' which meant that we would be going that night. This order was cancelled later in the day. The weather seemed no better the next morning, the 5th. In fact it seemed even more unsettled, but to my surprise I got 'Cromwell' again. I told everyone that we were going that night and we did all the things to prepare for battle including a low-fat meal to prevent sickness.

Just before take-off I went round each glider and gave them my 'Ham and Jam' farewell, not knowing when I would next see them again. I found it a very sad experience, and by the time I got to my glider, I had a lump the size of a football in my throat. 'Ham and Jam' were the code words for a successful capture of both bridges intact. Those two words became very important to us, during those days in the transit camp, and for ever since for us survivors.

At 2256 hours No. 1 glider took off, and by 2301 hours all six gliders were airborne, towed by Halifax bombers. I was with No. 1 Platoon and hoping we would reach the important canal bridge first. We cast off over the French coast, at about 6,000 feet, and from that moment our lives were absolutely in the hands of our glider pilots. After opening the doors at 1,000 feet I looked down on the lush green fields and could see the Normandy horses and cattle grazing quietly, which all had a tranquillizing effect. I knew exactly where we were because I had been studying the aerial photographs until I was starry-eyed. I recognized from the shapes of the villages, the churches and crossroads that we were absolutely on course. In any case one of the glider pilots had been giving the thumbs up, ever since we cast off!

As we came in to land most of us were scared, but our enthusiasm to get the job done overcame fear. The landing drill was to link arms with the man on either side of you, then butcher's grip your fingers, lift your feet and pray that your number wasn't up. On the first bump we lost the wheels, then we came down again on the metal skids and were airborne again, then another bump, with sparks shooting up from the skids hitting flints in the field. In the first tremendous crash the whole place seemed to revolve round me. I responded to my training and undid my safety-belt and as I staggered to the telescoped door I could not see and imagined I had gone blind. I thought, 'what a time for this to happen.' But I'd hit the roof on landing and this had jammed my helmet down over my eyes!

As I came out I had the most exhilarating moment of my life, for three reasons. First of all, less than 50 yards away I saw the tower of the canal bridge that I had been studying for so long; second, the nose of the glider was right through the wire of the enemy defences and, third, there was no firing, so we had been a complete surprise. Everybody realized this and took full advantage and ran to the bridge. I moved up the track to my command post. I heard two more gliders crash on the landing zone behind me; I could hardly believe my ears because they were so near. By now the leading section of No. 1 Platoon had hurled grenades into the pillbox, while the rest of the platoon, led by Den Brotheridge, doubled over the bridge. David Wood's platoon arrived and I gave then the number two task to clear the inner defences. The enemy had been woken now, but they were low-grade troops of mixed nationality and we didn't have much trouble with them, except the NCOs who were all German. Number 3 Platoon had a heavy landing, and when their commander, Sandy Smith, came up he was limping very badly. At the same time I got the message that Den Brotheridge had been shot in the neck and was apparently dead. I told Sandy to co-ordinate the two platoons on the far side and I would send somebody over to help him.

I then got a message from David Wood, the No. 2 Platoon commander, that he, the sergeant and his radio operator had all been hit by enemy machine-gun fire the other side of the pillbox and were out of action. After that I started to worry about the other bridge about a quarter of a mile to the east, because I could hear no firing from there, nor had I received any radio messages or had a runner from those three platoons. I was considering whether I should send at least a patrol over there to capture the river bridge. But then, as often happens in battle, luck changed for a while in that Captain 'Jock' Nielson, commanding the Royal Engineers, came up and told me that there were no explosives under the bridge. Almost simultaneously I got a message by radio to say that No. 6 Platoon had captured the River Orne bridge. So about 15 minutes after the first platoon had landed we started sending out our success signal 'Ham and Jam' over the radio! I got the operator, Corporal Tuppenderry, to keep repeating it, 'Hello Four Dog, Hello Four Dog, Ham and Jam, Ham and Jam, Ham and bloody Jam,' he shouted in all his excitement. While we were giving out this message I hoped that Brigadier Poett would pick it up as well because he had dropped at about the same time we landed with the 21st Independent Para Company – the Pathfinders.

At 0050 hours we heard the sound of our bombers flying low and coming in from the coast. As they got over the dropping zone east of the River Orne we saw 7 Para parachuting down; a great sight. As prearranged I blew a Victory V signal on my whistle. Some had landed in haystacks or in floods, but they heard this whistle. It must have meant a lot to them, because not only did it signify the bridges had been taken intact but it also helped them to orientate themselves.

In all the excitement, down the road from Ranville came an open German Mercedes-Benz staff car. Number 5 Platoon waited for it to come over the river bridge, then opened fire. When we got to it there were four badly wounded occupants. Inside there was ladies' lingerie, and it smelt of perfume. There were also plates of half-eaten meals so it must have been one hell of a party. It turned out that the German officer in the car commanded the bridge's garrison. He insisted, in perfect English, that, as he'd lost the bridge, and his honour, we kill him. The doctor came up and gave him a dose of morphine and put him to sleep, but he didn't survive.

Shortly after this two tanks came very slowly towards the canal bridge from the west. However, Sergeant Thornton of No. 6 Platoon blew up the leading one with a PIAT (Projector, Infantry, Anti-Tank) bomb, and the other retired quickly. The bomb had hit the ammunition inside and it went up like a fireworks display. Number 7 Para heard this and thought we were really in trouble because some of them arrived soon afterwards. As soon as 7 Para got across the bridge and into Benouville more fighting started straight away. Soon after first light wounded were taken into the Gondrée's Café, which had become a medical aid post. To celebrate us being the first Allied soldiers into occupied France, the patron, Georges Gondrée, went into his garden and dug up over 90 bottles of champagne to give to the wounded. The whole of my company decided they wanted to report sick!

The first aircraft we saw were three Spitfires at 6,000 feet. We put up a ground-to-air signal about our success and they came in low, circled the bridges, did a 'victory roll' and dropped a container full of the early morning papers from Fleet Street. The troops were fighting over the *Daily Mirror*, because it had a strip cartoon called 'Jane'. Jane was always in her undies, or nothing at all, and she had a superb figure, so everyone wanted to see what she was up to. There was no mention of the invasion of course, and that gave rise to a few quips.

For the whole of the morning and into the afternoon the canal bridge was under very accurate sniper and mortar fire and all movement immediately east of the bridge was 'at the double' between trenches and other defences. The first seaborne troops we saw were Lord Lovat's Commandos at around 1330 hours. They lost no time in crossing the canal bridge 'at the double' and so on to the other side of the river bridge where they were to fight gallantly alongside the red berets of the 6th Airborne Division who were ferociously forming a bridgehead east of the River Orne.

There was a Cockney section occupying a German anti-tank gun-pit, whose gun they were very keen to fire. The corporal kept running across the road to me with bogus targets, but I refrained from letting them fire – they were just like kids with a new toy. About half a mile away was a large water tower by a chateau and this corporal swore that there was a nest of snipers in it. I told him, 'Just one round.' We then heard a stentorian voice shout, 'number one gun', which made everyone look up (there was only one bloody gun there anyway!) and then a magnificent fire order followed by 'FIRE'. The whole of the top of the bloody water tower dispersed and blew into dust and debris. All the troops in the trenches, the commandos running over the bridge, the wounded in the café, came out throwing their helmets and hats in the air and cheering – a great grin on the gunner's face. But it's vital to shout in battle, because it relieves all the tension and on this occasion the cheering when the shot hit got us shouting at the top of our voices. What the German OP at the top of the chateau must have thought of those 'Mad

Dogs and Englishmen' I shudder to think. The chateau was known to be a maternity hospital and we were under strict orders not to fire at it.

The casualties for this operation were two killed and 14 wounded, which was a very, very low figure for such a hairy task. I think the three main reasons for success were first, the skill and daring of the glider pilots; second, we kept to an extremely simple plan; and third, the speed and dash of my wonderful *coup de main* party.

LIEUTENANT TOD SWEENEY, 2nd Battalion, Oxford and Buckinghamshire Light Infantry

After the 1st Airborne Division came back from North Africa we were at a football match and somebody pointed out Brigadier James Hill who had a DSO and an MC, and then someone else pointed out the famous Alistair Pearson. They both gave lectures to us about fighting in North Africa. Alistair advised us how to carry out a night attack, because the 1st Battalion had done one or two difficult ones. In his broad Scots accent he said, 'Well, the first thing you do is estimate how long it's going to take you from the assembly area to the forming-up position, then when you've worked out the time, you double it. Then you work out how long it's going to take you from the forming-up position to the start line; when you've worked that out, you double it. Then you work out how long from the start line to the objective, and when you've worked that out, you double that! And then,' he said, leaning towards the audience of generals and so on, 'you double the fucking lot.' This was absolutely marvellous advice from someone who really knew what he was talking about.

During our briefing for the landing there were maps round the walls, covered up with white paper. John Howard took bets on where we were going to land and, strangely enough, of the group there, only two people said the Cherbourg peninsula. The rest of us were saying Calais, Ostend etc., all the way up the coast. When John took the covers off the maps and we saw for the first time where our airborne invasion was going to take place it was very exciting. The idea was to land three gliders as close to each bridge as possible. We would all land within the two waterways, so that if the Germans did blow the bridges, then we wouldn't be cut off from one another. The plan overall was that the 6th Airborne Division was to capture the bridges, the high ground and the Merville battery and thus protect the left flank of the invasion beaches. The road that ran down from Troarn, where the sappers had to capture some small bridges and blow them up, ran across our two bridges, and straight along to the invasion beaches. The Germans would have been able to take the seaborne forces in the flank if they got across these bridges.

Brigadier Nigel Poett was given the task of seizing the actual bridges with his three parachute battalions of the 5th Parachute Brigade. He informed the divisional commander that he could not be sure of capturing these bridges intact because by the time his troops had dropped and got everything together it would take three-quarters of an hour and in the meantime the Germans could blow the bridges. He therefore requested a *coup de main* party of gliders which could land spot on. That's why John Howard's company was chosen to come under the command of Brigadier Nigel Poett and be part of his brigade for the initial landing.

While we were in the transit camp we went across to see the 7th Battalion because they would be reinforcing our positions once we'd taken the bridge. Their commanding officer was giving a briefing at the end of which he looked round the room and said 'Sweeney', so I and another chap jumped up. After the briefing was over I went over to him and said, 'I see we've both got the same name, but everybody calls me Tod.' He said, 'Well, actually I'm Lieutenant Todd, but everyone calls me Sweeney.' And that was Richard Todd the actor. We said to each other, 'See you on D-Day.'

On Sunday 4 June we were all ready to go and then it was postponed. On the Monday we packed up again and we had our so-called fatless meal so we wouldn't be sick in the plane. That evening we climbed into our gliders, very heavily loaded with ammunition. There were 28 men in each glider – 23 infantry and five sappers, plus an assault boat in case the bridges were blown and some Bangalore torpedoes and pole charges to assault the enemy defences. The information we had received was that the bridges were defended by about a platoon's worth of infantry, and that they were commanded by a fairly fanatical German officer from the 21st Panzers. In the last few days the RAF had flown low aerial photographic missions and, to our horror, in their photographs we noticed little white spots which were the signs of the anti-invasion glider poles. The glider pilots looked at them and said, 'Well, we'll just have to try and go between them and if they knock off one wing or both – too bad.' In fact when we got there although the pits had been dug the poles actually hadn't been put in. At eleven o'clock we took off from Tarrant Rushton to spearhead the invasion into Europe. It was rather like being picked to play for your country at Lords. The exhilaration buoyed us up and kept us going. We were all scared stiff, of course, but we'd been waiting and waiting for this stage from 1940 onwards and none of us had ever been into action before. My platoon whom I'd known for two years had trained and trained and now, at long last we were going. The men were all in good humour singing songs like 'Roll Out the Barrel' and we had some rations and a thermos of tea.

As we crossed the coast of France I was leaning in at the door of the cockpit when the pilot shouted, 'There you are!' and in the spotty moonlight I could just see the thin stream of the silver river – and then the two bridges! As we went down my batman got hold of my belt and I got hold of the door and tugged. We'd never done this before in the air because it was a rather dangerous operation. So it took quite a bit of effort to pull the door back and open up. As that happened the glider leaned over, so I found myself looking down on the fields of Normandy at cows munching grass! I strapped myself in and we landed. My glider pilot said, 'I'm sorry but I've dropped you short.' He'd hit an air pocket or something, so instead of landing within 15 yards we were 400 yards from the bridge.

We jumped out, did our usual drill and formed a ring round the glider. When everybody was out we dashed forward. There was no shooting, or anything, which was a bit of an anti-climax. We went doubling forward and went into a ditch full of water, so we all got soaked up to the waist. It must have taken me about four or five minutes to cover the ground and as we went rushing forward to the bridge we came across some shadowy figures who quickly disappeared. We went racing across this very narrow swing-bridge calling out our call sign 'Easy' and expecting as we went clonking across that it would blow up any moment. Then when I got to the other side there was another anti-climax because I heard the call sign 'Fox' which meant that the other platoon commander, Dennis Fox, who should have landed third behind me, was already there. His platoon had taken the bridge without very much opposition. I came puffing up with my two sections behind me and said, 'Hallo Dennis, how are things?' Now Dennis was a bit of a humorist and was obviously thinking of all the exercises we had carried out during our intensive training when he replied, 'All right, Tod, but I haven't seen any bloody umpires yet.'

I sent off the liaison officer who had flown in with us from the 7th Parachute Battalion to let them know that we had the bridge. We could meanwhile hear shooting going on at the other bridge. We then began searching the houses round about. I knocked on a door and a little old lady appeared. In my best schoolboy French I said, 'Nous sommes arrivés pour la libération de la France.' She took one look at me, standing there with this blackened face, airborne helmet, green camouflage jacket and slammed the door. I thought, that's a bit much when we've come to liberate you. We found later that the locals were afraid of the Germans carrying out anti-invasion exercises and trying to find out who were part of the maquis. The Germans would pretend to be British soldiers and she wasn't going to have anything to do with that.

When I got through to John Howard and told him we had taken the bridge, he said, 'All right, well, send Dennis Fox over to the canal bridge because we are having a bit of trouble.' So Dennis went off with his platoon leaving me in charge of the river bridge where we dug in.

The 7th Battalion began arriving, but they didn't come in as we thought because they had been so scattered. At dawn they took over the bridge which we had held all night. We then went into reserve and that was when what we'd be doing came home to me. In the RAP (Regimental Aid Post) was Den Brotheridge with whom I had shared a room for the last 18 months. During that time we had often talked about what we were going to do after the war, what it would be like to go into action, and so on. He had been the first platoon commander across the canal bridge and had been shot in the neck and was now dead. Two other platoon commanders, both friends, had been hurt but generally our casualties had been light.

One of our gliders, with Captain Priday the 2 i/c aboard, was missing. His glider had been towed too far east and so, when it was released, instead of seeing the River Orne, they saw the River Dives so the glider pilot followed that and put his glider down on what he thought was the Orne bridge. The men jumped out and raced over to the other side and captured the bridge. Then Captain Priday realized that he was on the wrong side of a completely different bridge. They then had to shoot their way back over the bridge again, because by now the garrison had been fully aroused and I think they lost one or two chaps. Captain Priday and his platoon finally made it on 7 June. Then of course we heard the invasion begin. The Navy opened up and heavy bombers were weaving like fighters dropping their bombs. Then silence and we knew the invasion troops were coming in.

Then up the river came a gunboat from the coast firing a 20-mm gun and hitting the bridge. Sergeant Godbold fired his PIAT and hit the prow of the boat which floated into the side of the bank. He raced down with a couple of chaps and took the crew prisoner. A rare naval victory! At about 10 am things started to go badly for the 7th Battalion which had crossed over the bridge and deployed to the west in the area which is called Le Port, next door to Benouville the village by the canal bridge. The Germans had attacked in strength and overrun their HQ and medical aid post. John Howard called Fox and myself into an orchard. We were told to await orders to carry out a counter-attack on 7 Para's position. We weren't all that happy about this. We thought we'd done our stuff. We'd got over all the alarm and excitement of the previous night and we were tired. The idea of counter-attacking a position, which a battalion was in the process of losing, didn't thrill us at all. As we sat there waiting, Richard Todd poked his head through the bushes and said, 'Hello, I said I'd see you on D-Day.'

About 11.30 am I heard the sound of bagpipes, so I nudged Fox and I said, 'Dennis, I can hear bagpipes.' He told me not to be stupid. However, two minutes later even he was convinced. When we got down to the canal bank there, to the sound of wailing bagpipes, came a piper, all by himself. A remarkable sight. About 100 yards behind came the Commando Brigade led by Lord Lovat.

That evening the rest of the glider-borne brigade arrived, which was a tremendous sight. They landed on both sides of the bridges and crossed over just as it was getting dark, to attack some villages down the road. That night we were finally relieved of the responsibility of the bridges by the Warwickshire Regiment. We went off to join our battalion who we thought were in Escoville. I went ahead with Corporal Porter and Corporal Bullen. We went skulking along the side of the road until we came to Hérouvillette where we found the whole atmosphere eerie; the regiment seemed nowhere around. As we went on towards Escoville I heard a metal door clang, and before we knew where we were, tracer bullets were coming towards us. It was an armoured car. Corporal Porter got down with his light machine-gun and Corporal Bullen and I began racing down the road 100 yards or so to the corner. Bullen was a great big country lad from Norfolk, heavy, slow-moving and I was a fairly slim, quite good 100-yarder: Bullen passed me! When I got back to John Howard I told him I couldn't find the regiment and that I'd lost Corporal Porter. We pulled back to Ranville where in fact we found the regiment; they had decided to lie up for the night and attack Escoville in daylight.

In the early hours of the morning we set off once more down the road again to Escoville, and there on the corner of Hérouvillette was Corporal Porter, who looked up at me with a rather sour look, as if I'd deserted him. But once I'd explained he was all right. We continued on down towards Escoville. The positions for the regiment had been chosen from the map and nobody had realized that the slope of the land went down into Escoville and then rose up beyond very slowly. That would not have mattered if the Canadians had captured the high ground at a place called le Bois de Bavent which overlooked us. But they hadn't, which meant that the Germans occupied it. As soon as we moved on Escoville we came under fire. We fought our way into the village, but no sooner had we got to our positions than we began to be mortared. The Germans had been training round these areas for months and knew all the ranges and key positions. We got quite a severe beating. I got up into an OP overlooking the high ground, and could see Panzer troops coming down the fields in perfect formation with their armoured cars. This was the only time I have ever seen the enemy as you would have in World War I. We called for artillery fire and we did our best, but we had the disadvantage of being just below the level of the high ground. In all our training in England we dug in positions on the outskirts of the village; you never occupied houses, because they belonged to the farmers. Consequently we dug in the gardens and the outskirts, and we were mortared very heavily. What we should have done was get into the thick stone Norman houses. However we didn't because at that point we were still thinking with a peace-time mentality, which is not surprising when you consider 36 hours beforehand we had been sitting in England. I lost about half my platoon that afternoon from mortar fire. The Germans were actually firing down the village street so it was difficult to move anywhere. Every time we did move we were shot at. I really thought we'd had it. We were knocking holes through the wall and every time you knocked a stone out, 'bang' a bullet would come straight through. John Howard came up to see why I hadn't gone forward. I told him why. He said he'd go and have a look. He went round the corner of this stone wall, and I heard a crack. Back he came, crawling on his hands and knees, his face white and a hole through the front and back of his helmet. On his head there is still a little blue mark. But B Company counter-attacked and pushed them back and we got out with our wounded. We went along tracks up the hill where we then dug in around Hérouvillette. We stayed there for about a week patrolling around Escoville. There was no sense in attacking again because we realized it was in a position which we could not hold. And in fact Escoville wasn't captured for about another two months.

We took up defensive positions at Hérouvillette. We were tired but it felt like the tiredness after a hard game of rugger. As we came up the slope from Escoville the commanding officer was cheering us in just like the headmaster after a hard game – 'Well done, lads.' But we were not too happy about our battle. The previous day we had achieved everything we attempted. We had captured the bridges, we had seen off the counter-attacks, we had held the bridges until relieved. Everything had gone well. Then in Escoville we had really been knocked off balance by the Panzer troops. We had felt like amateurs in front of these professionals with their skilful mortar fire, their superior use of ground and their fire and movement. However we dug in and awaited the follow-up – but it did not come. For some reason best known to himself, the enemy left us alone until 9 June. That day we sent patrols into Escoville and the reaction was the same as on 7 June. Infantry supported by armoured fighting vehicles again infiltrated the village. But this time they came on and towards evening attacked our positions at Hérouvillette. They opened their attack with heavy concent-rations of mortar and artillery fire. Then Messerschmitt 109s carried out a series of strafing attacks. Finally they attacked with tanks, self-propelled guns and infantry. However the respite given us for the preparation of our defensive position had not been in vain. The artillery, six-pounder anti-tank guns, medium machine-guns and mortars all had good shoots. The enemy got to within 100 yards of our positions but then withdrew, leaving two Mark IV tanks on fire. Four more tanks were destroyed at longer range and also two armoured cars. We were particularly pleased with our success as it levelled the score with 21 Panzer. They had scored in Escoville, we had scored in Hérouvillette. After that they left us alone on the Escoville front and turned their attention to attacking through Bréville towards Ranville.

On 10 June, from my position in Hérouvillette, I could see the Germans advancing down the slope from Bréville to Ranville. The 13th Para Battalion finally stopped the advance as we machine-gunned and mortared them from the flanks. Then on 12 June we had a grandstand view of the battle for Bréville, carried out by 12 Para, a company of 12 Devons and some tanks with the most enormous artillery support, including guns of warships lying off the coast.

We stayed in the vicinity of Bréville for the rest of our time in Normandy, until the break-out. The enemy were only 600 yards from us, so we found ourselves in a World War I type of warfare. Our main fear in the woods was these German Minenwerfers. Every morning as you woke you could hear the awful sound of these ghastly things coming over. Then there was the 88-mm which the Germans would fire to hit the trees and down would come an airburst. We very quickly learned to cover over all our trenches. Around early July we were based on Bréville and patrolling every night. One of the patrols was a standing patrol about 500–800 yards in front of our position, quite close to the German lines. It had been maintained for a few nights by A Company and consisted of an officer with four men. D Company were due to take over and so the only two platoon commanders left in D Company (myself and a chap called Chalky White – a reinforcement) were told to go out with the A Company patrol to learn exactly where the patrol was to go. It was arranged that we would all meet at A Company HQ, but when Chalky White and I got there the patrol had already left. Foolishly we decided to try to catch them up.

Now patrolling in Normandy, especially with a full moon, was a miserable, slow and dangerous affair. You crept and crawled and stopped and listened, and went on. It took a long time to cover a short distance and all the way through this 'no-man's-land' were dead bodies of Germans and cattle. We finally got near to the copse where the standing patrol should have been. We called out the password: 'Halt Hammer.' The answer should have been 'Tongs', but instead we received a rattle of machine-gun fire. We fired back, emptying a couple of Sten magazines. Then there was silence but in the fire fight I had received two bullets in my leg and foot, luckily without breaking any bones. Nevertheless I could feel the blood dripping and we obviously could not crawl back the way we had come out. So we decided to walk and limp boldly down the main road towards our positions, by the shortest route. This took us through C Company's lines and they were not expecting us. We walked into the position singing, 'God Save The King.'

BRIGADIER JAMES HILL, HQ, 3rd Parachute Brigade

I was somehow in the right place at the right time and early in 1943 I was given command of the 3rd Parachute Brigade which was then in its infancy. I was still having my wounds dressed from my injuries in North Africa and to obtain an A1 certificate I had to agree that I would not get a pension for the wounds I had received up till then. This suited me, because I hadn't joined the army to get a pension.

One day I was summoned to Divisional Headquarters by Richard Gale, who said, 'James, we have been given the one and only Canadian Parachute Battalion to join this division, and I want it to go in your brigade, so you have got to get rid of one of your battalions.' I went home absolutely delighted at the thought of having the Canadians, but sad to have to send my senior battalion, the 7th, to play a leading role in the formation of the 5th Parachute Brigade.

The arrival of the Canadians brought a new lease of life to the brigade. They were very similar to the 1st Parachute Battalion inasmuch as they were formed from soldiers who wanted to fight and the sooner the better, soldiers of fortune really. They didn't want to sit in Canada and miss the war, so they'd joined the newly formed Canadian Parachute Battalion. As one parachute battalion is no good to anybody they were very wisely given to us.

Some were very hard men and just what you would expect to come from the Canadian outback. There were 49 Red Indians, and about the same number of French-speaking Canadians. I went up to hospital to visit one Red Indian whose parachute hadn't opened. Almost every bone in his body was broken, yet he lived to tell the tale and fathered 14 children. They could be a bit boisterous and on one occasion, while returning from leave, one of them had crawled along the outside of the train and dropped a hand grenade down the funnel of the engine. I was hopping mad at that because it immobilized our leave train for a month.

I knew it was going to be tough in Normandy so I insisted on everyone being 250 per cent fit, and they were. I made sure that every officer could do two jobs and this proved absolutely invaluable. Every battalion and company had an A and B Headquarters, so that if one was knocked out, the other could take over. All the soldiers were trained to use other people's weapons and to drive Bren carriers – anything that kept the battle going. My four rules of battle I rammed home: number one, speed; we had to get across country faster than anyone else; two, control – no good commanding unless you have discipline and control; three, simplicity (in thought and action); and four, effective fire power or fire effect.

Well, the great day was arriving and all my battalions were penned in their camps, which they weren't allowed to leave. This period was very interesting to me. All day long the Canadians, with whom I'd pitched my tent, were playing games – baseball, throwing balls about – and I thought what tremendous vitality these Canadians had got. Then in the afternoon I would visit my English battalions and find half a dozen chaps desultorily kicking a football, and the rest asleep. I thought to myself, here is the difference between the Old World and the New; the élan and joie de vivre of the New World of the Canadian, and the maturity and the not worrying, not bothering and having a good nap while you can, of the British.

Attached to my Brigade HQ was my Commando liaison officer, Peter Haig Thomas, who before the war had been stroke of the Cambridge boat and the British boat in the Berlin Olympic Games. He was a very great naturalist who had gone to live with the Eskimos for two years in Greenland in order to study the Greater Snow Goose. I went out for a walk with him and we found three quarter-grown hares running about. He said he could talk to them so he left me and walked up very close to them, squatted down, and talked to them. As he walked back I had an intuition that I shouldn't see him again after D-Day. He was one of the most remarkable characters I'd met in my life. And, of course, shortly after the sun rose on that first morning in Normandy, he was dead – what a loss!

The evening before D-Day arrived and I went round to brief all the officers in every battalion and a lot of the chaps as well. My final words to them were, 'Gentlemen, in spite of your excellent training and your splendid briefing, you must not be daunted if chaos reigns. It undoubtedly will!' Chaos certainly did reign, and what I had said stuck in so many people's minds that they were not daunted.

The 3rd Brigade had three tasks: the first was to capture and put out of action the Merville battery, which commanded the beach defences, before the D-Day landings, and the second was to destroy five bridges over the River Dives (spread over some seven miles of waterlogged country). After that we were to hold a vital ridge which overlooked the whole of the Orne valley, exclusive of the village of Bréville, in the north, down to the west side of Troarn in the south. This was a fairly wooded ridge which entirely overlooked Caen and the Orne bridges. The third task we were given was to harry the enemy by strong fighting patrols to the south of Troarn, to make the intercommunicating roads unsafe for them.

On D-Day I was jumping No. 1, which gave me a problem. In camp, to keep the Canadians amused, I'd had a football with Hitler's face on it in luminous paint. Everyone knew I was proposing to drop this, along with three bricks, which they gave me with some rather vulgar wording painted on them, onto the beach to astonish the enemy. So there I was, as brigade commander, standing in the door of the aeroplane with a football and three bricks! As we got over the beaches, out went the football and the bricks and myself. As I orientated myself it appeared that I had been dropped with my stick bang in the middle of the River Dives. However, what the Germans had done in anticipation was to flood the valley of the Dives. On either side of the river were water meadows with very deep irrigation ditches. The Germans had wired this area before they flooded it so it was really a very impenetrable barrier.

I had tea-bags sewn into the top of my battledress trousers, so while I was trying to get out of this lake I was just making cold tea! The way we got out was that we each had six-foot ropes with a wooden handle at each end for tying things up. As we met up with others we linked up with these toggle ropes because if you went into a deep ditch and you weren't tied to someone, you drowned, and there were many drowned that night. After a four-hour struggle we got out, more or less on the edge of our DZ. The Canadians reported that they had captured the DZ and the German command post, so as far as I could tell, all was going well.

I realized I had to get back to my Brigade Headquarters as soon as I could, but I thought the vital thing was to find out what success the 9th Battalion had had with the battery. By now I had collected 42 very wet stragglers, and we set off down a track. It was a very mixed party from different battalions, including two naval ratings and an Alsatian messenger dog. It was about twenty to seven in the morning, when all hell broke loose! The naval bombardment of the beaches had started; it was worth a guinea a minute – unbelievable. Then suddenly I heard a noise and I shouted to the chaps to get down. Unfortunately our little lane had high hedges on both sides and no ditches. I threw myself on top of Lieutenant Peters, and realized that we'd been caught in pattern bombing from low-flying aircraft, and it was horrible. When, thank God, they'd gone, I raised myself on my arms and looked around. This little lane was clouded with dust and dirt and stank of cordite and death. Then I saw a leg in the middle of the road. I knew I had been hit, but when I took another look I saw it had a brown boot on, and I knew it wasn't mine. The only chap in the brigade who got away with wearing brown boots was the mortar officer of the 9th Battalion, Lieutenant Peters, and I was lying right on top of him and he was dead. His leg had been severed from his body, yet I was alive. I had been saved because I had a towel and a spare pair of pants in the bottom of my jumping smock, but my water bottle had shattered and I had lost most of my left backside.

From that column the only two people who could get on their feet were my brigade defence platoon commander and myself. I then had a problem as a commander. There I was surrounded by 30 or so dying or very badly wounded men. Should I stay with them or what? The answer was, of course, no. We were fighting a battle and we had to get on. We gave jabs to all of them with their own morphia. Then we collected the morphia from the dead and distributed it amongst the living. As we moved off those men, who were all to die, gave us a cheer. That moment will stay with me forever.

We went on and caught up with the 9th Battalion at the foot of the slope of the Sallenelles feature which they had been ordered to capture. I was reassured to hear that they had stormed the Merville battery with 150 men and had taken it. I was then put in the clutches of their medical officer Doc Watts, who patched me up. When he'd finished he told me that I should get further treatment and not go back to my brigade because I looked bad for morale! To which I replied, 'If you'd been four hours in the water, brewing cold tea, and had lost most of your left backside, you wouldn't look very good for morale either.' But he was very good and got me a lady's bicycle. I decided I would find Richard Gale, the divisional commander, and tell him what I'd seen and knew.

I sat somewhat gingerly on this bicycle, being pushed by a parachute soldier! It was a two-mile trip, fortunately downhill. Sometimes we saw Germans running across the road, sometimes British parachute chaps, but we just carried on until about midday when we arrived at Richard Gale's Divisional Headquarters. He did me the power of good because he said, 'Well, James, I am very pleased to be able to tell you that your battalions have all captured their objectives.' I was delighted. I told him my little story and was then seized by the ADMS who was a great divisional character, known as 'Old Technicolour'. He had fought throughout World War I and was covered in decorations. He told me I had to have an operation. I told him I would agree to this only if he would guarantee that I would be taken back to my Brigade HQ after it was over. He agreed. As I was passing out under the chloroform the first of the counter-attacks by 21 Panzer Division on our division came in. Three hours later I came to and the doctor collected me and put me in the back of his jeep, where I had to sit on my right side. I must have looked rather a mess because I had lost most of my trousers, and had bandages hanging out and, to add to the misery, I had a bottle of penicillin strapped to my side with little pipes going in.

We were driving out of Ranville when suddenly six Germans ran across the road. To my astonishment, Old Technicolour ordered his driver to stop. Then he pulled out a revolver and told his driver to follow him and off they went in hot pursuit, leaving their brigade commander sitting on his backside in solitary state in the back of a jeep! After about two or three minutes, and looking very sheepish, he came back because he hadn't captured the Germans. He'd wanted to get another addition to his string of gongs – all he got was a severe reprimand. We continued and at four o'clock I arrived at my Brigade Headquarters, where I found Alistair Pearson had taken over from me in my absence. He had been wounded through the hand, which was very painful, but was in good form. It would have taken more than a bullet in his hand to stop Alistair when his blood was up!

I took stock that evening. Alistair's 8th Battalion was about 280 strong; the Canadian battalion was in very good order and had captured their two bridges, and were now digging in at the Le Mesnil crossroads, about 300 men in all. The 9th Battalion, consisting of 90 good chaps, was still on the Sallenelles feature and was to be a day late in taking over the Chateau St Come between the Canadians and Bréville. But my Brigade Headquarters was depleted. I had no DAA & QMG, no brigade major and no padre, no Commando liaison officer and no sailors.

We got through the first night and the next morning who should be coming down the drive but my brigade major, Bill Collingwood, with his right leg stuck out at right angles, so that he walked in a most peculiar way. He'd been standing over the exit hole of his Albemarle when it had been hit. The blast had knocked him out of the hole and wrapped his static line round his leg as he fell into the night. He was spinning around under the aircraft with his 60 pound kit bag strapped to his leg. The plane had no option but to limp back across the Channel with the brigade major attached to it. The crew gradually winched him in before they finally got across the Channel to Odiham. Collingwood was pretty clued-up so with others he got hold of a jeep and went to the air-landing aerodrome and he came over in the wave of gliders that I had seen arriving the night before. I thought, 'This is the stuff that good brigade majors are made of' – an amazing feat of endurance and pain. But of course, with his injured leg, he couldn't really do his job, so with great regret he was carried off by the Field Ambulance and had his leg reset in the UK.

I was still concerned about having Alec Pope, my DAA & QMG missing. I was to find out later that he had been dropped on the wrong side of the Dives, had collected about half a dozen or more men and died fighting it out with the Germans. He was one of the finest men I ever met, my first brigade major at the age of 23 and every time I go to Normandy, if I can, I go to see his grave in a little tucked-away churchyard, at St Vaast-en-Auge, miles from anywhere. And, of course, Peter Haig Thomas, my Commando liaison officer, had also been killed shortly after landing. My Roman Catholic padre, Padre McVay, to whom I had given an Irish blackthorn shillelagh, was missing. He'd been captured by the Germans, and after a bit he got fed up with them and set about them with it, and escaped. They caught him and stripped him of his dog collar and sent him to one of the toughest PoW camps on the Baltic. He was a great fighting Roman Catholic padre and much missed in the brigade.

The two sailors who were to direct the guns of the *Arethusa* had been killed in the early bombing raid. We did have one 22 radio set and one very bedraggled naval rating, who didn't know anything about firing guns, but could work the 22 set. I now had to find somebody who could direct the guns of the *Arethusa*. I went across to Lieutenant Colonel Bradbrook's Canadians and I saw their very smart RSM, Clark. I thought, 'By God, he's the chap to fire the guns of the *Arethusa*.' Unbelievably, in a short space of time, RSM Clark was bringing down the shells within 400 yards of our front line and we had restored contact. It was marvellous, an RSM who had never heard of the *Arethusa*, and a wet sailor with no training. That just shows what initiative can do. Sad to tell, within 48 hours RSM Clark was dead. The next six days saw the toughest fighting I experienced throughout six long years of war – it was no picnic. From 2,000 fighting men during the first eight days my brigade lost some 50 officers and 1,000 other ranks. My Brigade HQ lost eight officers and 30 other ranks.

The fighting on our ridge became particularly fierce – Alistair Pearson and the 8th Battalion were separated from us by some two miles, denying the enemy the approaches to the ridge from the south. Their success was a remarkable feat and vital of course to our success. The 9th Battalion, whose numbers fluctuated during the battle from 90 to 270 to 190, held the wooded area and road adjoining the Chateau St Come. Brigade HQ and their defence platoon were in the middle. The Canadians held the Mesnil crossroads area immediately to the south. My Brigade HQ with their strong defence platoon, numbering some 150, and the Canadians with some 300 men were concentrated over a front of about one mile, astride the Bréville–Troarn road, running north to south on the top of the ridge.

Enemy probing attacks first concentrated on the Canadian battalion at Le Mesnil then swung against the 9th Battalion after the Germans had occupied Bréville on D+2. It was then that I realized we were up against a first-class German infantry division – 346 Grenadier Division – supported by tanks and SP (self-propelled) guns. During this period some six attacks were launched against the 9th Battalion from Bréville and the east – three of which were co-ordinated with attacks on the Canadian positions at Le Mesnil. There was constant patrolling activity and on one occasion my defence platoon accounted for 19 Germans. Unfortunately my intelligence officer, Major Wilkinson, was lost in the action.

My room was on the top floor of a barn with access only from the outside staircase. I sat on the top step with my left backside overhanging the steps, which was good as I smelt of gangrene poisoning. Imagine my delight at receiving a new pair of battledress trousers, with supporting underwear, on D+2. From my position I had a bird's-eye view of the German break-out from Bréville on D+4 and their attack on Peter Luard's 13th Battalion holding the north-east perimeter of Ranville. The 13th held their fire to the last moment and then mowed them down. For the next two days they filtered back through the rear of our positions. I knew it was irregular to see Germans creeping about but we had neither the time nor resources to chase them.

It was about this time that we were strafed by our own Typhoons – it happened twice. Unfortunately on one occasion the pregnant lady of the chateau, walking in the garden with her husband, was hit and died. Our doctors tried to save the baby, to no avail, and we buried her in a shroud in her garden with what dignity we could muster under such difficult circumstances. Soon after that the husband and housekeeper left and my Brigade HQ occupied the chateau.

Sitting on my steps looking down on the bank below I saw the adjutant of the 9th Battalion, Hal Hudson, lying on the bank looking like shrivelled parchment, waiting to be operated on by my Field Ambulance unit in the adjoining building. His story was unusual. He received some 18 shrapnel wounds in his stomach during the capture of the Merville battery. He thought 'I must kill one German before I die.' He imagined he saw a figure looming up and shot it with his Sten gun. It was in fact his foot! The pain was such that it took his mind off his much more severe wounds and thanks to that, and the treatment he received from the Field Ambulance and thereafter, he lived to tell the tale. He later became Chairman of Lloyds of London.

The 5th Battalion of the Black Watch were put under my command to capture Bréville. The attack went on in the early hours of D+5 and was repulsed by the Germans with heavy losses. I then told them to hold the Chateau St Come itself and co-ordinate their defence with the 9th Battalion. At this juncture the German Divisional Commander decided that our positions at St Come and Le Mesnil must be liquidated once and for all and a major attack was launched on D+6 on both the 9th Battalion and Black Watch positions and the Canadians. This attack was in strength, preceded by a heavy bombardment lasting some three hours, and it went in supported by tanks and SP guns at 1500 hours. The Black Watch were driven back and came back through the 9th Battalion and my defence platoon positions.

At this point at 1600 hours I received a message from Terence Otway commanding the 9th Battalion to say he was doubtful if he could hold out much longer. His position had already been penetrated on the previous day but the Germans had been driven out. I knew he would not send me this signal unless things were urgent and that something must be done about it. I had no spare bodies so I went to Colonel Bradbrook whose HQ was 200 yards away at the end of our drive and asked him to help. At that moment German tanks had overrun the road to his right and were shooting up his company HQ at close range. To his eternal credit he decided that he could deal with this problem and he gave me what was left of his reserve company under Major Hanson, a very hard and excellent commander, together with cooks and any spare men and we set off to the 9th Battalion area.

A young Red Indian aged 18, called Private Anderson, informed me that he was going to be my bodyguard. As we entered the wood between the road and the chateau I saw Padre Nicol of the Black Watch calmly walking up and down steadying his young soldiers. I understand that he later became Moderator of the Church of Scotland – a great man for all seasons. On entering the wood there were both Germans and Black Watch. We moved up to the far end of the wood near the chateau and I remember seeing a German tank cruising up and down at close range but we had no means of dealing with it. At this stage my bodyguard had been shot through the arm but insisted on carrying on. However, by this time, the attack on both the Canadians and the 9th Battalion was petering out. The German losses in

Two of the 3 gliders which carried the Oxf and Bucks Light Infantry and crash-landed on the banks of the Caen Canal

The army of Liberation had arrived. Dutch civilians welcome soldiers of the 1st Airlanding Recce Squadron on the 17 September 1944

Above: Still immensely confident, men of the 1st Airborne Division pose for what was, for many, their last photograph

Left: 20th September, Major Bruce Dawson, Brigade Major 4 Para Brigade, wounded and with his arm in a sling, had reached scant cover. He was killed by a sniper minutes later

Below: The parachute lines of a supply container hanging from a tree. In the background lurks a Sturmgeshütz III, a heavily armoured self-propelled gun

Two of so many who were to die at Arnhem. The fatal casualties of the 1st Airborne Division, 1st Polish Parachute Brigade, supporting elements and Air Force for this battle were 1916, of which 456 were never identified

An RAF photograph of the road bridge at Arnhem taken on the second day. Clearly visible are remnants of the Reconnaissance Squadron of 9 SS Panzer Division, destroyed attempting to cross the bridge

'As I was being taken away as a prisoner I turned to one of my Company Commanders, Douglas Crawley, who'd been with me in other battles, and said, "Well, Doug, I'm afraid we haven't got away with it this time." "No, Sir,"
he replied. "But we gave them a damn good run for their money."   *Lieutenant Colonel John Frost*

Left: Although the bridge had fallen the fighting continued, particularly in the Oosterbeek area where these men are seen clearing a house

Below: 'Despite everything they were proud to have held out for so long. Anyone who could walk had to walk, whoever had two legs had to drag another along. I could hardly bear to look at them, but I blessed them in my heart as I pushed our cart up the hill.'
Kate ter Horst

Below: The return to Europe. Hamilcar gliders and Halifax aircraft line up ready for the Rhine Crossing Operation 1945

both men and material were great and it would be said that we had won a great defensive victory.

Sadly, at 2100 hours a heavy concentration of shells fell on the 9th Battalion HQ and the CO was stunned and blown across the drive. Captain Greenaway and Lieutenant Pond were knocked out and Lieutenant Christie killed. This was a very sad end for brave men who had survived some eight days of concentrated fighting. That evening General Richard Gale mounted his counter-attack on Bréville, with the 12th Para Battalion, a company of the 1st Devons and a squadron of the 13th/18th Hussars, preceded by a monumental artillery bombardment which did considerable havoc to both the Germans and our own troops. Bréville was recaptured, the ridge was held, 346 German Division withdrew and did not contest the ridge again.

LIEUTENANT COLONEL ALISTAIR PEARSON, 8th Parachute Battalion

When I landed in England at Hurn Airport I went into the officers' mess and had lunch with Major General Richard Gale the GOC of 6th Airborne. He said, 'What are you doing here?' I told him I had been appointed Divisional G1 (Air). 'You'll make a bloody bad staff officer,' he said. 'I'm inclined to agree with you,' I replied, 'what are you offering?' 'I have just sacked the commanding officer of the 8th (Midland Counties) Battalion, which is in 3 Para Brigade commanded by James Hill. Would you like the job?' I said, 'Yes, that will suit me fine, but I don't think General Down will be very pleased.' He said that he would deal with him. I then went off for 28 days' leave.

After I'd been in Bulford for a week the battalion moved to Tilshead. General Gale sent for me and asked if I wanted anything. I told him I wanted to work an eleven-day fortnight, so that the men could have a longer week-end leave. He agreed to that and asked if there was anything else I wanted. I told him that I didn't want any senior officers breathing down my neck for three months. 'What do you mean by senior officers?' he said. I replied, 'Anyone senior to me.' He kept his word.

By the beginning of March 1944 I had the battalion very nearly fighting fit and certainly physically fit. We had limited rations, but we were fit. Lot of marching, lot of time on your feet. We had a series of tests; the hardest was ten miles in two hours with full equipment, weighing 50 pounds; we had to run to do it. That was hard.

Commanding officers and intelligence officers were briefed about 28 days before D-Day. We weren't told the exact day, but I knew with the moon and tides that it had to take place within six or seven days of the first week in June. I then had a mental aberration and got engaged. My wife-to-be said that as it was wartime we should have a short engagement and be married on 8 June. This, of course, coincided with D-Day, but I couldn't tell her that, so a lot of surprised officers of the 6th Airborne received invitations to our wedding. Joan had no idea what was happening and was not told until D-Day that she would not be getting married on the Tuesday.

I knew that we'd be fighting in woods so I asked my 2 i/c to find me one. He found a scrubby one about 50 or 60 acres somewhere in Oxfordshire. We shifted the whole battalion up there. I turned night into day so that they would get used to fighting in dense woods, with live ammunition. You have to work down known tracks and keep close together. It gave them confidence because patrolling at night can be very frightening – but it's a great ally, the dark.

About ten days before D-Day we moved to a transit camp, Blakehill Farm, which was alongside an airfield. We had to share this camp with a company of Irish Rifles. The camp was sealed and the only source of recreation was the NAAFI tent, staffed by about ten NAAFI girls. I told my adjutant that if any man was seen trying to get under the tent to get to the NAAFI girls they were to get a bullet in the arse. One of our chaps took this literally and put a bullet in the left cheek of one of the RUR – beautiful shot too. That stopped their nonsense!

We briefed the officers three days and the soldiers two days before D-Day. Then it was cancelled for another day so we had an extra day's briefing and I think that was invaluable.

The objective of 8 Para Battalion was to destroy the road and railway bridges at Bures and the main bridge at Troarn. We were then to hold the ground at Troarn as long as possible. When this was no longer feasible, I was to withdraw to a road junction on the Troarn–Bréville–Escoville road and from there there was no withdrawal.

We took off at 2200 hours in a Dakota. My air crew were Canadian flight sergeants, ex-bush pilots, 60 years of experience between them. Their CO told me that it wasn't going to be easy. He said that there would be so many different aircraft about that he could only go in once and then turn back. As we crossed the Channel you could hear a rattle on the fuselage. The chaps thought they were being shot at, but it was hailstones. The intelligence officer was standing in the door and as we crossed the coast, he shouted, 'I know exactly where we are, we're dead on course.' He was right because I was dropped right on the centre of the DZ. Because of my bad knees old 'Windy' Gale had had specially made for me by Quilters a large parachute so that I could descend more slowly, which I did. I was glad that it wasn't blowing too hard. When I landed one of my bloody soldiers had one up the spout of his Sten gun and put it through my hand. I was not best pleased. I never did identify the culprit.

The advance party on the RV fired the Very light and I made my way there and found my numbers very thin on the ground. I had planned to be able to move off by 0130 or 0145 hours but by the latter our strength was only 150, and it was not a balanced force. Instead of having two troops of REs and a squadron commander, I had one lance corporal from the REs, who was a cheerful chap and he was getting very worried about his bridge. He came to me and said, 'As we each carry a pound of plastic explosive, that will be 150 pounds – I think I could make a hole in the bridge with that!' I made up two ad hoc platoons. The first one was to work its way round the back of Troarn and do as much damage to the bridge as possible, the second was to go to Bures. They set off at about 2.15 am. I moved with what was left up into the edge of the wood. I left a couple of men on the RV in case any more appeared. I also sent two men to the road junction. We were collecting people who were coming in the whole time. I wanted to get away and into this wood before first light. On the main road I left Lance Corporal Stevenson and two men with two PIATs in a ditch. Just at first light I heard the PIATs firing. Corporal Stevenson had let three German half-tracks come as close as possible before firing, and had destroyed them causing considerable casualties. The rest of them had shot off back down the road again. When I went to see him he was worried about those who'd escaped. I explained that it was the best thing that could have happened as they would now be explaining to their CO that the road was held in strength. I'm certain that the lance corporal did as much to ensure the success of 6th Airborne Division as anyone else. Because if those half-tracks had reached Bréville and seen what was happening then elements of 21 Panzer would have been called in to occupy key points on the ridge and they would have taken some shifting.

At about eight o'clock that evening I heard explosions. The first was from the direction of Bures and the larger one from Troarn, and I concluded that demolition had taken place. Major Roseveare was the RE squadron commander – a very amusing chap. He'd landed on the wrong DZ at Ranville but he took the first jeep that he could find and filled it with all the explosive he could and seven men, and he battled down the road toward Troarn. On the way he cut through a road block of barbed wire. Then just as it was getting light he drove through Troarn. The bridge was at the bottom of a steep hill about 600 yards outside the village, so he got up great speed and drove onto the bridge and dumped the jeep. He fixed his beehive charges and blew a bloody big hole in the bridge. It was lucky because the bridge had a lot of cover, and big hedges nearby, but it was very well done. He had absorbed the briefing and maintained his objective.

In the afternoon more people, including A Company who had blown the other bridge, came back, so then I moved to the road junction. By three o'clock in the afternoon I had some 300 chaps and I was beginning to wonder how I was going to defend the junction, because I was quite convinced the Germans would attack and there was no way I could have stopped them. I decided the only way to hold this place was to take the war to them, and that we had to dominate the area. The method was simple. By day, each company would have a screen of standing patrols to locate enemy movement and each had to be prepared to move quickly to support the other on orders from Battalion HQ. We held this position until 11 June. We kept the enemy on their toes and it worked.

On the evening of D+1, the RSM of the 13th Battalion, a formidable man, appeared through the woods. He told me that an aircraft had crash-landed on the other side of the River Dives; some were dead and there were ten or twelve very badly wounded lying in a nearby chateau. I decided that I would go and get them. I had with me my 'donkeys', my mortar platoon, all very strong chaps, about 20 of them, and a jeep, so as soon as it got dark we set off through the wood. I knew a glider had crashed in the woods and that it would have a rubber boat. We got this boat down to the riverside and pumped it up by hand, which took a fair time. I was keen to get across. The first soldier to step in stuck his bayonet through the side of it – and down it went, with him in it. He clambered out. I was so bloody angry, I gave him a kick up the arse as hard as I could and he landed in the deep again. He struggled out and stuttered, 'You can't do that, sir. It's against King's Regulations. I'll complain to the brigade commander.' I said he could complain to bloody Monty himself if he wanted. With that the RSM hit him with a big stick! He then stuck him in the jeep that he'd hidden and told him to guard it with his life.

We scrambled across the blown bridge and made our way down the railway line and on to a road. The moon disappeared and it got very dark. I was leading this performance and I'd just got past this church in Basseneville when I realized by the sound that I'd lost half the men.

The scene was as the RSM had described; there were ten or twelve chaps, some of whom were capable of walking, others were very bad, but Warrant Officer Powell was particularly serious. I was wondering how the hell we were going to get them back, because I'd lost some of my donkeys. While the rest of my chaps looked after the wounded I looked around and found this big farm cart with huge iron-shod wheels on it. We got all the wounded on it as well as we could. I then offered the old lady 500 francs for looking after the men but she would not take it. Then I got between the shafts and harnessed myself in and with my chaps pushing we made our way back. The noise was horrendous – like a tank troop on the move. As we made our way back into the village I was wondering where my missing donkeys were. I felt that they were somewhere around. I said to the rest, 'Sing boys, sing "Roll Out the Barrel", that'll do it!' Just as we walked round by the church we were met by a corporal who said, 'Ooh, sir, it was a good thing you were singing, because we thought you were a German half-track vehicle and we were going to do it!' He was very disappointed!

We got the wounded back to the Aid Post at our junction. I made enquiries later and they'd all survived. People said we'd be lucky to get away with it, but we did. It was very good for morale too, because chaps knew they wouldn't be left.

On 16 June the Germans launched quite a severe attack in which they used half-track vehicles with a 105-mm gun. They also had a rocket gun, called a Nebelwerfer, which threw a lot of rockets at you. I got caught at the crossroads and heard these rockets coming, so I lay down in this ditch, which wasn't too deep, with my hands over my head. I thought, 'Oh Christ, I'm going to get it.' There was a hell of a crash in front of me and I felt I should be dead. Always afterwards there is a deathly hush and so I opened my eyes and there in front of me was one of these bloody rockets, but it hadn't gone off. I took off a bit fast. The Germans had advanced some way, but I'd anticipated where they would come in and brought up my reserve company and we did a flanking attack which was successful. But we did suffer considerable casualties from their 105s and mortars.

After that battle we were reinforced with officers and men from the Beach Brigade. They were very good material and were proud of being sent to a parachute battalion. Unfortunately, four of their officers were killed. One of my sergeants told me that they were so proud to wear the Red Beret and keen to maintain the standard expected that they became too brave.

For the next month or so we had a few days' rest at Pegasus Bridge and then moved around the divisional front.

I had a company sergeant major called Hutchinson who was very good, and I thought that he should have a commission. For this I had to take him to be interviewed by 'Windy' Gale, which I did. The interview was short, so the General asked me if I'd like a drink – he was always generous with his whisky and a master at picking people's brains. The more whisky he gave me, the more expansive I became about the proposed break-out. After dinner and a few more drams I was getting even more ambitious. Bobby Bray, his G1 was taking everything down. The next day I was back in my hole in the ground. James Hill, who was not in the best of moods, called me in and asked me bluntly what I had been doing the previous evening. I said, 'I had a drink with the General, sir, and then we had dinner.' He asked me what we had discussed, so I said, 'This and that.' 'Well,' he said, 'explain why I am to move you to reserve tomorrow.' I assured him that I'd not asked for that. Sure enough, we went back into reserve. The next day, however, I went to see James Hill who had just received an operation order. He handed me the order and I noted with interest that it was my plan for the break-out; the only difference was that 8 Para was to lead it! I thought to myself, 'the cunning old bugger'.

The crossing over the Dives was that night, and the next action of 8 Para was at Annebault, where we met stiff opposition. The enemy hit Battalion HQ, killing Major Cramp and 50 men. We moved on through Pont L'Évêque and other villages until we reached the Seine on 26 August. We then went back to Arromanches and got on a British ship. When I landed, George Hewetson was there. He told me I was getting married the next Saturday – which I did.

COMPANY SERGEANT MAJOR SID KNIGHT, 9th Parachute Battalion

I joined the 10th Essex when it was formed in June 1940 and it was in the summer of 1942 when we were on battle drill at St Albans that someone came round asking for volunteers to join a parachute battalion. The whole battalion was assembled, and after he made the appeal 300 to 400 men took a pace forward I believe. Two hundred and fifty went up to Ringway, and about 200 came through. By this stage many of us were already NCOs (I had been made up to a sergeant) so we really formed the nucleus of the new battalion – the 9th Parachute Battalion – when we formed up at Bulford. This was one of the reasons for the great camaraderie between us; we all knew each other and we were right at the centre of things, training the new intakes as they came in. I suppose you could say we were the spine of the regiment which became designated as the 9th (Home Counties) Parachute Battalion.

Eventually we built up to full strength – about 600 – and it was in April 1944 that Colonel Otway took over as commanding officer with his regimental sergeant major, Bill Cunningham. We knew there was something big afoot when we went off to train at West Woodhay. Of course the officers were in the know, but the rest of us weren't informed until the last minute that we were due to attack the Merville battery.

THE MERVILLE BATTERY 6 JUNE 1944

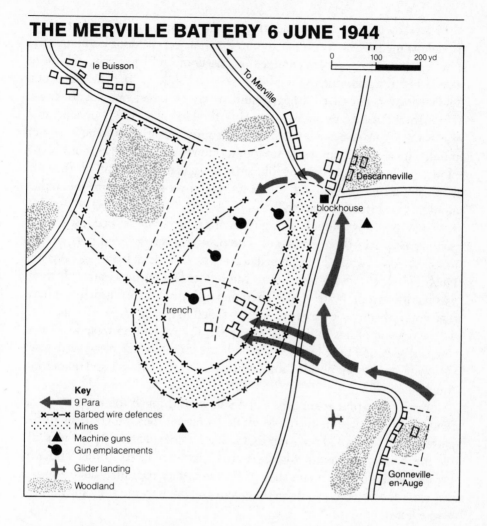

le Buisson

To Merville

0   100   200 yd

Descanneville

blockhouse

trench

Key
9 Para
x—x—x Barbed wire defences
Mines
Machine guns
Gun emplacements
Glider landing
Woodland

Gonneville-
en-Auge

About the day before we left it was explained to us what it was all about. Our target was a group of four massive concrete gun emplacements with full overhead cover and surrounded by a lot of barbed wire, an anti-tank ditch and a minefield. These guns were all facing the coast and covered Sword Beach where 3rd Division were due to land, so they had to be destroyed. My orders were to take a diversionary party of six men around the perimeter and make a noisy break-in at the main gate while the rest carried out a main assault through the breaches in the perimeter.

I was in the first 20 of the battalion to drop into Normandy from two old 'bath-tub' Albemarles which had taken off from Harwell. Unfortunately for me I was No. 10 in the stick and when I went to jump out, I couldn't move; somehow my harness had hooked onto a handle on the door leading to the pilot's cabin. Anyway, I hammered on the door and I just saw a chink of light when the door opened and I was loose so I slid out. But that delay of a few seconds meant that I dropped quite a way off target in a field of cows. Then these Lancasters started dropping their bombs, 400-pounders, so I was bouncing up and down in a ditch. It's funny, how things come into your mind, but as these bombs were coming down and the cows were being blown to bits and bellowing like mad I suddenly thought of this old Cadbury's advert, which said, 'Where is your chocolate? It's with the soldier alone in an unfriendly country!'

Anyway, things became a bit quieter after the bombs dropped, so I made my way round to the rendezvous. The planning was so good that when I dropped I knew where I was immediately. The first bloke I saw was Sergeant Hugh Salter, so we ran together to the rendezvous. When I arrived, there was hardly anyone there at all. Then one of my old mates turned up plus a few more. My diversionary party was attached to Headquarters Company so we were given orders to do what we could, but we had no weapons. I had just one pistol, one Bren gunner and one Sten in my party. Anyway, Colonel Otway then decided that we'd go off to the battery, and do our job there.

It was night-time, very dark and we all went through the lanes from the rendezvous at Varaville to the Merville battery. When we got near to the battery, everybody had their job to do. We numbered about 150, that's all. At the battery we found Major Alan Parry with Dusty Miller and Bill Harrold and a couple more; they were the battery reconnaissance party. I was close to the Colonel all the time, and Hal Hudson the adjutant was just to the left of him.

There was hardly any noise whatsoever, and the battery loomed out of the darkness. You could see the outlines of the four big guns facing the sea. We'd come over the barbed wire and there was an old perimeter track leading up to the battery so I started to make a movement around this road when machine-guns opened up from both sides. Someone shouted out, 'Get those bloody machine guns!' I had only one man with me and I took his Sten gun from him. We found there were three guns, one outside and two inside the perimeter, in front of No. 1 battery. I got the bloke on the outside corner by the forming-up point, then we went into the battery. It was very dark, but I could see that one of the gunners was by a whacking great lump of concrete that had been blown up. His tracer gave him away, so I got right round behind him and put my gun on him which soon quietened him down.

I had a go at the third one, whether I got him or not I don't know but it all went quiet. I went back to report to the Colonel and was just going towards the actual objective when I saw Major Parry on the right-hand side of the track wounded in the leg; on the left side was Captain Hudson and he had a terrible wound in his stomach. I think he must have been hit by a shell. I carried on with my diversionary party inside the perimeter and as we reached the main gate, we saw some Germans walking in, waving white flags. A couple of our blokes were shouting out, 'Shoot them'. Of course, I shouted, 'You can't shoot them; they've got the white flag up,' and so we rounded them up. I went and had a look in the batteries myself. Some chaps put two shells in the gun; one at the breech and one in the barrel! When the gun fired, the shells blew one another and the gun to pieces, I did not see the actual firing but heard the explosions.

At this stage we still only had about 80 men; we'd lost about 70 or 80 blokes in the battery, wounded or otherwise. There were medics there, who looked after them, but we didn't have time for them, to be honest. Then it went quiet, so then the next order was, 'Move out'. Originally the plan had been to go on to Sallenelles to take out the radar, but the Colonel decided that we didn't have enough men, so he ordered us to go towards Hauger, a village about half a mile from the battery. We were supposed to try and take Hauger but again we were so short of men that it was virtually impossible. There were high brick walls all around and we were being sniped at from the church tower. We had a couple of good snipers who accounted for one or two of them before they had a chance to do anything. But we were more or less pinned down there for the night.

From there, during daylight, we started moving towards the Chateau St Come which was the other side of Bréville. We were to take up position there in a compound called Bois de Mont. Well, again we had so few chaps that it was hard to fill the position. When our lads took over the chateau they found German food and money there, so we knew the enemy had been there recently. Our orders were to keep him out, so we dug into temporary positions on either side of the Bois de Mont road which runs between Bréville and Le Mesnil. A Company – what was left of it – dug trenches each side of this road. B Company were next to them on a lane overlooking the fields towards Bréville and C Company were in the rear. We set up a first aid post in a bungalow opposite the chateau after asking the Mayor of Bréville and his wife to leave. I was in a gateway covering the Bois de Mont road opposite the chateau drive with the rest of Headquarters Company. The Colonel said to me, 'You'll have to keep an eye on that left flank.' All I had was this Bren gun with a young chap named MacSorley and another little chap, name of Wilson, so I had to put them right underneath the hedgerow. Every now and again, up came the Tiger tanks along the road from Bréville firing at us like mad. The next thing was I'd lost these two brave lads. By now we'd managed to get some ammunition from somewhere, and I'd stacked it up all together. I had a PIAT as well, so I trained it on the ammunition. Padre John Gwinett, who saw me, said, 'What are you doing there?' I said, 'They're not going to have the ammo as well as us.' We were pegged down there quite a long time by those German multi-barrel guns, horrible things, then the Tiger tanks kept popping along the road.

Then, I think it must have been 11 June, the Black Watch came up and tried to relieve us and to occupy Bréville. They advanced with three Sherman tanks in support. I just lay there watching one Sherman after another getting blown to bits. Then all of a sudden the poor devils of the Black Watch were coming back through our lines. It's a wonder they didn't get accidentally shot by us. I think it was the open ground that beat them. At my end, I had about six of them break through the hedge. Of course I was thinking to myself they were Jerries breaking through so I was ready to have a go, and then I suddenly realized it was the boys. As they were about to pass me I said, 'No, no, no, you stay here now, get your rifles and fire with me.' So I took some of them under my wing for a little while.

Each day we were being built up by different units arriving in, six from here, seven from there. This was fortunate because we'd had heavy casualties. This went on for about four days and we'd had no proper sleep or anything like that. In the meantime, the 12th Battalion were ordered to attack Bréville to relieve us. They attacked from Amfréville and you could look down on them and actually see the battle taking place with our boys attacking. They relieved us tremendously by doing that and then they took Bréville. Marvellous job. I don't think we'd be here today if they hadn't done that. They lost an awful lot of men, though, some killed by our own gunfire, helping them out in the forming-up area. We then moved up to the crossroads at Le Mesnil and my little party dug in at the brickworks. Of course, the Jerries had a fixed line on it, so as soon as we got into the brickworks, boom, down came the shells and RSM Cunningham was hit. We picked him up and called the medics and put him on the ambulance. He looked at me and said, 'I'll tell you this, when we get back to barracks, I'll remember who the real soldiers were.' I said, 'All right, Bill, you get yourself better.' Later the medics came back and I asked, 'How is the RSM?' 'Oh,' they said, 'he's gone.' We'd already lost some men and now we picked up some more casualties while we were digging in. Terrible waste really, because Le Mesnil was our last place to go to before being relieved.

The Special Service Brigade relieved us and that's when we came back to the Caen Canal where we had a couple of days to lick our wounds. Colonel Otway was wounded and so he was replaced by Colonel Crookenden; I was made up to sergeant major. We stayed there about three or four days and then we got the next move to the Bois de Bavent, near the River Dives. We arrived in good shape; we'd had a nice clean up, had a rest, morale was all right and plenty of supplies had come through. But the Bois de Bavent was terrible – it was a place of death. It was the most fearsome place I've ever seen. It didn't smell of death, but had the look of it. We stayed there until we got the order in August that we were going to advance. We lost some chaps in the attack on Dozulé and in moving along the roads as there were plenty of areas for us to be sniped at or attacked because it was a wooded area and high banked. We then went across Pont L'Évêque and up into Beuzeville. We stayed in Beuzeville for a few days and then we were ordered home. We came down to Arromanches and boarded a ship. When we got to Southampton we disembarked onto the quayside, expecting to be greeted by cheering crowds. But all we saw were six WVS (Women's Voluntary Service) ladies who offered us a cup of tea – nothing else. We never heard a clap or a cheer all the way back to Bulford and I thought to myself, 'Ungrateful bloody lot.' But of course, we realized then that in Southampton and places like that, they'd had a terrific hammering from the bombs and it dawned on us then that they'd had more than their share of trouble as well.

SERGEANT DOUG WOODCRAFT, 9th Parachute Battalion

On the evening of 6 June 1941 I was a sergeant in A Company, 9th Parachute Battalion, who were providing the men for the three gliders which were to crash land on the Merville battery. Being subject to air-sickness I was not included in this party. I was a stick commander in one of the two aircraft that were to take the remainder of A Company to Normandy.

We took off around 2300 hours on a fine, but overcast evening and after about an hour and a half's flight the red light came on. Whenever I was stick commander I used to like to stand by the door to see the stick out and then follow, but this night it was to be my undoing. I had an entrenching tool secured to my right leg, which somehow got caught up in the strops, at the same time as the pilot started taking evasive action. Arse over tip I went, with my head and shoulders out in the slipstream, wondering just what the hell had happened to me. It took the combined efforts of the despatcher and navigator who came back to help to get me on my feet, by which time the pilot was heading off back to England like a bloody homing pigeon. My request sent by the navigator that he should turn and take me in again, was met by what I still consider an impolite reply, of just two words!

So with a great feeling of anti-climax back to England I came, just as dawn was breaking. I made my way into a deserted camp, from which I had departed a few hours earlier, and got my head down. I had hardly closed my eyes when I heard the sound of voices and, looking out, I saw the occupants of one of the gliders which had run into trouble and had managed to land in England. I joined this party and shortly after I found myself seated in a Horsa glider. I remember thinking what a bloody fine time I had chosen to make my first flight in one of these things.

To say I was unhappy is putting it mildly. The unaccustomed motion of the glider soon had me more airsick than ever and without a parachute on my back I felt naked and vulnerable. And then out of the haze the coast-line of Normandy appeared. Looking down I could see the huge collection of shipping offshore. Suddenly, the whistling noise ceased as the tug cast us off. There was a heart-stopping dive to earth, then we levelled out and made a safe, lumpy landing in a cornfield.

We tumbled out, took up a position of all-round defence and then a section at a time went back into the glider for other equipment and then we were off, running through the corn, making for the chimney on the skyline which belonged to the brickworks at Le Mesnil. By nightfall we were astride the crossroads at Le Mesnil and there we stayed for the next two days engaging the Germans who came in from the direction of Cabourg. Just about every parachute battalion in the 6th Division was represented there as stragglers made their way back and then we were moved to St Come on the morning of the 9th. I, together with some more strays, came up a track the other side of the road and made contact with the 9th Battalion for the first time since the evening of 5 June. The battalion was in a position of all-round defence with A Company on the right flank. I rejoined my platoon, already down to half strength, and found my platoon commander had been killed on the morning of D-Day.

In the early afternoon of the next day Sergeant Jimmy Frith and myself were briefed on a patrol we were to take up to the Chateau St Come which had been used as a German Regimental Headquarters. Our task was to search it and the stables, stay there, and report back by radio every 15 minutes the current position. Sergeant Major Beckwith had been in the chateau the day before and had found the regimental strong box, had opened it and had helped himself to the contents! We got the patrol together, comprising five riflemen and one Bren gunner, picked up a signalman from Battalion Headquarters and then split the patrol in half, three men each. Jimmy Frith and I tossed up who should search the chateau or the stables. I won and chose the chateau.

When we entered the chateau I saw the first signs that the Germans had been taken by surprise. I found myself in the dining room where, down the centre, was a long table still laid for the evening meal. They had just reached the sweet course for at each place setting was a half-eaten portion of rhubarb and custard. Chairs were thrown back and lay overturned on the floor, wine bottles knocked over and glasses smashed as they ran to get to their battle positions. We placed one or two items by the door which we thought might make our stay in Normandy more comfortable, although I still fail to see what use a large all-mains radio was going to be in our ditch!

Then we went upstairs. Hugging the wall, I cautiously started up, turned a sharp corner and got the shock of my life for there confronting me was a scruffy looking figure clad in a camouflage smock, parachutist's helmet with scrim hanging down over his face and pointing a gun at me. Before I could do anything stupid I realized I was looking at myself in a full length mirror! I leant against the wall for some moments to let my backside return to normal before going on.

The last room evidently housed someone of importance because there were large-scale maps of the area on the walls and a roll-top desk which I tried to open but it was locked. I got hold of a poker, inserted it in the lock and heaved and, as if that were a signal, bursts of automatic fire started up beneath the windows. Dropping everything we tore down the corridor and stairs just in time to meet Jimmy Frith and Lance Corporal Jack Watkins running in through the door. Jack Watkins was shouting, 'Look out, Jerry's out there and they've hit Jock.' At that moment, over Watkins' shoulders, I saw Jock run past and off down the drive.

By now our own Bren gunner was in action and Jack Watkins was sent out to stoke up some more fire whilst we got the signaller out. We did this by telling him to go to the far side of the room and to run like hell. By the time he got to the door he was flat out and away he went down the drive; we could see the sparks as bullets hit the cobbles just behind him.

We now had to get out but it was impossible to use the door as the Germans were concentrating their fire on it. The woodwork was rapidly being reduced to splinters and pieces of brickwork were flying about. We shouted to Watkins to get back down the drive and we would go out through the french windows on the other side of the room. When we reached these we found they were locked but by running at them together we went out on to the lawn amongst pieces of window frame and broken glass.

We picked ourselves up and ran for the wood the other side of the lawn and just as we reached it I looked back in time to see a small party of Germans come round the far end of the chateau in hot pursuit. Instead of running straight through and into the orchard we turned left and found ourselves in a vehicle park. We took up a position behind one of these and as the Germans passed some 20 yards in front of us we both opened up with our Stens and, without waiting to see the result, we turned and galloped down through the wood, yelling, 'Olly! Olly!', the rallying call of A Company.

So ended my first patrol. We had one man wounded, been thrown out of the chateau, but we had established one thing – the Germans were back.

We soon settled in our new position covering the road approach. Fortunately we were not attacked in any strength. When they came, attacks were of a probing nature. Just how close the Germans could get without being seen was brought home to me. I was crouched over a spirit stove, brewing up, when something made me look at my mate. Before I could speak he motioned me to silence and pointed just over my head, I looked up to see the bushes part and the head and shoulders of a German soldier come into view. How he failed to see us I will never know but all his attention was on the Vickers position. He raised his arm and in his hand was a stick grenade; before he could throw it my mate shot him. As he fell his helmet came off, striking me on the shoulder. In his wallet were photos of his wife and two small children who, unbeknown to them, had just lost their father.

Despite everything there were one or two lighter moments, one in particular was when we tried to do something about a German sniper who had been making life very awkward for us. Because of all the noise we were unable to locate him by the 'crack and thump' method. On this particular occasion he was having a go at the Vickers position and by the language from that area the occupants were not amused, so I positioned the Bren gunner and our sniper and ordered them to fire at any likely place. I then tied a mess tin to a stick and waved it backwards and forwards in front of a tree. I was on the point of giving up when 'smack', a bullet hole appeared in the tree trunk just above our heads. Each time he fired I carried out strict butt marking drill; I signalled bulls, inners, magpies and outers, each time marking the strike of the shot by placing the mess tin on the trunk and once, just to stop him getting big-headed, I signalled a miss by waving an aircraft recognition panel.

All the time the Bren gunner and sniper were firing into the trees opposite. Whether they got near enough to discourage him or he got tired of it all I don't know but he stopped and to this day one can plainly see a group of bullet holes in the trunk of that tree.

Soon after midday on 12 June a company of the 5th Black Watch took over the ditch and we moved back into the slit trenches we had dug on our arrival. All that long afternoon the pressure mounted, the noise was terrific, everyone firing. Then a most frightening thing happened, the Black Watch decided they had had enough and ran back through our position and things looked very black indeed, but we were saved by the timely arrival of Brigadier Hill with a company of the Canadian Parachute Regiment. They put in a counter-attack through the wood right up to the chateau and restored what was obviously a critical situation.

The next morning we were relieved by the Oxf and Bucks Battalion and some 200 of us, all that were left of the battalion, then moved quietly away to a position at the rear of the Canadians at Le Mesnil. We were not sorry to be leaving as this area had become a very unhealthy place to be.

The following day I was told to go into Escoville and see if it was still held by the Germans. So off we went, followed a track to the edge of the wood and there, 600 or 700 yards away, was the village. At the edge of the wood was a slit trench occupied by Jocks from the 51st Highland Division. I asked them if the Germans were in Escoville. The answer I got was in broad Scots, and had more fucks in it than a sergeant major's blessing. They didn't know, they didn't want to know, they were up to here with Normandy, give them the Western Desert any day. So, as the man said, go and find out.

It took the best part of an hour to make our way along a hedge through the thick undergrowth until we were almost to the village. I saw two Frenchmen digging a hole beside a very dead cow. After a bit I managed to attract their attention; they dropped their shovels and to my horror came running over, yelling, 'Tommy, Tommy!' at the tops of their voices, with me shushing away like mad.

We followed them into the village centre where there was a small café with eight or nine Frenchmen seated around, each with a glass in front of him, and there was a war going on outside! I shook hands with everyone, then the owner of the café came from behind the bar, moved a small carpet and, pulling up a loose floorboard, came up with a bottle of colourless liquid. I didn't know it at the time, but I was about to be introduced to Calvados – the real stuff – you could run the buses on it.

We all toasted De Gaulle, Roosevelt, Churchill and Stalin, each swallow causing a minor explosion at the back of my throat. All the time I was pointing in all directions and saying, 'Boche, Boche?' and everyone replying in a torrent of French. I was getting nowhere, when I suddenly remembered that we had been issued with a leaflet that contained a number of English–French phrases, and it was in my wallet. Also in my wallet, which I had forgotten about, were five contraceptives, loose, no packaging. As I opened it they fell on the ground; one Frenchman, with a yell of delight that could be heard in Caen, grabbed them up, held them high in the air, at the same time punching the air with his other fist, and shouting at the top of his voice, 'British Tommy jig-a-jig!' At this the small crowd started cheering and clapping. It was obvious there were no Germans in the near vicinity with all this noise going on, so I decided to get away as soon as possible.

Before we could leave the Frenchman went into a house opposite and returned with a dozen big brown eggs. My pouches were full with Sten magazines and my pockets had grenades in them, so I placed them carefully inside my smock, said 'Au revoir,' and left, to more applause.

On the way back we heard the now familiar sound of German mortars firing. As one man, the three of us dived headlong into the ditch and as the bombs burst around I suddenly became aware of a wetness spreading over my chest and stomach. My first thought was, 'God! I've been hit!' Then came the realization: I'd landed on the eggs. The air became blue.

About an hour later we got back, in a somewhat dishevelled state. I reported to my company commander and he took one look at me and said, 'What the hell has happened to you?' I saluted, presented him with a bottle of champagne, and said, 'Well, sir, it's a long story.'

CORPORAL DAN HARTIGAN, 1st Canadian Parachute Battalion

We came from units all over Canada to join the 1st Canadian Parachute Battalion. At Fort Benning, where we began our training, every few days we were offered a chance to quit and go back to our former units. It was often tempting, but the urge to get overseas as a paratrooper was stronger. I did not see a single recruit taking the fateful pace forward that would signal his intent to quit. Shortly before the permanent issue of overseas combat weapons, a general unit 72-hour weekend pass went into effect. It would have been better for the City of Winnipeg (the only city close by), the army and the men of the battalion if it had been done in stages. Soon the hotels were choked with red berets.

A Regular Army unit that was parading on the streets below with trucks, Bren-gun carriers and tanks, was soon being bombarded from several floors up by whisky bottles filled with water, and by pillows torn open so their feathers would scatter on the parade below. At the same time, spread over much of the Royal Alexander Hotel's façade were wriggling men going from the fifth to the sixth and the seventh floors on the outside of the building, climbing on bed-sheets tied together to make a rope – a result of one of the passing-out tests at Fort Benning where every man had to learn to climb a 50-foot rope or be thrown out of the course.

Things continued to move fast. We were sent home on embarkation leave, and then on 23 July left Halifax on HMS *Queen Elizabeth*. A few days after arrival, we were quickly mustered and shipped off to Carter Barracks, Bulford, near Stonehenge. There we were met by a tall, thin, youngish Brigadier Hill who possessed a firm jaw and looked like he meant business. Our methods of training changed. Instead of continuous crawling and dog-legging in simulated pincer movements, we turned to long forced marches, 10, 20, and 50 miles at a crack – with packs, weapons, and other battlefield equipment. Further emphasis was put on weapons' knowledge and handling, anti-tank grenade throwing, mortar firing, and target practice. There were exercises in assault training and preparation of defences. We were worked hard and we bitched regularly, but we enjoyed it.

Amidst all the hard work there were good times. Weekend passes came with reasonable frequency. Pay piled up during long periods of training where there was no way to spend it. Ten-day leaves came every three months. The English people were nothing short of marvellous. They took us into their homes, fed us, put up with our cultural differences, and without saying so, ministered to the need for reassurance that young people, a long way from home and facing danger, required. I will always remember and love them for that.

Our training jumps at Fort Benning had been made from the relative luxury of the Douglas C-47 Dakota. It had a large doorway in the port side which allowed us to make our jump from a standing position. Now, during parachute training in England, we had to learn a complicated system of shuffling along the floors of old bombers on the palms of our hands, towards a hole in the floor where we made an exit much like a groundhog ducking through his hole at the sight of his shadow. We had to lift not only the weight of our bodies on the palms of our hands, but also the 60 or 70 pounds of equipment each of us was carrying.

We also practised street-fighting. We were taken down to badly bombed areas of coastal cities like Southampton and Plymouth. We would race through the rubble firing live ammunition at cardboard silhouettes of enemy soldiers placed at strategic locations along the way.

The end of May saw us behind barbed wire in a security camp in southern England. Times were really getting serious. The briefings were so exhaustive we began to feel we had already been to Normandy ourselves.

We in the Canadian Battalion were given our objectives. Before the main landings could take place at drop zone 'V', near Varaville, it was necessary to neutralize the enemy troops positioned there in two pillboxes and a trench system which was about 100 yards south of the gatehouse of Le Grand Chateau de Varaville, on the eastern side of a road junction. On the opposite side was a 75-mm French field gun mounted on a rotating track. Both the gun and the trench system overlooked the main connection between the Cabourg and Periers-en-Auge road junction and the 'Y' formed by the Merville and Caen highways. The living quarters for the troops were in the Grand Chateau and in its gatehouse. Besides defending communications behind Cabourg, the 80 troops guarded a signals exchange which controlled defences along that section of coast, and was located in the fields below Bréville.

It was decided that C Company would seize Varaville before the main drops on dropzones 'N', 'K', and 'V', were begun. C Company would travel in twelve Albemarle bombers which would fly line astern, one minute apart, and would complete their drop by 0020 hours on D-Day – the same time that Major Howard's gliders would be landing at the Orne bridges. During C Company's drop there would be a 100-plane Lancaster raid on Merville battery and a strafing of the area by a squadron of Mosquito bombers.

The platoons of the company would rendezvous, line up on their jumping-off positions before the pillboxes, trench system, and living quarters by 0049 hours on D-Day. Bangalore torpedoes placed under the barbed wire surrounding the trench and gun position would blow. One minute later, at 0050 hours the enemy in Varaville would be destroyed. About the same moment the main drops of the 6th Airborne Division would begin.

C Company would consolidate its position at Varaville and destroy the bridge on the Divette, which would cut off the Periers-en-Auge and Cabourg roads. Following the main drop, one platoon of B Company would destroy the bridge on the Dives at Robehomme, another on a farm canal a quarter mile north of that, and would seize the road junction at Le Mesnil where the battalion would form part of the perimeter on the left flank of the main invasion bridgehead. A Company would protect the left of the 9th Battalion during its attack on the Merville battery, by cutting off the roads and pathways near Gonneville-sur-Merville. Headquarters Company would remain to secure drop zone 'V' and later be called forward to Le Mesnil.

C Company took off from Harwell in its twelve Albemarle bombers.

The Pathfinders of 22nd Independent Parachute Company and a special 9th Battalion Reconnaissance Patrol for Merville battery were flying with us in seven other Albemarles. It was twilight at 2230 hours when the first aircraft scooted along the runway. Here we were, C Company, just over 100 taking off in little bombers to drop behind Hitler's 'impregnable Atlantic Wall' and take on Rommel's soldiers. We were perfectly aware that attacking infantry should have a three-to-one ratio in its favour, but according to intelligence reports we were going in to do our job at close on one-to-one. We were loaded to the hilt with grenades, Gammon bombs, flexible Bangalore torpedoes around our necks, two-inch mortar bombs, ammunition, weapons and waterbottles which were supposed to be full of water, but were fractionally lighter. Our exposed skin was blackened with charcoal; the camouflage netting on our helmets was all tied up with burlap rags, and the space above the harnesses in our helmets was crammed with cigarettes or with plastic explosive. My section, made up of ten men as usual, flew in bomber No. 2. I was the section corporal. As soon as the aircraft was up and trimmed off, I made my way past the exit to the Plexiglass tail-section of the Albemarle. From there, I had a ringside seat for the trip across the Channel and gave my stick a running commentary during the flight.

A few minutes out, the first thing to report was that we were passing over a town where the streets, a few hundred feet below, were full of promenading people. That was the toughest moment of all, for each of us knew that we might never have the chance to do something like that, ever again. Somebody said, 'For Chris' sake gimmie a cigarette,' to which the sergeant growled, 'You know better'n that – stow the cigarettes 'til after Varaville.'

The engines of the little bombers, throttled back to jumping speed, barely purred as the aircraft slipped in over the beach. Below, there was a sort of grey sheen with black lines outlining blocks of territory. This we knew to be the flooding behind the beaches, with hedges sticking up through it, and running off to the west towards Merville. The bomber made a quick adjustment to the right and within a minute it was possible to see what we called 'Jackboot Hedge' with its sole up against Gonneville- sur- Merville at the beginning of drop zone 'V'.

As the red light switched to green we knew we were right on the money. In combat, the paratrooper's most pressing moment comes when his parachute opens and he has a short moment to realize that the commitment he has just made is irrevocable. For an instant there is a clear exhilarating feeling of the die being cast, absolutely!

C Company was on the ground only a few minutes when we knew that disaster was at hand. Many of the 4,000-pound bombs out of the Lancasters, meant for the Merville battery, came down too far inland, and were landing in and around the drop zone. Only a dozen men or so showed up at the rendezvous. Major Murray MacLeod set off for the enemy positions with the handful who were there. They managed to engage the enemy at Varaville within 30 minutes, so that the main drop could not be interfered with. In the next half hour or so about 20 more men of C Company showed up, and during the night a few more.

Eddie Mallon, a hard-rock miner from Northern Ontario, and myself, were treated to the blast of one of the 4,000-pounders. We were badly shocked, stupefied, for some period of time, and during the drop of the 9th Battalion we were wandering, trying to get our bearings. Soon we met an officer from the 9th Battalion. He too, was lost, and asked if we knew where we were. I think I answered, sarcastically, 'In France', and then tried to explain what had happened. He wouldn't believe that the RAF could drop a bomb anywhere but on target, and so we had a little difference of opinion. He then ordered us to go to the Merville battery with him – he had been able to gather only five or six of his own men. I, being a corporal in the Canadian force of two, tried to explain how important it was for us to get to our objective at Varaville but he straightened me out proper about being an officer in His Majesty's bloody army and you'll do as you're damn well told, and six men is too few to make a trek through the defences of the Atlantic Wall. Off we went and met Colonel Otway, who was in an absolutely foul rage because he could only find about the equivalent of a company of his battalion.

We reached Varaville at dawn, but our entire battalion had been badly scattered. Sixteen of the 35 transports dropped their men more than two miles away. There were never more than 33 of us of C Company actually alive and fighting at Varaville. Our company commander Major MacLeod was killed together with Lieutenant Walker and five other men. Captain Hanson, who had been dropped four miles away, took command. Shortly after 1000 hours the battle was won despite the fact that the company was missing two-thirds of its personnel and equipment. Two commando platoons from the 1st Special Service Brigade, which had come over Sword Beach, relieved us at about 1500 hours on D-Day, and we left for the Le Mesnil crossroads, which B Company had captured as planned. By the evening of D-Day, despite the severe scattering of its sticks, over half the battalion's personnel had reached the crossroads.

For the next three days we were continuously active 24 hours a day – on the attack, on fighting and reconnaissance patrols, on guard, defending ourselves against attack, or helping another unit. We stood to at 0600 hours in England on 5 June and did not stand down until the afternoon of 9 June – over 100 hours of continuous wakeful duty. We learned that lack of sleep was the worst of all deprivations – far worse than hunger or thirst.

The afternoon of the 8th brought rations at last, but still no sleep. The enemy kept shelling and threatening. Greenhorns became experienced combat soldiers and dug deeper. Water was gathered and stored in the trench. Enemy snipers began their work, and men died quietly, without as much as a murmur. With darkness, enemy reconnaissance and fighting patrols were put out in force, and it was all compounded by exhaustion and hallucinations that made it difficult to discriminate between fact and fiction.

My section was dug in on a narrow lane 100 yards from the crossroads, and in the semi-moonlight hedges seemed to become buildings, uneven trees jagged roofs, fields with dew shining on them lakes and streams, a cow a boat. When the sun came up on 9 June Lieutenant McGowan and Platoon Sergeant MacPhee led us out on a fighting patrol to the town of Bavent, a kilometre away, to determine the enemy's strength. The platoon was to approach the town, establish a firm fire-base with two sections, and send the third section (a sergeant and seven men – two had already been lost since the jump) right into the enemy positions to draw their fire. If this did not bring a reaction from the whole town, three men were to be sent running across an open field to encourage the enemy to expose their strength.

It was like a beautiful summer morning in any farm community back in Canada. We came right up to the town without a peep from the enemy, and we became over-confident. Suddenly, plans changed. An enemy machine-gun less than 100 feet away in a hedge let rip. What a jolt! Our eight-man section wound up in a huge bomb crater, with cursing, praying and instantaneous planning going on simultaneously. Sergeant Morgan heaved two smoke grenades in the direction of the gun. 'C'mon,' he bellowed to us. We rushed on into the smoke and threw Gammon bombs, which didn't reach the gun, but blasted the gun's crew into submission. The Bren-gunner and I raced up to a position above the main street, on a slight rise. The sergeant and his five men, firing from the hip, made for the first house, tossed grenades, followed them into the house and killed three of the enemy. While we had been entering the town an enemy machine-gun opened up from the opposite end of the main street and stitched a soldier across the chest. It was shocking to see how clean his somersault was as he went to his death. The machine-gun turned its attention to the sergeant and his remaining four men as they attacked the second house. Meanwhile, the two of us, with two-inch mortar and machine-gun, laid everything we could onto the enemy troublemakers. Sergeant Morgan encountered an enemy sergeant armed with a Schmeisser in the second house; both fired, and the enemy sergeant fell dead, but Morgan had two bullets in his gut. Shouting a command to abandon the attack, and covered by smoke from the surviving soldiers, he limped back to firm fire-base. He survived to receive his MM.

After one attack, the enemy retained possession of the town of Bréville, creating a bulge in the Airborne perimeter towards the open ground between Bréville and Ranville. It became a serious threat when the Germans assigned strong elements of their 346th Division to the task of cutting the Airborne bridgehead in two at what became known as the Bréville Gap. General Gale was lent an infantry battalion from 51st Highland Division to bolster his waning strength. The new battalion, nearly twice the size of an airborne battalion, was put on the south-east shoulder of the gap, near Chateau St Come, between 9th British and 1st Canadian Battalions. In the early evening of the 12th C Company was called upon to halt the deterioration in the area of the St Come Forest. There were only 54 men still available for action from our company. Brigadier Hill personally gathered up about 15 additional men from Battalion Headquarters and then accompanied Major Hanson, our company commander, into the counter-attack. As we passed through the Black Watch position, it was, 'The Canadians are here.' There was support from naval guns, but the situation was tenuous when we swept through the dense part of the forest with our bayonets fixed. When we regained the ground the enemy had won and pushed out a little farther, beyond where the first trenches had been, we found ourselves on the edge of a field on their front doorstep. We had brought no picks or shovels with us and were caught without trenches. If we deserved any real credit in this action it was now that we earned it, for the enemy brought up SP 88s and a couple of Mark IV tanks. In combination with heavy mortars, they punished us unmercifully, but we stood our ground and turned the enemy infantry back. It was a 'teeter-totter' situation. Brigadier Hill, being an experienced and determined commander, picked the right moment to send his chosen reserve in and this gave the extra little nudge that held the line long enough to turn the tide. We survived, mauled and wounded, though several of our men were killed there. We returned to Le Mesnil the following day.

We could take pride that the Germans did not make us take one step backwards through this whole affair. Although we had no trenches, and no heavy weapons to challenge their armour, we stood our ground, and fought back. General Gale must have been proud, too, for he gave our company a Letter of Commendation through Battalion Headquarters.

The Battle of Normandy continued for another two and a half months. Our battalion suffered 85 per cent casualties but had no complaints, and we gained a tremendous respect for the British Army. In early September we went back to England and rebuilt with new, well-trained recruits, ready for action again in the Ardennes.

LIEUTENANT NICK ARCHDALE, 7th Parachute Battalion

In 1943 I was 19 and while I was serving with the 60th Rifles a team came round looking for recruits for the Parachute Regiment. The two officers in charge were Major Pine-Coffin and Captain Blood; with such unlikely names I had to join!

After training I joined the 7th Battalion. As a young mortar officer I had a platoon of 28 men, ten of whom were NCOs. When we were on exercise or in action we lived with our men. On the odd week-end we did get away, we had a special leave train to London. A favourite nightclub was The Astor, where we had great parties, then to Rosa Lewis's hotel, where, if you were in favour, you got a bed and never got the bill!

The day came and in a field somewhere near the aerodrome we had a short service. Sergeant Roberts who was Welsh, was standing beside me and he had the most beautiful singing voice – a few days later he was killed. We got on the aeroplane and set off. As always there was a fair amount of tension as we were bumping about a bit and some of the men were sick. Somewhere over the Channel we opened the door and saw the white tops of the waves. Being the number one, I looked down and there were searchlights and gun flashes everywhere. However we weren't over the coast more than a minute or two. Just before I jumped I threw out a stuffed moose head, which we'd purloined from a pub in Exeter and was planned to put the fear of God into any German it hit! Then out we went.

I rather expected the Germans to be shooting at me as I landed but in fact found myself standing quite peacefully with my feet on French soil. It was quite amazing. Collecting about eleven of my platoon together we set about finding our three-inch mortar containers which had been dropped separately but failed to find any. I decided it was no good wasting more time, nor was there any sense in going to our rendezvous because it was too late; I made straight for the bridges along the canal path. We arrived at almost the same time as A Company who'd run to the bridges to relieve John Howard of the Oxf and Bucks. As always our brigadier was in the thick of things and we found him on the bridge, smiling and giving encouragement.

When our Battalion Headquarters had been established just north of the bridge, Geoffrey Pine-Coffin (now Colonel) told me to go up the canal to Le Port in case B Company was under pressure. Still very green I set off through the village, peered round the corner of a house and a bullet hit the wall an inch from my eyes and filled them with dust. A dear old French lady who had two wounded men in her kitchen, bathed my eyes. That incident had taught us a lesson. We'd done a year's training and suddenly it was the real thing; from that moment on we became very much better soldiers.

We were so thin on the ground that German patrols were getting through. I left Sergeant Freddie Fricker to establish a defensive position for Battalion Headquarters and went to try and head off these small German attacks. It was like playing cowboys and indians – only we were better at it than they were. I took two men with me and we had quite a lot of fun getting into the cracks, looking over walls, and doing a bit of shooting.

By today's standards, our wirelesses were absolutely hopeless, which meant that our CO had very little communication with the rest of his battalion. He sent me north again to locate B Company. I spoke with the company commander, Roger Neale, and got back to brief the Colonel, who then sent me off to A Company, who had been cut off. I got to them in Bénouville; they were in a bad state, with a lot of wounded and there was no way they could be got out. Nigel Taylor, their company commander was badly wounded, a platoon commander killed and another wounded in the head. In control at that time was Jim Webber, their 2 i/c, who was tremendously brave and inspiring. The Germans at times were only a hand grenade's throw away. We put up helmets on bayonets while others picked off whoever fired at them.

When I got back to Battalion Headquarters Jim Webber was there as well. I gathered all the available people from Battalion Headquarters to go back with me to A Company to help out. Luckily by the time we got back things were cooling off. We were all concerned for A Company's wounded. When it became quiet enough the leading elements of the Warwicks, who were to relieve us, sent up two White's scout cars to take out as many of the wounded as they could. These poor, wretched men were so full of morphine that their hands felt cold and stiff. I remained with A Company for the rest of the afternoon and evening. An SP gun had helped by knocking down the closest houses in front of us and things were fairly quiet. However that was not to last and just as a new attack started from the south and west another started from the north. We prepared for a last stand, assuming that B Company to the north-east had been overrun. We then realized that our assailants from Le Port had British steel helmets and amid shouts of: 'It's us, you bloody fools!' managed to stop the shooting and hand over our position.

In the next couple of days we moved down the canal. One afternoon we were sitting near a rather grand house, when a German tank appeared on the skyline. By now we had mortars and machine-guns and an SP gun in support. I said to the gunner with the SP gun, 'Let's shoot that tank.' I thought he'd pause a bit, because I was under the gun with binoculars, when, whoof! – off it went and nearly blasted me out of the ground! With that one shot, at quite long range, he knocked the turret off the tank! Great fun, but a bit unreal.

At one point we were called to counter an attack south of Ranville. For this the brigadier had called up the assistance of tanks from the 13th/18th Hussars. It was arranged that the 7th Battalion should go through the 13th, supported by tanks. It was assumed that there were no anti-tank guns in the Bréville direction. As there was no role for the three-inch mortars I just sat and watched from the start line. I was sitting on the edge of the road, in the ditch, and five minutes before the start the 13th/18th CO arrived and jumped into the ditch beside me.

B Company were delayed in their attack because the CO feared they might get caught up in the tank fire. By the time they began their advance the tanks had got ahead of the troops, and worse still there was an extremely accurate German anti-tank gun at Bréville and it wiped out one tank after the other. We just sat and watched them being blown up, which was very unfortunate. B Company, including a fearsome soldier called Drew who was armed with an axe as his main weapon, went hell for leather into the woods, killed about 40 and took many prisoners. We suffered only ten wounded, but the 13th/18th lost five tanks, nine killed and five wounded.

A little later we got up to the Bois de Bavent and took over from Colonel Alistair Pearson's 8th Battalion and moved into ready-made trenches with the Germans not 50 yards away and patrolled by day and night. Then at last we had the break-out and away we went. At dawn one day I was ordered to clear the opposition near a railway station. We fixed bayonets and set off. It was an extraordinary bayonet charge; we didn't run, shouting, we just kept steadily along, and went through them. My main concern was keeping a line so as not to shoot each other.

We finally moved up to Deauville, and our Normandy was all over. We learnt many things in Normandy, but perhaps the most surprising thing was just how one took death and casualties. It amazed me how quickly you became completely emotionally unaffected. It wasn't callous, it was a protective shield, I suppose. The other thing I found out is that very little time is actually spent fighting: most of the time you are doing nothing at all. That did surprise me, but of course if it was not like that there would be no soldiers in a few days.

CAPTAIN JOHN SIM, 12th Parachute Battalion

The 12th Yorkshire Battalion was raised from the 10th Battalion of the Green Howards and was part of the 5th Parachute Brigade, under Brigadier Poett. We were based at Larkhill, where we were involved in the basic training of the new battalion. We had to weld the newly forming battalion together with sectional, platoon, company and battalion exercises; it was a hard flog. Only 200 from the Green Howards had volunteered to parachute – mostly the senior officers and sergeants and men from HQ and Support Companies. So when I arrived as an outsider from a Yorkshire Regiment in September 1943, there were no rifle companies and we waited for drafts to join us from Ringway. They were fine men, but most of them were not from the infantry and many had not fired a rifle or Bren, or thrown a grenade. There wasn't much leave and most week-ends were spent training.

In the last two weeks in May, in between briefings, we relaxed. The weather was wonderful, the sun was shining and after all the extensive training we just unwound, sunbathed and played cricket. We wrote letters but they weren't despatched until we were on our way. We were also introduced to a new method of digging trenches. Each section was to carry a piece of tubing about three feet long, supplied with plastic explosive, safety fuse and detonator. The idea was that you took the turf away, bored two holes with the tubing, and dropped a piece of plastic explosive down. The explosion loosened all the soil which was then easily shovelled out.

The day before take-off was a long and exciting one with lots to do and now there was only the drone of the engines and the darkness, so I fell asleep. With 20 minutes to go my batman woke me. I struggled with a member of the crew to get the door in the floor open, which I had never done before! We then went through our normal drill inside the aircraft, and with five minutes to go we all moved up closer to the door. I was to be first out so I stood astride the door; to exit all I had to do was jump to attention. I found myself peacefully floating down without any shooting, onto a big field where I landed without any difficulty, next door to a horse! I got out of my harness and I was aware of other soldiers landing round me, but it didn't feel as if I'd landed in France and was involved in a live war. It was like one of our many night drops on Salisbury Plain.

It appeared to me that I had been dropped absolutely spot on, so I set off with two or three men, westwards, to rendezvous by a quarry, on the Cabourg to Caen road. When I got there our CO said the adjutant hadn't arrived and sent me back to the DZ with a flash torch to guide everyone in.

After a while I was called back to the quarry and was told by my company commander that very few of the battalion had arrived, that we couldn't afford to wait any longer and that I was to lead the battalion off out of the quarry and to our defensive positions south of Ranville. I set off with C Company but I wasn't aware of any battle going on anywhere; it was like an exercise. When we came to the south side of Ranville we had a very pleasant surprise because we found a hell of a lot of our chaps already there and digging in. They had landed in different places and instead of going to the RV had gone straight to their positions at Ranville. Major Stevenson, my company commander, asked me to see if there were any Germans in four houses nearby, where we were going to establish our Battalion Headquarters. I took a sergeant and two soldiers and when we got to the first house I noticed there was a light on inside. I knocked, and after probably about a minute, the door was opened by a middle-aged lady, in her day clothes. At two o'clock in the morning this was a bit unusual; behind her, her husband and two kids were also dressed in their day clothes. I said, 'Bonjour Madame, nous sommes soldats d'Angleterre; nous arrivons içi par avion, parachutistes; l'heure de libération est arrivée. Ou sont les soldats allemands? Les soldats allemands restent içi?' She looked blankly at me. I was a dunce at French at school, but I thought I'd done quite well. I had another go but now she looked dazed and terrified – we were all camouflaged up with blackened faces. I then asked my sergeant, a right raw Yorkshireman, if he could speak French; he couldn't and neither could the other two, so I tried again. I'd barely started when she burst into tears, embraced me and said, 'You're British soldiers, aren't you?' So I said, 'Yes, I've been trying to tell you this for the last three or four minutes. You can speak English well can't you?' 'Yes,' she said, 'I *am* English, born in Manchester, and I married a French farmer before the war and settled here.' I asked her why it took her so long to come out with it. She explained that there had been Germans masquerading as British commandos or parachutists in the area to test them out. Then she said, 'It wasn't until I heard your frightful schoolboy French and your backchat to your sergeant that I realized that no German could possibly have acted the part!' She told us there were no Germans in the area. I reported this back to Major Stevenson and set off for my position.

We started to dig ourselves in using our new plastic explosives. We had no wireless so I arranged a system with my company commander whereby I signalled with a Very light. About eleven o'clock that morning – I still felt we were on an exercise – 300 yards in front of us we saw a group of about 50 soldiers coming towards us. I thought that they were our own chaps, but they suddenly went into extended line and started to advance straight towards us across this open field! I then realized who they were. As they advanced they were on one of my defensive line targets, so I asked my naval observation officer to call down a stonk, but regrettably the ship had a priority target and couldn't help us. So the enemy continued to advance.

When they reached a fence about 70 yards to our front, I fired my red Very light cartridge straight at them. This was the signal for the whole position to open up rapid fire. Strangely, I felt no fear at all, I felt it was still an exercise and that these were English troops coming towards us and we were firing blanks. I just didn't feel that I was at war. When we opened up they all went to ground in the high grass, but we carried on firing in the general direction of where they had disappeared. I heard orders being given in German, so I sent up a red Very light to my right to let my company commander know that their attack was coming on my right. Mortar bombs rained along our hedgerow. Then suddenly as if from nowhere, two self-propelled guns were brought up close to the cattle fence and opened up. At the appearance of these two guns I was surprised that my six-pounder hadn't opened up. They were sitting ducks, but nothing was happening. From the area of the six-pounder a soldier came creeping along towards me, saluted while still on his hands and knees, and told me that the gun had been damaged on the drop and was unserviceable. I now had no means of picking off those two SP guns. I asked Sergeant Milburn if he would lay down smoke and go forward and attack them with a Gammon bomb – but unfortunately he was killed before he could go forward. There was then a lull. Then, surprisingly, the hatch on one of their tanks opened, and a German officer, arrayed in service dress and Sam Browne belt, carefully got out of his tank and started to light up a cigarette; he wasn't allowed more than a couple of puffs before one of my men shot him.

We were still being subjected to mortar fire and I was anxious about a flanking attack. After a while the sergeant who had been on my right flank came creeping along to report that he'd come up the hedgerow and couldn't find any of our section active or alive. We had run out of ammunition so I decided I would gather those still on their feet and dash back to the company line. When I called there was only the sergeant, three men and myself left, out of twelve. Half-way back our own mortars, which I'd been calling for, crashed down onto the enemy. If I'd just stayed where I was a little longer I needn't have come back, but I wasn't to know that at the time. When I got back to our lines the company commander and I decided that we ought to take a new section with an officer and re-occupy the position. When we got there the enemy had disappeared.

The platoon commander was capable of looking after the section so I felt rather redundant. I decided that I would take the dead from our action to Ranville church. Among them was a German soldier. While we were being mortared this lone soldier had come down towards us, from the castle fence carrying a rifle. I quietly said to my batman, 'Harris, you see that soldier coming down? Shoot him.' And he did. Much later I thought, 'How could I have given such an order?'

At nine o'clock that evening we witnessed a tremendous air armada of gliders coming in. The 13th Battalion had taken down a lot of the poles that were around the DZ so they landed without many casualties. We were now reinforced by three fully fledged infantry battalions. That night our battalion was relieved by the 12th Devons.

The following day we moved down the towpath of the River Orne to take over Longueval, occupied by the Royal Ulster Rifles, and to support them for their attack on St Honorine. Unfortunately the day ended chaotically because the RUR advanced, but artillery support didn't come down at the right time to support them, and at the end of the day they came streaming back to us in Longueval. We also came under fire and with two battalions very congested in this little hamlet, being mortared, we suffered a hell of a lot of casualties. We were told to withdraw and march back again along the towpath to a reserve position. It was now Saturday, D+4, and my first wedding anniversary. I felt my battalion was now being used as a dogsbody to fill in anywhere. Because of casualties we had to re-organize and I was transferred to B Company as only Major Rogers was left there and we had three officers in C Company. We were sent to the dropping zone on the outskirts of Ranville to relieve the 7th Battalion. On D+5 we went back to a quarry by the river for a day of rest, to change our underclothes and clean our weapons. Our quartermaster had arrived by sea with the cooks and our big packs.

Our tranquillity was broken when the rumour started going around that we were to attack Bréville the next day. After our evening meal, orders were given that we were to attack within the hour, in fighting order. At 8.30 pm with three companies, we led off at the double across the DZ with the smashed-up gliders and up the wooded ridge and finally came to rest at Amfréville, where, to our surprise, we were all led into a church. We sat there quietly, as you do, looking at the figures of the Virgin Mary, sucking sweets, wondering what was going to happen next. After barely ten minutes we filed out and Padre Joe Jenkins was standing there dishing out the divisional news-sheet, 'Pegasus', in which we learned how well the Russians were carrying on in their advance towards Berlin!

As we were marching along the track towards Bréville the artillery bombardment started and it was colossal. I'd never heard anything like it. The noise was terrible and then suddenly it all seemed to fall around us – I hugged a garden wall with my arms around my head whilst this shattering din went on – then suddenly it stopped and I gave the order, 'Right, all up, stand up, advance,' which we did. It seemed we hadn't suffered casualties, but as we advanced we passed a shambolic scene of soldiers of A and C Companies who were ahead of us, dead on the road, or wounded, staggering and crawling. They were in a terrible state, and had been caught on the edge of the bombardment. I carried on as if in a daze, as if I was cocooned in a protective screen. With this horrific scene of death all around, we just carried on marching in single file to get to the start line. As we moved on to this line, which was a hedge, I noticed sitting quietly in their trenches the darkened faces of the front line of the commandos. We lined ourselves up facing Bréville. I looked round and to my surprise there was Lieutenant Colonel Parker, our old CO. I said, 'Good heavens, sir, what on earth are you doing here?' He said that he'd come in by glider, had a job with the Airlanding Brigade, and heard that the 12th were going into battle. We'd just finished this conversation when Major Rogers ordered us to fix bayonets and prepare to advance. In extended line we moved forward across a field until we came to an orchard where we deployed and found a lot of Germans, dazed and shaking from the bombardment, and completely incapable of fighting. We occupied their trenches and took them prisoner. Without warning, we suddenly found ourselves again under a terrifying artillery barrage. I threw myself into a dip in the ground by a wall and put my hands around my head and prayed like mad. I thought it was the Germans counter-attacking, but later we learnt that it was our own artillery. Then, as suddenly as it started, it stopped. I staggered up and checked that everyone was all right – and they seemed to be. Then I saw Major Rogers half out of his trench. There wasn't a mark on him, but he was dead, killed by the blast. I laid him against the orchard wall and covered him up. In the meantime the church on our right flank was ablaze and the whole area was brilliantly lit by its flames. Above all this you could hear an eerie high-pitched note. People thought it was an organ stop that had jammed in the explosion, but whatever it was, it was there all night, a haunting, eerie sound. The enemy didn't counter-attack, the night passed quietly and I sent out active patrols.

After we'd captured Bréville I heard our tanks go in to assist those who were left of A and C Companies to defend the crossroads. At first light the quartermaster arrived with tea. My batman noticed I'd been hit in the arm. I went to the doctor who'd worked all night by the light of the flames of the church. He attended to my wound and stuck my arm in a sling and I was taken to Arromanches by ambulance. While I was there I went round a very large marquee, the whole of the floor of which was jam-packed tight with stretcher cases. There was not a single wounded man in there, they were all shell-shock cases. I noticed that pretty well all the men wore the African Star, and were from the 50th and 51st Divisions. They'd flogged all the way from Alamein to Sicily and Italy, and Normandy was probably the last straw. There was a limit to how much a division can take, without a reasonable period of quietness. Now, as these once-proud men heard the guns go off miles away, they jerked up out of their stretchers and quivered.

That night I was put on a ship and woke to find my landing craft had moored alongside HMS *Victory* in Portsmouth harbour. We were put on a hospital train and fussed over and mothered by charming ladies. Because we were young and very fit, many of us who were wounded in Normandy were back with our battalion for the break-out in August and for the advance to the River Seine.

LIEUTENANT JACK WATSON, 13th Parachute Battalion

I was a platoon commander with the 13th Battalion. I took off with my stick in a Dakota from Broadwell, near Brize Norton at 2330 hours. In the Channel, I could see below me ships signalling 'V' for Victory. Our battalion's task was to secure Ranville and to protect the DZ and LZ during the landing of the gliders. As I landed my parachute got caught up in the trees so had a fairly soft landing. I was lucky but I was alone! I collected my equipment together and saw the Ranville church tower and made for it meeting my men on the way. I could hear my CO and various other company commanders blowing their horns rallying us to our rendezvous. Each horn had a distinctive note.

I was with A Company and it was our task to get back onto the DZ and clear it of the poles, fill in the anti-landing ditches and set up landing lights for directions for the gliders. While we were doing this we could hear the fighting going on at Ranville which our battalion captured by 0230 hours, the first village to be captured in France.

At daylight we rejoined the battalion in Ranville. My next job, as a platoon commander, was to lay a minefield across the road that led from Le Mesnil. This was to deny any attacks that would come down the road to burst through Ranville and then into the bridges. In fact, that day we knocked out three tanks from our A Company position with six-pounders which had come along with their crews from the gliders.

The battalion also had three Alsatian dogs who dropped with us. One was killed and one went missing, but Bing survived. We used him with the sniper section and also on patrols to sniff out the enemy. Our padre, Whitfield Foy, was also missing – he dropped on the other side of the River Dives but he led a whole stick of about ten men back across the water and rejoined us. When he arrived the whole battalion cheered – he had been missing for two days. The call was, 'Hello Bishop, you're bloody late.' My company sergeant major, MacFarlane, who was also missing on the drop turned up two days later in civilian clothes riding a bike.

On the early morning of D+4 patrols from my battalion reported to Battalion Headquarters they had seen signs of movement as if the enemy were preparing for an attack from the direction east of Bréville. My commanding officer, Peter Luard, immediately issued orders to company commanders to prepare for a possible attack by the enemy. At about nine o'clock our forward positions reported the enemy were moving across the DZ/LZ using the mass of wrecked gliders as cover and were heading towards the direction of the battalion position and the Le Mariquet area – we were all ready for them. The enemy were allowed to come within 50 yards of the battalion line when the order was given to fire. The result was devastating – the enemy were falling like a house of cards – the terrific force of rifle and machine-gun fire took them by surprise and in no time they were a disorganized mass. They suffered 400 dead or wounded and we took some 150 prisoners and passed them back to the brigade cage. They were in fact a German Grenadier Battalion of 346 Division.

For the rest of that period we were well dug in around Ranville. We lost quite a few men through shelling and mortaring but we held our ground and eventually we were moved to Le Mesnil to take over the 3rd Brigade position. We remained in the brickworks there in a defensive position and at Ranville until the break-out in August.

Above the village of Putot-en-Auge there was an enormous hill called Hill 13, very strongly held by the Germans. This was a thorn in the flesh as far as the brigade was concerned because it dominated the main road to the Seine. We had to fight really hard to take the village on 18 August 1944. We were then ordered to attack the hill. We passed through 7th and 12th Battalion lines and formed up just below the hill. After a hard fight we captured it. We were then forced off it by the Germans who were much stronger and we also got caught by a lot of cross-fire from either side.

Eventually the 4th Special Service Commandos Brigade passed through and captured the hill; we just did not have the number of men to complete the task. We stayed a couple of nights at Putot on the other side of the village itself, sleeping in a field. Then we passed through 3rd Brigade and the next objective was Pont L'Évêque. When we arrived we found both the bridges were blown across the river and there was stiff opposition. In spite of this we actually got across the bridge by the remaining iron girder. Once we got into Pont L'Évêque the Germans withdrew – again the fighting was very hard with twelve killed and 33 wounded.

After Pont L'Évêque it was a running battle but we got to Pont Audemer and that was where our fighting finished, actually on the Seine.

We rested there and a signal came out saying that everybody had to hand back their £10 of French money to the quartermaster. Nobody gave theirs back apart from the commanding officer! The money came in useful because before coming back we had a day out in Honfleur and fed ourselves well and had a good party – on His Majesty! We then came back to England on an American Liberty Ship.

SERGEANT CHARLES ELSEY, 6th Airborne Armoured Recce Regiment
The 6th Airborne Armoured Reconnaissance Regiment was made up from about 100 volunteers of the 9th Lancers, 10th Hussars and the Queen's Bays which were the cavalry units of the 1st Armoured Division that had been scuppered in France in 1940. Before becoming part of the Airborne Division we were a commando unit based at Inverary in Scotland.

Before D-Day we had exercised extensively with the Glider Pilot Regiment and the RAF. When we first arrived at Larkhill there were no gliders to accommodate our six-ton Tetrarch tanks so we were frequently taken up in a small Hotspur glider to familiarize ourselves with this strange form of travel. I could sympathize with the paras who used to look in disbelief at this engineless 'plane' made up of wood and glue but equally sympathize with the glider pilots who could not believe that anyone would jump out of a plane at 800 feet dependent only on a piece of silk.

Eventually we were taken to see these beautiful whacking great Hamilcar gliders that were to carry our tanks and their crews of three and we had practice flights with the tanks in them. On the run up to D-Day we were incarcerated at Tarrant Rushton and for twelve days we were briefed about our objectives and our landing zone in the Ranville area.

The Paras went in first and captured the Merville battery and we went in later that day, towed by specially adapted Halifaxes. The airfield at

Tarrant Rushton had a bump at the end of it. If you hadn't got airborne by the time you hit this bump there was a thump and you went into the air. Ours was an easy take-off and as we gained height the countryside flowed away behind us – it was rather marvellous.

As we came closer to the French coast I opened a hatch in the floor of the glider and there, below, were hundreds of boats in the Channel and fighter planes buzzed all around us. Then we got into the tank for landing.

Our first big punch-up came on the second day, when we were moving to another position. There were four Germans in a ditch with machine-guns. I was the only one who saw them – nasty buggers – and they were shooting at us; even through the armour you could feel it. Now killing from a tank involves teamwork. I said to Ted, the driver, 'There's some on the left, turn left, go towards them – left, left, left!' Then, to the gunner, Bill, 'Traverse left, left, there's some Jerries in a ditch, left, left, see them?' 'Yes, I've got them,' said Bill. 'Fire, fire,' I said. 'Go left Ted, towards them. You're hitting them, Bill, you've got them. Drive over the ditch, Ted.' It was always like this, a combined operation – a driver to get you there, a gunner to fire, and a commander to find the target and say when to open up on it.

Commanding a tank was like looking through a bloody periscope and shaving, riding a bike, reading a map, talking on the wireless and doing ten other things at once! The gunner had an amusing act as well. He had a seat which went up and down; to his right was the big two-pounder gun, and to the right of that a machine-gun. He had two triggers – left-hand for the two-pounder, right-hand for the machine-gun. By moving his shoulder up and down against a pad, and bumping his seat up and down, he could move the gun. His eye was glued onto a telescope, with a brow-pad that held his head steady while his left hand turned a handle with two gears that traversed the turret, and with his left foot he cracked walnuts!

With the armour and the two-pounder you could wipe out any 'soft' target. Lorries, jeeps, and almost everything else were fair game – but you couldn't touch their tanks. If they fired at you you were dead; so you got out of their way as fast as possible. The Tetrarch was very fast – we used to tear around the streets at Larkhill at 30 mph. All in all it was an interesting little tank; it could even keep going if it lost a track.

We settled down just on the edge of Ranville in the grounds of a farm. We were doing a little recce every day, going out, probing. By night we would come back to our area – you could hardly call it a safe area because the 6th Airborne was protecting the left flank of the whole of the Normandy invasion. The most unusual recce job we had was when the colonel asked me to take out two tanks to protect the war correspondent, Chester Wilmot, and his BBC wagon. It was the day of the 1000-bomber raid on Caen. The colonel told us to find a place where Chester Wilmot could see what was going to happen. So we prowled about and found a nice little hillock which gave us a good view towards Caen, no more than two miles away. It was an awesome sight – the bombers came over and the sky was black with them. Chester Wilmot was doing his recording, and I sat next to him. When the bombing stopped, after maybe an hour and a half, our wireless picked up some tank talk, because the heavy tanks of the sea-borne brigades were now going forward into the devastated area. He recorded that. Then he began describing the planes coming in: 'Oh, another plane's been hit; it's all right, everybody's getting out!' He had to say that they got out, or the people listening back at home would say, 'Could it be Dad, could it be my brother?' We had a good couple of days with him – lovely fellow.

At last came the break-out. Everybody had been sitting still for weeks but this was it! The 6th Airborne, with the Airborne Armoured Reconnaissance Regiment in the lead, tore east along the coast. We had the support of the Norwegian Brigade; we carried them on the tanks where we could, and we had quite a few upsets with the Germans as they fled from us, though, thank God, we didn't come up against many of their tanks. We had paras all around us. They were glad to see us. An infantryman is glad to see a tank, they loved us because they could use the tanks for cover. We were towing trailers, but the colonel would not have much of that, because it decreased a tank's manoeuvrability. But by then the paras had acquired a lot of vehicles of their own – Bren carriers and odds and ends. Our colonel had even acquired a Sherman, God knows from where, and we were still looking for something decent to shoot at when it broke down, and we hadn't any spares.

We were tearing along. The thought in everyone's mind was, 'We are going to be the first into Paris! The 6th Airborne Division is going to be the first into Paris!' and we were getting through pretty fast, the odd fight here and there, just a tank or two. Then the division was told to stop and it seemed that everything else that had landed in Normandy just flowed past us, and they are the buggers who went to Paris. Within five days we came home. We swam at Deauville – it was beautiful – but we never did see Paris.

CHAPTER NINE
SOUTH OF FRANCE
Operation Dragoon
1944

AFTER THE FIGHTING IN ITALY THE 2ND INDEPENDENT Parachute Brigade underwent training at Salerno before receiving orders to drop in southern France. On 15 August, the Brigade dropped at dawn around the village of Le Muy, north of Frejus. They helped take this important position astride the supply line to the German coast forces, making it possible for the landing and rapid advance of the US Seventh Army. Having taken all their objectives and linked up with the ground forces, the brigade returned to Italy on 26 August to prepare for their next operation in Greece.

CAPTAIN TONY FARRAR-HOCKLEY, 6th Parachute Battalion

For the drop into the south of France I was the 2 i/c of B Company the 6th Battalion. During the night of 14 October the whole force was taken over to France by American Army Air Force. We had no doubts about the Americans' expertise as pilots, but because of Sicily had good reason to have doubts about their skill as navigators. When we were within 30 minutes of dropping zone everyone stood up and began to make ready. I was, by arrangement, the last to go out as I had to make sure that the containers got away. We'd had trouble with this in the past – and it was very important for us that they should be released. The red light came on then the green. As I got to the door I threw the container switches but one jammed and I had to fiddle around with it. The crew chief, I think, for a moment thought that I was going to refuse and made an encouraging remark. I got the switch up and just had time to shoot him a furious glance before I jumped out. As I did so I saw below me what was, to all appearances, the sea and I was seriously

SOUTH OF FRANCE AUGUST 1944

FRANCE

Lyons

R. Rhône

Grenoble

Valence

Montélimar

FRANCE

Gap

ITALY

Nineteenth Army

Digne

R. Durance

Avignon

Nice

Fayence

Cannes

2nd Ind. Para Bde
operational area

French
Commandos

Aix

Le Muy

Fréjus

Marseilles

Hyères

Toulon

US VI Corps
French Army B
US Seventh Army

French
Commandos

MEDITERRANEAN SEA

0   10   20   30   40   50 miles

concerned about this grey shimmering mass some way below me, to the point that I got out the mouth-piece of my inflatable life jacket. However, it proved to be a layer of low cloud. I was scarcely through that by more than four or five seconds when I hit the ground. Due to the switch jamming, I was some way beyond the end of my stick when I landed. I removed my parachute, got my weapon ready and using a compass began moving in the direction of our objective. I came across a lot of French people standing outside a farmhouse and I made them a speech in my best French telling them that the day of liberation had arrived and how splendid it was for them, etc. There was no answer and then one of the women nudged one of the men and said in French, 'Tell him to shove off!' There had been a lot of noise of aeroplane engines, which was what had brought them out – and they thought we were SAS or whatever, and they didn't want to be involved. This incident brought me very rapidly to realize that the French were not all 100 per cent ready to take up arms themselves.

I pushed on and shortly after dawn a shot passed my head. I took evasive action and found I was alongside a German ammunition depot. I then spent quite a bit of time dodging a party sent out to track me down. I made no valiant attempt to stand against them, but after evading tactics came upon an American airborne unit. Shortly after, I found B Company who had been dropped accurately: the American navigators were spot on that day and dropped us well. However, George Seal, our intelligence officer, had been questioned about a lake in the vicinity of our drop during our briefing. He assured us that it was not a problem as there was no water in it. Unlucky man, he fell in it right up to his neck in water.

We then engaged in some skirmishing against the Germans who were pulling back fairly fast, and that was that. The American Airborne Force remained for a time, but the 36th and 45th American Divisions came ashore and took on the pursuit of the Germans, pushing them up from the south.

It's been said that the operation was a waste of time – possibly. The one thing it did was to liberate that area, and provide the Allies with airfields and territory of use to operations in the north.

MAJOR DICK HARGREAVES, 4th Parachute Battalion

Our action in the south of France was part of a secondary assault taking place two months after the main invasion of Europe on the Normandy beaches. The Americans and French were landing on the beaches between Fréjus and St Raphael, and our task was to wipe out the enemy between La

Motte and Le Muy, and to intercept any German armour heading for the Allies on the coast.

We were due to drop before dawn on 15 August. It was quite still, and I remember looking out of the door – we appeared to be flying over the sea. I wasn't too happy about jumping, but we'd all been drilled to go on the green light; so I thought, 'Here we go.' The 'sea' was early morning mist – really white mist – and as I came down I saw trees poking through it; I wasn't sure then if they were islands or trees. I actually landed on top of a fir tree which wasn't a bad way of coming down, except I nearly knocked myself out tugging my kit bag down. But I was very lucky because I landed in the right place, while Dan Calvert who commanded A Company was dropped 20 miles off target. He reckoned there was no way he was going to walk it, so he ended up getting a bus in!

I could only find two platoons out of the three to attack with, but there were enough troops to do what I had to do. We had a major objective which was the hill overlooking the main road where we expected to intercept the enemy coming from Draguignon. We were in position by early morning and had captured the southern part of Le Muy by nightfall, together with many prisoners. The German reserves never bothered to come down, so the action was over by the 17th, with only a few casualties.

We waited there for two or three weeks, and it was then we had our first encounter with the political side of war. The Maquis, the French underground movement, were carrying out reprisals on the civilians who'd been collaborating with the Germans. We didn't really know what was going on at the time, but there was a nasty blood bath; people were being shot or having their heads shaved, and it was very unpleasant and very disturbing, but there was nothing we could do about it. We used to describe the South of France campaign as boy scout stuff, but it wasn't really.

MAJOR BILL CORBY, 5th Parachute Battalion

When the 5th Scottish Battalion, part of the 2nd Independent Parachute Brigade got to the South of France on 15 August the navigating equipment of the lead ship broke down so the pilot couldn't locate the beacon set up by No. 2 Platoon (Pathfinders) that had dropped an hour beforehand. He thought the best thing he could do was to take evasive action as if he'd been shot down so that the second aircraft would take over and give a more accurate dropping signal. Well of course it didn't happen; everyone followed him and the net result was that half the battalion, if not more was scattered all over the place, 20 miles this way, or ten miles that – and we had three or four killed on the DZ. This was very unfortunate but none the less all battalion objectives and brigade objectives were quickly taken despite the confusion of the landing.

However this same confusion probably added to the success of the operation. The Germans must have been misled by reports of parachutists all over the place in a large area and probably thought many more had landed than in fact had. This, coupled with the bombing of communications, bridges and defiles, probably prevented a German counter-attack on the bridgehead and added to our success.

I was lucky, I landed right on the DZ. There wasn't much shooting, but a few seconds after landing, when I'd stuffed my parachute under a bush, I heard somebody coming through the undergrowth. I quietly cocked my automatic and waited. When he got really close I challenged him and he answered in what was obviously a Welsh accent – he was a Welsh Battalion signaller! He could easily have been one dead Welshman. Meanwhile Tucker, one of my platoon sergeants, had dropped on the roof of the local German headquarters. Of course the opposition came out and started shooting at him so he shot back with his Sten gun, killing the German adjutant and wounding two others. Eventually they made a hole in the roof and came up through and warned him that if he didn't surrender they'd chuck grenades into his bit of the roof valley – so he decided to call it a day. They took him down to the guardroom where there were another two people who had landed in the same position. He told the Germans that they were surrounded by two divisions of airborne troops, so they might as well chuck it in. He was right. At 9 am the gliders with the gunners and sappers had come in along with another American battalion. It was a marvellous drop – the whole lot were in the air at once. When the Germans holding Tucker saw this they surrendered straightaway, and Tucker led all 80 Germans out as prisoners.

The scattered nature of the drop led to many skirmishes and brushes with the Germans as parachutists moved in towards their RVs and objectives. One such engagement took place when an element of the 5th Scottish moved out of their objective area at Le Mitan to cut German lines of retreat from the coast. This small battle took place at a crossroads on the Fayence road near Cannes where elements of B Company and Battalion HQ were blocking the road. Withdrawing Germans with fixed bayonets tried to break through.

Mortars were ferried up from the Le Mitan area in a French producer-gas lorry towed by a jeep with a towrope made of parachute rigging lines, and the Germans were seen off. The bayonet attack was broken up by RSM

McChellam who gave a fine exhibition of firing the tommy-gun from the hip in the middle of the crossroads as the Germans charged in. For this he was awarded a Military Cross, a rare and well earned distinction for an RSM.

After this things quietened down and eventually we were taken down to the coast and evacuated by Liberty Ship back to Italy; we had been in France only ten days.

CHAPTER TEN
ARNHEM
Operation Market Garden
1944

IN THE AUTUMN OF 1944 THE ALLIED ARMIES WERE APPROACHING the borders of Germany after moving swiftly across France and Belgium. Field Marshal Montgomery proposed a scheme to concentrate the Allied strength in the north in order to outflank the German defenses along the Siegfried Line and the Rhine. General Eisenhower, however, favoured a broad front approach. He was only able to allot the 1st Allied Airborne Army to reinforce General Montgomery's campaign to seize the main bridges over the rivers Mass, Waal and the Neder Rijn by airborne assault, thereby opening the way for the 21st Army Group to swing through and onto the plains of Germany to encircle the Ruhr. This was Operation Market Garden. The airborne part of this operation (Market) was to be carried out by the 101st US Airborne Division who were to capture the canal bridges north of Eindhoven, the 82nd US Airborne Division who were to capture the river bridges at Grave and Nijmegen, and the 1st British Airborne Division with the 1st Polish Parachute Brigade who were to capture the most northern bridge at Arnhem.

On 17 September the huge air armada carrying the first lift of the three divisions landed. The 101st captured their objectives after some hard fighting. The 82nd took the Grave bridge at once but it took four days hard fighting to capture Nijmegen bridge with the Guards Armoured Division. Due to insufficient aircraft the 1st Airborne Division had to be landed in three lifts and the Air Forces insisted that they land on DZs eight miles to the west of Arnhem.

The 1st Parachute Brigade advanced on three routes to capture the main bridge at Arnhem but met with stiff opposition. Only the 2nd Battalion, with elements of Brigade HQ and a company of the 3rd

Battalion, were able to get through and seize the northern end of the bridge.

The Airlanding Brigade remained on the DZs and LZs to protect the second lift on the second day of the 4th Parachute Brigade and the remainder of the division. The Polish Parachute Brigade were due to land south of the bridge on the third day. Heavy opposition was encountered from the 9th SS Panzer Division which moved to block the route between the bridge and the DZs.

The 1st Parachute Brigade with the 2nd South Staffordshire Regiment and 11th Parachute Battalion were cut to pieces during the heavy streetfighting in their effort to reach the bridge. The 2nd Parachute Battalion became isolated in the houses at the northern end of the bridge but they held out for three days and four nights until they were pounded into destruction by the ever- encroaching German forces.

The remnants of the division formed a tight perimeter around the village of Oosterbeek to the west of Arnhem. The Germans concentrated their strength against this perimeter, attacking it ceaselessly with mortar artillery and tanks. Despite heavy casualties and no re-supply the defending forces held on, in a position which even the Germans called the 'Cauldron'.

Due to bad weather the Polish Parachute Brigade could not be dropped until the fourth day at Driel, south of the river. Despite strenuous efforts they were unable to get more than a few hundred men across the river to reinforce the division.

Following the delay of the ground troops of XXX Corps in reaching Nijmegen and their consequent inability to aid the beleagured division, Montgomery was forced to order the withdrawal of the remnants of the 1st Airborne Division. This was effected during the night of 25 September with little over 2,000 men escaping out of the original force of 10,000. The fatal casualties, including those of the Air Forces, totalled 1,916.

FLIGHT LIEUTENANT ALEC BLYTHE, RAF

After D-Day we transported supplies to Europe and brought casualties back. We were alerted for a number of airborne operations which were cancelled because of the rapid advance of the ground forces. Eventually in September the assault on Arnhem was launched and most of us were to tow gliders. As it was a long way to do this we were fitted with long-range tanks in the fuselage of the Dakotas. There were no fuel gauges with these tanks and we had been briefed that the tanks would get us to the Dutch coast, where we should switch on to main tanks for the remainder of the flight. Somebody had miscalculated, because most of us ran out of fuel about mid-Channel!

ARNHEM 17-25 SEPTEMBER 1944

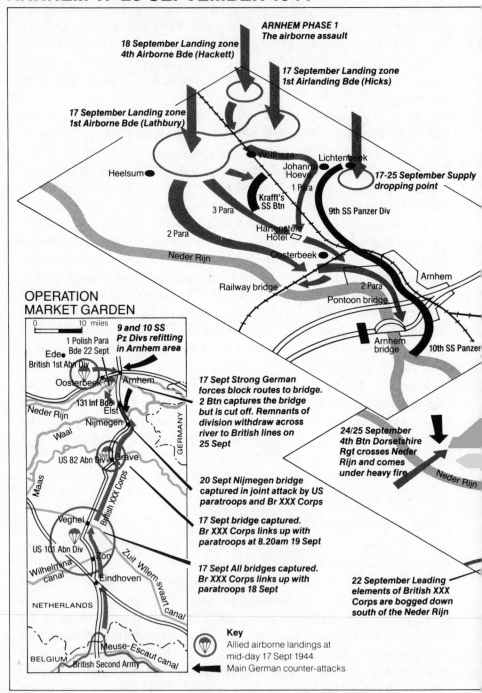

ARNHEM PHASE 1
The airborne assault

18 September Landing zone
4th Airborne Bde (Hackett)

17 September Landing zone
1st Airlanding Bde (Hicks)

17 September Landing zone
1st Airborne Bde (Lathbury)

Wolfheze

Lichtenbeek

Johanna
Hoeve

17-25 September Supply
dropping point

Heelsum

1 Para

Krafft's
SS Btn

3 Para

9th SS Panzer Div

2 Para

Hartenstein
Hotel

Neder Rijn

Oosterbeek

Arnhem

Railway bridge

2 Para

Pontoon bridge

OPERATION
MARKET GARDEN

0   10 miles

9 and 10 SS
Pz Divs refitting
in Arnhem area

Arnhem
bridge

10th SS Panzer

1 Polish Para
Bde 22 Sept

Ede

British 1st Abn Div

Oosterbeek

Arnhem

131 Inf Bde

Neder Rijn

Elst

Waal

Nijmegen

GERMANY

US 82 Abn Div

Grave

Maas

British XXX Corps

Veghel

US 101 Abn Div

Zon

Zuit Willem

Wilhelmina
canal

Eindhoven

vaart canal

NETHERLANDS

Meuse-Escaut canal

BELGIUM

British Second Army

17 Sept Strong German
forces block routes to bridge.
2 Btn captures the bridge
but is cut off. Remnants of
division withdraw across
river to British lines on
25 Sept

20 Sept Nijmegen bridge
captured in joint attack by US
paratroops and Br XXX Corps

17 Sept bridge captured.
Br XXX Corps links up with
paratroops at 8.20am 19 Sept

17 Sept All bridges captured.
Br XXX Corps links up with
paratroops 18 Sept

24/25 September
4th Btn Dorsetshire
Rgt crosses Neder
Rijn and comes
under heavy fire

Neder Rijn

22 September Leading
elements of British XXX
Corps are bogged down
south of the Neder Rijn

Key
Allied airborne landings at
mid-day 17 Sept 1944
Main German counter-attacks

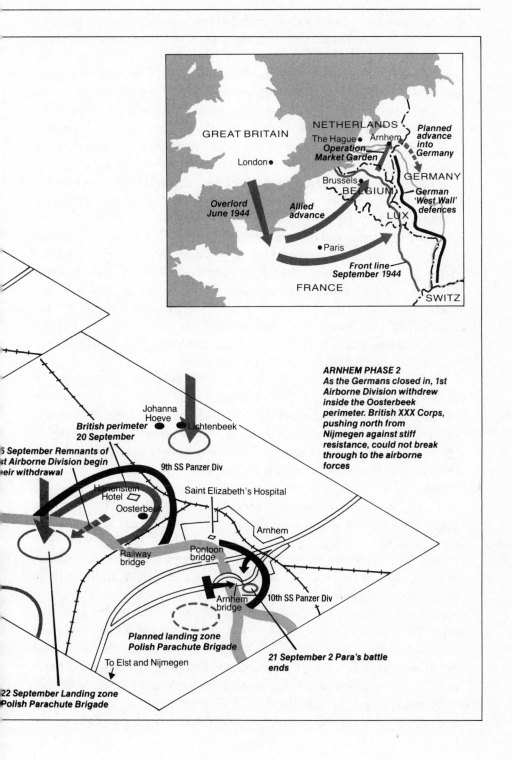

GREAT BRITAIN

London

London●

NETHERLANDS

The Hague● ● Arnhem

Operation Market Garden

Planned advance into Germany

Brussels●

BELGIUM

GERMANY

German 'West Wall' defences

Overlord June 1944

Allied advance

LUX

●Paris

Front line September 1944

FRANCE

SWITZ

ARNHEM PHASE 2
As the Germans closed in, 1st Airborne Division withdrew inside the Oosterbeek perimeter. British XXX Corps, pushing north from Nijmegen against stiff resistance, could not break through to the airborne forces

Johanna
Hoeve

British perimeter 20 September ● ● Lichtenbeek

5 September Remnants of st Airborne Division begin eir withdrawal

9th SS Panzer Div

Hartenstein
Hotel

Oosterbeek

Saint Elizabeth's Hospital

Arnhem

Railway
bridge

Pontoon
bridge

Arnhem
bridge

10th SS Panzer Div

Planned landing zone Polish Parachute Brigade

To Elst and Nijmegen

21 September 2 Para's battle ends

22 September Landing zone Polish Parachute Brigade

187

So there you were, towing a glider with 20 troops on board, suddenly losing power. Fortunately, almost to a man, the pilots immediately switched to the main tanks. We had a hand pump to force the fuel through and those lovely Pratt and Whitney engines immediately sprang to life. One wretched pilot's immediate reaction when his engines spluttered and started to stop was to pull the 'glider release'. I could see this unfortunate glider spiralling down until it landed on the sea. Meanwhile the pilot of the Dakota had restarted his engines and returned home. By some miracle the men in the glider were picked up by an air-sea rescue launch almost before their feet were wet.

The enormous train of tug aircraft and their gliders was most impressive. You were stimulated by a certain amount of fear, a certain amount of excitement at the very size of the force, and of course your adrenaline level was raised when attacked by ground fire. Whenever that happened a couple of Mustangs immediately appeared from nowhere and silenced the enemy on the ground. Despite the excellent support of these ground-attacking Mustangs, we had casualties. I watched a Stirling alongside catch fire, which from a small trail of smoke gradually grew until the aircraft was engulfed before crashing into the ground. Nobody got out. On that first day the opposition was comparatively slight and the glider landing was successful, despite collisions on the landing zones.

A second lift of gliders was flown in the next day, but I was not involved. On the third day we were briefed to resupply the 1st Airborne Division. It had been presumed that the Airborne Division would form a perimeter within the environs of Arnhem. In the course of the briefing we were told to drop at a particular DZ. Then as the briefing progressed the DZ was changed. Just before we took off we were told to drop as originally briefed!

Three Royal Army Service Corps despatchers pushed the panniers along rollers to the side door. When I went out to my aeroplane the despatchers were waiting. I said, 'Do you know where we are going?' They replied, 'No, sir.' I told them that we were going to Arnhem in Holland, which brought the response, 'That will be nice.' I replied, 'Well, it might be dangerous – we're liable to be fired at you know.' They just smiled. We used to speak of 'ten-tenths flak', meaning that the sky was just full of exploding shells. Well, as you approached Arnhem you got the impression that there wasn't wing-span room between flak bursts, not to mention the small arms fire – frightening! To my right a Dakota, I think flown by Flight Lieutenant Lord, caught fire. One of the despatchers was desperately trying to get out but he couldn't get through the door. Unknown to us the DZ was in the hands of the Germans. Whatever our troops may have done to attract our attention we probably wouldn't have seen. In any case, after the briefing change we would have ignored any ground signals as decoys.

Having dropped our load, we banked and weaved as violently as possible to avoid fire from the ground and headed home. When we got back to base my three despatchers were full of the joys and said, 'Well, sir, we thoroughly enjoyed all that weaving and turning on the way back!' Ignorance is bliss.

The resupply continued for a further six days and losses were severe but I never ceased to be amazed at the damage the Dakota could sustain and continue to fly. One came back with a hole in the fuselage large enough to push a chair through. Many flew all the way back on one engine. Others with lesser damage were repaired by the ever-willing and untiring ground crews to be ready for the next day's operation.

Arnhem was a disaster. We could have flown the 1st Airborne Division there in one day. It would have meant some of us flying two sorties in the day. In Burma we flew as many as three sorties a day. Had we delivered the division more quickly they would have had a better chance to form a firm perimeter and secure the bridge. Our resupply would have been successful instead of so much gallantry being wasted in sending supplies down to the Germans.

MAJOR IAN TOLER, Glider Pilot Regiment

There were endless delays and cancellations leading up to Operation Market Garden; order and counter-order and the consequent disorder were the order of the day. We spent the whole of one day loading and unloading our gliders; when the order changed for the sixth time that day, we just sat back and laughed. It was a good job we had some sense of humour. But we really were getting almost apathetic – we couldn't believe that it would ever come off.

In the end we had two days' notice to prepare the real thing. The plan for my glider pilots was to stay with their loads but one flight was to remain on the landing zone and then to protect Divisional Headquarters. One point was a bit dodgy though; I was told to take one flight (or 20 crews) straight to Nijmegen to help defend Corps Headquarters. All well and good, except that it would mean marching through twelve miles of enemy territory, assuming that we could get across the river! It was about the craziest order anyone had ever given, and I told them so in no uncertain terms.

The great day dawned fine and clear and I set off in a happy-go-lucky mood. We took off a bit nose-heavy, and it was a bit bumpy forming up; the neighbouring tug-pilot came a bit too close for comfort.

But when we met a squadron of 'Spits' and 'Tiffys' (Spitfires and Typhoons) going out, morale went sky-high. Suddenly we hit the slip-stream of some Dakotas and there was an almighty bump as if the glider had hit something solid. I thought the whole glider had gone, but calmed down when I found the controls were normal. Once we were flying over the North Sea we sighted the rest of the force, little specks in the sky stretching as far as the eye could see. Each 'speck' was carrying at least 20 men and a massive amount of equipment.

At last the Dutch coast appeared, and we saw black smudges ahead – flak – and we were heading straight for it. Morale pills would have come in very useful. Soon a Dakota burst into flames to port, and we saw the troops and crew bale out before the plane plunged into the flooded fields below. I concentrated on map reading and soon recognized the three rivers leading up to the target rendezvous. I told the tug pilot I was going into 'high tow', shouted thanks over the intercom and we were off, with a terrific juddering as if we were stalling, but dropping fast and heading straight for the landing zone. We landed well on target and as there was no opposition my co-pilot Shackleton and I got busy freeing the tail to let the load out. They didn't wait for the ramps to be set up, but were so keen they drove the jeep and trailer straight out over the three-foot drop to the ground! Gliders were all around us and the sun was shining. The quiet seemed ominous; there were only a few enemy around who surrendered as soon as we opened fire. They were a disconsolate bunch.

We were soon busy digging in, thinking in our inexperience that the enemy flak intended for incoming gliders was directed at us. Nearby the air was thick with paratroops. We had some sandwiches while I checked casualties: Angus's flight had got away with it, but a couple had been wounded from the other flight. That night I lay awake, too excited to sleep, and listened to our bombers going over.

Next morning was quiet and sunny: we washed and shaved at a local farmhouse, had breakfast and looked around. It felt just like being on exercise, only we saw the padre burying one of our men who'd died in the night. Perhaps it was the real thing after all. Later, two of my men turned up with a Bren carrier they'd salvaged from a Hamilcar; they were wonderful scroungers. Meanwhile news had come that General Urquhart had been captured. Brigadier Hicks was commanding the division and McCardie's South Staffords were to head for Divisional Headquarters with a view to supporting the 1st Parachute Brigade on the bridge at Arnhem. You used your own initiative as a glider pilot and I decided to stay with McCardie as I was supposed to find Divisional Headquarters anyway.

When the time came to move off we thanked our lucky stars for our Bren carrier and jeep; our rucksacks were hopelessly heavy and we didn't believe in carrying kit if we could help it. The jeep ended up pulling three trailers and a handcart, and we glider pilots made up the rear guard of the Staffords. Our advance was very slow along the main Utrecht–Arnhem road. It was empty of civilians and we felt pretty jumpy. There was a lot of firing in the direction of Arnhem – mortar, shells and tracer. All the civilians were in the air-raid shelters, one woman in hysterics, and with a house on fire down the road lighting up the whole area, Arnhem at night was beginning to look like Dante's inferno. In the end we stopped in a sheltered area and lay down on the pavement to rest. Amazingly enough, we did get some sleep, despite the stink of drains, continuous fire over our heads and mortars falling uncomfortably close. We were exhausted.

It must have been about two in the morning when I was called to the Staffords' temporary headquarters in a house which was in complete darkness except for a single candle burning in the parlour. It was a dramatic scene: windows full of bullet holes, one chap bent over a wireless and round the candle were McCardie, who looked a lot older than when I'd last seen him a few hours before, and Lieutenant Colonel Dobie, commander of 1st Parachute Battalion. The atmosphere was very tense; they'd had terrible communication problems but had just managed to get through to Lieutenant Colonel Frost, who was commanding the 2nd Parachute Battalion holding Arnhem Bridge. They had been reduced to about 80 men and were fighting for their lives: they must be relieved, as the success of the whole operation depended on their survival. McCardie was in a dilemma, though, as the divisional commander hadn't heard from Frost and had assumed he'd been wiped out, he'd ordered McCardie and Dobie to withdraw. I'd never seen two men look so grey and worn out – they'd suffered heavy casualties themselves – but they knew they couldn't let Frost down: 'We're going to go and help Johnny, come hell or high water.'

Zero hour was 3.45 am, and fortunately a message came through in time to tell McCardie that he'd made the right decision. Frost had got through to the divisional commander. I was all set to go with them but McCardie said my instructions were to protect Divisional Headquarters; I must go back. I must admit I was very thankful, but I felt I was deserting some very brave men on a forlorn hope. I wished them Godspeed and retraced my steps to where I'd left my lads lying in the gutter. Before we moved off we tried to locate the jeep with our supplies in it, but it was nowhere to be found and as dawn was approaching we had to sacrifice our stores and get moving. Not far along, there was a sudden burst of enemy tracer fire straight down the middle of the road. Thank God the Germans were so meticulous with their sights – and that we'd been trained never to march down the centre of a road; as we were all on one side – they missed us completely! No casualties at all so far, and we lay up in a garden until it was light.

Next morning we had no trouble locating Headquarters in a hotel! The atmosphere was pretty cheerful; they seemed glad to see us, and told me to rest up the men in a house in the hotel grounds. Someone cooked an excellent stew (rations were still going strong from our 24-hour packs a full 72 hours after landing!). That evening there were aircraft overhead – our first resupply – but I heard heavy flak and a Dakota went down in flames. We didn't know that the dropping zone was back in enemy hands.

Our peace was shattered by an order to take up defensive positions at once around the hotel. Shackleton and I went off on a recce and took over a small house, advising the occupants to leave. We spent a miserable night sharing a slit trench made for one; our legs were entwined in a most intimate fashion, we got endless cramps and every movement brought a shower of sand down on top of us. We slept sporadically – like animals, I suppose, waking up automatically at every noise or movement. That night a madwoman wandered around our position and away into the distance singing a wordless song in a high-pitched monotonous voice, continuing until she went out of earshot. It was as if she was afraid to stop singing at the peril of her life, and it was particularly eerie when the noises of battle died down; all you could hear was her weird voice in a background of complete silence.

The next day the sergeant major snooped around and returned with a beautiful BMW coupé which had belonged to the local Gestapo. We reckoned it would be ideal to drive into Arnhem in style in this beauty; we were still confident it wouldn't be long until we took the town, with the Second Army on its way.

After a recce I took up my headquarters in the cellar of a pavilion and the flight dug into their new positions. Next day the relative quiet was shattered by a whining, whistling noise and a series of sharp explosions, very loud and close. I dashed up the cellar steps to see Angus staggering towards me shouting, 'Andrews is dead.' Both of them had been in their slit trench a few yards from the pavilion when a mortar landed right on the lip of the trench, killing Andrews instantly and wounding Angus in the hand. I checked the rest of the flight and found they'd been plastered by a multiple mortar or 'Moaning Minnie'. Sergeant Raggett was killed in his trench by blast alone and two others had shrapnel wounds. I ordered everyone to dig down much deeper and get top cover on their trenches; lack of this had caused the casualties. An expensive lesson to learn, but it could only be taught by experience.

Shelling continued to be heavy the next day, and in moments of quiet the enemy tried another tactic, telling us through a loudspeaker that they'd captured Colonel McCardie and that it was pointless holding out. We replied with a burst of Bren-gun fire in the direction the voice had come from!

That day the shells were overshooting safely enough but on the following morning they really got our range. Our covering was blown in, my Sten gun blasted into the air and we were covered with earth; it was time to get out, and without a word we both jumped out and I ran three yards to the next trench saying politely, 'Mind if I join you?' as I dropped in. I was pretty shell-shocked by then – 'bomb happy'.

When I looked at the remains of our trench the next day I saw an unexploded shell lying just at its lip; if it had gone off, I wouldn't have been telling this story. I got back to Headquarters, where I spent the night, and at last came the order to withdraw. I was exhausted and was finding it hard to concentrate, and couldn't care less that I was unshaven and in a right mess. Colonel Murray was wonderful; he very tactfully suggested that if we were getting out that night we wouldn't want the rest of the Army to think we were tramps, and offered to lend me his razor. I got the worst off, and it was amazing how much better I felt both mentally and physically. And Colonel Murray was probably in a worse state of exhaustion than I; that was leadership for you.

A feeling of relief filled everyone as the time got closer for withdrawing, we didn't feel defeated as we'd lasted out nine or ten days when it should have been only 48 hours. As we approached the river the enemy started to mortar. Training told us to hug the earth, and thank God we did; I remember feeling something hot on the back of my neck but it wasn't until I undressed later that I found that my smock, shirt and vest had all been cut through by a piece of shrapnel. That's how near I was to being scuppered.

Getting down to the water's edge, I saw 'Shack' had been wounded and helped him into a boat; other boats were sinking due to shell or mortar fire so I decided to swim for it. The water was lit up by star shells and tracer, the fires of Arnhem burning in the distance, and mortar bombs exploding in the water – just like the scenes in the movies. Halfway across one of the Canadian Engineers' boats was chugging along, so not being averse to hitching a lift, I hung on, but in so doing lost my boots which I had hung round my neck in the approved fashion. That made it damned painful to march to the medical aid post, but it was worth it to get the wonderful cup of hot chocolate with lashings of rum.

LIEUTENANT COLONEL JOHN FROST, 2nd Parachute Battalion

In the briefing at Brigade HQ, near Grantham, on 15 September, Brigadier Lathbury's orders were that the 2nd Parachute Battalion was to take the three bridges over the Rhine; first the railway bridge, which was outside the town, then a pontoon bridge, and finally the main road bridge. I was to have some part of my force south of the main bridge, but the bulk on the north side. By the time we had this bridge, of course, we hoped that the rest of the brigade would have got into Arnhem and would be holding a perimeter north of the bridge.

I did think that having to take three bridges was asking rather a lot and I wasn't at all happy at having my force split by the river. I would have preferred if we had been given the task of taking the north ends of the bridges and somebody else had been told to take the southern ends, by dropping south of the river. Of course I never, never liked the business of having to drop so far from our objective, but even a cursory glance at the map showed that there was nothing more suitable north of the river than the dropping zone selected. But there was perfectly good terrain for dropping parachutists immediately south of the bridge. Shortly before take-off, we heard that the pontoon bridge had been dismantled and was not in use. My outline plan was for C Company to take the railway bridge, B Company the pontoon and A Company the main.

It was not an early take-off so we had time for a leisurely breakfast. In the mess everything was unhurried. One had the feeling that everything would go well. Outside it was a perfect day – clear, fine and cloudless. I checked everything with my batman, Wicks, and arranged for my shotgun and golf clubs to follow later in the staff car. As we moved down the drive the resident pheasants and partridges seemed indifferent, almost as though they knew that we would never be able to trouble them at any future date.

Anyway we took off from Saltby to do battle for a bridge that Montgomery urgently required. I was very optimistic because the German army had taken a tremendous hiding in Normandy and all the information was that they were a beaten force, retreating more or less in disorder back to behind the Siegfried Line into Germany, so I was expecting a fairly easy battle. We knew that XXX Corps, under 'Jorrocks', was coming up to cross over the bridges after we'd taken them. They were fresh, they had been rested, re-equipped, and one could see absolutely no reason why the thing shouldn't go according to plan.

As for us, we always had a few miscreants who absented themselves, but they had a sort of grapevine which seemed to tell them, wherever they were, that an operation was pending, so they ought to turn up. In fact one party of men arrived at Saltby in a taxi from London; morale was terrific. On the plane we read the Sunday papers, ate our sandwiches and smoked. Then, as we got over Holland, as the number one I stood in the door to make quite certain that we drop exactly where we expected, and we did. I had a perfect landing.

I made my way to our rendezvous to meet my battalion HQ where immediately I became aware of how badly the wirelesses were working. A lot of them had been packed away for some time, in anticipation of an operation, and they'd been netted for the terrain in Lincolnshire, which was open country. But as we left the dropping zones we were into heavily wooded country and soon into built-up areas as well, so they did not work at all well.

Before we got to Oosterbeek, where the railway bridge was, we did meet pockets of resistance which we dealt with quickly, without deploying, because once one diverges from the main objective people get lost, so I was determined to try and keep everybody as close into column as I could. One of the measures we took was to bring one of the anti-tank guns, which was normally at the rear of the column, up to the front to cover the main road. This was very effective against prowling enemy armoured cars.

When we got up to the railway bridge, C Company, under Victor Dover, who'd been briefed to take that, debouched from the column and under the cover of machine-gun and mortar fire got onto the bridge fairly quickly without much trouble. But, when the leading platoon was about half-way across, the bridge was blown up in their faces and they had to come back. The basic mistake of dropping airborne troops on the far side of a river, when you want them on both sides, now became apparent. Airborne troops were invented to land behind the enemy and not to cross obstacles in the face of intense fire.

Once we got to the main bridge it was getting dark so we quickly occupied buildings which dominated the north end and its approaches. Having established our position our main aim was to get across the bridge to the far side. A platoon of A Company started to move across. It was a horribly dangerous thing to do, even in the half light. As they started to move forward they were met by withering fire from a pillbox and an armoured fighting vehicle sited on the bridge. It was obvious that there was no future in a direct approach. Robin Vlasto's platoon 'mouseholed' through a number of buildings with PIAT bombs and then put in an attack on the pillbox with a flame thrower. The north end of the bridge was now clear, but just as we were about to make another attempt to cross, lorries drove up from the other side. We brought them to a halt near the burning pillbox which caused the lorries to catch fire. The Germans inside now became our prisoners. The heat from the burning lorries was so intense no further approach could be made that night.

With the bridge blocked I wanted to see if one of the other companies, who still hadn't emerged in my area, could get across the river. So I sent my chief engineer, George Murray, back to where the pontoon bridge had been to see if there was any way of getting across. He came back and reported that it was not possible, for no suitable barge or boat could be found. That made me all the more certain that there was no way of our getting across to the far side of the river. I then determined to make as tight a perimeter as we could to hold that north end, until XXX Corps came up from the south.

By dawn on the Monday, I felt quite happy about our situation at the north end of the bridge. I was confidently expecting the rest of the 1st Parachute Brigade and XXX Corps would be up with us in 24 hours. Not very long after first light a column of enemy armoured cars and half-tracks began to cross the bridge. This turned out to be the reconnaissance squadron of the 9th SS Panzer Division which really surprised me because we'd been given no information about the presence of such troops in the area. Things were not so good after all. Although three vehicles got through our anti-tank weapons, crews soon found their range and destroyed seven.

By this time we had about 50 men killed or wounded. We kept the wounded in the cellars beneath the main government building. I now wanted to concentrate as much as I could of the rest of my own battalion, because I realized that things weren't going very well for the rest of the brigade. I managed to get a message to Douglas Crawley of B Company to leave what remained of the pontoon bridge. He came up and strengthened the positions by the head of the main bridge, but I could get no word at all from C Company who were now in the area of the German headquarters which was in the western part of the town.

Then gradually the enemy pressure increased all through the Monday and Tuesday, so that by late Wednesday we were in a pretty bad state. We were running out of ammunition and there was no replenishment whatever. When you're fighting at close quarters, one thing you have to have is ammunition. I gave the order to fire only when absolutely certain of having a kill, but that allowed the Germans time to improve their position. We did get a certain amount of support from our own light regiment who were at Oosterbeek, three or four miles away, but that was the sum total of the support.

On Tuesday afternoon I was able to speak to General Urquhart on the radio. He had been incommunicado because he had gone to see what was happening to the 1st Brigade and had got bottled up in a house and was unable to take any part in the battle for that first day and a half. He wasn't able to hold out very much hope of relief. I told him about our shortage of ammunition, but I couldn't say too much because the Germans would have been listening in and if we started whining they would have moved in even quicker.

As the German attack continued, with 40-mm flak guns, the buildings one by one caught fire. Because they were largely built of wood they went on smouldering for a considerable time, so there was no refuge in the rubble, as there can be in buildings which are largely made of stone. There was no means of extinguishing the flames; they became no-man's-land. But we still kept the Germans off the bridge. Every time they tried, our mortars, artillery and machine-guns hit them hard. We eked out our 48-hour packs and found some apples and juicy pears. We also had to find food to give the 50 or 60 German prisoners. By the Geneva Convention one is meant to do what one can for them; but there wasn't very much we could do. They had to be watched carefully, because water was a problem and twice we caught them turning on a tap and leaving it running full blast. Water was not the only problem. The Germans had now brought up a 150-mm gun which fired a shell weighing 100 pounds from point-blank range. Every hit seemed to pulverize the masonry and scared us out of our wits. Something, I decided, had to be done quickly. It was lucky for us that our mortars scored a direct hit on the ammunition close by the gun, killing the crew in the explosion and disabling the gun.

All day the Germans pounded away at us and by now I was beginning to be very concerned about our wounded. Water had run out and many needed to be evacuated. During the day the Germans sent back to us, under a white flag of truce, one of our sappers who had been captured. He told me the Germans had sent him on trust to ask if I would meet the German commander under the bridge to discuss surrender terms. I said to him, 'That's complete nonsense, there's no question of that.' He then said, 'Well, sir, what shall I do – do I have to go back and tell them that, or can I stay and fight?' I told him to stay and fight and that they'd get the message anyway!

They certainly got the message because, towards evening, heavy tanks appeared, incredibly menacing and sinister in the half-light. Their guns swung from target to target, their shells bursting through our walls. Dust and debris was everywhere and the acrid smoke and smell of burning, combined with the intense noise, bemused us. But we had to stand our ground in order to meet any infantry advance. Casualties were increasing; our padre, Father

Egan, and Digby Tatham-Warter. Then our gunners brought a six-pounder round to the front and, combined with a bold move by the PIAT crews, we repelled their attack. Twenty yards behind us in the schoolhouse Major Tony Hibbert, the brigade major, and the rest of the brigade staff had to sit it out, sniping whenever they had a chance.

The last onslaught had left us weary. Arnhem was burning. It was as daylight in the streets, a terrible enamelled, metallic daylight. However, that night was more peaceful. But at dawn the attack began again. This was our third day of holding on under continuous enemy pressure. It was all the more demanding on our patience in that it followed on after the exhilarating journey from England, our early successful thrust into Arnhem, and the high expectations of reinforcement from XXX Corps.

It was during this attack that I was wounded by mortar fire, not badly, but extremely painfully, in both legs. After a time I was given morphia and taken down to the cellars. Freddie Gough assumed overall command at the bridge, but he used to come and refer any problems to me. We discussed doing a sortie and going northwards, but I felt it was much more important that we should stay in position, at the north end of the bridge, for as long as possible so as to give maximum help to anybody trying to cross from the south. So, even if we were left with no ammunition at all, we might have been able to do something to help them. There was, however, no way we could possibly move, we were absolutely sealed in by a ring of enemy infantry and armour.

On the final evening the Brigade HQ caught fire, but there was no water. Jimmie Logan, my head doctor came to see me and said, 'I'm afraid there is no hope of putting the flames out. Unless something else is done your 200 wounded are going to be burnt alive, including you, sir.' We'd almost ceased to be a fighting force because of lack of ammunition. The doctor then asked if he could try and make contact with the Germans so as to evacuate the wounded. The Germans agreed to a truce. Then everybody, including the SS, laboured with might and main, to get everybody out of the building, which by this time was blazing fiercely. After they'd got almost the last man out the building collapsed. Then our men dug positions in back gardens, hoping to be able to continue resistance somehow but when the morning came greatly superior numbers of German soldiers completely overwhelmed each group in turn.

I was taken to St Elizabeth Hospital but I knew that as soon as possible the Germans would evacuate us further. I'd taken off my badges of rank and hoped that I would be able to escape as a private soldier, but early next morning we were put into ambulances and driven right into Germany.

The Germans, and particularly the SS, were complimentary about the way we had fought the battle, but my bitterness was unassuaged. No enemy had beaten us before, and no body of men could have fought more courageously and tenaciously than the officers and men of the 1st Parachute Brigade.

CORPORAL STAN HALLIWELL, 1st Parachute Squadron RE

I was with the Para Engineers at Arnhem. When we got to the bridge it was dark. We saw these figures moving on it so Captain Livesey our platoon commander called out, 'Is that you, 2nd Battalion?' A burst of Schmeisser splattered against a wall, so it was obvious they weren't! He told us to occupy the office buildings, quite close to the ramp, leading up to the bridge, and we stayed there all night. Other Engineers had gone under the ramp, occupied a building on the opposite side, and ambushed some German armoured cars, which burned all through the night.

The following morning I thought we were a bit exposed using the windows so I reckoned it would be better if we knocked a hole in the wall at floor level and fired from there. I managed to get hold of a sledgehammer and while I was swinging this Ashworth was holding the long chisel. We got through the first layer of brickwork and I thought, 'One big blow and we'll be through'. It was still a bit dark, but I swung the hammer and brought it down, missed, and hit Ashworth smack in the face! You should have heard him! He lost three or four teeth and there was a lot of blood. I dragged him over to one of the medics, who asked what had happened. When I told him he laughed his head off. They plastered over his mouth and put a cigarette in and left him.

At one point about 30 yards in front of us was a tank with another close by. Major Murray studied it for a bit, and sent someone off for a PIAT firer. I thought there was nobody inside so Hicks and I ran towards it. As I got within 15 yards I saw one of its small guns traverse. I ducked down and my mate Hicks, who was right behind, was hit and killed. I don't know why, but I thought the best place was underneath the tank. As I lay there panting I could hear the radio, in German, talking to the other tank. Then he opened up with his main armament and nearly blew my eardrums. As if that wasn't bad enough, he began to start the tank. Then one of our lads hit it with a PIAT. I thought, 'Christ, I've had enough of this!' I crawled out and put my hands up, and was taken prisoner.

The Germans sent me back to Colonel Frost with a message! I agreed to go but at every corner I came to, some bugger fired at me. Eventually I found

Colonel Frost and delivered the message. He said, 'Well, if you go back, tell them to go to hell.' So I thought, 'I'm not going back to tell them that,' so I stayed.

From then on we were just being chased from building to building, hiding where we could. We sheltered in a room but the Germans set the roof on fire, and it just burned down on us – we were being roasted alive so we had to get out of that. We were really whacked. We hadn't slept for 48 hours. We had taken some pills to keep us awake, but we had used them all up. I'd lost everything because the Germans took my pack when they had me prisoner. I had nothing. We were pretty soon picked up and I became a prisoner once more. We'd done all we could.

MAJOR TONY HIBBERT, HQ, 1st Parachute Brigade

In July I passed out of staff college, and was posted to 1st Parachute Brigade as brigade major to General Lathbury. Morale wasn't exactly low, but everyone was getting edgy as they'd had six or seven operations cancelled since D-Day. I soon found myself rocketing down from Grantham to Moor Park once or twice a week to attend briefing sessions by General Browning on a series of operations which were first delayed then cancelled.

On 6 September we were given the details of the fifteenth operation in this series – Operation Comet. This involved 1st British Airborne Division taking on all the tasks which three divisions failed to complete ten days later. On its own, 1st Parachute Brigade had the task of capturing and holding Arnhem. I wish to God Comet had gone ahead. It could have worked; at that stage the Germans were still demoralized, still on the run and hadn't had time to regroup and reorganize. But Comet was cancelled.

On 10 September, the original D-Day for Comet, we were briefed for Operation Market Garden – a re-hash of Comet – but with three divisions instead of one, and with the whole of 1st British Airborne Division and Polish Parachute Brigade taking on the task of capturing Arnhem Bridge and holding it for 48 hours. There was a considerable gung-ho spirit and I'm sure that if somebody had offered to drop us in the middle of Berlin we'd have been as happy as sandboys. I believe Browning shared this over-optimism and was not as careful as he should have been when planning the Arnhem operation. Brian Urquhart (Browning's intelligence officer) came to see me after the briefing. He'd received confirmed reports that the 9th and 10th Panzer Divisions were in the Arnhem area, but Browning dismissed these and a doctor suggested that Urquhart was under stress and should rest. The operational plan was gravely flawed. Insufficient planes were allocated and of these something like 30 were taken to land the Corps Headquarters with Browning, south-east of Nijmegen, where they failed to influence the battle in any way. By dropping there he succeeded in putting himself out of communication with everyone in the critical first five days, and removing those planes from the 1st Division meant that we had to drop in three separate waves which ensured that the division could be taken out in bits by the Germans. A fatal flaw. The next disastrous decision was the refusal of the Air Force to drop the 1st Division anywhere near the bridge, on the basis of faulty intelligence which suggested that there were anti-aircraft guns on the bridge. Urquhart didn't have the experience needed to overrule both Browning and the Air Force. The only person who could have done that face-to-face was Eric Down, but he was no longer with us. These and other errors were leading to an epic cock-up.

After an uneventful flight we dropped on a lovely day with no opposition. John Frost, commanding 2nd Para Battalion, got off at good speed along the southerly route next to the river, followed by 1st Brigade HQ. Moderate fire opened up early on 1st and 3rd Battalion fronts. After we'd been marching for about an hour up roared General Urquhart. He was a reserved, gentle person but now he was really angry and asked me what the hell we were doing. I said we were advancing on the bridge, and he said, 'I can see you're doing that but you're moving too bloody slowly, get your brigade moving, Hibbert. Where's your brigade commander?' I told him he was up with the 3rd Battalion trying to push them forward faster, and off Urquhart went in a cloud of steam to find him. His parting words were, 'Unless we can get to the bridge before those bloody tanks this is going to be a cock-up.' I passed on the gist of the message to John Frost who was advancing along an unreconnoitred route and was up against more vigorous opposition than we'd been led to expect. We continued to advance behind the 2nd Battalion, and by now it was getting dark. We were in single file and were very strung out; it was our task to slip through to the bridge without getting involved in streetfighting and it was important we kept quiet as the Germans were only two streets away. However, every few yards Dutch civilians would come rushing out of their houses shouting 'Welcome!' at the tops of their voices and offering brandy and apples to the troops.

As we neared the bridge I managed to get radio contact with Brigadier Lathbury and told him that Colonel Frost, with the 2nd Battalion, was on the bridge and we (Brigade Headquarters) were about to join them. The route 2nd Battalion had taken was still clear so I suggested that he should side-step 3rd Battalion along the southern route and bring them onto the bridge. The first priority was to get to the bridge, and not to get engaged in street fights. But he said 'No.' They were too heavily engaged with the enemy and couldn't be disentangled at that time of night; they'd come through in the morning after resting. I believe that the moment that decision was made, our last chance of success was destroyed.

Meanwhile, Frost had captured the north of the bridge and established a perimeter while the Germans held the south very strongly. We set up Headquarters in a house 50 yards from John Frost's command post and took over the attic as it was the only place our wirelesses might work. There were six or seven of them and the place soon became rather conspicuous with aerials sticking out of every window and tile hole. At that stage we felt pretty cocky as we knew we'd achieved the first part of our operation order in taking the bridge: now all we had to do was hold it for 48 hours.

My first job was to inform Division that we were on the bridge. But that's when our real trouble started because not one of our wirelesses could pick up the faintest whisper from anyone in Northern Europe except John Frost who was all of 50 yards away. What use was I as brigade major if we couldn't get a single message through? I might as well take up a rifle, but I had to stay with the sets to be there when and if they started to work; we had to get the vital message through that we needed reinforcements, ammunition and food if we were to hold the bridge. It was also crucial that Division and XXX Corps were informed that we held the bridge. That evening we made two attempts to get a foothold on the south bank but both were repulsed with heavy casualties. Lieutenant Grayburn was wounded leading the attack over the bridge and was again frequently hit during fighting that evening and was finally killed by fire from a tank. He was awarded a posthumous VC.

By setting fire to buildings round the bridge we managed to keep the north end illuminated to prevent German infiltration. During the night Major Murray, commanding a detachment of Engineers, managed to reconnoitre the bridge and reported it was not prepared for demolition. So all we had to do was hold tight for 48 hours when 21 Army Group was due to relieve us from the south.

At 8 am on Monday a heavy barrage opened up on us and there was the sound of many tracked vehicles and revving of engines coming from the south. Most of us thought this must be the leading elements of XXX Corps coming to our relief, 24 hours ahead of schedule. But as the first vehicles became visible over the hump of the bridge the menacing black crosses quickly dampened our enthusiasm. During a brisk fire-fight two armoured cars, ten half-tracks, a tank and half a dozen lorries were knocked out and set on fire, completely blocking the north end of the bridge. The remainder of the column withdrew, leaving 70 dead but mortar fire and heavy artillery was now concentrated on us for the remainder of the battle and snipers and machine-guns kept up a steady fire.

At 3 pm one of our sets picked up 1st Para Battalion who reported that they and 3rd Battalion were fighting towards the bridge. They also told me that they had no news of Brigadier Lathbury. I therefore asked John Frost to take over command of the Brigade and to move in with me and he handed over command of 2nd Battalion. At 6.30 pm he ordered 1st and 3rd Battalions each to form a flying column with as much food, water and ammunition as they could carry to break through to the bridge by midnight. Our first priority was to hold the bridge.

At 7 am on Tuesday the barrage increased considerably as well as heavy infantry attacks on the perimeter with much hand-to-hand fighting. At 10 am one of our wireless sets got in touch with a Canadian unit in XXX Corps. We were able to report that we held Arnhem Bridge and that we were looking forward to their early arrival. They couldn't say on the air where they were but we got the impression it was still south of Nijmegen. Still a long way to go.

The fighting continued and supplies were getting desperately low, but our hopes were raised when at last, on Wednesday morning, one of our sets got through to General Urquhart. I sent for Colonel Frost to speak to him. The general thanked him for holding the bridge and asked him to convey his congratulations to all ranks. 'We're all proud of you. Just hang on and the Second Army will be through any moment now,' and John Frost said, 'Yes, but we need reinforcements if we're to continue the battle; we need ammunition and it wouldn't be bad if we had some food either.' Then the general suggested we should organize the local civilians to bring in food, ammunition and stores from some of the re-supply containers which had gone astray the day before. Colonel Frost told him that we were fighting in a devastated area, there were no civilians and we were surrounded in a perimeter of only 200 yards by a superior and somewhat aggressive enemy force, so it wouldn't be very sensible to go out on a foraging party. There were no containers nearby in any case. He reported that we had inflicted 300 to 400 casualties on the enemy.

That conversation didn't seem to me to be very productive and meanwhile enemy fire was increasing. I was scanning the road leading north from the bridge with my binoculars. Buildings were exploding with chunks of masonry flying in all directions, bullets were ricocheting from the walls and the road was covered in glass and debris. The noise was deafening.

Suddenly from a house about 250 yards up the road emerged a very dishevelled-looking woman pushing a brand new, immaculate pram, presumably with a baby in it. With her free hand she was waving frantically and I could see she was screaming hysterically as she weaved her way through the rubble. The small arms fire around her stopped instantly but the heavy guns continued. Miraculously she survived and when she got to about 100 yards from our HQ one of our platoons managed to get a Dutch-speaker to call her over and we got her under cover. The poor girl had completely lost her mind.

On Wednesday afternoon the position began to deteriorate rapidly. As the last of our buildings were destroyed or set alight, attempts to re-occupy burned-out ruins failed as the ashes were too hot. John Frost, Doug Crawley, Father Egan, Pat Barnett and Digby Tatham-Warter were wounded and Freddie Gough took over command.

By dusk Brigade HQ was being heavily shelled, the fires were out of control and the medical situation was getting pretty dire. In the basement of Brigade HQ we had by now nearly 300 wounded, many of them very seriously; they were packed like sardines and lying in the dark. They were now in danger of being burned alive as we had no water to tackle the fires eating into the house. Orders were given to evacuate the wounded from the cellar and to hand them over to the Germans under a flag of truce. The enemy took advantage of this situation to infiltrate our positions, and the perimeter defence was penetrated. The area round the bridge was ablaze and we no longer dominated it. We were down to around 100 unwounded and walking wounded, with about five rounds of ammunition per head.

We knew the division was still fighting five miles to the west and I felt we could be of more use back with them. I formed the survivors into patrols of ten men and an officer, with orders to return to the divisional perimeter. The first thing we found was that as the streets were covered in glass and rubble it was impossible to walk down them quietly. A patrol would go 'crunch, crunching' out; with ten people, you could hear the noise a long way off. In whichever direction the patrols moved, they ran straight into heavy German fire.

I took my section south-west, hoping to hit the river fairly soon, but, being last out, it was getting light and we made little progress before going to ground in a burned-out building. Some tried to bury themselves in the ashes and wait until the next evening, but if you have ever tried to bake a potato, that's what you felt like after about a quarter of an hour – so that didn't work!

The war correspondent Tony Cotterill and I plumped for a coal-shed which was so small that we hoped it would seem an unlikely place to look for two bodies. Unfortunately someone hiding near us fell asleep and started to snore so loudly that the Germans started ferreting around and soon Tony and I were hauled out, covered in coaldust, feeling very angry and foolish. They marched us off to the cathedral square where a depressing sight met our eyes. About 20 officers and 130 other ranks were being guarded by a large number of very unfriendly SS guards. This probably represented most of the survivors from the bridge. It was a great shock; we'd felt sure some of them would have got away.

That evening we were told we would be moved to another location; anyone breaking ranks would be shot. Freddie Gough put us through a quarter of an hour's parade drill before we set off: 'Let's show these bastards what real soldiers look like.' This boosted morale and restored our self-confidence which had been a bit shaken by the events of the last day. We marched very smartly, and as we went along we gave the local Dutch the Victory sign as they looked in need of cheering up too. This infuriated our German guards and they threatened to shoot us if we did it again – which we did whenever possible. We hoped by irritating them that we might get a chance to slip away, but there were too many of them around. They marched us to a small house on the outskirts of Arnhem and shoved us into a tiny room. It was here that Tony Deane-Drummond found a cupboard and we reversed the lock and left him in there with a few bits of bread and a jam-jar of water to keep him going.

A convoy of lorries soon arrived to take us to prisoner-of-war camp in Germany and this was our best chance to escape. I was in the last group to leave; our lorry was a three-tonner, open, with sideboards about three feet high and 30 of us, mostly officers, were crammed into it, along with two old Luftwaffe guards armed with pistols and rifles. There was a third guard with a Schmeisser on the front mudguard. The lorry tore off at about 60 miles per hour which was obviously intended to prevent us hopping off in transit. We continued to give the V sign to the Dutch as well as the odd German, and every time we did this the corporal on the mudguard lost his temper and stopped the lorry to tell us he'd shoot us if we did it again. But we carried on playing the fool, because every time we stopped it took some time for the lorry to build up speed again, and this was the opportunity we were waiting for.

We stopped for a third time for the usual tirade and I winked to Denis Mumford that we'd make a jump for it when the lorry got going again. I asked Pat Barnett next to me to keep the nearest guard busy and pulled myself over the side as the lorry started, the guard shouting, 'Nein, nein!' I hit the road fairly hard but nothing seemed broken though there seemed a lot of blood flowing. Denis was caught by the corporal's machine-gun as he climbed over a wall while I made a dash for the nearest side-turning, zig-zagging to avoid the bullets and crashing straight through the wooden fence at the end, Donald Duck style. Then I zipped through half a dozen gardens and decided to go to ground until it got dark. I covered myself with logs in a small garden hut and listened to the weapons still firing in the streets and the shouts of the search party. The noise eventually died down and, after a long time, I heard the lorry move off. My plan was to get well outside the town and approach a small farmhouse and try to find out where I was, get news of our troops and how to contact the underground.

Just as I was starting out I heard someone whistling, 'It's a long, long way to Tipperary' from a nearby house. I was tempted to go over but decided to stick to my original plan. After I'd gone what I thought was about two or three miles I found a small isolated farmhouse. I pulled hard at the bell and tapped on the window and eventually a small circular window in the wall slid open and a very suspicious man stuck his head out and shone a torch on me. I felt conspicuous in the torchlight and retreated hastily behind a bush while trying to convince him in German, French and English that I was a British soldier and would be very grateful for their help. I was wearing a groundsheet and my face was covered in blood and bruises and dirt so the glimpse he'd had of me can't have been very reassuring. It soon became clear I wasn't getting through and I left. I heard later that he thought I was a German deserter. When he heard the next day that I was a bona fide Englishman he burst into tears and spent the rest of the day bicycling about looking for me.

In the end I managed to contact the underground through another farmer and sheltered for three weeks with the family of Dick Tjeenk-Willink, a young member of the underground. It was here that I began to understand what the Dutch were suffering under occupation. So many of them had to live in hiding and the rest had to put up with the Germans stealing and looting and treating them with the greatest cruelty and arrogance.

During this time I met a local doctor whose daughter had witnessed my escape from the lorry and what happened afterwards. Denis Mumford, wounded by a machine-gun, had run into an orchard but was caught by a German. The corporal with the Schmeisser had completely lost his head and turned his gun on the back of the lorry, killing Tony Cotterill and another, and wounding eight more. He was threatening to kill the others when Freddie Gough stopped a German officer who was passing and got things under control. It's something that's been very much on my conscience ever since.

It wasn't long before the underground were hiding quite a number of escapers in our area, including Brigadier Lathbury. Altogether, there were about half a dozen officers of 1st Brigade, and we formed a new Brigade Headquarters in a butcher's shop in Ede. Every morning, dressed in an odd assortment of civilian clothes, we met in the back of the shop to prepare plans for a mass escape. A wonderful Dutchman, Alex Hartman, worked for a Dutch electricity company which had a private telephone line to Nijmegen which was held by our troops. Every morning he sent messages from our escape headquarters to the Second Army. This was a hazardous business because the calls had to be connected through a company switchboard which was manned at this time of day by a Dutch Nazi, so Hartman was really taking his life in his hands as he had to trust this chap. Fortunately the Nazi's patriotism overcame his political feelings. Through this telephone link we were able to plan an escape route down to the Rhine, and Second Army promised to send boats across to meet us. Altogether there were 130 escapers, of whom all but ten belonged to the 1st Airborne Division.

We were determined that we should go out as a fighting patrol, and arranged over this telephone line to have weapons and uniforms parachuted to us near Ede.

On the night of the escape, I was in charge of a group of 60 who were due to rendezvous in a hut in the middle of the forest. I was delighted, when the last party came in, to find that it was led by Tony Deane-Drummond, safely escaped from his cupboard. We changed into uniform in the hut and collected and cleaned our weapons. A wonderful Dutch Resistance leader called Wolff appeared out of the darkness with three magnificent old charcoal-burning lorries for transport. The lorries were open, with sides about two feet deep, and as we were all in British uniforms, and with our weapons, it seemed unwise to be seen sitting boldly upright in the lorries. We found a great pile of potato sacks in the hut and I ordered everyone to lie face down in the lorries in two layers: the people at the bottom would have a rough old ride as the lorries had few, if any, springs! Then we would lay the potato sacks on the top. There was some reluctance to volunteer for the bottom layer.

The Dutch drivers took us all the way through the woods to Renkum past two German posts where we were stopped and then down to about a mile short of the river. We stopped in a little lay-by, and I went round to the back and said, 'Everybody out, and keep bloody quiet because there are

German posts all round here.' Needless to say – you know what British troops are – there was a certain amount of 'Fuck you', 'Christ, watch out . . .' 'Prison camp would be better than this!' While they were getting out and making too much noise a German cycle patrol came along with a lot of tinkling of bicycle bells and cries of ''Raus! 'Raus!' When the troops heard all this tinkling of bicycle bells they politely stood to one side, and allowed them to pass. The patrol didn't seem to notice a thing! We then had to make our way in pitch darkness, led by Dutch guides, to the crossing point of the river about two miles away. This entailed moving between German posts no more than 100 yards apart in places; it was a heavily protected area. Digby Tatham-Warter told the escape party, 'Now, you have got to hold onto the coat, or whatever, of the man in front and don't for God's sake let go. The important thing is to be absolutely silent – the Germans are only a few yards on either side and there are 130 of us to get through.' Well, we were climbing over hedges and dropping down ditches about eight feet deep and climbing up the other side; it was difficult to do it in silence. The Germans must have heard us, probably saw us, but maybe they felt that anyone who was making such an enormous amount of noise must be one of their own patrols. Either that, or there were so many of us that they felt the sensible thing to do was to keep quiet, because if they started shooting they would probably get shot at even harder. However, the moment we got down to the river we ran into two German patrols. This time we fired and they disappeared pretty rapidly.

Exactly at midnight a Bofors went off over the river, we shone our torch back, and the assault boats came and took us over. On the other side we were ferried away by jeeps along a road parallel to the water. I volunteered to sit right on the front bonnet to guide the driver as, of course, there were no lights. We were going fairly fast when the driver went slap into another jeep coming from the opposite direction. I moved my legs and feet at some considerable speed or they would have been chopped off at the knee. As it was, I just raised them in time, did a triple somersault, landed in the road and bust my leg, and spent the next three months in hospital. So a thoroughly unsatisfactory battle ended in a thoroughly unsatisfying anti-climax.

CORPORAL RAY SHERIFF, 3rd Parachute Battalion
At Bulford the 3rd Battalion were trained like a regiment of guards. That was J. C. Lord's handiwork – our regimental sergeant major. He always had the usual Saturday morning parade and he'd put us through hours and hours

of drill, making us get it absolutely perfect. He'd stand there on a table which made you feel uncomfortable to start with, gripping his pace stick, shouting order after order. It wasn't that we loathed him, but you didn't like anybody who shouted at you!

Once I had to go to his office and he said, 'Why don't you try, Corporal? You'd made a good NCO if you would only pull your socks up, show a bit more enthusiasm.' I never really did, though.

We were at Spalding before going to Arnhem and we were all confined to barracks for quite a long time; there were about 16 alerts during that time, so the chaps were getting fed up with being confined to barracks. Now you could nip off into Spalding – there were lots of pubs there – and at one stage the nipping off got so bad that Lord said he wanted two NCOs to go round these pubs and get the men back. So another NCO and I were detailed to go round together. We looked through the blackouts and in one particular pub we saw two of our chaps with a couple of females. I said, 'Right, we'd better get in here and get rid of those.' So we went in and sent the blokes off and then we went after these two females. We walked all the way back with them and they said, 'Come in.' My mate went to another house up the street, and I went with this particular one and she got me some egg and chips, which was super, and a cup of cocoa. Then, we went upstairs. Trouble was, I was all kitted up in full para gear. I had my smock with all the big pouches, grenades, my jacket, then a string vest, big boots . . . I finally got this lot off and got into bed when all of a sudden there was a knock on the front door and I said, 'Who the hell . . .?' 'It's probably my husband.' I said, 'What shall I do?' She said, 'Don't worry, he'll be drunk for one thing and the second thing he'll want something to eat, so when you hear us down there, just get dressed and nip out the front door.' I got dressed and stuffed most of the things in my pockets, put my boots on, no socks.

It was a moonlight night. I looked and there was a lovely patch of freshly dug soft soil below the window. I didn't fancy going down the stairs, because I might meet the husband coming up so out I went, did a lovely landing. Just as I was getting up easy someone put their hand on my back. I thought her husband had come out the back door, so as I was coming up I swung round and hit this bloke. It was only my mate, who'd come to get me! He'd gone back to camp and had found out that we were on the move, at two o'clock. He had a bike, so I sat on the cross-bar and he rode us back to camp. Just as we were going past the orderly room, who should walk out but J. C. Lord. Of course, he didn't have time to do a lot then because everybody was on the move and we had to go and pick up our chutes from the hut, but he said, 'I shall want to see you after this operation.'

Lord seemed to have a habit of turning up when I was in trouble. In Africa, I was wounded – hit in the chest – so I took out my field dressing, stuck it on and sort of half rolled and struggled to the bottom of a ravine to get some help. I was walking along, crouched over, clutching this dressing and bleeding pretty badly when who should appear in front of me but J. C. Lord. 'Corporal Sheriff,' he said, 'if you can't walk in a soldierly manner, lie down!' So I lay down to attention, arms at my sides while he stood over me, holding a Sten gun in his right hand. I really thought he might just shoot me. But he said, 'What's the matter?' and I said, 'Bullet in the chest, sir', hoping for some sympathy. He looked at me and he said, 'You haven't shaved!' I said, 'No, sir, I haven't.' 'Why?' 'The Germans attacked at reveille; I didn't have time.' 'No excuse!', he said. He knelt down and took out a packet of Woodbines, put one in my mouth and then went away and got a couple of stretcher bearers who took me off still lying to attention.

On the second day at Arnhem I was blinded. I lost all bearing; I was being bundled about from one place to another. At one stage I was put on a table in a kitchen and I was shouting for water. They wouldn't let me have it – they reckoned I had a stomach wound – but I didn't and I was so bloody thirsty. Terrible. In another house one of the medics said to me, 'Would you like a biscuit?' There were plenty of biscuits, so I said, 'Yes'. I ate one of them but I didn't have sufficient saliva to swallow it – I couldn't get it down. It must have been two days or more since I had swallowed anything at all, so he said, 'Would you like some jam on it?' I thought that might make it better, so off he went and came back with two biscuits covered in jam, which I ate. It wasn't long after that I was violently sick and I couldn't understand why. I put it down to shock.

When we got to Stalag XIB we were talking one day and one bloke said to me, 'I remember seeing you, Ray, in that house,' and I said, 'That wasn't the one where I had the biscuits?', and he said, 'That's it. Do you know why you were sick? When we first went in there, we brought a German in who'd had both his legs blown off, and we put him in this bed with white sheets. When he died, we had to throw him out of a window as we couldn't go outside. And on the bed there was a sort of red cross where his legs had been, so we added to it with strawberry jam making a clear red cross on the white sheet, and hung it out the window.' When I'd said I wanted jam, they'd gone and taken it off the sheet. So it was German blood, stale blood – that's what made me sick. For many a year after I never had strawberry jam.

I came to Stalag XIB quite late on as I'd been dropped off at several hospitals to see if they could do anything for my sight and to operate on my bad leg. The day I arrived it was freezing cold – mid January by then – and the Germans put me on a pile of straw in a wooden hut. Although I was blind I could tell the place was crammed with bodies, all wounded; it stank to high heaven. Terrible. I knew by now I was blind for good, and I sat on this straw, surrounded by the noise of foreign voices feeling very alone and pretty scared.

The world at that moment was very dark. I fell half asleep – then I heard someone come marching up towards me and through that maze of horror came the clipped and orderly voice of J. C. Lord. 'Hello, Corporal Sheriff, how are you?!' I couldn't believe it, I thought I was still dreaming. I instinctively wanted to get up, stand to attention. He said, 'That's all right, Corporal, stay where you are, there is no need to get up.' But I staggered to my feet and managed to stand to attention and said, 'It's lovely to hear your voice, sir.' That moment was the turning point for me; life would be OK again. It was a real life-saver.

PRIVATE JAMES SIMS, 2nd Parachute Battalion

Before we got on the aircraft they gave us bacon sandwiches and tea – I don't think they could have given us anything worse! It was a terrific atmosphere, just like a picnic; everyone was really keyed up. I suppose nerves played a part to a certain extent, but everyone was shouting and laughing. Along went a truck with a camera crew on the top, filming us all jumping up and down, cheering, putting on a show for the families. It was just like a Sunday School treat. Of course we didn't know what was in store for us, but morale was sky-high; at last we were going, having been stood by for something like 16 operations.

Of course, I wouldn't have been on it, only for a trick of fate. There were three of us – a fellow called 'Brum' Davies, myself and a young Geordie, we were all only 19 – and Colonel Frost said, 'You're too young to go in the battle, but if you follow the Second Army with the baggage train, you'll see something of what war is all about. When we're victorious you'll meet up with us north of Arnhem.' At the last minute, however, three old sweats went absent thinking it was just another false alarm and they couldn't find them. They went round the fleshpots of Nottingham shouting their names out through loud-hailers, trying to get them to surface, but they didn't want to know. So we got roped in and had to go.

On the DZ I met Sergeant Kalikoff who had lost his kit bag. I couldn't help laughing because he had made us practise days on end with our kit bag attached to our leg so we didn't lose it, and he was the only one that had! I hoisted my 60 pounds of mortar bombs on to my back, together with pick, shovel, rifle and small pack and looking like a Christmas tree went off to find the others. We formed up and got an ironic cheer because we were about the last to arrive. The rest were already starting off on the way into Arnhem – Colonel Frost was there, Lieutenant Woods, and already we had casualties, with one or two missing. We had four mortars when we took off, but only two ever got into Arnhem. We were pretty sure one bloke went in the Rhine with the base-plate attached to him.

We started off into the town; everyone thought it was a sort of walk-over really, because we had been told we wouldn't meet much resistance, only line-of-communication troops and second-rate German personnel, which I don't think exist! One thing that did hold us up a bit was the Dutch people greeting us and giving us drinks, tomatoes, flowers and saying, 'We've waited four years for you!' From a window a really beautiful dark-haired girl looked down at me and whispered 'Goodbye,' which gave me a shiver – I could have done without that. Our officer got quite annoyed because we found it a job to get along through the crowds, we had to get on and take our objectives. The Germans left odd machine-gunners behind to hold us up. These men were very brave. They were obviously going to get it, but they did their job. You see, we were trained to dive into the nearest ditch or take cover if the enemy opened fire, whereas the Americans were trained to stand up and fire back, which takes some doing. I think the Germans and Americans were attacking armies, while the British and the Russians were more defending. That was what made Arnhem such an epic – because it was the best attacking troops in the world (the SS) against the best defending troops (us).

Our own platoon was strung out along this hedge, and all of a sudden this girl screamed and ran indoors. As she slammed the door a German machine-gun raked the hedge and caught 'Brum' Davies in the stomach and he fell dead. We lay there exposed behind the hedge, while Lieutenant Woods dashed for the cover of a house and fired at the German machine-gunner. He shouted for us to get up and move; it took a tremendous effort to do that. Our sergeant, Joe Hamilton, kicked our backsides and told us to get on with it – a very brave man. Another time we were at a sort of crossroads, and when the enemy opened fire, whether it was because it was getting dark, or because they were using incendiary ammo, bullets lit up my officer's face – they were that close. I pulled him back and then ran back to get assistance. I stopped at a jeep and said, 'What mob are you?' This chap said, 'We're the Royal Army Service Corps,' and I said, 'Christ, have I run that far?' Everybody laughed, and I turned round and made my way back to

Lieutenant Woods. He climbed into a Bren-gun carrier and ordered the driver to head straight for a machine-gun that was giving us trouble. He fired straight at it and got the gunner.

As we ran we passed an SS police barracks with several men dead outside. Slumped across a machine-gun were two bodies in Luftwaffe blue. They were a boy and girl about my age. She was lying beside him with the ammunition belt threaded through her fingers, her blonde hair stained with blood.

We gathered ourselves for the assault on the road bridge, which was about another 200 yards away. The rifle companies were expected to take it; we were just there with the mortars to support. But by the time they neared the bridge they were badly depleted through casualties, and so it was decided that we would go in as reinforcement. We could hear the rifle companies ahead screaming 'Wahoo Mahomet!' and firing and bombs going off. So Lieutenant Woods said, 'Right, follow me,' and he started off with us all spread out in a line behind him with fixed bayonets. Luckily for us, by the time we got to the road bridge what was left of the rifle company had taken the houses at that end. Some of the mortar platoon were so charged up with blood-lust that they didn't know where they were or anything, so Lieutenant Woods had to smack them and shout at them, and gradually they became human again. It was really quite weird.

Colonel Frost told my lieutenant to get himself a house and gather what was left of the platoon, and everybody else got different houses and barricaded them. We had got the north end of the bridge under our control, but we couldn't capture the other side. The mortar platoon had only two mortars, which were put on this island in the middle of the road where we dug slit trenches. There were two mortar crews, about three men in each, and about six of us in these slit trenches. The remainder of the platoon were holding a house just across the way.

This was all about tea-time, but it was quite dark. I was sharing a slit trench with this chap who had been at Dunkirk, Narvik, and God knows where – he'd been everywhere. His name was 'Slapsie', after Slapsie Maxy Rosenbloom. We had a bit of army slab cake between us and I was fed up with this digging. We were exhausted, but he said, 'Tomorrow morning it won't seem half deep enough, keep digging.' I said, 'Well, how are we going to get out of the damn thing?', it was getting so deep. I slept all through that night and when I woke up Slapsie was sitting there, looking at me, full of admiration. He said, 'Be careful but take a look over the top.' When I looked there were dead Germans carpeting the road. I said, 'Where have they come from?' He said, 'They attacked during the night – I couldn't wake you so I had to stand on you to defend the position, you slept through it all!' Slapsie thought I was a cool customer and I began to get this completely undeserved reputation for being cool under fire.

There were Germans forming up to attack across the bridge, and we engaged them. With Lieutenant Woods we made an OP in what we called the 'White House'. He gave the fire orders, and since our walkie-talkies wouldn't work, I was shouting them down to Joe Hamilton and Joe couldn't understand why he could hear these orders when he knew he wasn't hearing them through the set! I was shouting them out of this window – I had to be very careful, there were a lot of snipers about. My officer noticed a little concrete emplacement from behind which came a puff of smoke. It was obviously an enemy mortar. They were utilizing the mortar's high traject-ory, firing at our positions. We gave the orders and one of our mortar bombs must have landed right on the base-plate, and blew it up. Our men were very expert, but had we known the Germans had all this armour we would never have taken mortars, we would have taken more anti-tank guns, instead of which we only had about three which were manned by the Airborne Artillery. If we hadn't had them I don't think we would have been there as long as we were. They did wonders.

We saw an ambulance coming up the road. A chap in the White House fired at it and the officer who was behind said, 'You damn fool, don't you see the Red Cross?' As he said that the doors opened and out came all these fully armed SS, charging. They didn't even get to shelter – they were all machine-gunned in the street.

There were individual acts of great heroism, I saw a German tank coming down the road. This para – he was quite old – came out of a house and got down in the gutter, lying full-length, with his PIAT. The tank was so close to him that it couldn't depress its machine-guns. He just fired and hit it. The whole thing sort of lifted up, blew up and caught fire, and he just walked back in.

We had a Welshman in the White House who was a sniper. He waited practically the whole morning to get this German, who was in a church behind a grille. He waited with his rifle trained on this spot, and never moved, and eventually the German either wanted to relieve himself or had cramp and got up on one knee, and he caught him. After one German attack an SS man was left in the road. He was badly wounded yet he pulled himself hand over hand right across the road to the pavement, to where he had only to put one hand out and he'd have been in his own lines. This Welsh sniper just put a bullet through the back of his head. That upset me – not only me, it upset quite a few of us; nobody likes snipers – and I said,

'What the hell did you do that for? He was out of the battle.' The Welshman said, 'Well, he was the enemy, he was a German wasn't he?' But then other things happened that sort of evened everything out. Two of our Airborne medics carrying a stretcher ran out to get another German soldier – this was the next day, Tuesday. The stretcher-bearers were unarmed, and what they were doing was obvious. But a German machine-gun opened fire, and the front man crumpled in the gutter. The man at the rear just made it back. It was an act of murder.

Then this Scots sergeant came into the building. He'd come with Colonel Frost, and I don't know why, but he wasn't very keen on me. He said, just casual like, 'Oh, you know the Mortar HQ, slip over there and get my small pack, I've left it behind.' This road was being swept by machine-gun fire, but you didn't disobey an order, and all I could do was say, 'Right, sergeant'. Somebody let me out of a window on a side street, and I had to use the dead body of a German as a stepping stone. He'd got all his medals on and my heel plates clicked against them. I was a good runner but I think that was the fastest I have ever run in my life. German machine-guns had a far faster rate of fire than ours and as one opened up on me it sounded as if bullets were eating the ground up quicker than I could run. It turned my legs to water. Anyway, I made the mortar pit, and tumbled in on top of these men who were having tea out of an elegant tea service. 'Would you like a cup,' they said. My hands were shaking so much with fright they had to hold them steady round the cup and make me drink. They had settled down for the rest of the war. After I'd had my tea I reluctantly left them and under fire ran to a house where a sentry told me I was on fire. I had actually been hit by an incendiary bullet. Another bullet had gone into a tin mug in my small pack which obviously saved me. I had been hit twice without knowing a thing about it. There was a fellow there, young Peters, he was brewing up and he had two holes in his Denison smock – a sniper had shot at him twice, and he hadn't known, he was so busy making his tea.

Inside the house I found the pack, but I never went back. The battle deteriorated and things got to such a state that when I set out again I got no further than a slit trench on the island. I spent my second night at Arnhem there. A while later, I got back to the mortar platoon house, where I learned Slapsie had been killed. I couldn't believe it. Slapsie was indestructible. I was stunned, so much so that when Sergeant Smith saw how it had affected me he gave me a great swig of cherry brandy. I must still have been feeling all warm and comfortable when I volunteered to go and get the Bren gun left on the island. It was about 15 yards there and back. I ran out, and there wasn't a sound. I grabbed this Bren gun, but there was no magazine. When I got back the sergeant wasn't too well pleased. I rather half-heartedly offered to go again, but he decided not to tempt fate twice.

I lay on a bed squinting down the barrel of my rifle trying to see through the smoke. When it did clear I could see tanks blazing and dead bodies everywhere – mostly German. There was another para on the bed and between us was a big box of rich Dutch chocolates. The bed was piled with beautiful silk underwear and stockings and as I ran these through my hands I wondered if I'd ever feel the soft skin of a woman again. As I looked in the corner of the room there was one of our lads laid out. He'd been hit full in the face by a sniper's bullet. Someone had put a handkerchief over it. Only a few weeks ago I'd falsely signed him a sleeping-out pass so that he could see his girlfriend.

On Tuesday night we heard tanks coming across the bridge. Somebody said, 'It's the Second Army,' because that's the route they should have come, but of course it wasn't. It was Tiger tanks bulldozing all the wreckage so they could get at us. They put tracer fire over the White House which was their two-minute warning that they were going to shell us. We could either get out or stay put. Of course, with the Paras, there was no question of surrendering. They hit with one shell and the whole building seemed to shake, and with the second shell, the walls went outwards, and the floors and roof fell in. There was one scream and this solid sheet of flame went up. We all stood up, automatically, and turned towards the door, and Sergeant Jackman said, 'Where do you lot think you're going?' Silence. 'Right,' he said, 'everybody downstairs. Sergeant Kalikoff, choose six men to hold the house till the last. The rest of you get outside, and dig in.'

I got hold of a pick, and just as I went to break the ground there was a tremendous explosion. A shell landed just behind me and six fellows were literally wiped out, killed straight away by the explosion. Everything went red, my head seemed to swell up and felt as if it would burst out of my helmet. I knew I had been hit, then I heard a voice behind me say, 'Christ, I'm blind, I'm blind.' This Irish chap was holding his head and subsiding into this half-dug slit trench – he just collapsed. I said, 'Hang on, Paddy, I'm coming,' and I turned to walk over to him, and just fell down and passed out. Two fellows came later and carried me down into the cellar in HQ. It was a terrible sight because there were all these wounded men, more or less one on top of another. It was a sort of warehouse, and there were these great big ledgers – they were so big that when they opened them up they were like beds – and they put men on them. All I could think of was all these neat entries made out by some Dutchman, and we were ruining them all, bleeding to death on them. I was having a weird dream about Valhalla and

God knows what, and I must have screamed out. The orderly came over to me and said, 'Oh, you're still alive' – he obviously thought I was going to die, the other two on either side of me were dead by now – but I was stuck to the floor by another man's blood. When they pulled me off the deck there was a thick sticky, tearing sound, and the orderly said, 'I think you had better come back in the land of the living.'

They placed me on a ledge in the main cellar beside a badly wounded Scotsman and some others, and I kept on lapsing into semi-consciousness. One minute I was listening, taking it all in, the next I was miles away, in a dream world. I don't know how much time went by, but I kept on hearing British boots charge past, shouts, battle cries in English, effing and blinding and explosions, and then that would vanish and I would hear jackboots running over and shouts of 'Sieg Heil', Schmeissers going, more screams and shouts. This went on all the time – just as if they were fighting over our bodies. By now the building was burning, right down to the first floor almost, and we were in dense smoke. The colonel ordered all those that could to make a break for it. They roped together those that were blind but otherwise fit, and some of those who wanted to carry on. Then the medical officer contacted the Germans. A German officer arrived – he was high-ranking, with all the epaulettes, the Iron Cross – and he looked absolutely shocked. He sized things up, rapped out orders, and German efficiency took over – down they all came. The Germans carried everybody out. When we came out of the building I was astounded to see how far the fire had got. There was no roof, and the flaming timbers were falling down all round us.

Then this great big German soldier, with a silk scarf round his neck, came up to me and said, 'Good fight, eh, Tommy?' You'd have thought we had just finished playing football – you wouldn't have thought we'd been in a battle trying to kill one another.

Eventually after a number of days I found myself a prisoner in Stalag XIB. The conditions were pretty terrible, there were practically no medical supplies and there were no German medical orderlies. Myself and another badly wounded man had to do everything for the men in our hut, two of whom had amputations. As we both had leg wounds (mine were to remain open until I returned to England eight months later) we had to hop around as best we could. There was one RAMC orderly who came up from the main camp each day and told us what to do.

One morning I saw RSM Lord of the 3rd Battalion coming towards me. He was tall, slim and immaculate in battledress, with red beret exactly an inch above the eye. His badges and buckles shone like jewels and his black boots were like glass. I automatically adjusted my collar which was undone and put my beret on straight. I had never met the RSM. 'What battalion are you from?' he asked. I told him the 2nd Battalion. He asked me about the other wounded men and his expression hardened. Then suddenly he gripped me by the shoulder and said, 'Don't let them get you down lad,' and then he was gone.

RSM Lord always treated German officers and NCOs correctly, but did not bother to disguise his contempt for them, referring sarcastically to the Germans as 'the detaining power'. His task in Stalag XIB was a very difficult one. The Airborne accepted him without question, as did also any Guardsmen, but there were men from almost every unit in the British Army, as well as some Canadians, Australians and New Zealanders. Some of them felt that now they were prisoners they should no longer come under army discipline.

Enforcing discipline was extremely difficult as a man could not be confined to camp, or his pay stopped. Extra duties would have been no punishment, as boredom was our main problem and most of us would have volunteered for any extra work if we could have got it. For the most part the RSM had to rely on the good sense of the men, plus threats of post-war punishment. He did not hesitate to make an example of anyone who transgressed, and I remember that when one soldier refused to wash, the RSM had him stood up in a sink stark naked and buckets of cold water were thrown over him whilst two 3rd Battalion NCOs scrubbed him down fore and aft with yard brooms, and it was below zero.

We received in food about half a pint of watery swede soup daily, plus three small potatoes at midday, and one slice of sour black bread with a smear of margarine and a spoonful of ersatz jam at tea-time. We were supposed to receive one Red Cross parcel each per month, but in fact had only one between four of us. If one was lucky and belonged to a foursome that decided to use some of the articles provided, and trade the rest for bread, then you could just about survive. Even so, in seven months I went from eleven stone seven pounds to less than seven stone, and so did others, but many just lost the will to live.

RSM Lord had made an office out of Red Cross packing cases, and on his door was a notice which said, 'British RSM. Knock and wait.' A German warrant officer was in front of me and he walked into the RSM's office. I heard a scuffle and the RSM shouting, 'Can't you bloody well read!?' then the German warrant officer came hurtling out to land flat on his back. His cap was tossed out behind him, and the door slammed shut. As the German was armed I feared the worst, but he got up, dusted himself down, grinned and walked to the door and knocked. The RSM shouted, 'Come in', and that was that. This incident more than any other, as far as I was concerned, illustrated how good RSM Lord was at understanding the enemy. There was nothing the average German understood better than a good kick up the arse by someone in authority.

RSM Lord had been wounded in the right arm at Arnhem and when his arm was better he told us he had decided that he would salute any German officer he saw. He said, 'In future, when I see a German officer I shall draw myself to my full height, look him straight in the eyes and I shall salute in the correct fashion. However, gentlemen, as I do this I shall say to myself in a firm voice, "Bollocks!"' We thought this was wonderful. From that moment on we were saluting every German officer we could find – I tell you we were looking for them. They were as pleased as Punch – they thought we'd really come round to their way of thinking. That one word 'bollocks' summed it all up. Now we began to believe in ourselves again. We needed food, medical help, warmth, but above all we needed hope and that's what J. C. Lord gave us – hope.

I was in another prison camp when the 8th Hussars arrived on 8 April at Stalag XIB. J. C. Lord was the first man to greet them. He marched out looking immaculate. This grimy and dirty corporal jumped down from his tank and marched towards him and stood rigidly to attention, to report himself. The guards were disarmed and J. C. Lord lowered the swastika of the Reich and hoisted a homemade Union Jack which had been laid on the coffin at so many funerals. Like those in Stalag XIB, we in Uinstedt had survived, we were overwhelmed with relief and I think every one of us, in his own way, was thanking God it was over.

MAJOR CHRIS PERRIN-BROWN, 1st Parachute Battalion

The task allotted to the 1st Battalion at Arnhem was to secure the northern approaches to the town. After landing we set off from the dropping zone early in the afternoon along the line of the Utrecht–Arnhem railway, moving nicely for about an hour. We had crossed the railway and were heading in the direction of the Arnhem–Amsterdam road when our leading Companies, R under Tim Timothy and S under Ronnie Stark, came under heavy fire from infantry and armour deployed across our line of advance. It soon became clear that we had run into a force moving from the north of Arnhem which was heading back along the route we had come in order to attack the dropping zones. The country was light woodland and we became more and more heavily engaged as we tried to probe our way forward. R and

S Companies began to absorb fairly heavy casualties. My company (T) was in reserve and we didn't suffer so badly, though I lost the first of my platoon commanders. By dusk we knew that if we persisted northwards we were never likely to achieve our objective in the time, as our strength would be dissipated by diversions.

We had been unable to contact Brigade HQ, but around midnight our signallers picked up the 2nd Battalion calling from the bridge for urgent reinforcements. Our CO, Lieutenant Colonel Dobie, made his own decision to abort our efforts and move southwards straight into Arnhem in an attempt to reach Colonel Frost at the bridge.

We had considerable difficulty in disengaging ourselves since the enemy had closed in behind us. As we probed northwards, however, by dawn we were moving through the suburb of Mariendaal, aiming to join the lower road along which the 2nd Battalion had passed the previous afternoon. My company was now in the lead. Accurate sniping and intermittent small arms fire was causing us some annoyance but not enough to stop our progress until we hit Den Brink. Here we ran into a strongpoint with a pillbox, and mortar and small arms fire coming from a factory building in the open ground. My two leading platoons were stopped in their tracks and Lieutenant Hellingo reported that both he and Lieutenant Davies had been wounded. At that moment Lieutenant Colonel Thompson, commanding the Divisional Light Regiment of Artillery, dropped down by my side and offered to concentrate his guns on this target. I called Hellingo and told him what was going to happen. The moment the guns opened up he was to pick up his men and make it back to the cover of the houses, which I would occupy. This all went to plan. There was a considerable battle going on in the area of the houses lining the left-hand side of the road and this I took to be the 3rd Battalion, making its way forward.

From entering the built-up area at Den Brink the main road ran for about a kilometre straight through to the St Elizabeth Hospital. Hellingo and Davies were both incapable of walking so I split my remaining force in two, taking half myself and putting my 2 i/c, Jimmy Ritchie, in command of the other party. We set off on the embankment side under a continuous hail of fire, leap-frogging each other from house to house. We had to check the houses as we went because, if we hadn't, not a man would have reached the end of the row.

The main problem with street and house fighting was the enormous increase in the rate of ammunition consumption. As we entered a building from which firing had been, or was still coming, we didn't just knock at the door or ring the bell. We burst in the door or window and pitched in a grenade and followed in as fast as possible, spraying the premises as we went. Now the amount of ammo the airborne soldier can carry is pretty limited, so the one and a half kilometres of house-clearing from Den Brink to the hospital just drained away our unreplenishable supplies. Our only available source of reserve ammo was the pouches and pockets of dead or wounded comrades; it was not an enjoyable business robbing your dead friends.

As we fought our way through our casualties were heavy. Nobody is in such dire need of companionship as a dead man. So, as soon as one of our lads had cleared his floor, or whatever, he'd undo his chin-strap and sit down to comfort his dead pal. This meant that his section corporal was continuously re-entering houses to roust him out and chivvy him away from his dead mate, and to keep him moving. The sergeant in the meantime was searching for his missing corporals, while the platoon commander was trying to continue the war. In this manner we eventually reached St Elizabeth Square, only to find the whole damned area a parking place for a squadron of enemy tanks, armoured cars and flame-throwers.

At the end of the row of houses the square overlooked a sloping open embankment, running down to the river. Along the edge of the square enemy tanks could pour an uninterrupted fire down on anything trying to move forward. We'd reached our limit so I withdrew into the cover of the houses and reported the situation to Dobie following along behind with the remnants of R and S Companies. Night was again falling and we'd been in close combat for upwards of 40 hours. We formed a strongpoint and had a brew of tea, the first since five o'clock on Sunday morning, and it was now Monday night. We searched back along the way we'd fought to recover our casualties and await orders.

At about 7 pm Dobie called an O Group. He had been to a meeting with the battalion commander of The South Staffords. They would be pushing forward through Arnhem on our left and would, it was hoped, reach St Elizabeth Hospital during the night. At first light the next morning we were to attack below the square towards the housing and the pontoon bridge, in the first leg of a rush onwards to Johnnie Frost at the main bridge, some 400 yards further on.

The Staffords' battle went on throughout the night and it wasn't until about 6.30 am on the 19th that Dobie came forward to us with R and S Company remnants and ordered us forward. We tore across the open ground with everything bar the kitchen sink coming down on us from the square above. We reached the houses just as a section of tanks debouched ahead of us and lined up on the road leading across our front to the derelict pontoon bridge. We poured over the garden walls and up the garden slopes into the occupied houses above us. How we got in I'll never know, but we took those houses. I had some seven men left. We went up to the bedrooms overlooking the street, just in time to see a Jerry tank manoeuvring to get its bloody gun through the ground floor window below our feet. We had time to put our fingers in our ears before the bastard fired and we dropped through the ceiling of the room below. As I pulled myself out of the rubble I got a rifle butt in my ear and found myself a prisoner. We'd done all we could, but it wasn't enough.

MAJOR JOHN WADDY, 156 Parachute Battalion

On our return to the UK from Italy at the end of 1943, we trained hard for the coming invasion of Europe, and it was, therefore, a blow to all of us in 1st Airborne Division that we did not take part in the D-Day landings, but merely stood to on the airfields as an immediate reserve in case there was trouble in the bridgehead. During those long summer months we became increasingly frustrated as we waited for action. We planned and prepared for a number of likely operations which were cancelled. One near Caen was highly dangerous, with the DZs littered with panzers, and there were other targets – Brest, Le Havre, the forests south-west of Paris, canal bridges on the Belgian border; and in early September, Operation Comet, the later Market Garden task but to be carried out by the 1st Division only and the Polish Brigade.

On the morning of 17 September we were all thrilled to see large formations of Dakotas wheeling over our base at Melton Mowbray: it was the first lift of the operation flying in, and we knew the operation was, at last, on. Even then during the night there was a postponement in time of take-off. It was strange early next morning as we drove to Saltby airfield seeing the townspeople of Melton Mowbray going to work as we went to war. Even then at the airfield there was further delay due to low mist. Our American aircrew finally came out, and I checked the aircraft with the pilot, who was dressed immaculately in service dress and cap, but wasn't sure if he had to fly in north-to-south or south-to-north! I told him to sort it out, but he said, 'Shit, I'll just follow the rest.' At last we were off, flying in huge circles to get into the formations of nine aircraft in Vs – what the Americans call 'nine-ship elements'. We crossed the Dutch coast when there was a little flak, and flew on over the fields flooded by the Germans, waving back at the Dutch families huddled on the roofs of their farmhouses. The aircraft formations tightened up as we flew about 50 miles inland, bearing north-east over S'Hertogenbosch on to the final heading for our

DZs, 30 miles away. Here the fighter escort, 1200 aircraft in all, closed up expecting attack from the Luftwaffe; we started to fly through light flak and small arms fire; puffs of black smoke could be seen bursting among the aircraft ahead and there were a few near us, but we were hit only once with no damage. Flying as low as 700 feet, I could see the white upturned faces of the German flak gunners. An aircraft just to starboard received a direct hit and, on fire from nose to tail, passed just under my aircraft and crashed in a huge ball of white and red flame below, just missing two terrified carthorses. RAF Typhoons were also diving below our aircraft and strafing the German guns.

Finally we crossed the last river, the Rhine, hooked up and ready. I had a RAF flight sergeant from Ringway in my aircraft to help (several had come with the 4th Brigade as a result of a private arrangement between our brigadier, Shan Hackett, and the PTS. They were ordered by the RAF not to 'fall out' of the aircraft). This sergeant was great, and he might have been dispatching over Tatton Park, dressed in a shapeless RAF battledress and scuffed shoes. At last, with a huge shout of 'GO' from the whole stick, I jumped, to be followed down the slipstream by a call from our RAF friend, 'Give 'em hell from Ringway.'

I did my usual untidy landing, getting entangled in my Schmeisser carried in the harness. I had landed just north of the new autobahn under construction, and so had a good half-mile walk to our battalion RV on the north-west corner of Ginkel Heide in the woods. I trotted slowly towards it, collecting some of my soldiers: I passed my company 2 i/c strolling up a track, saying, 'Hurry up, Monty, there's a war on.' He replied, 'So I see.' The aircraft formations continued to roar overhead and the air seemed to be full of parachutes – over 2,000 men were dropped in a little over ten minutes. The American aircrews were superb and, despite the flak and now the small arms fire, they flew on in perfect formation but I could see at the end of the DZ, where there was a considerable belt of fire (and where the 10th Battalion had to fight for their RV) that as each 'V' of nine aircraft completed their drop, they poured on extra power to climb out of danger and into a more dispersed formation.

At the battalion RV the well ordered drill of rallying the battalion was working well. My company had to push out patrols to the north to protect the RV from enemy reported in the nearby Ede barracks. One was captured but when interrogated in German, answered in perfect English; he was a Pole. After about an hour the battalion was ready to move, less about 90 men missing, either from aircraft shot down, or killed, wounded by enemy fire or injured from the drop: one of my platoon commanders was missing, later found shot on the DZ. Just short of the Wolfneze crossing and as dusk was falling we joined up with the glider lift of the battalion: HQ and support company jeeps and carriers and anti-tank guns, which had landed on a LZ south of the railway. Soon after we were strafed by some German ME 109s. We continued to move forward slowly in the dark and the first fatigue was starting to set in, despite our fitness; it had been a long day with an exciting flight and drop, and a march forwards with everyone carrying heavy loads of 80–120 pounds.

Our leading C Company met strong opposition as it approached the railway cutting at Oosterbeek and the night was full of orange and mauve tracers, and soon burning houses lit the sky. Our battalion was ordered to halt and to move again at first light: fresh orders were issued. C Company were to push on again to take the high point (high for Holland!) in a wood just north of the railway, and I was to give fire support from the houses by the railway station. It was a slow job moving through the hedges and fenced suburban gardens of the neat houses, where surprisingly we met some Dutch families calmly sitting down to breakfast. Soon a fire-fight ensued, including tank fire against our houses, but our supporting fire role had been completed and we had to withdraw all the way back again along and over the railway and into the Johanna Hoeve woods.

I reported to my CO on the edge of the wood to be briefed. He had just been visited by Brigadier Shan Hackett, who had left with him saying, 'There are a lot of English faces down at the bridge eagerly awaiting us . . .' which in his words meant that we had to get a move on. I was told of C Company's position and that A company had attacked past their left onto the road running south to Oosterbeek, and I was ordered to pass through and move on to the Lichtenbeek feature in the woods 300–400 yards beyond the road. I was told that there were only a few snipers.

Later, I found out that A Company had been held up by heavy fire from the road, and that John Pott (who had won an MC in 1943 leading his company in Italy in a gallant attack against a strong position of German parachutists), had made a left flanking attack to reach the road to fight a desperate battle among the houses beyond the German armour and infantry. He with a group of his men then got on to the Lichtenbeek feature, and held it for several hours under repeated attack, until finally he and most of his men were either wounded or killed, and finally overrun.

I advanced with two platoons forward either side of a main ride in the woods, and only after a short while we encountered very heavy Spandau fire and bullets were ricocheting off the trees in all directions. I came to a clearing of felled timber, and by a pile of logs there was a Platoon HQ of A Company, all dead. Ahead a quick-firing gun was slamming HE shells into the scrub where my left-hand platoon was trying to edge forward, and they were taking heavy casualties. I then saw the gun at the end of the ride about 150 yards ahead on the road – it appeared to be a twin-barrelled 20-mm flak gun on a half-track chassis. As it was opposite my line of advance I decided to move forward myself to try to knock it out, with some of my soldiers and with Tom Wainwright, OC Support Company (what was he doing up there?).

Hearing the noise of fighter aircraft Tom suggested a dash across the clearing while the enemy's heads were down but the aircraft, as they passed very low overhead, had that prominent black cross on their sides – they were ME 109s and not Spitfires or Typhoons. God knows we could have done with the latter there! Nevertheless we pushed on through the scrub until we were within about 15 yards of the gun; the Germans were all shouting at one another and I could hear the empty shell cases rattling down on the deck; one could now sense that there were a lot of other armoured vehicles on that road.

Just then the soldier on my right was hit smack in the forehead by a bullet, and I saw that there was a sniper in the tree above the gun. I had only my .45 Colt and no Schmeisser and so I fired five rounds at him and he, or someone else, shot me in the lower stomach. When I came to, and started to crawl away he fired another shot, hitting the ground near my hand. I collapsed and lay doggo, until I heard a crashing through the bushes and a large Rhodesian private, Ben Diedricks (we had about 20 Rhodesians serving in our battalion since our stay in the Middle East), picked me up in his arms and carried me back some 200 yards to Company HQ. At the battalion RAP our doctor, John Buck, must have thought that I had had it for all he did was to chuck me his silver whisky flask! At the Field Ambulance casualty post half a mile back I was given a plasma transfusion, which was better than the whisky, and then, wrapped in a billowing parachute, I was taken on a stretcher jeep to Oosterbeek to the Tafelberg Hotel where 181 Airlanding Brigade Field Ambulance had set up a main dressing station. The billiard room was used as the operating theatre, and after I was operated on, I was moved out into the dining room. After about a day, as more wounded came flooding in even faster, I was moved out to a nearby house.

As no resupply had been received, the initial quantities of food and medical stores were fast running out. The Germans shelled and mortared the perimeter throughout the day and of course the dressing stations, being in the front line, were being repeatedly hit and the wounded were being wounded again or killed. The nights were cold and it had started to rain, a dismal drizzle: there were very few blankets and most of us were lying half-naked on the floor (having had our clothes cut off by the medics) or sharing mattresses from the hotel. Smells are usually held to be one's most evocative memory, and I can still smell today that mixture of wet earth, burnt cordite, brick and plaster dust, and pus that permeated those days. Towards the end of the battle there must have been over 3,000 casualties in this situation on the perimeter. A large proportion were evacuated to German hospitals towards the end during a short cease-fire organized by the ADMS, our head doctor, Colonel Graeme Warrack and a German medical officer. Graeme Warrack was truly a tower of strength and a source of encouragement to all of us lying helplessly in these battered houses. He was one of the greatest unsung heroes of the battle, as were his medical orderlies, who carried on without rest for over a week in their task of caring for the wounded, despite the fact that the dressing stations were under fire from snipers and from mortar and tank fire. On one day the room in which I was in received a direct hit, killing about six men and wounding others including myself, and this was followed by a rush of steel-helmeted Germans through the house. A counter-attack was launched and the Airborne troops drove them out, and this was repeated several times until finally we were in German hands. Two Germans came in and set up a fire position in the wrecked bay window, but soon one of them was hit by an airborne sniper firing from a house across the road. A huge German feldwebel came in and lectured us on the evils of our soldiers firing at a house flying the Red Cross flag, and then he proceeded to shout at the wounded German, who was moaning pitifully. The next day in the morning the whole area around us was subjected to an even heavier concentration of fire, but this time it came from our own medium artillery (5.5-inch), which had been providing superb close fire support around the perimeter over the last few days: this was a very unfortunate lapse. Our room again got a direct hit and particularly the wounded German. I woke up, wounded again, under a pile of rubble but most of the others were killed except for a glider pilot-officer, who had had both legs smashed when his glider had crash-landed, lying screaming underneath a large piano across his shattered legs. Our house soon caught fire and the medical orderlies carried us out. I found myself on a house verandah behind, and close to, a gruesome sight of some 30 bodies stacked in a pile; they must have been those who had died of wounds or had been killed by mortar or shell fire in the dressing station.

A jeep suddenly drove up and out jumped a Sergeant Chivers, not only from our own 156 Battalion, but also from my original regiment, the Somerset Light Infantry. He said, 'Good God, Major Waddy, what are you doing here?' and I said, 'Just get me out of here.' I was, with some other casualties, loaded onto his jeep and driven down a road strewn with wrecked vehicles and fallen tree branches. I thought that we had been relieved by Second Army, but too soon the jeep turned a corner, and drove into a space behind what I now know to be a fire station, and there in a huge semi-circle were some 100 SS soldiers with machine-guns mounted on tripods. The wounded and the stragglers were being rounded up by the Germans, in company with Airborne medical staff and the padres, all of whom had stayed behind to carry on their care for the wounded. If battle honours could be awarded to the RAMC, then Arnhem/Oosterbeek should be one of its finest feats.

All the wounded, and there must have been over 4,000, were taken to a large empty barracks of the pre-war Dutch Army at Apeldoorn where the division's medical staff were establishing a British hospital nearby. I was taken to a German hospital full of their wounded, mainly from the SS Panzer divisions that we had been fighting, but one might have thought that they were on our side by the way they helped our soldiers as they came in and were put into their wards. A lightly wounded SS corporal helped me onto a bed, took off what was left of my blood-soaked and dusty clothes and, seeing that I was hit in the jaw, then carefully peeled and cut up an apple to feed me. I asked him to find out what had happened to a young soldier of the 1st Battalion with a badly smashed face who had been with me; next day the SS man came and sadly told me that 'der Junge' had died.

The German doctors and staff were very correct and attentive throughout my six weeks' stay in that hospital, although their medical resources were limited, consisting mainly of paper bandages and lashings of acriflavine; anaesthetics especially were in short supply for anything other than major surgery. Colonel Graeme Warrack visited us twice on his rounds of other hospitals and he said that the German Army were ten years behind in battlefield surgery. One day two German surgeons at the end of my bed discussed whether they would amputate my foot (amputations were apparently an all-too-common remedy in the German Army and an elderly German orderly gave me an example of heavy German humour – 'never report sick with a headache'). The two doctors abruptly broke off their discussion when one said, 'The major speaks German'; anyway the matter was solved by a large, blonde, German nursing sister who later pulled out a two-inch-long mortar splinter in one excruciating moment, complete with some sock knitted by Ann, my fiancée and now my wife.

There were one or two dramas: once after a RAF Spitfire had put a burst of cannon fire through the operating theatre, killing a German nurse and a

British soldier, I got a bollocking from the hospital matron about the British disregard for the Red Cross on the roof: she was a formidable lady like so many of our military matrons. On another occasion, a soldier from our own battalion, Private Greer, the battalion humorist, climbed out of his bed one day, walked across the ward and turned a picture of Hitler face to the wall, saying, 'I can't stand looking at that bastard any longer.' At first, the Germans laughed. 'He's mad', they said, meaning Hitler of course, but the arrival of a German nursing sister changed the situation and we all got another rollicking. Eventually, sometime in November the last of the Airborne wounded were shipped or rather railed out of Holland into Germany – the inevitable 'das Transport' had come. Colonel Warrack's hospital in Apeldoorn had been emptied, and he himself with a number of his doctors had at the end slipped away into the efficient and caring hands of the Dutch underground, and most would finally make their way home to safety.

We left Apeldoorn station in a German hospital train, the centre two coaches of which contained British wounded. The journey through the shattered railway system of Germany down into Graz in Austria to offload the Germans ('nichts fur Tommy', we were told) and back up to a Stalag hospital took over six days. The painful tedium of the journey was relieved by the usual irrepressible humour of the British soldier. The panels on the outside of the coaches were soon chalked with huge Victory 'V's which caused consternation as the train pulled into platforms crowded with German military and civilians. At one station, some of our soldiers had blown up condoms and drawn on the end Hitler's well-known features, and when these were displayed to the waiting throng on the platform, at first they evoked some merriment until the arrival of an officious Nazi official.

Stalag VIIIA, Moosburg, was a mixed camp for Russians, French, Polish and British soldiers, but it had a hospital (or what passed for one), and here I spent another three months before being passed fit enough to go out into the compound, where some 120 officers were held, mainly airborne and from special forces taken in south-east Europe. Food was almost non-existent in the whole camp but much more so in the Russian compounds which were at starvation level, and this enabled the Germans to recruit Russians into their army as late as April 1945.

As the spring of that year blossomed, the sounds and sights of the approaching fronts became more evident. We had a superb grandstand view, almost daily, of the massed daylight bombing raids by the US Air Force on targets all around us; and for several hours each night we could hear and feel the RAF heavies doing their stuff. After the war, the Allied bombing offensive has been denigrated as having achieved little in the strategic field, but certainly from what we saw and heard from the Germans in our camp, it had a significant effect on their morale.

Finally, in early May, artillery fire was heard during the night a few miles off and in the morning tanks could be seen several miles from the camp; before long they swept past and through the thick pinewoods in a headlong advance to Munich and beyond. It was George Patton's army on the move, and highly efficient it looked. About noon a huge Stars and Stripes flag was seen high on the church tower of the hill-top village of Moosburg: in front of me was the figure of a broad-based American Air Force officer, who remarked, 'Well, kiss my naked ass, it's the flag.' We were liberated. A few days later, we were flown out to Rheims, courtesy of the USAAF, and from there back to England, after a day's delay, by RAF Bomber Command, after they had recovered from their VE-Day celebrations. At an airfield in Buckinghamshire we were met by the charming ladies of the WVS with a cup of tea and a packet of ten Gold Flake cigarettes: we were home, almost.

LIEUTENANT EDWARD NEWPORT, 1st Battalion, The Border Regiment

When we landed it was quite extraordinary; the Dutch, who thought the war was ending, were out on the streets in force. We kept saying to them very politely, 'It's nice to see you, yes, but I do think you ought to look to your trenches and your cellars. Don't imagine that this is the end of it. The Germans don't react that way and we are expecting trouble.' They couldn't understand why we were so polite compared with the Germans. The Germans had no scruples. If they wanted to take over a house, they'd open the door: 'Aus – get out.' We would knock on the door. When the lady came to the door, we'd say, 'Do you speak English?' 'Oh, yes.' 'We are terribly sorry, but we want to use your upstairs bedroom. Do you think you could move out your valuables, or stack them at one end, and we'll remove the curtains.' Whereas the Germans would just put a gun straight through the window. So they really weren't used to English politeness!

Something like 600 gliders had landed on this piece of common land which we were supposed to defend. It was fairly open so we had to go to the very edges of suburban Arnhem to put up our defences. Sure enough the next morning at about eight o'clock we were startled by a loud crash: the first enemy tank firing at us from the edge of a wood about 1,000 yards away. The Germans had decided to attack. This was my first experience of being dug in and seeing an attack coming in on us. It was awe-inspiring and frightening. I remember firing and thinking that this was the first time I had actually seen someone killed by myself. I had two feelings about it really. One was, 'What am I doing this for?' Then reminding myself, 'If you don't do it, then he's going to do it to you.' And after that I seemed to reconcile myself to it. But that first experience didn't come easily to me. To see a German and then think, 'Poor sod,' when I'd shot him down. And they couldn't get to us; they went to ground and my company commander came up on the radio to me and said, 'This is where we should use our mortars.' That was devastating. A lot of the enemy actually ran back as fast as they could to the woods; they didn't like the mortars at all and they didn't try that approach again.

The next day we thought there would be a large force waiting for the next lift that came in, but surprisingly the enemy didn't put up a great deal of resistance. They probably didn't think there was enough room for a second lift when they saw all the gliders on the ground.

Now stage one was over we started to advance to the outskirts of Arnhem. This was slow progress because every now and again we would run into Germans; we'd go 300, perhaps 400 yards, and then the whole column would have to stop. Eventually the whole division was directed to form a horseshoe perimeter from the Rhine right out into a suburb and then back down to the Rhine again so that we held about three-quarters of a mile of the river. From now on it was essentially an artillery battle – the only Germans we saw were the occasional patrol. Once the Germans realized that we were in this relatively small, primitive division, they concentrated everything they had on us and never let up. It was really a wearing-down process. I was there for ten days, and the only time the bombardment seemed to fade was in the evening. We used to say, 'They're having their evening meal. Get yours quickly or else you're in trouble!' That was the only time you could scurry around, repair damaged defences and dig holes a bit deeper. Then it would start again, only louder. It was very, very wearing.

As the hours and days passed, food got low, ammunition got low and morale began to get a little bit tatty at the edges. All of the people around me behaved remarkably well except one man, a Glaswegian. At one stage D Company's southern edge of the wood was under great pressure and they were getting the worst of it. A runner came up and said, 'Would you please send four men over to reinforce them because they have had a lot of casualties?' So I detailed four men, one of whom was this man from Glasgow, and he refused. He just sat in his place and didn't speak. The other men were watching this and I knew this was a crucial test of my leadership. I remembered stories from my father in World War I about shooting people who were cowards, and I thought, 'Are you going to make a great demonstration?' But I couldn't pull a pistol on him and shoot him or anything like that. I gave him another chance, but he said, 'I'm not going, sir.' I said, 'All right, I'll leave you there, but I'll tell you something, your comrades will never forgive you. You think about that.' And do you know, they never had anything to do with him after that. They didn't speak to him and tell him what they thought of him; they just totally ignored him. He had become a pariah.

A great friend of mine, Bob Houston, was in a position only about 100 yards behind me holding my back. Every evening when there was the lull I used to wander over to him in his trench and say, 'How's it gone today?' and we would compare notes, and try to joke a bit. One evening I went over in the usual way and I looked down into his trench. I thought he was asleep, but in fact he was dead. He had been hit by an eight-pounder. He looked very much at peace, but it was terribly sad. His platoon sergeant (who was now commander of the platoon) came over and I said, 'How long has Mr Houston been dead?' And he said, 'Oh, since early this morning.' I said, 'Then why haven't you bloody well buried him? Get it done.' And stalked off. But I instantly felt that this was no way to behave; I felt a real heel. When there was another lull I went back and found the sergeant and said, 'Sorry. I was so upset because he was a great chum of mine and I lost my temper, but do bury these people straight away and put something over them – a wooden cross.' That is what we did.

The latter stage of the battle became a war of attrition and took on quite a regular pattern in that very early in the morning they would start their bombardment, so if you didn't have your breakfast (or what answered for breakfast) very quickly, you didn't get anything. That would continue for quite a long time and perhaps some time in the morning they would try one attempt to break through. I was on the edge of a wood with about 400 to 500 yards' field of fire across some pastureland, and quite often in the last few days a tank would appear somewhere on the edge of the wood and make as if to come forward as a cover for an infantry charge. But we put up such a strong resistance that they would usually turn back. We never actually managed to destroy a tank though. Tiger tanks were virtually impenetrable from the front.

All this activity was very fatiguing and my gun crew were really getting to the end of their tether. Food was now getting very short, and although there were some valiant attempts by the RAF to resupply us, the stuff quite often, frustratingly, went into German lines. Long, long afterwards when I was eventually captured I remember feeling so annoyed when I was offered a cigarette, a Players No. 1, by a German. I said, 'Oh, you like English cigarettes,' and he said, 'We've plenty of these.' Everything we had – ammunition, food – was supposed to last for 48 hours and then we were meant to be either resupplied or relieved by the ground forces. But we were now into about our sixth or seventh day and the only food we had was what we could scrounge from houses around us. Everyone was doing the same thing, of course, so it wasn't very successful. We were starving, in fact.

One day we got a message saying that the artillery could give us some support – not our own artillery but heavy artillery, firing at extreme range – and there was a possibility that the odd round might fall short. What did we think about this? Should we say yes? Of course, the soldiers said, 'What's one odd round of our own? Let them join in the fun.' And so they did just that. We were told when it was happening and we heard a lot of it going over our heads into the German lines, which cheered us a great deal. The odd one did fall on us, but it was a drop in the ocean compared to the stuff we were suffering most of the time.

I had one experience which was particularly frightening. I was in my slit trench and I thought I heard a twig snap behind me, so I turned round and there, not five paces behind me, was a line of seven German soldiers coming backwards in my direction. They thought they were out of our lines and were facing the enemy. You might say they were sitting ducks, but although I had a Sten machine-gun down the bottom of the trench I suddenly remembered that its one failing was that it was given to stoppages if it got dirty. Of course we had been in so much dirt and muck and filth for so long that for quite a time I had had to clean it every two or three hours to make sure it was firing, but I hadn't done this for quite some time. The thought went instantly through my mind, 'If you now fire on these people and it doesn't work, you're a dead man.' That was all in a split second, and I just sank slowly down into my trench and watched as the nearest German's foot went right past the trench as he walked back. He never saw us. But it did give me a nasty shock, that one, I can tell you.

Eventually one evening at about 5.30 there was a lull and a runner came over from Charles Breese, the company commander of D Company, to say there was an 'O' Group in ten minutes and I went across. 'Well then,' he said, 'I've got some good news and some bad news. Which will you have first?' We all said, 'The good news.' He said, 'Well, they are going to withdraw this evening. The bad news is that we are going to be the last contingent to go because we are going to cover the withdrawal and stay on the north side until the others are all over and then, if there's still time, we go away.' Just as Charles asked if there were any questions, a mortar bomb went off in a tree and a piece came through my helmet and into my head. I was very aware that somebody had hit me with something over the head, and of blood pouring down my face. Of course, blood always gives the wrong impression – you think you are stuck like a pig and near death – and I recall a feeling of, 'That's it, that's it, I've had it.' I now know that I was concussed. I don't know how long I was in this condition, but eventually I began to recover my senses properly and they bandaged me up. I noted the hole in my steel helmet, and thanked God that I was wearing the thing. Eventually so many things had to be done that my injury became a secondary consideration, and we began to pull out.

The withdrawal across the Rhine was very orderly and well conducted. It started at about midnight and I got down to the Rhine about a quarter to two. There were not a great number of people left, just an orderly sort of queue, all lying down near the river, waiting their turn. They were called for when a boat arrived, and there was no panic of any kind, no rush for the boats. It took about five minutes to get across so there was a sort of shuttle service every ten minutes. Eventually, our numbers had dwindled where I was to about 50, by which time most of the people were from our own company, the last of our defensive screen. I now noticed that the light was getting better. A boat had just loaded. I went up and a Canadian just said to me, 'Sorry, chum, that's the lot. No more now. The light's getting too good.' I just stood there and I don't know whether I felt frustration, irritation, panic or what. I just felt completely drained as I watched him disappear into the mist that was coming up over the river. I went back to my men. I think this was the last time I addressed any of my own soldiers, and I said to them all, 'That's it, I'm sorry to say. There are no more boats, and it's no good hanging around here. Get out of the open before it gets too light or they will see us. It is now every man for himself. Go back to Oosterbeek – be careful how you go – and try to find a Dutch family who will hide you. When I say "hide", I mean really hide, because I know what's going to happen in the morning, when they really understand that we've gone. They will search all the houses, all the woods, everything, to find any remains of us at all. So, don't just think you can step into a wardrobe and shut the door and they won't look in there when they come upstairs. It's got to be something a bit more sophisticated than that.' Then I said, 'Well, good luck to you all and see you back in the UK.'

They all disappeared, and only then did I think, 'What a fool; I should have at least asked my batman to stay – I might have enjoyed the company.' I started to wend my way back up to Oosterbeek and I remember reaching the end of the tape where the wood started and I suddenly felt extremely

233

low and abandoned. I still had my weapon in my hand, and I thought this is not a good thing to have now at all. Get rid of it. So, I found a well and threw it down, and was now without anything. I had no headgear because I had a bandage around my neck and I felt absolutely hopeless and helpless. Still caked blood down my face, hadn't washed for at least four or five days, was even slightly unshaven; grossly hungry and feeling very lonely. The end was really quite an anti-climax. I came round the side of a building and as I did so there, straight in front of me, was a German patrol of seven men. They stopped and I stopped, we both looked at each other, and I slowly raised my hands. That was the end of my war.

MAJOR TONY DEANE-DRUMMOND, 1st Airborne Division

As soon as we heard the facts about Operation Market Garden, we knew it was the biggest gamble ever. But we took the risks with our eyes open; we were relying on the fact that there weren't going to be any Germans at Arnhem at all, except a few fourth-class troops – no more that 500 – covering the whole area. The price for success would be great, but success was not to be.

The positioning of our dropping zone broke every rule in the book; the number one lesson we'd learnt from previous operations was that you had to drop on your objective, or within a mile of it at the most, otherwise it just wouldn't work. And here we were dropping seven or eight miles from the bridge, in the belief that there wasn't going to be any opposition at all. So it was a complete gamble, and a gamble that failed.

The day came and as I jumped 50 aircraft ejected their loads all around me. It was a most inspiring sight and one which I shall never forget. I touched down in some heather, and already the next 50 aircraft were roaring overhead. It was magical, the way 1,000 parachutes appeared from the planes and floated down above our heads. We had landed on a large open heath covered with heather and surrounded by pine forests which scented the air beautifully, unlike the tang of aviation gasoline hanging around from the aircraft.

I was second-in-command of the Divisional Signals and it wasn't long before reports were coming in that 1st Parachute Brigade were facing quite some opposition on their way to the bridge. At Divisional Headquarters, we were worried, even on that first afternoon; we were having trouble with our wireless sets which were only designed to carry signals up to three miles and it was eight miles to the bridge. To make it more frustrating it was a problem I had foreseen, but which had been brushed aside. All we could do was change the frequency of our transmissions and I was asked to go and tell 1st Para Brigade about the change.

So the next morning I set off with my batman, Lance Corporal Turner. We found the battalion on the outskirts of town, preparing to fight through the two miles of enemy-held streets to get to the bridge. They were already under concentrated fire from mortars and snipers; the enemy had obviously realized our intention and was resisting with surprising force. We did not realize then that Field Marshal Model had witnessed our drop the day before from his headquarters only a mile away at Oosterbeek. He had immediately ordered armoured reinforcements from the Ninth SS Panzer Division just north of Arnhem. Blissfully unaware of this fact, we prepared confidently for the attack. I decided to attach myself to the battalion and go through to the bridge with them; like everyone else, I completely failed to appreciate the strength of the force we were up against.

The going was rough right from the start, and Turner and I ended up taking over control of a company which had just lost its commander. They had the task of clearing the river banks along the Rhine, so I encouraged them to keep moving up to the next group of houses 400 yards along the bank while the rest of the battalion caught up with us. Like all street fighting it was a bloody business, and by the time we got to the houses only 20 men had survived out of the whole company. The rest of the battalion was way behind us.

By nightfall nearly all our ammunition was gone, and I realized our position was hopeless; the battalion was now over 800 yards away. So I split the men into three groups and told them to try and infiltrate back through the lines and join up with Battalion Headquarters. My group of four decided to swim to avoid the deadly streets, so we broke into a house near the Rhine to have cover near the water. Just as we were checking the place, we heard Germans breaking down the front door, so we dived into the loo and locked the door on the inside. To our dismay we heard them establishing a sniping post in the attic above our heads and digging two machine-guns into the pavement outside. We had no choice but to stay put, so we took turns sitting on the lavatory seat for the next three days and nights. Every now and then a German would come and try the door, but when he found it 'engaged' he politely went away and tried elsewhere.

In the end I could stand it no longer and said we'd have to try and set out on the fourth night. We were all pretty hungry and some of the men were jittery, but we planned to swim the river, rendezvous on the far side at the blown railway bridge and rejoin our division. We crept out at 1 am between bursts of firing and seconds later we were in the water. The current separated me from my three companions as we crossed but just as I was coming up to the rendezvous, whistles blew for a stand-to. I was in the middle of a German platoon and fell slap bang into an enemy slit trench. They looked as surprised as I was; I'd got right into the heart of their position undetected.

So the game was up – as in Italy, I was a prisoner again – and once more I had to go through the indignity of being searched by the enemy. They marched me off to Battalion Headquarters and sat me down in front of a middle-aged German subaltern.

'I must to you questions ask. You will answer.'

'Oh.'

'Your name, please?'

I told him.

'What day you jumped?'

'I can't say.'

'How many more are you?'

'I can't say.'

His eyes bulged behind his glasses and his neck went very pink.

'OK, you no speak. We will see.'

They soon gave up on me and I was driven off to captivity, over the main bridge where so many men had lost their lives and into the outskirts of the town. Eventually we reached a large suburban house which was being used as a prisoner-of-war cage. Inside were 500 men, including Freddie Gough and Tony Hibbert; they told me more about the events of the battle and only then did I realize what a failure it had been.

All the time I was looking for ways of escape. Having been through all this before in Italy I was determined not to go through it again if I could help it. My thinking was that the British Second Army would overrun this place in about two days, so one solution would be to hide in the house until they released me.

The only possible hiding place seemed to be a wall cupboard in one of the ground floor rooms with a concealed, flush-fitting door papered to match the room. It was about four feet wide and seven feet high, but only twelve inches deep, although it was possible to stand in it after removing the shelves inside. I reversed the lock so it would be locked from inside and concealed the keyhole by pasting a bit of wallpaper over it. I filled up my water bottle and a two-pound jam-jar I'd found; some of the officers offered me their bottles but I had to refuse them as I felt they'd need them for when they escaped. For food I had a pound tin of lard and a small loaf of bread. Little did I think that I'd be trapped in that cramped space for 13 days and nights before being able to get away. I daresay that if I'd never been a prisoner before, I would have given up after a couple of days. But, to hell with it, I wasn't going to be a prisoner again. As it was, I thought I'd reach my limit after three or four days; I wasn't in best condition for an endurance test.

On the evening of the 22nd, the Germans came round taking all names, so to avoid this I started standing in my cupboard. There was no room to sit down, of course, so I started the drill that was to become almost automatic over the next fortnight. First I put my weight on one leg, then the other; then I leaned on one shoulder and then on the other. I could sleep all right, but sometimes my knees would buckle beneath me and bang against the door. Every bone in my body ached and the lack of food, water and rest made me quite lightheaded.

To make matters worse, the day after I got into the cupboard the Germans started using the room as an interrogation centre, with the table right up against my cupboard. It was quite bizarre; only half an inch of wood lay between me and the rest of the world outside. I heard every prisoner being interrogated, and I was quite surprised by the responses of many of our men. The Germans would ask quite innocuous questions about families, that sort of thing, and then would sneak in a question about something of military importance. Most people told them a few non-military facts, but two men didn't hesitate to pass on everything they knew. At night there was no respite – the room was used as sleeping quarters for the guard – but I was determined to hang on until my luck changed as it had never failed to do before. I eked out my supplies bit by bit, allowing myself a mouthful or two of water every four or five hours and just a bite of bread. Water was the real problem, as after about nine days my mouth was so dry that I couldn't eat at all. I was able to urinate into a gap in the floorboards and I was amazed that my system kept going despite the fact that I was drinking so little.

By the thirteenth day my water was almost gone, my mouth was bone-dry and I had terrible cramp most of the time. I'd really had enough and knew I must try to get out that night – or fail in the attempt. Anything would be better than this hellish cupboard.

My luck was definitely in. I stood there, ears pricked, listening for every movement in the room. About 6 pm I pulled on my boots and smock which took three-quarters of an a hour to do silently; dressing in that cupboard was a work of art. As I finished I heard the guards stumble out of the room muttering about a 'fraulein'. I carefully pushed the door open an inch to have a quick check. But, damn it, there, right in front of me was another

German snoring in a chair. I almost despaired, but just at that moment there came the sounds of troops and giggling girls clattering upstairs and into the room above. The gramophone was turned on and soon there was quite a party, which woke my sleeping German and drew him upstairs in search of the fun. My legs felt incredibly weak as I climbed out of my 'prison' and crossed the room. Under cover of a passing lorry I dropped out of the window and crawled into some bushes for cover until dark.

When it was black enough to start moving I crept through the garden and into an orchard where I was soon stuffing myself with delicious apples. I could feel my energy returning; it was such a joy to be free from that terrible cupboard. I was very weak, but now I had a real sense of hope and my brain seemed to be back to normal at last. I suppose I shouldn't have been surprised when I got a pretty brusque brush-off from the first few houses I tried for assistance, but I felt incredibly depressed. I had thought that all Dutch were pro-British, but the reality was that some were pro-Nazi and many more were quite simply afraid. The risk of harbouring a British soldier was horrendous; you'd be shot and your family sent to a concentration camp. When I realized this, it made me respect the people who did help me even more.

Eventually I found myself scavenging food from saucers outside people's back doors – obviously cat scraps. I decided I'd take my chance with those who left the fullest saucer as they must surely be the most generous-spirited! So I waited until dawn in a garden shed until the houseowner came up to get some firewood. 'Good morning!' I said in my best German. To give him his due, he didn't look at all surprised to see me, and to my huge relief he was willing to help. He called his young wife and she came over looking rather cross. But when she caught sight of me she screamed and clutched her husband in panic. I don't suppose I was a very pretty sight, with my two weeks' growth of red beard and dirty, tattered battledress. It was the first, and I hope the last, time a woman screamed at me in fear!

Soon afterwards I was in hiding again, this time under a pile of seed boxes, covered with sacks, much cheered by a large plate of boiled potatoes and gravy which my hostess brought me; it smelt like a banquet fit for a king. After wolfing it down I fell asleep under my sacks. I awoke to the sound of military boots and accusing German voices coming towards my hut. Someone must have given me away! I froze as they searched the barn and my host continually denied their accusations that he was sheltering a British officer. Fortunately they only checked the most obvious hiding place – the hayloft – which I'd rejected for that very reason, and then left, muttering curses. Soon my host was back and begging me to leave in a

Above: October 1944 and men of the 4th Parachute Battalion advance through an olive grove towards Athens where they were to be involved in a thankless and bloody campaign against the highly organised ELAS troops

Below: Street fighting in Athens. Many of the slogans such as KKE were daubed on the wall by the terrorists with the blood of their victims

Above: The 5th Parachute Battalion occupied the Acropolis which dominated Athens

De-crating a jeep dropped with the 3rd Battalion, The Parachute Regiment at El Gamil, Port Said, 5 November 1956

1200 hours, Aldershot, New Year's Day 1965: C Company, 2nd Battalion are recalled for immediate departure to Borneo. Not all are quite prepared for it

Above: Internal security work in Palestine 1956: after terrorists blew up a Defence Security house, killing 3 soldiers, suspects were held in a barbed wire cage by 3rd Brigade, 6th Airborne Division

Left: Men of the 3rd Battalion active in Cyprus in 1956. They have arrested a priest suspected of collusion with EOKA

Below: Men of the Parachute Squadron, attached to the SAS, with their Iban trackers somewhere in the Malayan jungle in 1955

The 3rd Battalion very much under fire from dissident tribesmen in the Radfan in 1964. Note, centre left, the 3.5" rocket launcher, a powerful weapon against rock-built sangars

shaking voice. He was petrified and it was hardly surprising. So I thanked him from the bottom of my heart for all his help while he loaded me with milk and sandwiches and directed me to open country.

More doors were slammed in my face that night, but at last I was taken in by a real hero, an elderly Dutch security guard. He was very proud to have a 'Tommy' in his house and I sat in his kitchen, covered in dirt, stuffing bread and jam while he tried to tell me his life story in Dutch. Meanwhile his wife sat in her nightdress and curling papers with a constant smile on her face. For several days they sheltered me and fed my insatiable appetite for food and sleep with meals big enough for ten men and an attic bedroom where I revelled in the luxury of clean sheets. Up until then I'd been living on nervous energy – pure adrenaline – but now all I wanted to do was rest and sleep. I hadn't realized before how weak I was. Later I was tottering around the house when a glimpse of myself in a mirror gave me a shock. I could hardly recognize myself; my face was so thin and lined I looked almost like a corpse. Bronchitis hit before long, no doubt caused by my weakened state, and I was laid up for four days unable to eat.

It was at this stage that I moved to a different household in Velp that was better organized for sheltering escapers. They were a gallant family – a local schoolmaster, his wife and two children – as they already had two other refugees staying with them. I've never met a more brave and God-fearing man than Mr Huisman, and his wife was incredible; somehow she managed to care for seven people squeezed into a tiny two-bedroomed villa, while keeping the house spotless. I was there for several weeks and it was during this time that I was put in touch with other British officers hiding in the area. So I heard of the plans for Operation Pegasus, getting all the escaped troops in the area together and back across the Rhine. It was rather frustrating not to be involved in the preparations – reconnaissance and so on – but I had to be patient and wait for the great day.

We had a wonderful party the night before we left. Some friends came round with bottles of Arak gin and a local baroness sent round a bottle of champagne for the 'poor British officer who is so thin'. All the Dutch got extremely merry and sang patriotic songs at the tops of their voices. I was overwhelmed with gratitude to all those people who had sheltered me so bravely. I shall never forget them. The next night I was in uniform once again being carried back across the Rhine in a boat full of friendly faces. This was my fourth Rhine crossing in six weeks: I had flown over it, swum it, been driven across it as a prisoner, and now I was carried across it in a boat. I preferred the last method, although I did not regret the first.

Back in England I phoned my wife who was by then six months

pregnant. She had been told by my colonel three weeks before that he didn't hold out much hope for me; an eyewitness had seen a mortar bomb explode where I was standing. But she always believed that I would return safely, and I did.

CAPTAIN JAN LORYS, 1st Polish Parachute Brigade

We were supposed to go on 19 September, but owing to bad weather we were delayed for two days and we received new orders on the 20th; instead of jumping near Elden, opposite the main bridge, we were to jump in Driel. Originally we had been meant to cross over on the bridge, and were even promised a cup of tea on the dropping zone and a bus ride across. Now we were told to drop near Driel, and cross by ferry to help the 1st Airborne Division. It was a sign that something had gone very badly wrong on the other side. Little information was coming through – communications were very poor – and General Sosabowski demanded to know what was happening. He was assured that the ferry was being kept for us, and that all was as planned.

On the 21st we finally got into our planes. I was with General Sosabowski, in the Headquarters as G2. As we took off it was very cold, and the General brought out oranges for us from somewhere. How he got them I don't know, but he had a box of them and treated us all in the plane. We were in good spirits because we were finally going into action. When I jumped I saw the tracer bullets coming up to us, and the artillery and mortar fire, and I knew, my goodness, we were not on exercise this time, we were in action at last. I landed safely, but when we started assembling our units we discovered that many of them were missing; we could not account for a whole battalion and more. It was a shock. We saw one or two aircraft still heading east, and we thought others were also misdirected toward Germany. Only two days later did we find out that 41 of our 114 planes had turned back to England. Air Command had decided that the weather was too bad and sent orders to all our aircraft to return. For some reason only 41 planes received the order and turned back. They were carrying mainly the 1st Battalion, but also some elements of the 3rd Battalion and Headquarters. These men had to wait until the 23rd, when they were dropped near Grave.

Anyway, we started marching to the Rhine, looking for the ferry to cross the river. But the ferry was not there; there were no boats either. Radio communications were very difficult, and so during the night one of our liaison officers with the 1st Airborne Division, Captain Zwolanski, swam the river to report to the General. He told him the position, which was very bad, shocking. Later, the chief engineer came, and they both asked us to cross as soon as we could. We were told that Division would attack to widen its bridgehead on the river and that boats would be found. But nothing materialized. At dawn General Sosabowski decided to move back leaving the second-in-command to wait along the river in case something came up. The main body of the brigade moved to Driel, and he ordered Headquarters to organize defences around the village. We started digging in, and it was not long before the Germans began their attack, from the east, in battalion-strength with five or six armoured cars. We had no anti-tank units at all, because all our transport, heavy equipment, and artillery, had landed on the north side of the river days before. So we never had their support, and when the Germans started attacking we had only machine-guns and PIATs, which are no good at more than 15 or 20 yards. And we had only as much ammunition as we could carry on our backs. Some of our units soon began reporting they were short of ammunition and we had to order, 'Stop shooting!' right down the line. But eventually two British armoured cars reached us overland from Nijmegen, and they opened fire. When the Germans saw we had anti-tank weapons they pulled back their armoured cars.

Throughout the day we were trying to collect boats. Patrols went to our dropping zone where there were still some containers, and they found a few small inflatable boats. During this whole time, day and night, we were under regular fire from German artillery mortars. North of the river were wooded hills from which the Germans could see everything – any movement was immediately picked up. We managed to collect four or five boats and one or two more came from the other side, from the Airborne Division. As the night of the 22nd fell we started crossing, but these inflatable boats took only two men; they were only small dinghies and we had no oars, we were using little spades, our trench tools, as paddles. It was a shocking affair. Only 50 to 55 men got across, and during this whole operation the Germans were having a good time picking us off.

On the 23rd we managed to get a promise of boats from XXX Corps. Our Chief of Staff went south – he was a sapper himself, an engineer – and he made arrangements with the engineers of XXX Corps for boats to reach us about 9.30 that night. They came at about midnight. We had organized our brigade, made up groups of 18 men and marked out approaches with white lines. Our engineers had been working all day and when we got to the river the boats were built for only twelve men. Throughout the night we had to reorganize from 18-man to twelve-man units. We had to carry and drag the boats a good 500 yards from the trucks to the river, up and down across dykes with steep, high banks, through the wet and slippery night. Throughout this reorganization we were under fire but General Sosabowski was walking up and down this high wall giving orders because the men who could not get on were standing about in crowds and were like ducks in a shooting gallery for the Germans. We managed that night to get about 250 across. Daylight came and it was impossible to do anything more.

During the next day General Horrocks came up to our brigade and met General Sosabowski. The latter explained to Horrocks that it was no use trying to make small crossings, that the division was in very, very poor condition, and there needed to be a big crossing, a whole division. Later that day our general went to a meeting at General Thomas's headquarters. The interpreter who was there told me about it. The conference was opened by Horrocks, who said that General Dempsey had ordered another attempt to cross the river, which would be made by General Thomas, and Thomas unfolded his plan. The crossing was to take place at two sites: the Polish Brigade would cross at the same place they did before, and the 4th Dorsets would take their boats further west, opposite the ferry. Behind them would go the 1st Polish Parachute Battalion which had jumped the day before. The Dorsets and the 1st Polish Battalion would join the British 1st Airborne Division with fresh supplies. General Sosabowski repeated his opinion that one battalion, even supported by another, would change nothing. He proposed a big crossing, by a whole fresh division further west. Only this would save the operation, but Thomas apparently rejected this idea.

Sosabowski returned to Driel. No boats arrived, and that was the end of the whole operation.

Next day came the order for the division to withdraw. It had been terrible for us. Not just that we were in a hard battle – after all, war is hard – but because by then, in September 1944, the Germans were practically beaten and were retreating. We thought that we were going in to beat the Germans, and instead we were beaten ourselves. Waiting all those days, it was disappointing, very disappointing. We thought that we would be beating the Germans.

For many years a feeling of frustration, a feeling that we didn't really manage to beat the Germans, was to haunt many of us – me definitely. We were so full of vigour. The whole Western Front was marching forward, but instead of going forward, we were stopped. We did what we could – we couldn't have done much more. It was the brigade's first operation, its first battle, the soldiers behaved very well and we did make an impact on the battle. We secured and held the south side of the river and by doing so we enabled the remnants of the 1st Airborne to be evacuated from the north. We were very sorry that we didn't win the battle, but we are still proud.

SERGEANT DICK WHITTINGHAM, 1st Parachute Battalion

I was a sergeant in the mortar platoon of the 1st Para Battalion. My section consisted of myself and nine others; we'd been together since July 1940.

We took the north road to Arnhem as we were supposed to hold the high ground north of the bridge. At five or six o'clock in the evening on the first day my company ran into an ambush and we all got split up. So of course we had to go to ground and three of us were wounded. For the rest of that evening we didn't get very far; it was all stopping and starting. In each section we had 44 ten-pound bombs – that's 60 pounds in weight to carry on your shoulders besides all the small arms and everything else.

By Tuesday we came under Lonsdale's force. Our advance had been stopped by the enemy and by this time we were rather short of ammunition so I was getting worried. But the rest of my mortar team managed to purloin a jeep full of three-inch mortar ammunition so now I had dozens upon dozens of bombs. I wasn't frightened any more. My field of fire was an open field about 600 yards deep and beyond this were woods where I thought the enemy would try to form up an attack. So we started to bomb the woods. We bombed and bombed and bombed again. We only stopped to allow the smoke ring around us to disperse; it made us an easy target. All of a sudden the attack came in; about seven tanks, armoured cars and supporting infantry, started coming across my field of fire, and I opened up on them. We kept firing until they got within 200 yards, and then the enemy infantry broke ranks and the tanks and other vehicles went away to the north.

At this stage Lonsdale decided to come back into Oosterbeek itself. We took up position on a dyke overlooking a big open field near the church. We spent the night there, surrounded by dead cows lying with their legs sticking up in the air and bellies torn open. The next day Lonsdale withdrew us from that position. We went into the church and read his famous words on the blackboard, 'Have half an hour's rest and carry on.'

I searched for a new mortar position which was difficult because a mortar pit had to be five feet deep and the soil around was so sandy you couldn't dig more than two or three feet deep. Then I came to a Mr and Mrs Breman's house. At the back was a tiny courtyard about three yards by nine bordered by the large house, a high brick wall and several barns all about 20 feet high. So I knocked at the door and the blacksmith – Mr Breman – came out. I asked him if he minded us being there and he said, 'No, it's quite all right.' And we were only about a yard from his back door, which led down to his cellar, which made the position even more ideal. There was even a pump in the courtyard. They were so helpful; they welcomed my men in the house and shared all their food – their chickens and winter stores – with us until nothing was left. That's why we called Mrs Breman 'mother'. The Dutch people had such a hard time of it, and although we didn't realize it at the time, we brought even more havoc. There were civilian casualties, and we ruined nearly 50 per cent of their houses and buildings. But despite all that it was they who felt sorry for us.

Usually the Germans would try to creep up on us by sheltering in holes in the ground, but we'd adjust our range and open fire. But on one occasion they got into dead ground only about 80 yards away which was too short for our three-inch mortars; they had a normal range of 200 to 1,600 yards. I was determined to get them. We reduced the number of main secondary charges to two, then one. Still the bombs were 'overs'. So in desperation I ordered, 'Primary charge only'. The primary charge was only supposed to ignite the main charges, but we sent this one off and it just crept through the air. And when I say 'crept' I mean 'crept' – it was hardly moving – we saw it going up and up and up and we were sure it was going to fall back down on us. But it slowly turned in the air and landed slap on target! The rubbish was still coming back so I fired a couple more bombs to seal the fate of those still out there. That was our narrowest escape.

While I was looking for another observation post I got caught by a sniper bullet. Luckily enough, it only grazed my head – just blood, no brains! But on the Saturday before we withdrew I got seriously wounded; coming back from reporting to Lonsdale I was shelled and my leg was hit. My men managed to get me down into the cellar and I saw no more of the rest of the action.

I returned after the war to see the Breman family and only then did I realize what a mess we had made of their house and their lives. I started to say how sorry I was, but she stopped me and said, 'It does not matter, because for a few days you made us a free people. You will always, always be welcome.'

PRIVATE ROBERT PEATLING, 2nd Parachute Battalion

As we moved towards the bridge we had an almost unbelievable fairy-tale welcome. On that sunny Sunday afternoon the villagers came rushing out to greet us showering food and drink on the 'deliverers'! They thought their war was over. It was my first time in action and I did not have long to wait before I saw our first casualty, a private soldier lying as if asleep by the roadside.

When I reached the bridge it was a hive of activity; the enemy were holding the other end and that was not in our book. B Company had not reported themselves by radio and the signal platoon officer, Lieutenant Ainslie, was told to find them; I was to be his escort. It was pitch black and the enemy kept sending up flares, which may have helped them but did not help us. After some time and not finding B Company we returned. Meanwhile there had been much activity over the bridge; we had been stopped from taking the far end and Colonel Frost wanted some boats to cross the river.

Sergeant Major Bishop must have thought I was a company runner for after another party had failed to find a boat he sent me with Major Wallis to reconnoitre. A machine-gun opened up on us and when the firing stopped Major Wallis had gone. I continued looking for a boat but had not caught up with him when I heard marching feet. I crossed to the doorway of a house facing the river and waited. I saw what was obviously our chaps with a sergeant leading a long column in single file. He told me he had not passed anyone else on this lower road and so I decided to return to the bridge with him. He had 22 prisoners with him, it was a military police section and they were going to the Arnhem police station. I took up the rearguard and was going to drop off as soon as we were challenged by the 2nd Battalion. We picked up another lone warrior, Sergeant Harry Parker of the 3rd Battalion, and on arrival at the police station said we were off to the bridge and our proper position.

A military police lieutenant said that we must wait there until he sent an escort for us both; he then left us. By the Tuesday afternoon we were completely surrounded, outnumbered, and the sergeant in charge ordered everyone to stop firing and surrender, a very painful moment for all. I raced for the roof and then changed my mind and settled for the rafters in the attic. The Germans searched the building, shooting into every room but as luck would have it they did not venture up the narrow staircase that led to the attic. After about 15 minutes they left with their prisoners and ours. I had won the first round.

Now that I was on my own I took stock of my position. From my roof lookout I could see nothing but fire and smoke down by the bridge, not a healthy sign. At times during the day our aircraft were about and the anti-aircraft fire intense.

I collected together all loose ammunition and two Sten guns that had been left. I had shaving gear, a full water bottle, four biscuits and a meat block. I had my emergency tin of chocolate and luckily found another left behind by someone who was now a prisoner. The water system had failed so I took water from a lavatory cistern and in the process flushed it, so I scooped the water from the pan! It started to rain so I put various utensils under the shattered tiles on the roof. I found a notebook and started writing a letter home, then changed it into a diary form in order to keep track of the days. I found a clock in an office and brought it up to the attic.

Flying Fortresses of the USAAF came over on three days and dropped some earth-shuddering bombs by the bridge, taking off more tiles from my roof. I searched the policemen's personal lockers and found some scraps of food, cigars and pipe tobacco. I had never smoked before and found that the smoking kept the hunger pains at bay. To help pass the time I collected as many stamps of Holland I could find in the various offices, soaked them from the envelopes and put them in my diary, as any good philatelist would.

October came and it was wet, cold and miserable and I had no news of what was happening. I usually went out into the town scavenging for food before 4 am, while it was quiet.

On 30 October I was still waiting to hear the battle moving my way when I had visitors to my attic who caught sight of my washing bowl and other everyday items for living, and walked across the rafters towards me. They moved away again, downstairs, but returned very shortly afterwards. As they came towards me I stood up and challenged them; they were Dutch policemen. The senior, Lieutenant ten Hove, said he would not help but would not stop the other man, Lieutenant Hans van Maris, from doing so. They told me that the division was no more, that 6,500 were prisoners and 3,500 were dead, that the army was still at Nijmegen 20 miles away.

About an hour later Johan Penseel arrived with clothes for me. He identified himself with the V for Victory tap on the door, waited while I shaved and we left for his home at Velperplein 7, an electrical shop. Lieutenant van Maris walked in front with his cycle, giving the all-clear sign at each junction. My new hideout was a void between two rooms with high Victorian-style ceilings and above two cupboards, reached through a trapdoor in the bedroom above. Mr Penseel said he would be back with some food, wonderful! He came back with his two sons, John, 24, and Marinus, 21. They brought a saucepan of steaming vegetables, coffee, cooking apples and a blancmange. I ate as we talked. I'd not eaten a proper meal for six weeks and had lost two stone so when they left I ate more and more until all food was gone and I lay on my back writhing in pain for being so stupid.

Some days later two resistance workers came to live in the house with me, Klaas Schuttinga and Nico van der Oever, both 23. We had a supply of vegetables and a meagre weekly ration. I became the cook. They went out daily to do any job that they were asked and because they wore stolen police uniforms they travelled quite freely.

Herman Bresser took my photograph for an Ausweiss (identity card). Brother Paul edited 'World's Press News' an underground newspaper and was a frequent visitor. All these lads had been imprisoned and sent to Germany to work but had escaped. Fires were deliberately started in the town by Germans and one very near to Velperplein got out of hand and we evacuated. While pushing a handcart up a steep incline a German soldier came to help me and talk, John Penseel quickly changed places with me!

Christmas 1944 was memorable for me. I joined the Penseel family in the vaults of the Amsterdamsche Bank on Velperplein. They had adopted a Jewish girl of seven whose parents had been taken away; we were great friends for the day and exchanged Christmas gifts.

The Town Mayor (Hauptsturmfuehrer) decided not to renew my Ausweiss for the Technische Nothilfe after 31 December and it was thought best that I should leave the town. At 10 pm on a cold and frosty New Year's Eve I said farewell to the Penseel family and sitting on the carrier of Nico's cycle with Klaas in attendance we presented ourselves at the control barrier on the Apeldoornscheweg. According to my Ausweiss I was a deaf and dumb electrician; Nico and Klaas did the talking. I was handed over to Jan Himmerling at Woeste Hoeve for safe keeping and Nico and Klaas returned to Arnhem.

The following day we visited various houses at Hoenderloo, Otterlo and Barnevelt. Eventually I met Herman van Esveld and was invited to stay on his farm at Kootwijkerbroek. To my surprise I met John Haller, a glider pilot and Harold Riley, a brigade signaller. We slept in a hollow haystack with Paul, a Dutch radio operator from SOE. We were too many for safety so I had to move on, and Johan van Dijk of Achterveld said he would have me for a few days until I made the run across the Rhine. I was known to his six children as Oom Kees from Limburg to explain why I did not speak the same dialect as they did.

On 16 April rumour had it that troops had turned in our direction. (Achterveld became no-man's-land for three weeks after I had left. The two sides met in the village school to agree the Armistice.) I left at first light with a sandwich from Mrs van Dijk, wearing civvies and carrying the police chief's 9-mm Browning. I set off carefully using cover where possible and after several hours saw troop movement on a road. They stopped short of me and I stood up with my hands outstretched, shouted, 'Ik ben Engelsman' and then remembered it was time to speak English. It was the 49th Lower Edmonton Regiment who were out patrolling in front of their battalion.

Off to Zutphen for interrogation, new uniform, bottle of whisky, medical inspection, B1 malnutrition. Two days later in a Dakota I landed at Croydon Airport. 'Have you anything to declare?' challenged a customs officer. I rudely answered. 'Where the bloody hell do you think I've been this past seven months?' and he stepped back. I had arrived back home!

Three months later and back with the regiment I received a letter from a lieutenant colonel in MI9 in London saying that my diary had turned up in the house of a Dutch farmer in Essen, Barnevelt. And then came the bad news. Most of the Arnhem Resistance Group (LKP) that I had joined had been rounded up on 2 January by the SD and started on their way to concentration camps; they were tortured for knowledge of Bob the Englishman. Toon van Daalen, Johan Penseel and Nico van der Oever were saved from the camps and were returned to hospitals in Holland, all in poor health. John Penseel and brother Marinus died in Ludwigslust concentration camp in March 1945. Klaas Schuttinga was suffering badly from dysentery in February 1945 and was parted from his friend Nico. Klaas was never heard of again. The others managed to avoid capture. I can never forget them.

CAPTAIN FRANK KING, 11th Parachute Battalion

For three months the 11th Battalion lived at almost constant alert, with no leave, continual planning and restricted access to nearby towns. We had a great fear that the war would be over before our assistance was called for and the girls of Melton Mowbray were already beginning to label us 'Home Guards'.

Market Garden changed all that. Our objective was the far bridge at Arnhem, and as soon as the soldiers were briefed the camp was sealed by military police. Contact was broken with the outside world and the telephone lines cut, so there could be no spoken goodbyes – soldiers wrote their farewell letters, but knew that they would not be posted until they had landed in Holland. It was always annoying for married men not to have that last word with their wives but once briefing had taken place, security had to be paramount. The overall plan left a few unanswered questions. We were pleased to have the far bridge; that seemed the place of honour. But it was a long way from 21st Army Group's present positions and although Monty had promised likely relief within 48 hours, it was clear that many things might upset this forecast. There were only enough planes to carry a third of our division. Because of the distance this meant that our arrival would be spread over at least three days. And because Air Force intelligence indicated that the bridge area was probably covered by anti-aircraft defences, drop zones were agreed reluctantly well to the west of the town. 1st Brigade, Divisional HQ and much of the Airlanding Brigade in gliders were to have the honour of the first day, whilst we would follow early the next morning.

Our brigade should have left Lincolnshire at dawn on D+1 but the airfield was blanketed with thick fog. When, eventually the red light came on we quickly sorted ourselves out and, as No. 1, I took up my position near the door with my batman close behind.

With five minutes to go the crew chief should have been busy re-checking all our equipment. He was a nice young American encased in nylon body armour, but at that moment he made me angry because he was lounging in his seat, a picture of contented idleness. 'Bloody Air Force,' I thought, and shouted at him. There was no reaction. It was only then that I noticed a large and growing pool of blood beneath his seat. He was dead, shot through the floor of the plane. When I looked out of the door I had a further shock – our port wing was on fire and we seemed 200 feet from the ground!

I shouted to my sergeant major to open the crew cabin door and when he did so all we could see was smoke and flames. I immediately gave the order to jump and we crashed the red light, an indictable offence but it probably saved our lives. I landed very heavily and, nursing my bruises, counted the rest down. We were two light. Our pilot was a conscientious and brave man; although the plane was now a veritable fireball, he flew straight and level until he disappeared low over the horizon.

With our heavy loads and no trolleys we plodded towards our objective. The inevitable small boy joined us and we soon came under fire but only had one casualty – the boy, shot through the stomach. We carried him to a nearby house and left him with the startled occupants.

We were now in an awkward situation; most of my soldiers were mortar-men who only carried a pistol for personal protection. So my large army of 17 men possessed only one rifle and two machine carbines between them. Meanwhile an enemy patrol was snapping at our heels but luckily they were not very bold. We made good progress towards Arnhem and en route came across Lieutenant Keith Bell and his C Company men who'd also been shot down. At dusk we decided to rest in a small copse until dark.

On the edge of this copse a Dutch farmer was milking his cows. Although communicating with him was difficult he did put us in touch with three young men who would act as guides. We had 20 miles to go and just before midnight we rested in a farm house where we had a splendid meal. Never had food tasted so good.

Meanwhile, Lambert Ledoux, a Belgian and the French-speaking member of the guide party, explained that the battle in Arnhem was going badly; the British were completely surrounded and we would have little chance of reaching them. He also told us that they could take us no further – they were in danger of being shot if they were caught out of doors after curfew but he offered to hide us until the situation became more clear. After some thought, we thanked them for their help and food, but we must, we said, go on.

We had not gone far before we realized that the redoubtable Ledoux was still with us. A few miles further on we heard the sound of digging so Lambert and I crept forward to try and identify the diggers, but we couldn't make out what language they were using. Lambert motioned me back and crept forward. Suddenly he shouted, 'Les boches'. There was a burst of firing; a sound of running feet; some angry German shouts and then silence. We said a silent prayer for Lambert and then quietly withdrew. He was a brave man.

Veering north again we struck the railway which would take us directly to Arnhem. Suddenly we came across the welcome sight of dozens of parachutes draped over gorse bushes and lying on the ground. We had reached the drop zone and at once came under fire from our own side – the wounded soldiers who'd been left at the DZ. We found bodies too, of members of 4th Brigade, who'd faced an opposed landing.

From now on neither guides nor map reading were necessary – we merely followed the brigade litter. Parachute soldiers are always grossly overladen and take early opportunity to lighten their loads. Sweet and chocolate wrappers came first and then, as the going got longer and harder, the odd respirator or other item of kit not deemed necessary for killing Germans.

By mid-morning we had almost caught the end of the brigade tail, so we took the opportunity to have a quick breakfast and to tidy ourselves up; we desperately needed the rest and it was important to arrive in good order. I found Brigade HQ, apologized for our late arrival and enquired after our battalion but nobody knew where it was. Near midnight a cheerful driver arrived in a Bren carrier to collect ammunition for the troops at the sharp end and he professed to know where my battalion was. Quickly I obtained permission to go and look for them. We hurtled through the night without lights until we reached our destination just north-west of the railway bridge at Arnhem. 'Your 11 Para,' said the driver, 'are over there,' and gestured into the darkness. I set off in that direction and struck lucky – I stumbled into C Company and my old platoon sergeant.

Dawn brought a gloomy picture. I expected to find myself in a well-prepared battalion position. But of some 35 officers only two were left. The 700 soldiers had shrunk to less than 100. I learned that in its struggle to reach 2 Para on the bridge the battalion had met heavy opposition on the outskirts of the town. This remnant – mostly C Company – was all that remained.

Later that morning a supply drop came of much-needed food, ammunition and medical stores. We watched helplessly as wave after wave of aircraft flew steadfastly into heavy ack-ack fire, incurring many casualties, and then dropped our desperately needed stores into German hands.

At about lunch time we gained a new commander, Major Dickie Lonsdale. Shortly after his arrival we saw our first tank which began to shell our position. I was told to take some soldiers and shift it. We had no anti-tank weapons in our position except a PIAT, but its crew was dead so I left it behind and took five soldiers who were near to hand. We moved off cautiously and to my relief made the first house undetected, burst in through the back door and made straight for the cellar. We were about to clear it by tossing in a grenade when we noticed a very tearful housewife and some young children. Upstairs I heard several quick shots which had disposed of two snipers. In the second house we approached the cellar door quietly and threw it open. Inside was a very surprised German soldier who was carrying his rifle carelessly at 'the trail', which is just about the worst possible way of carrying a rifle to allow quick action. I calmly pointed my pistol at his chest and told him to put his hands up. He was a far smarter soldier than I had credited. In one swift movement he tipped up his barrel and fired one-handed. I could feel my breast bone exploding. In a reflex action I also fired twice; with a .45 Colt at point blank range there was no need to inspect him. Blood was now also gushing from a hole in my chest about an inch above the heart.

There was more shooting upstairs. Two more snipers had been accounted for in the front bedroom. We then inspected the rear. About six feet below one of the bedroom windows was our tank – not in fact a tank at all but a large tracked SP gun. Its commander had his head and shoulders above the hatch and was warily observing his front. We hastily withdrew into the room and prepared our secret anti-tank weapon. It consisted of an army sock packed with plastic explosive and detonated with the fusing device of a 69 grenade. We opened the window and dropped our bomb at a point just behind the commander's hatch. There was an impressive bang, a great deal of smoke and one very dead-looking commander.

On our way back – for some unaccountable reason – we stumbled into a chicken pen and had to force a way through the wire. Just as we started to crawl through, a German stick grenade hurtled through the air. There was a tremendous bang and I received fragments in the leg but one of the soldiers had taken most of the blast on his thigh. We dragged him clear and had what seemed an interminable journey over 300–400 yards back to our position. I was told to repair to the medical centre in a house near Oosterbeek church.

The aid post was a splendidly solid Dutch house belonging to a solicitor who was absent with the 'underground'. His young wife, Kate ter Horst, had willingly agreed that her home be turned into a hospital. My heart went out to her and her young children. What was obviously once a beautiful home was now a shambles. Bodies, alive and dead, filled every room and passageway. Dirt, blood, smells and groans were everywhere. It was reminiscent of the Crimean War and she was a modern Florence Nightingale.

I passed the next few days in a deliberately comatose state. With no resupply there was little food and the Germans had turned the water off at the mains. Although there was a pump not far away in a garden, it was constantly monitored by German snipers. After two precious medical orderlies had been killed trying to get to the pump some of the wounded tried but they too paid their toll. The doctors were marvels – they never seemed to stop and never seemed to sleep although they were inundated with patients and short of all supplies. But the heroine of the hour was undoubtedly Kate ter Horst. She had, I believe, five young children yet somehow she not only kept these amused and happy in her dark cellar but read us psalms, chatted and cheered us all whilst her home grew more damaged, soiled and sordid.

Eventually the house was over-full and still the wounded came in. Many were serious cases and inevitably a system of culling took place. Lesser casualties were asked to leave. They left in some sorrow not knowing where to go.

My own position was not a particularly happy one. Medical supplies were now at a premium and I could expect no more meaningful treatment. A shot of morphine had brought a tremendous feeling of well-being on each of the first two days but a greater one of depression when the practice ceased. I decided to leave. I found my way to a house on the perimeter where there were some glider pilots. I remained with these new friends for several days until one early morning I was awakened by harsh German voices and discovered to my surprise that I was the sole occupant of the house. I was taken outside and placed in a small open vehicle. I asked a guard who spoke English, 'What happened to my friends?' He said, 'Don't you know? They have gone. They crossed the river last night. They left only the wounded behind!'

I was shattered and angry but on reflection decided that it had been a sensible decision. To break contact at night is a difficult manoeuvre. Stealth, silence and speed are all essential. Wounded passengers would jeopardize the safety of all. But it seemed a poor way to end a great adventure. Taking stock I decided that I had little to be proud about. I had led a company of soldiers to Arnhem and had scarcely fought with them. It was clear that our mission had failed and that the very people whom we had set out to liberate would now pay dearly for our failure.

And at what cost? It was many months before I discovered. Over 10,000 set out. Only 2,163 crossed the river on that final night and more than 1,200 lay dead upon the northern bank, including every officer but one in my own company. However General Eisenhower did write to the divisional commander: 'In this war there has been no single performance by any unit that has more greatly inspired me than the nine-day action of your division. Your officers and men were magnificent. The Allied forces salute them!'

KATE TER HORST

It was a peaceful Sunday in September. From our vicarage garden we could hear the organ playing in the church of Oosterbeek-Laag, and our five children were enjoying the sunshine in the apple orchard. Suddenly a couple of fast fighting machines flew low over us, shattering our peace and making the baby cry. Then an angry staccato sound filled the air – they were firing! We rushed the children indoors and heard the planes come lower and lower over our roof, bullets rattling on the slates and whistling around the house. In the distance we heard heavy explosions. What could be happening?

When the shooting died down we went outside. The sky was full of huge bombers flying from the west in marvellous formations. They seemed to be towing something behind them – very long planes with no landing wheels. Suddenly they were coming down gracefully as the bombers turned and climbed. They were gliders! An air-landing! We were mad with joy – could this mean liberty from the Germans, who were running away towards the east?

We ate supper in the large kitchen from which we could see the road. Suddenly a group of villagers gathered, all looking and pointing in one direction. We couldn't believe our eyes; along the road, like a long green serpent, came our British liberators. The leader laughed under his camouflage helmet, spread his arms out and said, 'Give us a kiss!' I remember their big smiles and great long legs, each step seemed twice the length of the Germans – moving so calmly and yet in perfect order. We stared and stared; we were used to the noisy German marching, but these men moved so quickly and quietly. There were orange streamers and flags, flowers and cheering people hugging each other with joy.

At seven the next morning, two Red Cross cars came into our grounds. The men weren't wearing helmets, but dark red berets. A young man – Dr Martin – jumped out and asked politely whether he might set up a small Red Cross first aid post in our house. 'We don't need much; only the lightly wounded will be treated here. I hope we won't have many casualties.' While he was speaking supplies of stretchers, linen first aid cases, tins of sugar and tea were brought in.

Outside, the house was surrounded by soldiers busy making tea. They cut large slices of beautiful white bread and the children got some, as well as some real chocolate. In the beautiful meadow beyond the orchard (which we called 'little heaven') the Tommies were digging a large hole. My eldest boy was enjoying himself watching a piece of field artillery being dragged into it. The gun barrel was pointing towards Arnhem South and soon the first command came: 'Fire!' A flame. And a cracking roar.

On Tuesday the firing around us increased and we could not leave the house. The first groups of wounded were brought in, lying side by side on their red canvas stretchers. Most of them were cheerful and smiled at me. The kitchen was very busy, full of tea-making soldiers. Our Aga did good service and an old pump in the scullery was a great help as the water tower had been shot to pieces. In front of the Aga stood Ernest (known as 'Scan' by his friends) a sturdy Londoner and father of six. He was wonderful – the doctor's right hand, and the focal point for any hungry tired soldier, for he was the cook. Although he was a sergeant, he seemed to take control of the whole situation. He told me I should sleep in the cellar that night for safety, and I knew I must obey.

Suddenly my husband appeared. He had been helping the officers, and had come to say goodbye; the British were being forced to withdraw with their artillery into the woods, so that our house would again be in German territory. The captain would not let my husband stay.

At seven that evening we prepared our night quarters, covering the cellar floor with mattresses and rugs. With five children, myself and some neighbours it was very full. I awoke in the close, hot cellar in the middle of the night, to sounds of gunfire and shouts of, 'Wounded! Wounded!' But nothing could prepare me for what I saw the next morning when I opened the cellar door. I was struck dumb with amazement; our house had been transformed overnight. The long corridor was filled with wounded, side by side on their stretchers with just enough room between them to put a foot down. With difficulty I got through to the kitchen, which was full of activity. On the granite floor were six or seven wounded, the doctor examining them. Scan was making tea, orderlies were washing up and the large table was covered with dressings and bandages. Medical orderlies ran in and out while the doctor calmly gave his orders. But he was worried; the pump only gave a little water and that wasn't clean. The nearest supply was 60 yards away.

I went through the rooms . . . wounded everywhere, in the dining room, the study and the garden room, the side corridor and even under the stairs and in the lavatory. There was not a single corner free of them. Splinters of glass from the broken windows covered the wounded like sugar. I felt so helpless; if only I could be a proper hostess and give them a real bed to sleep in and at least fresh water to drink. It was a terrible thing for me when they refused to use the things I offered; I wanted them to tear up my linen for bandages, use my stores of food, but they didn't want to – they said I'd need it for the children.

When I came upstairs again that afternoon even the stairs and landing were crowded with wounded soldiers. No-one could get through; the top floor was full and they were even lying in the attic. My house was protecting over 300 people. There were no sweets for the children that day; all the rations had gone and there had been no fresh supplies. But there was still a large copper of real English tea on the Aga and Scan found time to think of us and sent us a jugful.

Towards evening I went to the back door for a breath of fresh air, and I saw them for the first time – the dead. Six or seven of them, maybe more, most of them lying face downwards, with tousled hair over their muddy faces. They lay like forgotten bags dropped on the path to the kitchen. Could it go on like this for much longer? We expected the Second Army at any moment.

That night I told the children stories to make them laugh before they slept. We always had a lot of soldiers sheltering with us, many in the cellar and some even fell asleep on the coal. One of them stretched out his arms for the baby and took it on his knees. I could see by the light of the candle how he was sweating and black from the slit trenches. It was impossible to keep even the most primitive hygiene in our dark cellar, and before I knew it I said, 'No, that won't do – you're too dirty,' and put the baby back in his wooden cart. How could I have done it? Perhaps it was the last time he would look into a child's eyes. The next moment he was outside again, helmet on and loaded Sten gun under his arm.

When I could, I told the older children about life upstairs. I told them about Captain Frank King whose stretcher lay on trestles, so there was room for one to sit and talk to him which was impossible by the other stretchers. He would tell me, smiling, about his children and asked me about my children downstairs. The children drew a little picture for him, which he folded carefully and put in his pocket-book with his family photographs.

That night yet more wounded were brought into the kitchen where they lay groaning and panting. One was turning blue, and Dr Martin bent over him, pressing his weight on him, digging for the thread of life which had sunk away so deep. Another of the wounded screamed out in fear as the house took a crashing blow, but the doctor did not look up until slowly a deep gasping sound rose from under his hand.

The next morning it was very still and the heat in the cellar became almost unbearable. I went upstairs for a breath of air. A carrier came into the kitchen with a bucket of water. Fresh water! He handed me a jugful and I emptied it in one draught. I noticed him staring at me and I turned away, ashamed, thinking, 'Can't you control yourself? There's no-one here without a burning thirst.' To make it worse, Scan came up to me and asked what was wrong with the pump. The water was quite red. We both had the same dreadful thought; could it be the blood of the dead men washed through by the rain? All we could do was disinfect it; it would be suicide to fetch water from 60 yards away. That afternoon Scan stopped me and said, 'There's a red parachute on the roof – that's what caused the red water.'

A small hand pulled at my skirt. 'Mother, will you fetch my dolly Poppeljis for me?' My eldest asked for his fretsaw and a piece of wood. But the firing was heavy, bullets rattling and shells thundering around us. On the landing a soldier rested his head against the wall and looked at me with his blue eyes staring out from a mask of congealed blood. His features were invisible. I didn't even have any water to wash him with. These men lay exposed to the wildest freaks of chance. You'd think the devil himself was at work; all over the house the wounded lay disfigured, shaking with fever and martyred with the pain and thirst in all that hellish noise.

I had a bottle of currant juice and I offered it to 25 men in the big room. It was pure, thick juice, excellent for the thirst. The bottle was passed from hand to hand and came back half-full. I couldn't believe it; they were dying of thirst. So I joked with them: 'Are you soldiers? Can't you finish a single bottle?' It went round again. On the back wall somebody got up and helped his neighbour who had no hands. Such kindness and thoughtfulness . . . these boys had radiant hearts. Such a contrast to the hardness of the Germans. Despite everything, seeing such things made me very happy.

At last I remembered I was looking for toys. I had to step over a few stretchers to reach Poppeljis. I found the fretsaw but had to go up to the attic to get a piece of wood. It was awful up there; holes in the roof and noise enough to make you crazy. Thank heaven there were no wounded up there; so many wounded had died that there was room for them lower down.

Downstairs, the children were delighted with their toys, but the doctor was pale and depressed. We were now under our own fire and a shell had killed several wounded near the window where Captain King lay. The men around told me he hadn't been hurt but had been moved back into the house. I searched everywhere but could not find him. When I got back the doctor told me that the Germans were pressing in closer and closer to the ring of British near the Rhine. 'Don't worry,' I said. 'This house won't be smashed.'

But it was unbearable, to see this terrible pain and suffering. I remember those bleeding faces; you'd think they'd be crying or shouting but there was no fuss at all. I was full of admiration for them. I just wanted to bless them all, those simple boys.

Up to that moment there had always been a sense of order and duty among the soldiers who sheltered for a short time in the cellar. But now they crowded together and made no show of going out again; German tanks were approaching, they told us. That night our cellar was crowded with men while heavy firing sounded around us. We began to sing our national songs and then all kinds of English verses. The soldiers said they didn't feel 'singy' but still, they tried. Then we tried to sleep. But it was unbearably hot and stuffy; there were 40 people in that hole. The baby vomited suddenly in his cradle; now even his mattress and cushion were dirty. He lay tired and white in my arms. I was terrified in case the Germans would see the soldiers and throw in hand grenades, but I couldn't bear to wake the sleeping men and send them away. Later I managed to find some warm water and bath the baby, and his dull eyes brightened for the first time in days.

As darkness fell that day the crazy firing got worse, not better. We felt surrounded by an iron ring of cannon getting steadily nearer. The noise was incessant and we were too miserable to speak. We sat in silence and thought of the boys outside; our cannon were still firing, so they were still standing by their pieces in this murderous fire. The heroes! – they wouldn't give up.

A great silence fell and we momentarily thought of leaving. In the cellar we discussed everything, and slowly our confidence grew. Courage was infectious, and unanimously we decided to stay on. We felt so deeply thankful, and together we read a psalm written for fighters: 'Thou shalt not be afraid for the terror by night; nor for the arrow that flieth by day' (Psalm 91). These words brought such healing to our hearts, and after saying the Lord's Prayer, we lay down to sleep, leaving our fate in God's hands. Before sleeping, I went upstairs to tell the padre how we had been strengthened. He had no time to read to the men, so he gave me his little Bible and asked me to do it for him. So I went to every room in the house and read them this strange old psalm which now seemed so clear and simple. At any other time in our lives the meaning would have been hidden from us.

The next day snipers penetrated into the hedges and fruit trees around the house, and fired shamelessly into the rooms and corridors crowded with helpless people. It wasn't long before the doctor was wounded. He was so unself-pitying and was sure he'd be up and about in a few hours. Then it happened – a crashing blow filled the cellar with dust and debris. Above us we soon heard desperate sounds of digging as they tried to release trapped men beneath the rubble. I managed to get upstairs, and saw that the shell had blown a great hole in the garden room. Along the wall lay a few survivors, covered with brick dust; they could hardly understand what had happened. I brought one of them a drink. 'A Nightingale,' one of them whispered. A lump came into my throat; if only I could have done more. But I had to let them lie there in misery.

The doctor had now been wounded in four places and his resilience was gone. He was given morphia. I knew it was only a matter of hours until the end, so I looked for some clothes for the baby. I opened a drawer of fresh, white untouched linen. The scent of baby soap and lavender rose from it, and I bent over to breathe in the sweetness. It was like a dream; I couldn't believe it had ever smelt like that in my house.

That night, unknown to us down in the cellar, General Urquhart gave the order to retreat. At dawn there was an eerie quiet. I looked outside and saw a German soldier standing on the doorstep. The order had come to clear the house and it was time to leave with the children; you never knew what a German would do to your children. We loaded a handcart with our few possessions. Then I went indoors to say goodbye to our Airborne friends. We whispered good wishes to each other. Despite everything, they were proud to have held out for so long. As I was wrapping the baby in an army cape I saw the Airbornes step outside. Anyone who could walk at all had to walk, whoever had two legs must drag another along. And so they marched out. I could hardly bear to look at them any more but I blessed them in my heart as I pushed our cart up the hill. Our hearts were full of courage as we joined the stream of refugees walking through the sunshine. We took deep breaths of the fresh air and I rejoiced that all my five children were around me, safe and unhurt.

CORPORAL DANNY MORGANS, 1st Parachute Battalion

One brigade, three battalions, to clear a city. That's how it was on that Sunday, with 1st Brigade; the Airlanding Brigade staying out on the dropping zone to protect it for the arrival of the 4th Brigade. We were on our own and no wonder we were swallowed up by that city – like penny packets. I was a corporal in T Company, 1st Para Battalion, and by Tuesday or Wednesday morning we were being pushed right out of the centre of Arnhem. We didn't realize how close we had got to reaching the bridge before we had to pull back to Oosterbeek.

In the city I was given a mixed section of half a dozen men and told to hold a house covering a road junction until 1400 hours. This was to allow other units to withdraw in the direction of Oosterbeek. It was a beautiful house, belonging to an elderly couple, and I suggested they should leave as it was about to become very dangerous. But the owner said, 'We will stay.' So I persuaded them to shelter in the cellar and then set about putting the house in a state of defence. It was a heartbreaking task; we literally had to wreck this beautiful place.

First the windows had to be smashed, so the glass couldn't be blown in on us. Then the furniture was piled into barricades inside the room. Everything that was watertight, from the bath to buckets, vases and jugs, had to be filled with water; the Germans were using incendiary ammunition to burn us out. Very soon the place was an organized shambles. Suddenly the old gentleman appeared in his wrecked lounge. He was carrying a tray with glasses and a bottle of Advocaat. He solemnly filled up the glasses and handed them round to the men who'd just wrecked his home – I apologized for what we had done and he replied: 'It is not you, my son, it is the war.' And he returned to his cellar. To this day, if I am taking a drink (and I was teetotal then!) and get sentimental, I call for an Advocaat and think of that marvellous Dutch gentleman. He treated us as honoured guests even when we'd just destroyed the life-work of him and his wife. We had to withdraw from that position and I always regret not having let them know we were leaving. I still don't know whether they survived that day.

When we got back to Oosterbeek we joined Major Dickie Lonsdale's mixed force and heard his speech in the old church.

From the church we took up positions in gardens nearby. Dick Whittingham had our last mortar next door at Bertha Breman's house. She remembers us as very dirty and tired, and we remember the Bremans as the only Dutch in that part of the Benedendorpsweg who hadn't evacuated. They wouldn't shift, despite everything, and they helped the wounded. It was there I got injured by a mortar bomb in the head and the knee. Head wasn't bad – I'd always been told I had a thick head and it paid off in the end! The knee was a compound fracture though, so they took me over to Kate ter Horst's house, which was the MDS.

The mess over there was indescribable. I was stuck out in the back-yard at first – there was no room inside – but as people died inside they'd move you further in. I spent a couple of hours under a glass porch which wasn't a lot of fun. They put a blanket over my face to keep off the glass splinters. Then they got me into the kitchen which was the operating theatre. But they had no bandages and no anaesthetics; the doctor came up and said, 'Sorry, we can't do anything for you.' So they put me out in the passageway, and I saw Kate passing through – a lady, climbing over the bodies.

But the worst part was when the officer came in and told us that the division had been ordered to evacuate and they had to leave us behind. We didn't feel betrayed, but just thought of the shame of being prisoners of war. We knew we'd done all we possibly could, but we had no idea of the overall picture; we only knew what had happened in our little area. But we couldn't worry about it at that stage as we were so terribly tired. It was only when we got to prisoner-of-war camp that we realized what a disaster it had been. What we really worried about was that people at home would say we'd done a lousy job.

I once said to Bertha Breman, 'I can't understand why you made such a fuss of us, why you made us so welcome. We didn't liberate you. We killed your people, destroyed your homes.' She replied, 'Because you came.' I said: 'But we made such an awful mess of the job.' She put her hand on mine and said: 'Say no more – YOU CAME.'

CHAPTER ELEVEN

GREECE
Operation Manna

1944

I N SEPTEMBER 1943, FOLLOWING THE SURRENDER OF ITALY, ELAS (the Greek National People's Liberation Army), the military wing of the Greek Communist Party, seized huge quantities of weapons abandoned in the area of Italian occupation. By August 1944, when the Germans began to withdraw, the communists controlled nearly 80 per cent of Greece. Winston Churchill despatched British troops to Greece to support a stable government acceptable to the Western Allies, to accept the German surrender and to pave the way for a large-scale relief operation.

Operation Manna was launched on 4 October 1944, when British troops landed at Patras. Four days later the Germans left Athens. On 12 October 1944, a company of the 4th Parachute Battalion dropped on Megara, northwest of Athens, in extremely windy conditions to seize the airfield for the arrival of the remainder of the 2nd Independent Parachute Brigade for an advance on Athens, which they entered on 15 October. Thereafter, until January 1945, the brigade was engaged in clearing up remnants of the German forces throughout Greece, restoring civil order, and subsequently fighting in Athens a particularly thankless and bloody campaign against ELAS which cost them heavy casualties. The task of clearing out ELAS was a difficult one. Quite often, battalions and companies were completely detached from each other under sniper and mortar fire but the brigade held fast until the relief divisions arrived from Italy. The brigade was withdrawn and returned to Italy in February 1945.

GREECE OCTOBER 1944 – FEBRUARY 1945

MAJOR TONY FARRAR-HOCKLEY, 6th Parachute Battalion

Our task was to force the Germans out of Greece, rather as we had forced them out of the South of France. It was known that they were ready to go but that they needed pushing. We needed airfields there and we needed to try and get right round onto the Balkan flank, to exploit it if the Russians were held up, and if things went wrong in North-West Europe. Mr Churchill always had up his sleeve the idea that we should attack the soft under-belly, through Italy and through Yugoslavia.

After a difficult landing in high winds at Megara we made our rendezvous and began the march into Athens. We had been warned that there was schism between those who supported the old government and the Greek royal family, and a strong vigorous group of communist-led guerrillas, the EAM-ELAS. When we got into Athens, the crowds gave us a colossal reception. I had one of those extraordinary war-time experiences. In the crowd I saw a sergeant in the Commandos who had been a friend of mine in ordinary days, and I just had time to say, 'Good Lord, Stefan, how good to see you – what are you doing here?' We shook hands before the crowd separated us, and I've never seen him again. The Greeks were going mad and the difficulty was to contain and keep together our soldiers; there were a number of very attractive Greek girls trying to secure them for parties, which didn't help. The three battalions chased after the Germans. The 4th and ourselves (the 6th) were confined mostly to the direct route up north of Athens, while the 5th Battalion went off by sea to Salonika. The 6th Battalion was halted to secure south central Greece. Thebes became the centre of operations. We cleared out small pockets of Germans from the surrounding countryside. I took control of the town of Thebes, and was in effect the military governor, where we did a great deal of initial relief work before the official agencies came. There were two villages where they did not have a single blanket between them nor seed to put in for the following year's growth. We were able to obtain relief supplies and make sure that they went directly to them.

Our work in Thebes was continually hindered by the guerrilla brigade in the area – almost 5,000 in ranks. They were led by dedicated communist officers. They attempted to impose their rule on the villagers, which they had no mandate to do, and to impose a government in the town of Thebes, which we denied them. We succeeded in minimizing their authority, pending some proper arrangements from Athens.

As we came into the winter we were told we would be withdrawing to take part in the next operation in Italy, so 2nd Parachute Brigade was ordered to reassemble in Athens for embarkation. Just after we got back into

Athens we were suddenly ordered out quite late at night to round up a body of Greek former guerrillas who were converging on Athens. They turned out to be Colonel Nikiforas (a pseudonym: literally, 'Victorious') and the men we had encountered in Thebes. There was a very unpleasant scene by firelight as we rounded them up and told them to hand over their arms. They did this with great ill-grace until my commanding officer, who had attempted to be friendly, gave an order to our soldiers to put a round in the breech of their rifles. Needless to say they all escaped later from their rather flimsy confinement; quite shortly the whole of Athens was besieged by the communist guerrillas and we found ourselves fighting them and holding them off. In places, we discovered they were arresting civilians arbitrarily, as we had seen happening in Thebes – and killing political opponents and their families whose bodies we later discovered. In the struggle for Athens, all our three battalions were heavily engaged; the 5th mainly in the Acropolis area, the 6th Battalion in Omonia Square and the 4th adjoining. My own company was at the top of the road to Piraeus, throwing back these people who were trying to push in and take over Athens. During this fighting, OC, C Company was shot through the head, and I, while acting as OC B Company, had been wounded in the arm and chest but had recovered from that. Suddenly, at the age of 20, I was told by my CO to become OC, C Company permanently. I felt a seasoned old soldier. For ten days we remained in defence, fighting at night as much as by day. Then after reinforcement from Italy the whole Athens' garrison began to attack.

We had learnt the technique of mouse-holing – blowing a hole through houses to get at the enemy without going up the street. One morning we were mouse-holing through a chemist's shop and as we went through I saw one or two rogues taking cards of scissors etc. I stopped in the middle of this attack, very vexed, and said to my sergeant, 'Get a hold of your soldiers and have all those goods handed back before we go on another step,' which he rapidly did. The whole war seem to stop for a moment as a reminder of the importance of discipline. We rapidly took our first objective, but then had to get out into the open street, where almost immediately I lost a number of men and the leading platoon commander, a South African called Stofberg. He looked very grey and I saw he had caught a burst of which several had hit him in and around the crutch. I opened his trousers and could see the rounds had passed through the fleshy inner part of his thighs and I said, 'Stoffy, it's all right – nothing vital's been hit,' and I was happy to see the grey look pass from him! We threw out the ELAS, mainly by infantry action, but helped by some of the Sherman tanks which were in the 23rd Armoured Brigade – Ark Force. Eventually the ELAS realized they were beaten. Air attacks began on them as they got out into open country, and the battle of Athens was over.

At that time there was a lot of political talk in the UK, including a certain amount in the TUC, that British soldiers were not fighting Germans but were taking on Freedom Fighters who had fought the Germans and had recovered Greece. The General Secretary of the TUC, Vincent Tewson, and one or two others, came out to Athens. The 2nd Parachute Brigade, officers and all ranks mixed, crowded into a theatre in Athens where Tewson said to us all, 'Well lads, I want you to answer these questions. Anybody can get up, irrespective of rank.' He then asked what they thought about putting down the guerrillas. The officers really left it to the soldiers who made it clear that we had not been taking on a gallant lot of Freedom Fighters, but a group who did not enjoy popular support and some of whom were murderers of their own people. Tewson left satisfied.

After we had driven the ELAS back out of Athens, we found places where they had butchered political opponents. Columns of people had been lined up and knives and axes had been used on victims. It was the most horrible and sickening sight and it made a deep impression on many of the soldiers. Thankfully, soon after this the remainder of the 4th Division arrived in relief. We were put into boats and taken back to Italy.

The 6th Battalion's strength was 528 all ranks throughout the fighting in Greece, but we lost 130 of that number killed or wounded badly enough to be taken to hospital – so it was quite tough fighting. We had about three weeks of intense street fighting. The enemy had the advantage of knowing Athens well, and they outnumbered us by about five or six to one. But it would be true to say that we had the advantage of better training and in the Parachute Brigade the quality of the soldiers was absolutely first rate. The fact that we did not give ground at all in our area was one of the main things which made them realize they were not going to get in.

LIEUTENANT COLONEL VIC COXEN, 4th Parachute Battalion

The 4th Battalion dropped on Megara airfield on 12 October. I had a lot of casualties on that drop. There were strong winds blowing but I thought we'd just have to take our chance on it. If I had been quicker on the uptake I would have had us dropped in the olive groves near the airfield – one or two people might have been hurt, but they wouldn't have been dragged; and dragged they were – one man, Donald Marsh, was found on the lee side of a small rocky hill; he had quite literally been dragged up one side, over the top and down the other. My batman, Fusilier 'Titch' Stanley, was dragged the whole length of the airfield, until his chute caught in the barbed wire at the bottom. Half an hour later, rather bedraggled, with very little skin on one side of his face, he arrived carrying my rucksack, which I'd lost on the descent. Three were killed but 30 or 40 were injured, with legs and arms broken. All casualties went into houses near Megara where we left a couple of the medical staff. The Germans had already evacuated Athens, so when we arrived I set up headquarters in the main hotel there. I was soon replaced by an Administrative Brigade and I moved my HQ to Gaudi Barracks, so one minute I was having tea with Princess Frederika and next minute I was lying on the floor at Gaudi, which was unfurnished.

Soon afterwards we went off to chase the Germans out. I went out with the SBS (Special Boat Squadron) with Lord Jellicoe, and we started off after the enemy up through Larissa and Lamia, by which time we were quite close to their column. They were blowing all the bridges, and roads as they went, so it was not easy to follow and we didn't always have a lot of petrol. The battalion was in three companies, but at one stage it was rather like having a company each at Bristol, Southampton and Plymouth – we were that sort of distance away from each other. We tried to persuade the Germans to surrender at Kozani. I sent in Geoffrey Morrison, who was fluent in German, with Lord Jellicoe, to try and persuade the retreating Germans to surrender but they were convinced we were brigands; a pity, as in trying to prevent them (the best part of a division) we lost a number of men including Rupert Teed, a splendid young life.

Another attempt was made to stop them at the Klythe Pass. I managed to borrow enough petrol to get round to the pass before the German columns. There were a lot of Andati there, who said that they would help in the fighting, but as soon as they saw the German column twelve miles away on the horizon they disappeared to a man without firing a single shot. We had been forced to abandon our jeeps as an appeal to Italy for petrol had resulted in an airlift of greatcoats, so my troops had to march. It was hopeless – I had to sit almost with tears in my eyes and watch the German column go through.

After the Germans had passed through the Klythe Pass there was still a column coming up through Florissa. When 'B' Company arrived we sent out a platoon to blow the railway which ran from Florissa to Edessa. We had very little explosive and could only blow one track in two places. The first armoured train compartment rode the blow, but the passenger compartment slipped off the track and we opened up with mortar and Bren-gun fire. The crew of the armoured engine was quick off the mark because they uncoupled themselves and disappeared northward with all speed. The remainder, about

400, surrendered – poor devils. They were part of a Caucasian division, who in due course were returned to Russia where they were all shot.

On the road near Monasteri I got a message. 'Churchill to Coxen: On no account will you go into Yugoslavia.' Yugoslavia was a Russian sphere of influence, so I met a car-load of Russian representatives on the border and we drank vodka and whisky together. That was all I saw of them. We then turned round and by stages got ourselves back to Athens. As fast as we were clearing the Germans out and freeing everyone, the communist brigade, who were very well organized, were steadily moving in and taking over the towns. We witnessed the reprisals against so-called collaborators which the Andati were carrying out everywhere. Our engineers emptied some wells in the Metixuria, into which several hundred bodies of men, women and children had been thrown.

It took us six or seven weeks of continuous fighting to clear Athens of the Andati. You started with a small ring in the centre surrounded by barbed wire barriers, and you slowly moved the perimeter out, searching all the houses as you went. You would have a lot of firing coming from these houses, so you'd attack and take over, only to find a family having breakfast. They'd hide their rifles and ammunition under a bed, or quite often they'd fire ten shots out of the window and nip out of the back door and off up the street before you got there.

Behind each of our battalions there was a Greek force whose task was to identify the enemy. They were very rough and by the time they'd found the communists in a house they'd have given everyone a hard time. If we handed any of our prisoners back to the Greek battalion, they'd reach the PoW pen as corpses. There is little doubt in my mind that had we not gone to Greece the communists would have taken over. By and large, Germany had only used Greece as a communication route to the Middle East. So, provided the Andati kept clear of the roads, they were in no great danger. There were two major groups of Andati; the ELAS, by far the larger, who were communist-backed and inspired and were geared to take over the country when the Germans left, and the EDES, who were royalist and who were largely destroyed by the ELAS. The ELAS were very well organized and we had supplied them with arms. Our arrival was a signal for the Andati to come in from the hills and occupy the towns and villages. Twenty men with a Sten gun can take over a village, 50 a small town. In the towns the communist cells now surfaced. The ordinary people were intimidated and while there was no open hostility to our troops chasing the Germans out, there was very little co-operation from the ELAS unless it suited them, like provision of food etc. When they realized that our strength was two brigades, then there was a closing in on Athens until it would be fair to say we really controlled the centre of Athens, the airfield and part of Salonika; the rest was under domination of the communists. I was flown back to Italy with a recce group to prepare for brigade operations in Northern Italy. I managed to get in touch with the Army where I confirmed the reports that were coming through about ELAS. The next day I got permission from the Americans for the plane that had flown me over to fly me back. When I arrived I returned to the centre of Athens by tank. The clearance of Athens was difficult and costly. I had 156 casualties in my battalion, 90 per cent of which were inflicted by the Greeks, whom we had come to rescue from the Germans. A large number of the Andati were probably boys of 15 to 16 – brain-washed kids – who didn't know why they were fighting, but a kid with a gun is as dangerous as anyone else. My doctor was shot dead by a 14-year-old boy while he was standing by his ambulance.

By January the situation was stable enough for us to hand over control and return to Italy.

MAJOR BILL CORBY, 5th Parachute Battalion

The 4th Battalion had a very nasty drop a couple of days before us in a strong wind, and had quite a lot of casualties. We followed the 6th Battalion a day or two later and the reception in Athens was quite astonishing; we had decided to go straight through the middle of the city, but it was hopeless, we just couldn't get through for crowds of cheering people.

Soon after this at the beginning of November, 5th Scottish Para Battalion with an element of Brigade Headquarters was moved to Salonika by a Royal Navy cruiser, to deal with emerging difficulties with communists up there. The battalion landed in assault craft on the beaches south-east of Salonica. There were explosions in the sea on the run in, possibly mines being blown up by the Navy, but there was no opposition, despite the presence of many ELAS faces in the town.

A day or two later our cruiser steamed right into the harbour close to ELAS headquarters. From the shore her six-inch guns looked very threatening. That night I woke up in the early hours to the sound of marching and singing. I looked out of the window to see a considerable force of ELAS communist troops, with horse or mule-drawn transport, moving out of the town to the north singing their favourite marching songs. A few days after that, the battalion was moved to Drama in north-east Greece to deal with the communists up there.

By the end of November trouble was really brewing in Athens so we were returned by cruiser as quickly as possible to Piraeus. We were transported to the centre of Athens to form a tight perimeter around Corps Headquarters in the Grand Bretagne Hotel. My company, B Company, were ordered to hold the block of buildings to the north of the hotel. We were told that there were a large number of communist troops around us, and that they would probably launch an assault the next morning. The next morning nothing happened – we stood to in anticipation, but they didn't attack. But 10 Platoon, in a building overlooking University Square were fired on from a building across the square. They soon cleared that lot of opposition and found that the communists had occupied a Greek hospital. In one of the wards, which had taken a generous share of the Bren-gun fire covering the assault, 10 Platoon found a Greek lady in labour. Fortunately she was unharmed.

The rest of the day passed quietly and that evening B Company were ordered to occupy the Acropolis which dominates that part of Athens. The leading platoon found it unoccupied except for one very scared Greek policeman. The company then occupied the rest of the Acropolis. The hardest job was carrying not only ammunition and rations but 300 large cans of water up the steep steps at the entrance. Before morning we were ready with everything inside.

Sniping mortar fire started early in the morning and this continued for several days, causing casualties, both killed and wounded. D Company at this stage were near the Theatre of Dionysus and to the south of it – they had moved forward as soon as we got to the Acropolis and occupied the area immediately below us and they were fairly heavily attacked. We supported them as best we could and had quite a pyrotechnic display one night with our two-inch mortar flares to light up the attack. D Company realized the opposition had to come through one particular place so they trained three Bren guns and a PIAT on it, and when the enemy came through they let fly with the lot. They must have come through en masse but although they were a gutsy lot, they didn't do it again!

After a few days of this, B Company was ordered to clear the communists/ELAS off the rocky, scrub-covered hillocks to the south-west of the Acropolis entrance about 300 yards away and 9 Platoon, under Lieutenant Brammell, did this at dawn one morning with fixed bayonets. They returned having dealt with the communists without suffering casualties.

Shortly after this, I was ordered to leave the Acropolis to take charge of a Greek Home Guard battalion near Omonia Square in support of 6th

(Royal Welsh) Para Battalion. I was with them for ten days or so and then returned to B Company who had by then left the Acropolis and moved to Piraeus Road a few hundred yards south-west of Omonia Square and on 6th Battalion's left flank. Here the company patrolled and probed forward to the north and were fired at by communists from nearby buildings.

The overall break-out started a few days later. The leading platoon of D Company under Lieutenant Bertie Page passed through our 10 Platoon position and were immediately heavily fired on by an enemy light machine-gun. Bertie was wounded in the foot and fell in the road while others disappeared into doorways. Sergeant Mason of 10 Platoon, B Company immediately sprinted down some 70 yards of open street, picked up Bertie in a fireman's lift and brought him out at a fast trot back to cover. The D Company attack proceeded with a tank in support and cleared forward to its objective. We then followed on D Company's right flank to our objective, clearing through several streets and blocks.

Next day B Company were ordered to lead the break-out from Athens to the northern outskirts following approximately the line of the railway. The break-out was successfully achieved with little or no opposition. I think the opposition had had enough the previous day.

It was a seven/eight week affair, all street fighting with the complication of not really knowing what your enemy really looked like or, of course, where he was, coupled with the usual difficulties of dealing with distraught civilians. The battalion started in the battle about 400 strong, I suppose, and suffered 100 casualties, or 25 per cent.

MAJOR JAMIE GOURLAY, 4th Parachute Battalion

The drop at Megara was the roughest I've ever had – I was dragged in and out of craters not knowing when to turn over on my back to open the quick release box and get free. We moved off, leaving many casualties behind and were taken by fishermen, under persuasion, in their boats across the Bay of Salamis to Athens.

The Germans had just pulled out so my company spent that night in a four-star hotel previously occupied by the Germans. That was the start and the finish of luxury. We were loaded on to coaches and lorries acquired by the SBS, and moved north by devious routes to the Kozani area. C Company's transport broke down less frequently than others, and we were lucky enough or not to be there first.

That evening our commanding officer, Vic Coxen, gave me three possible objectives: to blow a bridge south of Kozani; to attack the town of

THE MANY FACES OF NORTHERN IRELAND

Right: Lance Corporal comforting a student after bomb blast

Catholic ladies supplying tea in 1969

A patrol of the 2nd Battalion returning to Bessbrook barracks

The devastation at Warrenpoint, 1979

This page

Left: The 2nd Battalion leaving Aldershot for the Falklands

Below: The 3rd Battalion aboard a landing-craft on San Carlos waters, having disembarked from HMS Intrepid, 21 May 1982

Opposite

Above: The 2nd Battalion advance to Furze Bush Pass prior to their attack on Wireless Ridge

Below: Men of the 3rd Battalion's Regimental Aid Post tend the wounded of both sides, as a helicopter approaches to collect the stretcher cases, at the base of Mount Longdon

Men of 3rd Battalion celebrate the retaking of Port Stanley following the surrender of the Argentinian forces

The next generation. The RAF Parachute Jump instructor has just opened the door of the Hercules transport plane a young recruit, like so many before him, contemplates his first jump

Kozani or to attack a hill to the north. I thought the last seemed most in my line, and something the company knew about. Our task was to hasten the withdrawal of the Germans through Greece. Our immediate objective was the top of this hill.

The climb started with a cliff-face which proved to be practically vertical. The ascent was slow, moving from one position on to the next. How my signaller managed to get to the top, carrying a No. 18 set on his back, I will never know. Eventually we reached the top of the cliff-face, and were confronted with a more gradual incline. I reorganized the platoon formation for the approach to the final assault. It was now just before dawn and the element of surprise was on our side. We moved off up the slope in complete silence. Suddenly, an enemy trip-wire was accidentally operated, lighting up the sky with a brilliant flare. We had arrived; it was a strange sort of exhilarating relief which broke the tension. As darkness settled again we moved on, Company HQ with the leading platoon. During the final assault my second-in-command, Rupert Teed, had joined the platoon, when both he and Sergeant Wilmot were badly wounded.

The platoon, in spite of the losses, advanced steadily on towards a bunker from where most of the fire was coming. As they moved in the Germans there surrendered. Company HQ moved on to an adjacent building where further prisoners, surprised by the speed of the attack, were taken without resistance. All the prisoners were then held in this building. In the final assault on the bunker position every man in that platoon showed the greatest possible courage. Having secured the hill-top, we set up Bren guns firing tracer bullets on to the road which the main German column had to use for their withdrawal. They were about a platoon in strength and were met with heavy fire, forcing them to withdraw. Jimmie Greenhalgh, commanding No. 11 Platoon, was wounded in the attack. Shortly afterwards our position came under heavy shell-fire from the Kozani area.

The company had been unable to dig in on the rocky ground and suffered heavy casualties. A complete section on the left flank were wiped out by a direct hit. The persistent shelling was clearly in preparation for a further attack. Surely enough it followed, this time in greater strength. It was eventually repelled, but only after inflicting more casualties on the company, including another platoon commander who was killed while bravely defending his platoon area.

In spite of many calls to the enemy to come and 'collect their NAAFI rations', they eventually withdrew. While visibility was still reasonable we were joined by a Vickers machine-gun unit, commanded by Jock Gammon the originator of the Gammon bomb. Almost immediately visibility went; a very thick mist settled down and remained for the rest of our stay. With many casualties already, I decided to vacate the hill and withdraw to base. I ordered the platoons to make their own way back independently and the machine-gunners to remain, covering their withdrawal as best they could in the mist. CSM John Smith then got a stretcher-bearer party to collect Rupert, who was by now very weak, and they set off down the hill. I went to pick up our prisoners from the building where they were held but they had already gone; I thought one of the platoon had taken them.

As we approached the valley, visibility improved. Our withdrawal was being covered by Ian Patterson's SBS, firing a scout-car-mounted heavy machine-gun. The company was widespread over the countryside but eventually we arrived at base bringing the wounded. Sadly Rupert died that night. He was a remarkable man of courage and kindness, combined with a great sense of humour and, incidentally, the heavyweight boxing champion of the battalion.

That same day we buried our dead. Later I drove up to the top of the hill to the building where the prisoners had been held. Inside I found a trap-door in the floor leading down to the cellar. Here I found our prisoners who had gone to ground during the heavy shelling prior to the final German assault. As was the case in many battles, the battle of Kozani was won by the private soldier – by every one of them there.

CHAPTER TWELVE
ARDENNES
1944

I N DECEMBER 1944, THE GERMAN ARMIES LAUNCHED A MASSIVE counter-attack through the forests of the Ardennes. The plan was to drive across the River Meuse and on to Antwerp to split the Allied armies and their lines of communication.

The 6th Airborne Division, rested and re-trained after their success in Normandy, were ordered over Christmas to move at once by sea and road to take up defensive positions between Dissant and Namur (*see* map of the Rhine Crossing, p. 278) in order to defend the crossings of the River Meuse. By the time the 3rd and 5th Parachute Brigades were in position, the German advance had been brought to a halt. Just before New Year's Day 1945, the brigades were ordered to advance against the tip of the German salient.

The German Army, however, was still full of fight and it became necessary to attack. On 3 January, 13th Parachute Battalion was ordered to attack the village of Bure which was strongly held by the Germans. After some very heavy hand-to-hand fighting, the battalion forced the Germans to withdraw but at the cost of heavy casualties.

In January the division withdrew to Holland and carried out active patrolling along the River Maas before returning to the UK in late February.

MAJOR JACK WATSON, 13th Parachute Battalion

The 13th Battalion moved out on 23 December 1944 from Larkhill Barracks, Salisbury Plain, for the Ardennes. The Germans were breaking through and Monty needed some very quick reinforcements. We had to get down there very quickly to help stop the gap, hold up the German advance and assist the Americans.

We got our kit ready very quickly, entrained at Salisbury on Christmas

Eve, then went straight down to Dover and across by boat to Calais where we were picked up by RASC transport. We travelled by open trucks, old coal trucks, and it was bloody cold. We were taken down into the Ardennes to Namur. We hadn't been able to tell our families that we were going. The padre's wife had come all the way down from Newcastle and as she got in at Salisbury we were on the other platform moving off. A young officer who'd been left behind had to tell her that her husband had gone to the Ardennes!

We had our Christmas dinner in the 'Chateau Ardennes', and it was a very pleasant way of enjoying Christmas, especially as there was a lot of snow around us – one got the festive feeling. On 1 January our battalion received an order to move to Pondrôme, to attack a village called Bure, and then secure another village, Grupont. I was sent for by my CO, Peter Luard, and briefed – I was commander of A Company. The plan was to spend one night in Pondrôme and then go by transport to Resteigne. There we would de-bus and march to Tellin. There were six inches of snow and it was cold, below freezing, with ice on the roads, but the men were in good heart. We marched to a wood which overlooked Bure, our first objective. This was the furthest point in the German offensive to which the German tanks had advanced. Our task was to evict them from Bure.

The forming-up was A Company on the left, B Company on the right, and C Company in reserve. My task was to attack Bure with B Company to secure the high ground. We were formed up ready to go in at 1300 hours on 3 January. It was a bloody cold day, still snowing heavily, and even going through the wood to the start line was very difficult because the snow was as much as three or four feet deep in some places. We were wearing normal battle equipment, parachute smocks, helmets.

We formed up on the start line and looked down on this silent and peaceful village. The Germans knew we were there; they were waiting for us and as soon as we started to break cover, I looked up and I could see about a foot above my head the branches of the trees being shattered by intense machine-gun fire and mortaring. They obviously had the guns on fixed lines and they pinned us down before we even got off the start line. This was the first time I'd led a company attack and within minutes I'd lost about one-third of them. I could hear the men on my left-hand platoon shouting for our medics. We were held up for about 15 minutes because of the dead and wounded around us but we had to get moving. We were about 400 yards from Bure, and so as soon as I could I got my company together and gave the order to move. We had to get under the firing and get in the village as soon as possible. On the way down I lost more men including my batman. One man took a bullet in his body which ignited the phosphorus bombs he was carrying. He was screaming at me to shoot him. He died later.

We secured the first few houses and I got into one with my Company Headquarters. What I did not know was that B Company had also suffered badly in the attack. Their company commander, Major Bill Grantham, was killed on the start line together with one of his platoon commanders, Lieutenant Tim Winser. His company sergeant major, Moss, was mortally wounded. The remaining officers, apart from Lieutenant Alf Largeren, were wounded. He led the much depleted company to their objective, but was later killed during the first day, trying, with hand grenades, to clear a house held by a German machine-gun post.

Once I had got into the village it was difficult finding out just what was going on. I pulled in my platoon commanders to establish that they were secure and to start movement forward. It was eerie. We would be in one house, myself on the ground floor and my signalman telling me that there were Germans upstairs, and at other times they would be downstairs and we upstairs. It was a most unusual battle.

Our numbers were getting very depleted as we moved forward from house to house. I eventually got to the village crossroads by the old church. In the meantime I had informed my CO exactly what was going on, and he decided to send in C Company, who were in reserve, to support me. By that time their 60-ton Tiger tanks started to come in on us. It was the first time I had seen Tigers, and now here they were taking potshots, demolishing the houses. I moved from one side of the road to the other deliberately drawing fire. A tank fired at me and the next thing I knew the wall behind me was collapsing. But a PIAT team came running out, got within 50 yards of the tank, opened fire and smashed the tank's tracks. They were very brave. It went on like this all day – they counter-attacked but we managed to hold them. They pushed us back – we pushed forward again.

It became difficult to keep the men awake – after all they were tired, we had no hot food. All through our first night they were shelling and firing at us, and we were firing back. When we told HQ we had German tanks in the area they decided to bring in our own tanks in support, but they were no match for the Tigers. We had Shermans, and by the end of the battle 16 of them had been blown up. We were reinforced by a company from the Oxf and Bucks, commanded by Major Granville – by that time I was down to about one platoon in strength. The Oxf and Bucks went forward but they were not out there very long before they were forced back into our positions.

I will always take off my hat to Colour Sergeant Harry Watkins. How the hell he found us I do not know, but he did. We were still scattered in the houses along the main road in the centre of the village. He brought us a stew which was good and hot, and we were able to get men into small groups to have food and then get to their positions in the houses.

At one point in the battle Sergeant Scott, RAMC, went forward in an ambulance to pick up casualties. A German Tiger, which had been fighting us all day, rolled forward alongside him, and the commander seeing him unafraid said, 'Take the casualties away this time, but don't come forward again, it is not safe.' Even Sergeant Scott knew when to take a good hint!

Over the following day we suffered five more counter-attacks supported by Tiger tanks. By that time we also had artillery support, and we could finally make the Germans' life difficult too. Once we started shelling they countered with their own artillery and tried to blast us out of the village. Fortunately most of my company had experienced heavy shelling at Ranville, in Normandy, so they knew what to expect. I told Major Granville to move forward beyond my own position to find out what was going on. As he did so the enemy attacked again with two Tigers. We held that attack and then it all went very quiet, though the Germans left one Tiger behind as an irritant. It was time at last to secure the other half of the village, together with C Company and the Oxf and Bucks going from house to house ferreting them out. It was very much hand-to-hand fighting.

By about nine o'clock on the evening of the 5th we had the whole village in our hands with my company eliminating the last enemy post. We took up defensive positions, but that same night we were told to withdraw. We found out afterwards that the 7th Battalion had come in from a different direction, met with little resistance and taken Grupont. It meant that we did not have to go any farther. So very early on the morning of the 6th, just after midnight, I got all my company together and we withdrew to Tellin – very wet, very tired, unshaven. The battalion lost about 68 men killed and about half of them were from my company. They were buried in a field in Bure by our padre, Whitfield Foy, a few days later.

CHAPTER THIRTEEN

THE RHINE CROSSING
Operation Varsity
1945

THE FINAL BARRIER TO GERMANY HAD BEEN REACHED BY March 1945 and on the 24th, the 6th Airborne Division, together with the US 17th Airborne Division, dropped in the Wesel area to secure and deepen the 21st Army Group bridgehead east of the River Rhine. Once landed, the division's objectives were to occupy the high ground of the Diersfordter Wald, the village of Hamminkeln and certain bridges over the River Issel.

The 3rd and 5th Parachute Brigades landed first, followed closely by the gliders of 6 Airlanding Brigade and Divisional troops. The division landed as a complete force on its objectives, avoiding the mistakes of Arnhem. Due to heavy anti-aircraft fire and dust and haze on the landing zones, the glider pilots often lost visibility and consequently there were heavy casualties on landing. In this, the most successful and final major airborne operation of the war, all objectives and link-up with the ground forces were achieved within 24 hours. Thereafter, between 26 March and 2 May, the division advanced 350 miles, mostly on foot, to the Baltic coast where they met the advance elements of the Russian forces at Wismar.

BRIGADIER JAMES HILL, HQ, 3rd Parachute Brigade

The largest and most successful airborne operation in history took place at ten o'clock on a glorious sunny morning on 24 March 1945. That day, the Allied Airborne Corps formed a spearhead for the British and American

THE RHINE CROSSING MARCH 1945

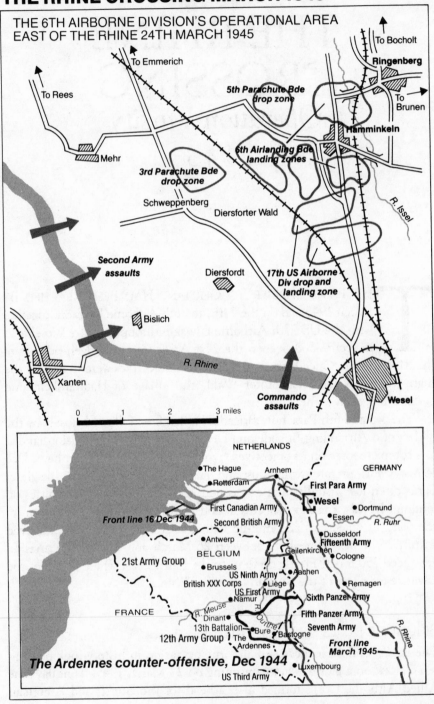

THE 6TH AIRBORNE DIVISION'S OPERATIONAL AREA
EAST OF THE RHINE 24TH MARCH 1945

To Bocholt

Ringenberg

To Emmerich

To Rees

5th Parachute Bde drop zone

To Brunen

Hamminkeln

Mehr

6th Airlanding Bde landing zones

3rd Parachute Bde drop zone

Schweppenberg

Diersforter Wald

R. Issel

Second Army assaults

Diersfordt

17th US Airborne Div drop and landing zone

Bislich

R. Rhine

Xanten

Commando assaults

Wesel

0   1   2   3 miles

NETHERLANDS

GERMANY

The Hague

Arnhem

First Para Army

Rotterdam

Wesel

Dortmund

Front line 16 Dec 1944

First Canadian Army

Essen

R. Ruhr

Second British Army

Antwerp

Dusseldorf

Fifteenth Army

BELGIUM

Geilenkirchen

Cologne

21st Army Group

Brussels

US Ninth Army

Aachen

British XXX Corps

Liège

Remagen

US First Army

Namur

Sixth Panzer Army

FRANCE

R. Meuse

Dinant

Ourthe

Fifth Panzer Army

13th Battalion

Bure

Bastogne

Seventh Army

12th Army Group

The Ardennes

Front line March 1945

R. Rhine

The Ardennes counter-offensive, Dec 1944

Luxembourg

US Third Army

armies that breached the formidable enemy defences on the banks of the River Rhine at Wesel.

As we boarded our aircraft, everyone sensed that they were entering a battle which would mark the beginning of the end and as we had drilled into the minds of our men in preparation: 'When attempting any great endeavour, the important thing is to see it through to the end.' This we were determined to do. Ten thousand aircraft all told – bombers, fighters, reconnaissance, troop carriers, tug aircraft and gliders were involved in this great battle and its preliminary bombardment, all linked and controlled by radio communication. What a difference in skill, technique and planning from our original 1st Battalion drop in North Africa in October 1942.

Flying in tight formation, 540 American Dakota parachute aircraft carried the 7th, 8th, 9th, 12th and 13th Battalions of the Parachute Regiment, the 1st Canadian Parachute Battalion, and six parachute battalions of the US Army – twelve parachute battalions in all. In 1,300 gliders, the British and American glider brigades and divisional troops rode into battle.

There was a quite remarkable affinity and hence co-operation not only within the units of our own division and the Royal Air Force, but also with the pilots of American Troop Carrier Command with whom over the previous two years we had had much practice. For example, we asked them to drop the 3rd Parachute Brigade, which I commanded, consisting of 2,200 fighting men, in a clearing 1,000 by 800 yards in a heavily wooded area held by German parachute troops. The drop took six minutes to conclude and was dead on target. The 5th Parachute Brigade, commanded by Brigadier Nigel Poett, enjoyed the same splendid service. Our division, therefore, when it emplaned on that glorious sunny morning was full of confidence – very experienced with D-Day, Normandy, the Ardennes and Holland behind us. We were well disciplined and were able to take advantage from lessons learned from four previous airborne operations.

On arrival, amidst the sunshine and great clouds of dust rising from the preliminary bombardment on the banks of the river, some 50 aircraft and ten gliders were shot out of the sky and a further 115 aircraft and 300 gliders were raked by ground fire. However, the 1st German Parachute Army on whom our corps descended, was routed, and links established with the leading follow-up formations who were now enabled to deploy across the Rhine.

The price had been paid and the sacrifice made. A total of 1,078 men of the 6th Airborne Division had been carried off the field, either dead or wounded, before the sun set on that lovely March day. The total airborne casualties, American and British, amounted to some 2,500 killed and wounded and 500 missing, many of whom returned to fight another day. The German casualties were estimated at 1,000 killed, and 4,000 prisoners were taken, along with some 90 major artillery pieces and many 20-mm guns in multiple mountings and hundreds of machine-guns. All these would have been available to impede the deployment of the British and American armies crossing the Rhine.

We were well led by General Eric Bols, alongside the 17th American Airborne Division and came under command of the corps commander, the great American general, Mat Ridgeway who, later on, took command in Korea and became American Chief of Staff.

Thirty-seven days later on 1 May, having fought our way on foot across some 275 miles of Germany, forcing crossings on both the River Weser and Elbe, and keeping pace with the armoured division on our flanks, the division captured Wismar on the Baltic, and were the first British troops to link with the Russians. The war in Europe was virtually at an end.

SERGEANT DAN HARTIGAN, 1st Canadian Parachute Battalion

Having come inland from the coast at about 1,200 feet I looked down to see a strange countryside. What I saw wasn't just a western European winter landscape, but ravaged terrain. The vegetation cover was so sparse and looked a somewhat burgundy tinge; mud oozing through turf. I'd never seen anything like it. It was quite surreal.

For a few miles along the flight path and stretching towards the French coast on the Channel, as far as the eye could see, were hundreds of thousands of crater rings. There were so many it appeared almost incomprehensible. Yet there they were, sullen on the surface of this ravaged landscape. We had heard of no heavy artillery attacks in this area, certainly nothing of this concentration of fury.

Then it dawned on us quietly that we were flying over the World War I battlefields. It was a sobering sight, which filled us with melancholy for the suffering which must have gone on down there. Yet here we were less than 30 years later going to fight the same enemy. It took some time to come back to reality.

CORPORAL DOUG MORRISON, 1st Canadian Parachute Battalion

As soon as I dropped with the rest of the Canadians I set up my Vickers near the south-west corner of a field close to the drop zone. There was a farmhouse about 200 yards to our front, and for most of the afternoon it was occupied by the Jerries.

A glider came down in front of the house and as the troops jumped out the Jerries picked off the first three or four. Although we fired away with our Vickers they were out of the line of fire. The remainder of the men inside the glider stayed there but were subjected to a steady stream of fire from the farmhouse. The thin shell of the glider didn't give them any protection.

I sent a runner to our rear where we had a three-inch mortar position to ask them to lay down smoke between the glider and the farmhouse. I hoped this would give the men in the glider some protection. But after ten minutes we still hadn't got any smoke and the situation was now pretty desperate. Then without a word to anyone Corporal John Chambers jumped up and took off across the open field towards the glider. He was under fire from the time he began his dash, was knocked down once, but got up and kept going until he reached the glider. He took out a smoke grenade, pulled the pin and tried to throw it over the glider towards the farmhouse. Unfortunately, the phosphorus grenade didn't clear the wing and rolled back down close to him and exploded. It spewed molten phosphorus all over him. He had a fair amount on his face and in his hair. (His helmet had fallen off when he was hit and went down on his run out to the glider.) We could see him rolling around on the ground, scooping up handfuls of earth and putting it on his face and hair to extinguish the phosphorus burning him. I felt helpless because all I could do was keep firing at the house, but the enemy troops could stay far enough back out of range. They just kept up a steady stream of fire on the glider.

Charlie Clarke then jumped up and he took off for the glider. He was hit before he was half way to the glider, but he too got up and managed to make it to the partial protection of the fuselage.

About this time the mortar platoon was able to lay down smoke between the glider and the farmhouse. A number of us went out and brought back everyone including the wounded John Chambers and Charlie Clarke who were handed over to the medics. Clarke soon died, but John Chambers recovered.

MAJOR TOD SWEENEY, 2nd Battalion, Oxford and Buckinghamshire Light Infantry

The 6th Airborne Division took off on the morning of 24 March for the biggest airborne operation of the war. We were in Horsa gliders towed mostly by bombers. The Oxf and Bucks were to seize a railway bridge and road bridge over the River Issel and then take a number of German defensive positions. We circled for about an hour to allow the other aircraft to join us, and then set off across Essex over the Thames and past Canterbury, where my wife was asleep in bed at seven o'clock in the morning with our three-month-old daughter. We flew across the Channel towards Brussels where the American Airborne Division joined us.

For the week or so before as Monty moved all his men and equipment up to the river he had had an enormous smokescreen laid down, and then there was a tremendous artillery bombardment and for the actual crossing 200 bombers had dropped 1,000 tons of bombs on Wesel. So as we came over on that crisp clear morning there was an unexpected cloud of dust and smoke still hanging over our area. The Typhoons with their rockets couldn't always see their targets, and in the area of the landing zone and the parachute dropping zones most of the German gun positions were still intact. As the gliders came over they had to drop below the dustcloud and fly around to locate their landing zones. When the first parachute brigade came over they dropped satisfactorily. The paratroops dropped from a low height, and they were down before the flak could open up, but they lost many of their men from fire on the ground. The next parachute brigade came over and they too dropped without much loss. But the Airlanding Brigade, the artillery and the divisional troops, which were the third lot to come over, faced an enemy that was by this time prepared for them. The German anti-aircraft gunners had a marvellous target – big, slow-moving gliders going around looking for their objectives. It didn't matter too much exactly where I landed because mine was a headquarters glider. So we went zooming down, twisting and turning, but landed all right. We opened the door at the front, put the ramps down, got the jeep out and then came under the most tremendous fire from a whole lot of steel helmets, which we could see on the side of a field by a half-made-up road. I realized that we had ended up on the wrong side of the River Issel which we were supposed to be defending – I was between the autobahn and the river with a jeep and a trailer and five men and nothing else. I said, 'Forget about the jeep and trailer. Take the radio and we'll get across the river!' We made it across and I got the men down into firing positions. Meanwhile the gliders were still coming in all over the place. The whole battalion had flown in together, and that included gliders carrying jeeps full of mortar bombs and petrol. If the jeep and trailer were hit and set alight the glider became a flying bomb; a lot of them just blew up. While we were watching all this taking place around us, in came a glider which landed safely and out stepped a platoon of my own regiment. By now I had worked out where I was. I got hold of the platoon commander, Hugh Clark, and told him to put one section ahead and two sections at the rear. Then everybody else I split into two parties – one party to carry and one party to be carried – they were in all sorts of condition. Suddenly I saw snaking through the woods from the opposite direction a lot of grey figures with steel helmets. I was up with the leading section and I got them down and said, 'Don't shoot until I give you the word.' It was lucky I did so, for as they came closer one of these men turned his arm and there was a big Stars and Stripes on it. In the half light their helmets made them look like Germans. We on the other hand had been told to put on our red berets as soon as we landed. I approached the Americans and said, 'Have you got an aid station nearby?' And they said, 'Oh yes there's one up the road. In fact you're in the American area.' We offloaded all our wounded and made our way up to our headquarters, where I reported to my commanding officer. My battalion flew in 600 strong and had 110 killed in the landing. In the Reichwald Cemetery today you will see just to the right of the cross a plot of 110 graves – all from my battalion. A lot of them were men I had known since the beginning and now just 44 days before the end of the war in Europe they were dead. I remember that night the adjutant was trying to work out the effective strength of the battalion and he couldn't make 300.

Now one funny thing that happened concerned a quartermaster, Bill Allsop. He shouldn't have been flying into action – he was quite old, about forty, but he'd been the quartermaster and of course the commanding officer wanted him. As he was coming in to land, he saw first the left-hand pilot slump over his joystick and then the right-hand pilot do the same. They had both been shot, and the glider was hurtling down to the ground. So he pushed one of them aside, and since he'd seen what happens when landing he sat down and as the glider came in he pulled the joystick back. He had no idea how to apply the brake or the rudder or anything else, but at least he straightened the glider out and it ran on and on before coming safely to rest. He was seated in front of the ticket office at the railway station (our headquarters) and he stayed there all day without saying a word. He was in shock, absolutely devastated by what he'd done. The commanding officer had a sense of humour and put him in for a DFC. He didn't get it, which shows a lack of a sense of humour on the part of those higher up.

The parachutists hadn't had so many initial casualties, but they had quite a number in the subsequent fighting, because it took quite a bit of time to sort things out. The rest of that day was just a question of resisting attacks and sending out patrols. That night the Germans began a real assault, with tanks, and we had to blow the bridge over the Issel which we had seized that day to stop them coming across, which left only one of the bridges open. The next day, the 25th, we were still in a defensive position and only that night did the first of the 52nd Lowland Division come up and begin taking over. It was 48 hours after we landed that we were finally relieved of our duties. We were absolutely flogged out. But then we had a day's rest, cleaned our weapons, cleaned ourselves up, and then set off on a ten-mile march. That night we had an O group at about eleven o'clock and the commanding officer had his company commanders, intelligence officers and all the rest around him. Gradually, one by one, we all fell asleep. Then somebody woke up and got us all going again. It must have been a sight — like one of those scenes of dead men in a circle around a table.

Then we set off and marched all the way through Germany to the Baltic. We literally marched the entire way. We crossed Germany via Osnabruk and Celle and I suppose we had a little battle about every ten miles when we were in the lead. Then every now and again we'd get a couple of days' rest while the rest of them pushed on ahead. We had a bit of trouble crossing the Weser, but at the Elbe another division went ahead and we just marched over a bridge. Until we came to the last two days of the war we moved tactically. Then we received instructions to get up to the Baltic as quickly as possible to cut off the Russians heading for Denmark. So for the last day of our war, instead of fighting our way along we commandeered any vehicle we could get hold of, off-loaded all our stores from the jeeps and trailers and just motored along to our objective.

All afternoon, coming past us, down the other side of the road was the German army in perfect formation, marching with their rifles properly carried, their tanks, their guns, their womenfolk and so on, getting away from the Russians. We were not taking the slightest notice of each other and yet two days before we'd been fighting. They didn't acknowledge us at all. They just kept on going. The 40 miles from just beyond the Elbe to Wismar and Lake Schwerin we covered in that one day. Within 24 hours of our arrival the Russians turned up.

I was deputed to take a party of our soldiers from the brigade over to the Russians to have a celebration. There were 40 or 50 of us, and we went to their Brigade Headquarters, but of course we had terrible language problems, and our interpreter and theirs had to speak German to each other. We stood around and these tough-looking Russians with shaved heads came up and started showing us the collections of watches they had all the way up their arms. It was all horse-drawn vehicles, and messengers were coming to and fro on horseback.

The Russians cleared out a couple of houses and brought in

German women to lay the table with linen table-cloths and glasses and then we were all invited in. The senior officers and brigadier sat down and we had the British and Russian officers seated alternately around the round table, and then out in the rest of the house were the private soldiers – Russian/British/Russian/British – all seated around. There were toasts to Stalin, Churchill and Roosevelt and we gradually got more and more intoxicated. By the end of two or three hours we were all well gone. All the soldiers, Russian and British, had their arms on each other's shoulders and were singing. One or two of our men became a bit difficult and wanted to kiss the Russian women, so I thought we'd better get away before they had their heads chopped off; if a chap was in too bad condition we called for stretcher bearers and took him off to his billet.

About five days later we went back across the Elbe. The Germans who had been stopped and put into camps were horrified we were going because they would be left in the Russian zone. A lot of them were trying to get away to cross the river with us.

We flew back to Bulford on 17 May and were given a month's leave. Then we were told we were going to the Far East and we started doing training on Salisbury Plain. We had things we called JEWTs, 'Jungle Exercises Without Trees'. Our advance parties went off to the Jungle Warfare Training School, and then the Bomb dropped.

PRIVATE ERNIE ELVIN, 7th Parachute Battalion

It was a daylight drop but you could hardly see the ground for all the smoke. As we came down the enemy were onto us straight away, machine-gun bullets crackling all around us and through my canopy. I was a Bren gunner and I pretended I was dead – and I slumped forward, kept my kit bag on and hit the ground with a right old whack. I was lucky I didn't break my leg.

So we got organized and away we went. My most vivid memory of the dropping zone is coming across a battery of 88s. There were about twelve paras there from 12 Battalion, all alongside this gun. You'd have thought they were just resting; some were sitting, some were lying down, some were leaning. But they were dead – must have been killed by the blast of this gun. Concussion. Not a mark on them. People got a bit upset; they couldn't understand how it had happened. But we had to keep moving and head out from the DZ to the Battalion RV.

The 7th Battalion rather enjoyed the first few days of the advance because you could do as you liked. You could get a pram or a wheelbarrow and put all your gear in it. You were scruffy, you were filthy, you had more

German weapons than you had English – I mean, we were like brigands. Then after five days it was: 'Right, snap out of it, smarten yourselves up, chuck all that rubbish away; you're paras, you know.'

Then the advance really got under way and it was move, move, move; across country, on foot, brushing away any resistance, but keeping away from all the big roads. At one stage we were travelling on Churchill tanks and the only real excitement was when two of them kept catching fire; they were worn out. The order was to stop the Germans getting across the river Leine at two bridges, one at Bordenau which 12 Battalion had to take and the other at Lion Bridge, Neustadt am Rubenberg, which was our objective. But we other ranks didn't know anything about this at the time.

We had just reached an aerodrome in these lorries when all hell was let loose. The lorries went up in flames and I ran away from the transport as fast as I could, just as I'd been taught to – it was automatic – and I threw myself on the ground with only a few blades of grass for cover. Fire was coming from some outbuildings nearby so I trained my Bren gun on them and I could see the bullets hitting the red brick and the dust flying up. The firing from there seemed to stop, but a lot of men were getting shot up. A few tried to take cover behind some dead sheep but they were wounded because the German bullets just went straight through the sheep into the men. By the time the Jerries withdrew, the commander of 6 Platoon was severely wounded, two men were killed and quite a few injured. One of the men killed was my platoon commander, Lieutenant Pape, a Canadian on loan to our battalion.

When we got to Neustadt, 4 Platoon, my platoon, was leading. We got to the outskirts of the town and found what we thought was the road leading up to our bridge. But it was the wrong bridge. Of course in the pitch black we didn't know that, and Sergeant McIvor, who had taken over after Pape was killed, shouted, 'Wrong bridge, wrong bridge, come on, over you go.' So we doubled up and made to cross the bridge. I had just got across when the next minute I was lying on the ground with my Bren gun, the barrel smashed, and a lump of concrete about a yard square lying alongside me. I never heard an explosion, never saw a flash, but when I shook myself and got up, I realized the bridge had been blown. There were only about nine of us left, and blood all over the place. We helped carry the wounded over to this lady's home on the end of the bridge, a Frau Erika Naujoks.

When we'd got all the wounded under cover Lieutenant Gush asked for volunteers to swim back across the river to let the rest of the company know what had happened. I volunteered and Phil Crofts went with me. We stripped down to our vest and pants with just a 9-mm Browning round the waist. When I got into the water the current was so fierce I thought I was going to drown. I didn't realize until the morning that the river was in flood. I never would have gone if I'd realized. I ended up 75 yards downstream, on the other side, absolutely exhausted.

We trotted back to the road and Sergeant Major Lucas came out of a house which had been made Company HQ and asked what had happened. We told him, and then he said, 'Well, you'd better go back again.' Fortunately Major Reid was there and he said, 'Don't be ridiculous, Sergeant Major, those men are exhausted. You can't expect them to swim back across that river.' At daybreak we dressed in civilian clothes and got back across the river by boat.

When we reached the other side one of my platoon sections was laid out, the whole lot of them dead. One of them had been a looter; instead of his pouches being full of grenades silver knives and forks were spilling out of them. All they had of one bloke was his head and arms, but at least that meant they could identify him. An elm tree just at the entrance to the bridge was full of the remains of the men who'd been blown to pieces. It looked as if a hundred crows were sitting there. The blast had blown them up sky high.

Our company commander, Major Reid, was completely shattered by it all. Twenty-four men had died that morning and another eleven were to die of their wounds. We were down to 30 men in our company, so for three days they let us do as we liked. We were put up in a hotel and lavished with eggs and brandy. After reinforcements came we were detailed to do another drop. But there weren't many paras looking forward to that job. I think we had the stuffing knocked out of us; we knew the war was coming to an end and we just didn't want to take any more chances. Soon after, the operation was cancelled. No-one was sorry. Only days later, there were thousands and thousands of Germans in massive columns, eight abreast, just marching down the road with their hands on their heads. Nobody brought them in – they just gave themselves up. We later linked up with the Russians. The war was over, just like that.

SERGEANT DEREK GLAISTER, 7th Parachute Battalion

When we got to the Rhine, it was murder, because Jerry knew we were coming; every farmhouse was occupied by Germans. They put a lot of smoke down, so instead of coming down to 400 feet which is the lowest height you can drop from, we had to go up to 1,000 feet. We were also travelling quite fast. I was No. 20, last man out, so you can imagine how far off target I was.

Miles out. I and ten others came down near a farmhouse which had an 88-mm gun just outside it. Just before my feet touched the ground a bullet smashed through my left elbow, so I lay on my stomach and pretended to be dead. I saw nine of the others come down, some into trees. The Germans shot them as they hung there helpless – it was a sickening sight.

I was in big trouble; I am left-handed and my left arm was useless. But when five Germans came towards me I got hold of my Sten gun in my right hand, and as they got close I fired and I think killed them all. Then I made for the farmhouse hoping to get some help, but as I peered round a corner I saw German rifles poking out of every window. I tried to give myself some cover by throwing a smoke bomb, but just as I was making for the nearest ditch, a German SS officer came up and shot me in the back from ten yards away with a Luger pistol. Of course I spun round and fell down, and this officer grabbed my left arm and shoved it through the straps of my webbing, then he took of my water bottle, flung it in the ditch and looted whatever he could. I was worried that he'd finish me off with my knife but I had the presence of mind to lie on it and when he'd gone I got hold of it and threw it in the ditch.

I lay there feeling pretty rough – my left arm was like a great black pudding by then, all swollen up – and watched those poor fellows swinging in the trees. Then one of our gliders came over, but the 88-mm cracked it open like an egg and the jeep, gun, blokes all fell out. Point blank range – they couldn't miss at 50 feet.

Towards the evening I was still lying there, in one hell of a bloody mess. I was finding it difficult to breathe because the second bullet had touched my lungs. Then a couple of captured airborne soldiers came by – a glider pilot and Lance Corporal Butler from my own battalion – and they asked their German escort if they could pick me up. So they gave me a shot of morphine, which helped, and put me in this wheelbarrow. They carted me along in this farm wheelbarrow along a bumpy old road until the Germans took them away for interrogation and I was wheeled on to a big mansion near Hamminkeln.

At dusk a German lorry came along and two Jerries picked me up like a sack of spuds and dumped me in the back of the truck on top of some dead blokes sewn up in sacks. They must have thought I was dead. That was the first time I fainted; my wounds had opened up and were bleeding again.

I came to in a German toilet with my head near the pan. That was where all my troubles started. Two orderlies took me into an operating theatre and pulled my clothes off which was very painful. They'd just been operating on some chap and they slithered me straight onto the aluminium table which was still covered in his blood. Then they put an ether mask over my face and out I went.

I woke up five days later, my arm in a Nazi salute in plaster and paper bandages all around my back. No medicines or antibiotics. My back had opened up again as the stitches had come apart so I was carried off to be restitched. When we got to the top of some massive stairs I was tipped off, deliberately I'm sure. I landed at the bottom on my head, breaking my nose and smashing the plaster. There was a hell of a row about it and those orderlies didn't appear again. They stitched me all up again and put another plaster on, still in a Nazi salute. Then they had a go at my nose with no anaesthetic. They probed about pulling bits of bone out but they went too close to my eye and damaged it so I've got permanent pain and double vision from that.

I lay in that hospital until the British arrived. They flew me over to the RAF Hospital at Wroughton and sent for my wife and parents as they didn't expect me to live. My father was also in hospital at the time, having his leg amputated as a result of World War I. When my mother and wife came into the ward they walked right past my bed; they didn't recognize me. I had pneumonia by then, so they put in a tube to drain off the fluid and sent me by ambulance to an orthopaedic unit. The tube came out in the ambulance, so they just pushed it in again, nearly choking me when it reached my lungs.

When at last they got around to getting the German plaster off, one of the nurses fainted; the stench was bad enough, but the plaster was full of maggots, put in by the German doctor to eat the dead flesh. No wonder it itched. A surgeon took one look at my arm and said, 'Off' – just like that. But there was a lady doctor, Miss Wagstaff, who said she'd like to have a go at saving it, since I was left-handed. The surgeon said it would take years and still might not work, but they tried. It took three years in hospital and 55 operations to get me where I am now, which is 80 per cent disabled.

LIEUTENANT COLONEL FRASER EADIE, 1st Canadian Parachute Battalion

It was not until 1 July 1942 that Canada's Minister of National Defence gave final approval for the formation of a parachute battalion. A call was made for volunteers from the existing Canadian military units in Britain, where five divisions of Canadian volunteer soldiers awaited the invasion of Europe, and from reserve and active units still in Canada. By July 1943 the unit was in England and mustered in combination with the British 6th Airborne Division.

A most fortunate event was the young battalion's placement in 3

Parachute Brigade under command of Brigadier James Hill, DSO, MC. Hill was a regular soldier, battle-tested in North Africa with the 1st Battalion the Parachute Regiment. Quite apart from his soldiering qualities he understood his new, somewhat wild and woolly charges, and his ability to have firm discipline accepted by them brought the young Canadians quickly up to the standard he demanded of the 8th and 9th Parachute Battalions in his brigade.

The battalion fought well in Normandy. It sustained 117 casualties on its first day of battle, and was down to less than half strength when the division returned to England to re-fit in September 1944. The winter of 1944–5 saw the battalion in the Ardennes and Holland. By February all ranks were back in England for a stint of leave.

The battalion returned to its quarters in Bulford on 7 March and immediately began a period of weapons training and battalion battle drill. All the sub-units had been brought up to strength in both equipment and personnel. During the morning of 23 March, the battalion, complete with all their fighting gear, travelled to the airfield at Chipping Ongar. Reveille on the 24th was at 0200 hours. By 0630 hours the troops were suited up with equipment and parachutes awaiting the orders to emplane. The NAAFI wagon hove in sight with mugs of weak tea that many accepted, primarily for something to do. Then the call came from the aircrew, '30 minutes to loading time'.

At this point nature appeared to take over. One by one the soldiers headed off the runway to the grass verge, off equipment, down trousers and relief. I doubt that more sheets from Army message pads were used during the entire 37 days of operation in Germany than were used that morning on the edge of the runways at Chipping Ongar.

Once airborne there was nothing to do but wait. I reminded my stick of the brigadier's warning that once on the ground there would be complete confusion, that every man knew his job and must get to his RV post-haste. No buggering around in the midst of somebody else's battle. We could see the Rhine coming up and it was 'red light on, and stand in the door'. The stick was already up and pressing hard to the door to ensure a tight exit. My batman, Private Del Parlee, was right behind me. We were jumping one and two. He looked up at me and said, 'Looks like a nice day out there, wish I'd gone fishing.'

The artillery of the 52nd Lowland Division were still firing on their targets as the crew chief yelled 'green light on'. This was it. Each man was on his own until reaching his RV. The German ground troops engaged the paratroopers as they descended from a height most of us later felt must have been between 600 and 700 feet. We had hoped to exit at around 450 feet. A couple of well-placed rounds snapped with great authority around my ears. I wanted desperately to determine the direction of the shots but discretion was much the better part of valour, so I hung limply in my harness with my best friend, my ever-present tommy-gun, hanging from one hand. Nothing more seemed to be directed at me and I landed in a rather clumsy fashion within 50 feet of where both the CO and I had chosen to hit the ground.

I rose up, squeezed off two bursts and did my best to catch up to Private Hoskins who was hell-bent for the RV. It was probably about 200 yards to the woods and B Company, RV, but running in ploughed ground with what felt like a ton of equipment, seemed to take forever. About halfway along, I ran into one of our three photographic sergeants standing upright behind his tripod cranking away with his 16-mm movie camera. I told him that he'd best bag his ass out of there if any of us were to see his movies when this particular shambles was all over.

I reached a wood jutting out from the main wood which was a German strongpoint and a prime objective of B Company of the 8th Battalion. Several Canadians were spread out on the northern and eastern perimeter of the wood getting involved in somebody else's battle. As I tried to extract them and get them on their way to their own objectives, I couldn't help but feel the need to give the buggers a squirt or two of my dear old tommy-gun. Just then Captain Sam McGowan, second-in-command of B Company, showed up. He had taken a round squarely on the front of his steel helmet which had ringed around the liner and exited leaving only a minor scratch on his forehead.

This was no place for either of us. B Company was our job, and Sam took off. Just as I grabbed a couple of men to get the hell out of there, Lieutenant Rick Burden of C Company showed up, and in his aggressive way was preparing to take on the show single-handed. We dissuaded him, and he gathered up a few of his C Company pirates and headed for the road along the northern end of the woods.

Lieutenant Jack Burnett from B Company caught up with me as we both prepared to take off, but before he had gone two steps he was down and finished. I chased after McGowan and on reaching the RV met up with an NCO from A Company who said the CO had not arrived. I told him to take off with what troops were available and make for the objective, Burgen-forth.

Lieutenant Vic Fleming of B Company came into the RV flat out, and the two of us gathered what troops we could and headed through the woods to the village. By the time we arrived, McGowan had completed his task and had locked in his Bren positions to protect the area from any enemy retreating from the river. A Company had done a super job in clearing the house in Burgenforth and locking in their Bren positions with B Company. There was still no sign of the CO.

C Company meanwhile had their hands full. Heavy fire was pouring into their positions. A fighting patrol was already on its way to Hignendahl's Farm on the road leading from their area to Emmerich. The patrol established a firm base there, which also provided an excellent OP for the gunners to engage the heavy German weapons to the north. The Vickers guns provided excellent fire, and it was reassuring to hear their slow rhythmic beat as they engaged their targets.

By noon all companies had secured their objectives, but enemy fire that continually swept the east and south ends of the drop zone still had to be silenced. Our doctor, Captain Pat Costigan's medical crews really excelled in their rescue and evacuation of casualties through to our aid post, a somewhat battered church in the village. Those needing further major medical attention were moved to 224 Field Ambulance, who had set up an operating theatre in the priest's house across from the church. Corporal Fred Topham of the battalion medics displayed tremendous bravery in caring for and evacuating the wounded. He was awarded the Victoria Cross for his deeds of compassion and valour despite a very painful face wound.

Shortly before noon the Bren positions of A and B Companies observed a platoon strength of Germans retreating from the river and as they approached our positions, the Brens opened up. It was short and fierce. A counter-attack came in on C Company in the afternoon, but that wild and aggressive unit soon put a stop to the nonsense.

The recce elements of 15th Scottish Division started arriving in late afternoon and were followed throughout the night by tanks and infantry heading east. Company casualty returns started arriving at Battalion Headquarters by 2000 hours. Still no sign of the CO. I could only hope he had been taken prisoner. Total returns showed 20 killed; 38 wounded; 7 missing.

The next day was spent clearing the DZ. 15th Scottish had passed our position and we were on our own to carry out an assessment of battalion strength. By now it was known that Colonel Jeff Nicklin had been killed on the drop by small arms fire. At the beginning of the war he and I had volunteered together for active service with the Royal Winnipeg Rifles. We had seen the formation of the 1st Canadian Parachute Battalion and by March 1945 we had been in battle together and could read each other like a book. I had lost my closest friend. On 27 March the brigade captured Bruenen without serious trouble. For the next two days the battalion moved forward through the towns of Raesfeld, Erle and Rhade, on to Lembeck, where it rested for two days.

On 30 March the brigade, along with Churchill tanks of the 4th Battalion Grenadier Guards, started toward its first major objective on the drive to Wismar and the Baltic, the Dortmund–Ems canal. The column moved quickly through Coesfield, Billerbeck and Altenberg toward Graven. Whenever resistance was met, A Company would be off the tanks in a flash, and under cover of the hull guns of the Churchills they would dispose of any enemy, while the turret gunners handled light armoured vehicles that chose to challenge the force.

It was a very confused night in Graven. A Company met heavy small arms fire from defended positions on the river. A German leave train arrived at the local station loaded with troops from the Russian front, who were all taken prisoner. A large ammunitions dump was blown which lit up the sky for miles around. On the streets it was hard to tell our own troops from those of the enemy, and occasionally a German soldier would fall in with a small group of Canadian paratroopers, which was his bad luck.

Rain began during the night and lasted well into the next morning. The 9th Battalion had passed through the Canadian position during the night and the brigade crossed the Ems on a temporary bridge and headed for the canal. We soon came under very accurate fire from ack-ack batteries defending a small aerodrome near the town of Ladbergen, on the east bank of the canal. The air bursts were devastating, and at 1400 hours the battalion, led by C Company, crossed the canal, silenced the batteries and took the town.

On 3 April the brigade was ordered to advance to Wissingen. The village was taken by the 9th Battalion, but fighting had been fierce and the place was a shambles. The following day the brigade moved out. Our objective was now Minden.

The brigade moved on quickly to Barkhausen, when at 1700 hours five Tiger tanks opened up on the lead recce tank, killing its commander and driver. The 8th Battalion took off to the right of the line of march and pressed towards Minden until pinned down. The town had originally been an American objective, but the Americans stood down to let the Paras have a go. The brigadier ordered the Canadian Battalion into action.

We preferred to move in darkness and crossed our start point at 2330 hours. By 0400 hours on 5 April Minden was declared clear. Jerry had pulled out during the night. Naturally we assumed that it was the sight of the maroon berets that prompted his quick departure rather than any hint of a proposed US air raid.

On 7 April we crossed the Weser and moved on foot to meet the Churchill tanks. Once more aboard the tanks we made our way to Spreissingholt. The tank crews were beat, and at 2345 hours harboured for the night.

At 0600 hours we were at it again with the tanks. By now most of the battalion were on foot. On the route through Wunsdorf we began to see more and more German infantry giving up the ghost and surrendering. At this point Brigade HQ intercepted a signal from the reconnaissance unit of the 15th Scottish Division which was being torn apart in the village of Ricklingen, about two miles ahead of us. We had to get there fast.

A Company was aboard the tanks and took off. The balance of the battalion dropped all extra equipment and headed out at the double. By 1630 hours the company had secured the town, the balance of the battalion cleaning up what was left of a now badly beaten enemy. Once again this was an American objective. Despite being pleased to see the armoured cars of the US 44 Cavalry Division eventually arrive the troops couldn't help but pass some snide remarks as the Yanks took over. We pulled back and were able to have a well earned rest.

At last light on 14 April we were on the outskirts of Celle, where 15th Scottish had made a shambles of the town. We bogged down for the night and awaited further orders.

On 17 April, again with the Grenadier tanks, we did a wide flanking movement around Uelzen and headed for Ratzlingen. Here the battalion put in a set-piece attack with A and B Companies up, C Company in reserve, tanks in support, field artillery as well as a medium battery under command. What luxury, and what an attack! Casualties, while never pleasant, were light: one killed, four wounded.

Orders were received on 29 April to proceed to Lauenburg. The Royal Engineers had put two excellent pontoon bridges across the river and our forward formation had already disposed of enemy resistance. Once across the brigade moved right to take up positions for the night. By last light the Canadian Battalion had occupied Boisenberg. During the night, American artillery persisted in shelling Boisenberg. This did little to enhance our relations with our North American neighbours. The next day Brigadier Hill appeared with orders for us to take the lead and to reach Wismar before the Russians. With us were the Sherman tanks of the Scots Greys and a transport column of very large troop-carriers of the Royal Army Service Corps.

I told Major Stan Waters, B Company commander, how urgent it was for us to be in Wittenburg by 1200 hours. I followed immediately behind Stan's tank in my jeep. Stan Waters was a Calgary boy. His cowboy instincts took over, and he drove the tanks on at maximum speed so that we cleared Wittenburg by 0900 hours! At the entrance to Wismar, we got confirmation from a released Canadian PoW that there was no fight left in the enemy, and we were on our way to the far side of town. Companies were dispersed to ensure Wismar was completely in our hands. The remainder of the brigade would join us later.

Badly whipped German soldiers were streaming into town from the east, fleeing from the Russian forward armoured units. They were absolutely terrified of being taken by the Russians. Only a few hours after our arrival the Russians finally drew up at the east entrance to the town. They were somewhat put out when told that the 1st Canadian Parachute Battalion already occupied Wismar, in the face of their own orders to press on to Lubeck. The Canadians had no intention of leaving, or letting the Soviet armoured units through.

On 8 May the war was officially over, and thanks were given to the Almighty that our days of fighting in Europe had at last come to an end. Fortunately, 1st Canadian Parachute Battalion were able to convince the authorities that the battalion complete with its reinforcements should return home as a unit. Approximately 1,100 all ranks embarked on the *Isle de France* and arrived in Halifax, Nova Scotia on 20 June 1945. By the end of September, while the battalion was in camp at Niagara-on-the-Lake, Ontario, orders came to wind up the affairs of the unit. Once this was completed, I remained as the final member of the battalion and arranged for my own discharge. My departure ended the existence of a gallant unit of fighting men, unique in Canadian military history.

CHAPTER FOURTEEN
PALESTINE
1945 – 8

THE REORGANISED 6TH AIRBORNE DIVISION WAS ORDERED TO Palestine as part of the Imperial Strategic Reserve stationed in the Middle East. The division eventually was to consist of nine parachute battalions in three brigades. The division, though intended by the War Office to be kept clear of internal security duties, was inevitably drawn into the thankless and bitter conflict against Jewish terrorists who were trying to create a situation whereby unlimited numbers of immigrants would be allowed into the country. In 1947 the United Nations agreed that Palestine should be partitioned between the Jewish and Arab inhabitants. On its return from Palestine, the 6th Airborne Division was finally disbanded.

MAJOR DARE WILSON, HQ, 6th Airborne Division
We, that is, the 6th Airborne Division – went to Palestine as an integral part of the Imperial Strategic Reserve for the Middle East. It was well situated and we were expecting to enjoy many advantages in a country with so much to offer. For us these included good airfields and the prospect of excellent airborne training in the wonderful climate. But it hit us fairly sharply soon after we arrived that our role was likely to be rather different; in no time we were becoming embroiled in the internal security situation. This was a real turn-around for the men who'd come almost straight from major conflict where the principle of any action against opposition was the use of maximum force. Once in Palestine that principle was almost immediately reversed; with internal security any action taken must be based on minimal force, whatever the situation. And this new role was directly involved with a tense political situation which was liable to flare up at any moment – it was our first real encounter with political terrorism.

PALESTINE 1945-8

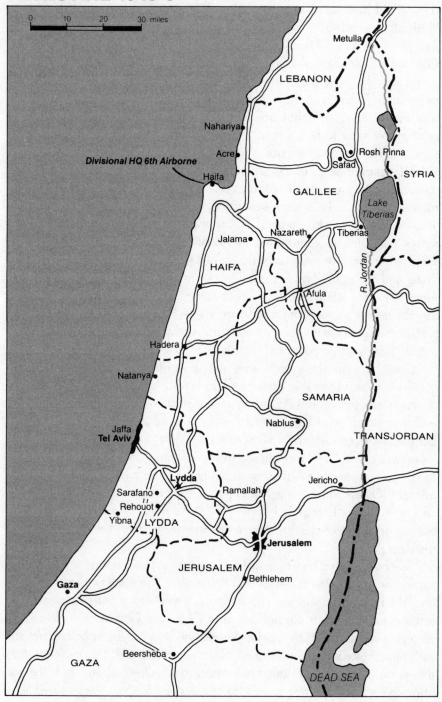

0   10   20   30 miles

Metulla

LEBANON

Nahariya

Acre

Rosh Pinna

Divisional HQ 6th Airborne

Safad

Haifa

SYRIA

GALILEE

Lake
Tiberias

Jalama

Nazareth

Tiberias

HAIFA

Afula

R. Jordan

Hadera

Natanya

SAMARIA

Nablus

TRANSJORDAN

Jaffa
Tel Aviv

Lydda

Sarafano

Ramallah

Jericho

Rehouot

Yibna   LYDDA

Jerusalem

JERUSALEM

Gaza

Bethlehem

DEAD SEA

Beersheba

GAZA

We spent much time explaining the situation to the men so that at least they would have some understanding. The British Government had in its White Paper of 1939, limited Jewish immigration to 75,000 over the next five years. In 1944 it had extended the time period, but not the number. Obviously with the hell of Nazi Germany behind them many Jews sought refuge in the Promised Land, but by 1945 the quota was practically exhausted. To the Jews the imposition at this stage of an immigration quota was unnecessary and inhuman. It was a situation that could only lead to conflict; we were to face a small but tightly organized opposition intent on changing the course of events.

The main underground organization was the Hagana – virtually a Jewish national army – with an almost universal membership of able-bodied Jewish men and women. They were well equipped and armed, but were essentially a moderate group who planned and trained with commitment behind the scenes but avoided confrontation with British forces whenever possible. It was the extremist organizations that posed most of the problems – the Stern Gang and the Irgun Zvai Leumi. They seemed to think they could achieve more through violence than by other means and they specialized in armed attacks against the security forces, with The Palestine Police – an efficient and highly courageous force – suffering many casualties in cold-blooded attacks against their posts and patrols.

Conditions in the camps were pretty primitive. Initially the British garrisons were expanding apace and incoming units would invariably be tested by the indigenous Arabs. By means of stealth, unsurpassed expertise and with much good humour they infiltrated the defences of new arrivals. During takeovers, which locals seemed to know about in good time, these jokers had a field day. Nothing was beyond them; marquees would disappear in the course of a single night with double sentries passing them every few minutes. Given a little longer, and particularly in the south of the country, structures normally regarded as permanent would disappear on the backs of the ass or camel of the Bedouin with little more than the hard-standings remaining.

So obviously we had to guard the property. This became an increasing battle of wits between ourselves and the Arabs. The Arab worked by stealth and seldom attacked sentries – he really was a specialist at penetrating the best defences undetected. It was not unknown for soldiers (and in one case a senior officer) to wake up looking at the sky with no sign of tent or belongings and with only the beds and the blankets over them remaining. On occasions even the pistol would be missing from under the pillow of any but the old campaigners. This meant a guard rota of one night in three – very tiresome.

A lot of the duties we were involved with were very unpleasant, and caused a lot of tension between the Jewish community and the units who were trying to carry out orders with humanity. We were often called upon to search houses because intelligence suggested that there were weapons concealed in a certain settlement; you can't do this without causing some damage, and while the soldiers were convinced they'd leant over backwards to minimize damage, the householders who had to sort out the mess at the end of the day saw it in a very different light, which led to an intense dislike for the British. An even more distasteful, odious task was guarding the refugees who'd arrived from Europe in those overloaded ships, and taking them off to detainee camps.

In these charged situations it was understanding and good humour that won the day, and not a show of force. I think this is where the British Army has got remarkable reserves in tolerance and understanding, and it was the quality of restraint which really came to the fore when the men were under considerable pressure, a quality only found among soldiers with confidence born out of discipline and experience. Discipline is also the *sine qua non* when the going gets rough. When the car-park guard of 5th Parachute Battalion were shot up in their tents by the Stern Gang and seven men were killed the unit concerned were under considerable stress, so, for 24 hours the commanding officer, on his own initiative, kept the men occupied in barracks so they couldn't get any ideas which would have let the side down. I think you would have to search far and wide to find another army which would show the same degree of restraint under this sort of provocation. I believe that the British Army is unique in this regard.

MAJOR JOHN WADDY, 9th Parachute Battalion

Not long after our arrival in Palestine in October 1945 we became involved in the frustrating task of internal security. The Jews were determined to make Palestine their home, and if Britain got in the way then they would fight us: indeed, many of their clandestine and even pseudo-official organizations had been preparing for it for some years, even when Eighth Army had their backs to the wall at Alamein in 1942. In November 1945 riots were engineered, and manipulated by the Jews in Tel Aviv to make the airborne troops look like the oppressors especially when they had to open fire, causing casualties. Terrorist gangs, with other groups, started to ambush and mine roads. These actions were all part of the classic insurgency activity and were designed to make the security forces react against such incidents, and in the process, by searching settlements or curfewing and screening the people, they would antagonize the local population.

The Jews, with the connivance, if not under the guidance, of their 'authorities' held the initiative: one month they would attack and destroy trains and the track on the main Haifa–Egypt railway, and six or seven battalions would then be forced to spend several weeks guarding the railways (and at the same time eating all the luscious Jaffa oranges). Our activities would then return to normal, and then the Jews would attack all the bridges over the River Jordan; so we guarded the bridges. Then they attacked the airfields and destroyed over 30 of our aircraft, thus putting a virtual end to what little parachute training had been possible. What was left of the RAF force disappeared down to Egypt and we guarded the empty airfields.

In between cordons and searches and curfews we were able to carry out some training but on the whole our true military life was fruitless for some two and a half years. At the start, there were many members of the division who had served throughout the war. Some, like me, had spent periods of time in Hitler's 'hotels'. We had arrived in the Holy Land looking forward to enjoying peacetime soldiering in the sun; instead we found ourselves embroiled in this campaign of hate, which also entailed loss of life and limb. It was therefore understandable that all of us, officers and soldiers, soon built up a distaste for the Jews, and not only for the terrorists but for the population as a whole, because they were all in it in their effort to make it difficult for us, and thus to force our government either to give up or to allow the immigrants into Palestine. In the end, this was what happened and Attlee for once did the sensible thing and said to the UN, 'You help us sort out this problem, or we get out.'

The Jews were the first people, postwar at any rate, to prove that terrorism pays as a means of gaining national or political ends. It must be admitted that the Airborne Division perhaps took stronger action than other formations in dealing with incidents or with the activities of the Jewish terrorist or 'defence' organizations, and I think that is partly due to the rugged manner in which our troops were trained for the more violent actions of airborne warfare. We were labelled as anti-Semitic or even the SS of the British Army. We were called the 'Kalionots', a Jewish word for a poppy – a red flower with a black heart. Our soldiers, in jest of course, reacted sometimes to this by singing the Horst Wessel, with other suitable words.

After the first year, most of the war-enlisted members had gone home, other than the regular cadres of officers, WOs and NCOs, and the ranks were largely filled by national servicemen, who, I must say, were marvellous, and every bit as good as their wartime colleagues. No other soldiers in the world could have done our job and maintained discipline, and above all, a sense of humour.

One of the most difficult things was to maintain the soldiers' alertness at all times against terrorist action; a precaution, which over the past 40 years has become more instinctive among security forces, particularly in Northern Ireland with its similar situation. I tried to hammer it into their heads on every occasion, and it was therefore most embarrassing that in a brief moment when I myself was off guard I was shot in the back by terrorists. Later I was visited in Haifa hospital by my company sergeant major who said, 'Sir, the boys will never believe you now, when you tell them to be always suspicious . . .' No one had any regrets at leaving the Holy Land when the last Airborne troops sailed out of Haifa harbour in April 1948, leaving the Jews and the Arabs to fight it out among themselves. We didn't hate the Jews: we were sorry for many of the immigrants, and especially the old people and the children, but we were annoyed at the impertinence of their leaders in ruining the peace which we had fought for. We felt that they were a lot of ungrateful shits.

MAJOR BRUCE LEE, 8th Parachute Battalion

On arrival in the Middle East, the 8th Battalion of 3 Parachute Brigade was stationed initially near Gaza, in southern Palestine. The advance party had already learnt that security in Palestine, not only of arms and ammunition but of all attractive 'useful' items, was paramount. Security against Arabs was understandable to soldiers, in a sense it was a game. It was different in the Jewish urban and settlement districts. At that time it had become quite apparent that there was going to be a major internal security problem to do with Jewish immigration, and Arab objections to it. So, along with the rest of 6th Airborne Division, we were moved to various parts of southern Palestine, while the infantry division was stationed in the north. The 8th Battalion moved to a camp at Sarona in a village outside Tel Aviv. The camp was a main base of the Police Mobile Force (PMF) an all-British force of armoured cars and vehicles equivalent to an armoured car squadron plus strength with good wireless, Tel Aviv being an all Jewish city, adjacent to Jaffa, which was all Arab. Obviously this was going to be an increasingly difficult internal security assignment.

The battalion settled in quickly – there was always one company on stand-by, one company on ordinary training, and one company doing various internal security patrols closely with the PMF. The situation then rapidly worsened with increasing Jewish attempts at immigration, well over and above their legal quota. At that time none of us in 6th Airborne Division really realized the size of the Jewish problem – the immigrants that would be coming from Eastern Europe. It wasn't just a simple immigration problem – the Diaspora was over and they all wanted to get to Palestine.

In November of 1945 there were some serious riots in Tel Aviv, and the situation had got beyond the control of the police. The 8th Battalion were directly involved in these, and it was the first time British troops had to disperse European, let alone Jewish, mobs. We went in the classic IS manner, with the banner 'Disperse or we fire' and all the usual warnings. It wasn't a nice business at all, in an urban situation. During the next six months or so the battalion was involved in various IS operations in Tel Aviv – mainly active patrolling with the Palestine police, and cordon and search operations for terrorists after a terrorist act; the nearest villages would be cordoned and searched, and sometimes arms were found, sometimes not. The terrorist enemies were the Stern Gang and the Irgun Zvai Leumi (IZL).

A rare coup for us occurred after a group of some 30 terrorists attacked and attempted to blow up a small police station at Yibna on the coast ten miles south of Jaffa. These small 'coast-guard' stations had become targets for Jewish terrorists because they were in the front line for detecting illegal immigrant ships. However, this particular group must have got their timing wrong because, come daylight, they were spotted by Arabs withdrawing across desert to the sanctuary of the Jewish part of Tel Aviv. The Arabs reported this to the police and the 8th Battalion. The standby company was already committed elsewhere. A scratch force consisting of elements of HQ Company and others in camp, led by the CO, George Hewetson, left in transport within 15 minutes. The force, then on foot, arrived near the sighting, chased across the desert, and, aided by an Auster AOP, caught up and surrounded in sand dunes 30-odd terrorists. A brisk fire fight ensued and they surrendered. These were an IZL gang including some women. British troops in Palestine had never before managed to catch any Jewish terrorists, because usually they just disappeared into the Jewish settlements. It was a definite feather in the cap of the 8th Battalion.

All operations and patrols were different. A somewhat untypical operation was what had become a weekly search for the terrorist clandestine radio station Kol Israel – Voice of Israel. This station was very mobile, broadcasting from different houses and flats in urban areas at regular intervals at the same time, 1400 hours, for half an hour or less if threatened. Finally the station was surprised one day by the patrol, acting on information, and the operators captured. They were Stern Gang and armed, but surrendered. George Hewetson, in at the action, himself found a terrorist hiding in a lavatory.

After about six months the battalion moved from Sarona and operations in the Tel Aviv area, to a camp at Qastina in South Palestine where 3 Parachute Brigade were now concentrated. The brigade were near RAF airfields and available for the Imperial Strategic Reserve role of 6 Airborne Division, with possible tasks anywhere in the Middle East. Although in the Strategic Reserve role and carrying out normal training as much as possible, inevitably as the terrorist campaign continued and relations with Jewish population worsened, the battalion became increasingly committed to internal security, mainly in South Palestine and again in the Tel Aviv area.

It was all very frustrating and difficult for airborne soldiers trained to aggressive action to understand. Morale and discipline were extraordinarily steady. All officers, WOs and senior NCOs had battle experience. A slowly increasing number of young officers and soldiers were joining by mid 1946.

For some periods the troops were literally confined to their tented camps, with barbed wire all round. There was little recreation. Sometimes for weeks on end we never left camp apart from carrying out training, cordon and search operations, road blocks, railway and airfield protection; so it was very unrewarding and unreal for soldiers, most of whom had taken a very active part in the liberation of North-West Europe. Nor should one forget that a lot of venomous Jewish propaganda was levelled at the soldier in the red beret. One prominent person in the United States, I believe the Mayor of New York, proudly said, 'Every time a British soldier is killed in Palestine, I take a holiday in my heart.' They made a real point of singling us out for abuse, ignoring the infantry division in the north. We were not violent with them, but were always keenly patrolling and were probably more active.

SERGEANT CHARLES ELSEY, 6th Airborne Armoured Recce Regiment

When we arrived in Palestine with a mixture of Tetrarchs and Locust tanks we were put into camps in the desert. They set up an open-air cinema for us. It was bloody hilarious – the Arabs were running it, and you had to pay a couple of piastres to get in. An Arab had set himself up with a little counter with a few boxes in front of him, with sweets and drinks. So when the film came on, if you felt like a packet of fags, or chocolate or something you would go down to him. But he hadn't quite reckoned with the 6th Airborne Division, who were a load of villains; when the lights went out, and he was watching the film, there were people creeping down and helping themselves, so by the interval he hadn't got anything left! He was calling to Allah!

Sometime after our unit had been taken over by the 3rd Hussars our camp was raided by extremists. We had proper buildings of sorts – sergeants' mess and officers' mess – and opposite those, two whacking great marquees full of ammunition. Parked near the marquees we had all our tanks. I was a sergeant by then, and I remember sitting in the Mess, and somebody shouting out, 'The Jews are raiding the ammo tents!' I was near the front door of the Mess, so I rushed out and ran over towards the ammo tents, thinking the whole Mess was behind me – but nobody had bloody well followed me! I ran over and dived down between two of the tanks. There was shooting going on all over the place, and I looked up and just between the two tanks in front was a lance corporal with a pistol. I didn't recognize him, but I said, 'Get down!' The bastard, it wasn't one of us, it was one of them! – dressed up as a British soldier. He fired! – just missed me – and he ran. There was shooting going on all around and later on we found they were all dressed as British troops – there was a sergeant major, several sergeants, a couple of corporals and about ten in dungarees. They had driven two trucks in and they were quietly loading ammunition on to them. Just as that happened, an officer ran from the Mess, and dropped down beside me. The two trucks with the ammunition now drove off the square and came past us. The officer had brought down two pistols one of which he gave me and as they passed us we fired into the back, and we got a couple of them; one fell dead. We found a wounded one later on, and we heard that a second one had died.

For the soldier, Palestine was a difficult time – it was one big game of playing policeman. It was the sheer frustration of not being able to be soldiers as we'd been throughout the war.

CHAPTER FIFTEEN

MALAYA

1955–7

I N 1954, AT THE REQUEST OF THE DIRECTOR OF OPERATIONS IN Malaya, an Independent Parachute Squadron was raised from volunteers from The Parachute Regiment. They were to reinforce 22 SAS and to replace their Rhodesian squadron for operations in Malaya against the communist terrorists, who were attempting to take over the country. Some 80 officers and men were selected to form this squadron and they served in Malaya on operations with 22 SAS until May 1957 when they returned to their respective battalions in the UK.

PRIVATE PETER GERAGHTY, The Parachute Squadron, 22 SAS
From 1948 the communists (CT) dominated Malaya and particularly the jungle areas, indoctrinating the aboriginal tribes. The SAS, reformed from the Malayan Scouts, fought this tenacious and elusive enemy by penetrating deep into his territory. Not only were they harassing the enemy but in order to win back the support of the local aboriginal tribesmen the SAS conducted a 'hearts and minds' campaign.

In 1954 the Director of Operations in Malaya, General Sir Geoffrey Bourne, recommended that the Parachute Regiment should supply a special squadron to replace C (Rhodesian) Squadron, 22 SAS who were coming to the end of their tour. It was decided that the volunteers should come from all three battalions of the regiment so that no particular one should be favoured.

When they asked for volunteers from 3 Para to form this independent para company we all volunteered, every single one of us. There wasn't any form of selection. One day my name appeared on detail to go. Everybody said to me, 'You jammy bastard, you.' All the old soldiers were browned off because they'd been in Egypt for three years. We went on the piss in a

THE FAR EAST 1944-1965

Kohima •
Imphal • • Sangshak

INDIA

R. Chindwin

CHINA

BURMA

R. Irawaddy

Rangoon •

THAILAND

Bangkok •

ANDAMAN SEA

FRENCH
INDO-CHINA

SOUTH CHINA SEA

Penang •

1

MALAYA

• Kuala Lumpur

Kota Tingii
• • Singapore

SUMATRA

Brunei

SARAWAK

• Nanga Gat
• Kuching

Plaman Mapu

INDONESIAN BORNEO
(KALIMANTAN)
2

INDIAN OCEAN

JAVA

1 Malaya 1955-7
2 Borneo 1965

0   200   400 miles

North Camp Hotel for a couple of weeks, and that was quite a novelty, because we normally drank in Aldershot. It was like being in another town; nobody had cars or transport then, so it was quite a big difference. Then we marched to North Camp railway station with the full band and drums playing, got on the train and went to war.

We went somewhere – I don't know where – stayed overnight, got on a plane, and landed, got out and it was a great big RAF camp in the middle of nowhere in Iraq. We spent the evening down the NAAFI and got pissed; went to Karachi, got off, got pissed, got back on the plane, went to Ceylon, got off, got pissed, got back on the plane and then arrived. Then they sent us to Jungle Training School at Kota Tinggi which was absolutely fascinating. After that we were sent into the jungle and then went to Kuala Lumpur and joined up with the SAS. There were A, B and D Squadrons and we were renamed the Parachute Squadron. We operated four-man patrols for the whole tour. The only difference between us and them was that we retained our regimental cap badge. But we were very much part of them.

The normal infantry regiments in Malaya basically made no more than say four- or five-day patrols in the jungle. If they went on what they called their really long patrols they went for ten days. We were doing a totally different thing. We were going in what was called deep penetration, where they put you down right smack in the middle of the jungle and just left you for six, eight, or ten weeks and the only contact with the outside world was the old HF62 radio set on skywave. Every seven or ten days over came a plane, down came the parachutes and that was your rations and you carried on. You had no physical contact with anyone else. In our troop, we had a troop commander, troop sergeant, two NCOs and the rest of us were toms. There were about twelve of us altogether, four abo porters to carry the radio kit, and two Iban trackers. We didn't shave and we didn't smoke.

The idea was for us to live in a large area to stop CTs living in it. If we came across any cultivation or areas they lived in, we destroyed it to stop them using it. We met the abos who lived in the jungle, and in the north, right up in the Camerons we met tribes I'm quite sure had never seen people like us in their lives. Little kids in the villages used to come and look at me because I had very blond hair and a long beard, and blue eyes. Mind you I hadn't seen anything like them either!

We usually went out at first light parading at the squadron stores. We got an empty bergen, jungle hat, OG shirt, OG trousers, socks, boots. The only personal kit we would have was a toothbrush and our jack-knife, and in my case, as a radio operator, a pencil and log book. On top of that was the proper military equipment, for example a compass, weapon, ammunition. You could choose what personal weapon you wanted. Apart from the first operation I carried an American carbine which was not very good at stopping anyone, but was nice and light to carry. Then off you'd go by helicopter or by truck. You'd get off at the side of the road and get straight in. We were only in small groups and we knew they would be in bigger groups which made us quite vulnerable. So apart from looking for them, we were also trying to avoid them.

When they teach you jungle training at the school, they teach you to have a dry set of clothes which you keep in a plastic bag. So every night you put your basha up and you take all your clothes off and you powder your feet and you put on your dry set of clothes and you get into your hammock. But in reality that didn't work for us. We binned all the spare army kit, never used the issue hammocks at all. For the first week we'd rough it. Then when they dropped our supplies we'd cut four panels of a parachute, fold them over and stitch them up with para cord, cut two six-foot poles and slide them through the side which made a stretcher and that's what we'd sleep on. One each, off the ground. Then we'd put up our poncho, cut a piece of wood, bend it to hold the hood in place, tie the corners with para cord and you had a waterproof basha. Then we'd strip off, and because your kit was either wet with sweat or rain you'd put a couple of sticks in the ground and hang up your boots and socks, but they'd still be wet in the morning. We used to sleep in green, very lightweight cotton underpants which we called drawers Dracula. We'd wear the same pair of pants for maybe weeks. At night we'd sleep in a sleeping bag made out of two parachutes stitched together.

When we wanted a change of kit I used to call up on the radio. I would put in for a shirt and trousers and a pair of boots for every man; because we could wear out a pair of boots in a week. They'd just split, or fall apart. We also used brown canvas hockey boots. After drying and powdering your feet you wore those at night. During the day your feet were always wet, crinkly, horrid with leeches in the top of your boots. Your feet and ankles got into a bit of a state. You also had to make sure that you didn't become ill. This was the hardest thing because you weren't on a very good diet and you were working hard carrying a lot of kit and because we only washed when we could flop into a river, we were in a fairly insanitary state.

For air-drop days it took ages to clear an area because we only had machetes and usually I was left behind with the abos and the LMG man and perhaps the troop medic to clear a blooming DZ. I tell you air-drop days were really dramatic times, because if your scoff and kit landed in the trees there was no way to get it down. We used to put up air marker balloons. NAAFI supplies would also be dropped, which we'd ordered, but at the end of the tour you'd have to pay for them. They'd drop the straightforward rations, which for a ten-day drop would consist of nine days' hard rations and one day's fresh. You know, bread, meat and vegetables. So we would sit there and eat that there and then. When we'd eaten we'd have to move. We'd had an aeroplane fly over and we'd been there two days so we couldn't stay there any longer. So we then had the soul-destroying job of having to pile the parachutes together, all the rations we didn't want, the paperbacks which a very kind WVS lady had sent and burn them. Because we were entitled to a tot of rum a day they'd often drop us a big jug in a wicker basket – that had to go on the fire too! We'd put six or seven days' rations into our bergens, grind off into the jungle for three or four days, absolutely knackering ourselves, set up another base camp and a little patrol area and then a few days later go through all the same performance again.

We had our first casualty, a lad called Ossie Phillips, who was in an ambush and was shot through the upper leg and had a ball removed. It took two or three days before we could get him out. We had a troop medic but he was like me, he'd been told, 'you're the medic'. So there he was trying to look after him and me trying to get through on the radio. In the end they parachuted in a medic with plasma, which was a very hazardous business. Then we cleared an LZ and the lad got out.

I was quite ill on one of the ops; all my hair fell out and I went almost completely bald, which when you're 19 is quite worrying. An Auster came and dropped me some pills to take for this bloody thing. Then I got toothache and if you've got that for six weeks life is agony. That's when I discovered oil of cloves. Toothache can drive you mad; I remember I had one really bad bout of toothache when we were in the Cameron Highlands. Major John Watts said to me, 'You'll have to go and have it treated. There's a road about 6,000 metres away, we'll send a patrol with you. There's a convoy passing by twice a week. You can flag it down, jump on, go home, get your tooth pulled out and they'll bring you back.' So we waited until this armoured car came along and out we came in all this ragged kit, long-haired, unshaven and the buggers opened fire on us. I tell you it cured my toothache straight away! I never complained again, I went straight back into the ulu (the jungle).

It was always interesting to go to Singapore on leave, after an operation, because there were all these healthy matelots and RAF guys, army guys from the other regiments, all down in the Britannia Club at the swimming pool. And there we were, all white, very skinny, scrawny and scabby, and covered in spots. It wasn't just leeches that were the bugbear; to me the worst thing were red ants. They'd get into your basha, millions of the bastards and you'd just have to move. The two most fearsome things in the jungle for me, what really got me down, were sandflies and hornets. If you got an area where you were absolutely covered in sandflies life was total misery, and if we were attacked by hornets on patrol we carried out the same drill as anti-ambush, we all split up, ran away and came back and re-joined! I've seen a lad stung in the eye and he couldn't see for about three days. Horrible things, hornets.

We were always reporting sightings of animals, but no one believed us. We reported things like white rhino, pythons bigger than anyone had seen, tigers that you could saddle, but we became a joke because it was always our troop that saw the bloody things. I mean, if you're lying in ambush for two or three days on a track, you'll see all sorts come down there, because the animals use it. It's their highway in the jungle. I saw a tiger which was so big that I looked at my piddling little American rifle knowing its capabilities against a human being and I thought, 'What chance have I got against that.' I was highly relieved when it went wandering off down the track. The other thing was the big buffaloes and crocodiles in the rivers.

When we came out of the jungle for leave we got cleaned up then the following day you were given your pay for however long you'd been in the jungle and put on the train. The senior NCOs used to go to Penang and the officers and we soldiers used to go to Singapore on the overnight train, which was quite an experience. We went armed with pistols, in uniform, because the whole train could have been ambushed. We used to get pissed and up to all sorts of shenanigans, running along the roofs and doing all sorts of silly things. When we arrived we'd hand our pistols in and then down to the NAAFI Club where we gave all our money in to the manager who put it in the safe and gave us a few dollars back so we could have a few beers. They had the world première of 'Rock Around The Clock' in Singapore, right in the middle of our tour. But we'd never heard this music. There were all these juke boxes which were all playing The Platters and Bill Hayley.

Singapore was full of very delightful girls, and all types and things were ridiculously cheap and we had all this money. I think we were getting about ten dollars a week, we were actually rich and having an absolute ball. The army were clever about VD in those days. If you were going out to have a bit of nooky you booked out through this small room in the guardroom, you filled in a book and got a little package which contained a Durex and a little tube of cream. I think you had a little instruction as to what to do, which went, 'Try to wash yourself afterwards and then go and urinate in bursts, holding it to give yourself a good clean out, and then squirt this tube of cream over it.' You can imagine what it was like when you were three parts pissed and went through this drill!

If you got a dose in those days it was considered a self-inflicted wound and you were put on a charge. The reason you booked out and put your name down was because if you did get a dose and you'd used this kit, you were absolved. 'The name was in the book, sir, I signed out, sir, I fear it must have split or something, sir.' I'm not sure if many of us actually knew if we got a dose or not because just before we went back to the jungle the troop medic used to give us penicillin shots, which of course was the cure for it, in those days. The other cure was to stay off the booze and the women for two or three months or going back into the jungle was the perfect cure.

In two years I saw a lot of jungle – it was either work or play – I tell you, for a young soldier it was a marvellous life.

CHAPTER SIXTEEN
CYPRUS
1 9 5 6 – 7

IN LATE 1955, GREEK TERRORISTS (EOKA) OPENED THEIR campaign for *Enosis* (union with Greece) and in January 1956 the 1st and 3rd Battalions were flown to Cyprus to augment the island's security forces. They were followed, in July, by the 2nd Battalion and 16th Independent Parachute Brigade, prepared for trouble expected in Egypt and the Middle East. The brigade was engaged in a continuous round of anti-terrorist operations in the Troodos mountains and the Kyrenia hills. These operations were interrupted in November 1956 when the brigade took part in the Suez campaign. In December 1956 the 1st and 3rd Battalions returned to England while the 2nd Battalion remained in Cyprus on operational duties where it scored two notable successes in the EOKA campaign until, in February 1957, it too returned home.

LIEUTENANT COLONEL BALA BREDIN, 2nd Battalion

I took over command of 2 Para in February 1956. About a couple of months later the 1st and 3rd Battalions went off to Cyprus and we were left behind for a month or two. While we were waiting in Aldershot I had a phone call from Evie Deane-Drummond, whose husband, Tony, was a major out with 3 Para in Cyprus. She rang me up and said, 'I've had a terrible telegram from the Ministry of Defence, saying that Tony has been very badly wounded and he's on the DI (dangerously ill) list. Can you do anything to find out any more?' I told her I would do all I could. What had happened was that when he was driving, wearing only a beret, some ill-intentioned EOKA chap had dropped a brick on his head from the top of a house. It had stove in the side of his head. Initially they reckoned he was going to die, but within a few days all the hospital staff were saying he isn't going to die now, but he'll probably be a vegetable. Then they said no, he's beginning to perk up a bit,

CYPRUS 1956, 1964

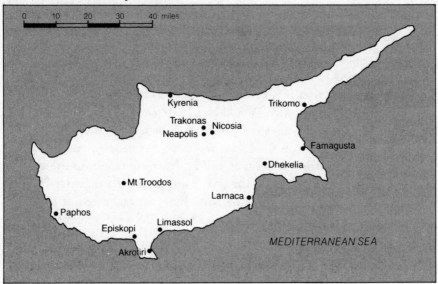

he might even at some indefinite future date be able to work. Then they said, well, he might even be able to stay in the army as long as he transferred to a sit-down job somewhere. It went on like this for a few weeks when Tony summoned the doctors and nurses and said to them, words to the effect, 'Look, I've been listening to the kind of nonsense you have been talking for the last couple of months. Now here are my instructions; you will get me fit for parachuting in the next year – is this quite clear? Now, clear out and don't let me hear any more nonsense.'

Well, the following year he won the gliding championship of Great Britain. He is I think probably the most determined man that I have ever met. Having escaped a couple of times and spent 13 days hiding, shut up in a cupboard in Arnhem, it was going to take more than a brick to kill him.

Anyway, in high spirits we arrived in Cyprus to get down to the business of trying to cope with EOKA, which after Palestine was right up our street. It was strenuous, because of the mountains, but it wasn't the unpleasant business of rounding up villages and towns. We laid lots of ambushes and we cudgelled our brains to think of bigger and better plots to catch EOKA. We were, throughout this time, commanded by Brigadier 'Tubby' Butler. He did something which is desperately needed in the army today, he made soldiering fun, while maintaining efficiency.

313

We were down in the south-west corner of Cyprus, waiting to be told of some operations, when we were told that someone was coming from Brigade Headquarters by helicopter. At the time I got the message I was in the sea, with the O Group, and most of the battalion, so I said, 'Fine, put out a couple of stripes on the beach for the helicopter and have people with the usual flags waving to tell him where to land. Get a swimming costume and a Lilo and when whoever it is lands, tell him to excuse us, but we are in the sea only 100 yards or so away. Would he like to put on the costume and join us in the water and we'll have the O Group. If he wants to deploy maps and things he can put them on the Lilo. Here are some pencils, and he can get on with it, and put the battalion at half-an-hour's notice from the time he arrives.' Well, it worked like a dream. It was Major Tony Farrar-Hockley who arrived in the helicopter – he was absolutely staggered at what was going on. But it saved a hell of a lot of time. We went straight from the beach, climbed into our stuff and were up in the hills, refreshed and ready for work. No other battalion could have done this. They would have all got themselves smartened up and put out white tablecloths and God knows what. It was a very good example of the sort of thing that Butler did, which was passed on to us.

We got a tip from an informer, caught by Peter Field, that there was a place near the top of Mount Olympus called Platras where quite a few important chaps had a hide under one of the houses, so we surrounded the village with a company or so. With the little posse of the informer and the interpreters was a remarkable chap called Lionel Savery who was a gunner, but attached to us as an IO. The informer, after some reluctance, showed us the house which was a perfect picture of domestic bliss. There was a woman sitting in front of a roaring fire with her baby in her lap. We searched and we searched and we couldn't find anything. Then somebody noticed that the fire was on a brick platform which might be covering something. So the whole fire was cleared and sure enough there was a trap-door immediately underneath. We prised this trap-door up and Peter Field shouted down. No answer. Then the interpreter shouted in Greek and Turkish, 'If you don't answer they're going to drop a hand grenade down.' We all then stood back in the room to watch what would happen, and out they came! Not Nikos Samson, but the next best one, followed by about six more, of whom four were real top chaps. I took my hat off in a way to their leader. He came out, blinking, then looked round the room and his eye lit on Lionel Savery. He said, 'Captain Savery, I think, sir, isn't it?' He was the chap who had been trying to ambush Lionel Savery for some months.

Lionel Savery had collected round him a little gang of ex-EOKA terrorists, who had been captured, and who had said, 'Well, all right, we will come in on your side.' He would go out with this gang and look for EOKA chaps in the villages. He always wore a sheepskin coat and he and the gang used EOKA weapons. I used to ask him where his hair finished and the sheepskin coat began. Lionel's gang would go into the village and settle down in some café and have a drink and tell the locals to make quite sure that they were informed if any police or troops approached. Then as an aside they would say, 'None of the rest of the boys around are there, at the moment?' Once in a dozen times some chap would say, 'Oh yes, there are some of your friends I think at the next café just round the corner.' So then they would advance and a gun battle would ensue. The platoon which we'd placed close by would rush in quickly to reinforce the situation. Old Lionel Savery was very good on his own. However after we left he got quite badly wounded in one of these operations, but he got a very good MC, and the other chap, Peter Field, got an MC as well.

LIEUTENANT PETER FIELD, 2nd Battalion
After the Suez operation 2 Para returned to Cyprus to take part in the anti-EOKA terrorist campaign. One of the centres of EOKA activity was the Troodos mountains and although the Army had a presence there, it was too small to expect much success in this very large, rugged area. The battalion was based in Platras, a small tourist village of mainly wooden buildings, not far from Mount Olympus. We took over the village completely, each company occupying a hotel; there were no tourists to worry about! This was the first time that a major base from which to mount operations against EOKA had been established well inside this mountainous area. We knew that we were not to be there for long and I remember the CO, Lieutenant Colonel Bala Bredin, saying that if we could get one or two terrorists before we left, he would be satisfied.

We had a very able military intelligence officer attached to us, a man called Lionel Savery. Our own battalion intelligence officer was an Arnhem veteran, Nick Nicholson, and the two worked very closely. In a short time they created a remarkably successful intelligence effort. They were supported by Greek-speakers, usually Turkish policemen, and gradually as little bits of information were pieced together, patterns and pictures emerged of EOKA activities and sympathizers. Information came from other sources as well, perhaps Nicosia, and it wasn't long before each patrol had something definite to find out or to check. The two IOs and the intelligence section worked hard and around the clock. We began to have small successes, but every success came from this intelligence effort.

I think the classic for me was when we went after one particular group in a remote mountainous area. It was a large-scale operation and some of us were to be taken in by Sycamore helicopters. The area was to be cordoned in the early morning, then we were to close in. Bala realised the security problem in such a large operation; the group would escape if their suspicions were in any way aroused – we could easily lose them. My platoon was therefore asked to enter the area the night before and see what we could find. One particular village was thought to be a likely hiding place for the group. We left at about 2000 hours the night before and arrived near the village at about three o'clock next morning. A cordon was put around the 30-odd buildings with men on the cordon being about 70 yards apart. Then a small group moved into the village and searched houses selected by the intelligence section. We would tap on the door and as soon as it was opened, we would slip inside. The shock and surprise seemed to stun the people into keeping quiet. If any did start to make a noise, we shut them up immediately. After checking the occupants we moved to the next house on the list, leaving a tom behind to make sure they didn't raise the alarm.

We searched the main suspect houses and found nothing. Then I knocked on the door of the last house on the list. It was opened by a man in pyjamas and when he recognized me, he panicked. I pushed him aside and ran up the stairs into a large room where five men were asleep. There were Thompson sub-machine-guns and rifles stacked against the wall. The men had obviously come in for a night's rest. The four toms with me rushed into the room and it was a free-for-all fight – lots of noise and confusion. Two shots were fired and two terrorists were wounded, and they all surrendered. This was a good example of what can be achieved with good intelligence, good training and a bit of luck.

Intelligence began to snowball as the two IOs collated more and more information. On one occasion the information came from Nicosia. A man had agreed, for a substantial reward, to show us where another gang was based. My platoon arrived at the spot in the middle of the night but I couldn't find anything even when using a torch. The informer pointed to the ground and said, 'Lift that'. There was a trap door which I would never have spotted on my own. There was no-one there but we found a large amount of explosive, ammunition and general equipment.

The informer took us to another place but by this time it was quite light. We were in a deep open valley and I was very anxious that we would be spotted. We climbed up one side of the valley hoping to find an approach with better cover. Near the top I saw some footprints and we followed them.

The footprints led to a newly dug hole in the side of a steep slope. There was a trap door with some bushes, rocks and shingle covering it. The hole was fairly small and I was sure that the birds had flown. We sat down and waited for the others to join us. I had a cigarette, then impatiently decided to have a look at what was below. I went down the shaft which was about twelve feet deep. At the bottom of the shaft there was a tunnel which I could move along on hands and knees. I used my torch to spot any trip wires and my pistol was in its holster. I rounded a bend and in the light of my torch saw three or four men with their weapons at the ready. I have never moved backwards so fast in my life! I got back to the top and called them to come out. This they did – there was no escape for them.

In Platras there were several local people for whom our arrival meant a return of some trade and business. I don't think they had sympathies for either side – they just wanted to make a living. One came most days selling fresh bread carried on his donkey. On one occasion he seemed agitated and the sentry decided to check his baskets. He found explosives prepared as a bomb. EOKA had frightened him into carrying the bomb into our base. He finished up in gaol. It was alarming to think that he could have got inside our base.

We carried on with our patrols which most of the time were boring and very tiring in the hot weather. We were also trying to prepare ourselves for Suez. I divided the platoon into small groups. Private Faiers and Sutherland, did not do exactly what I told them and went back to the farm where we'd been the day before. They spent the day prodding, poking and digging and found a weapons cache in a wall. These toms had no NCO with them and had been given an area to search which did not include the farm. They had 'interpreted' my orders. I think they got a well deserved beer from me that night!

CHAPTER SEVENTEEN

SUEZ
Operation Musketeer
1 9 5 6

IN JULY 1956, EGYPT NATIONALIZED THE SUEZ CANAL, AND REFUSED to allow free access to ships of all nations. Following the successful Israeli offensive across the Sinai desert to the Suez Canal, the British and French governments put into operation a plan to seize the Canal. The 3rd Parachute Battalion, in conjunction with French parachute units, were ordered to carry out a parachute assault. Flying from Cyprus and landing 24 hours ahead of the seaborne force, the 3rd Battalion secured El Gamil airfield by *coup de main*, cleared the road to Port Said and sealed off the native quarter. They then linked up with the 2nd Battalion who arrived by sea and assisted with the securing of the town and the advance down the Canal, which was halted only by political pressures on the two governments.

MAJOR FRANK KING, HQ, 16 Independent Parachute Brigade Group
When 16 Parachute Brigade returned from its tour of duty in Egypt I had come to the end of my three years' parachuting engagement and was due for staff employment. I was lucky. I was merely transferred from 2 Para to Brigade HQ to fill a then vacant appointment as GSO2 (Air). This was an interesting but not arduous task, with responsibility for all the airborne and parachuting aspects of the brigade's training and, more importantly, the operational planning that went with it in the event of war. So when in 1956 the Suez crisis erupted I was immediately involved in a turmoil of unexpected activity.

After a concentrated period of up-dating training, the whole brigade with its war-like stores moved by air to Cyprus. Whilst the bulk of the

SUEZ 1956

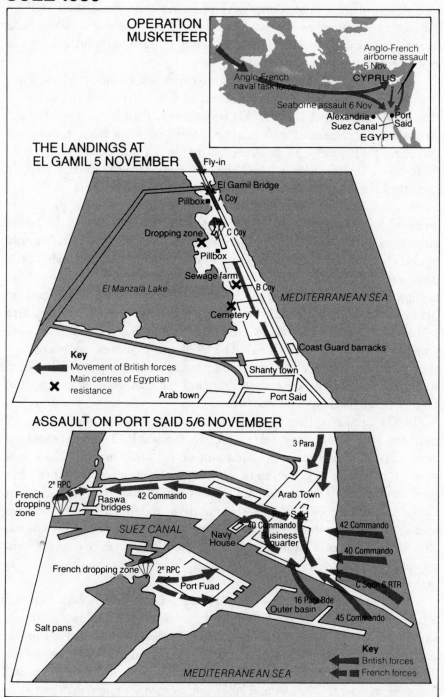

OPERATION MUSKETEER

Anglo-French naval task force

Anglo-French airborne assault 5 Nov

CYPRUS

Seaborne assault 6 Nov

Alexandria ●
Suez Canal
● Port Said

EGYPT

THE LANDINGS AT EL GAMIL 5 NOVEMBER

Fly-in

El Gamil Bridge

Pillbox ■ A Coy

Dropping zone ✕ C Coy

Pillbox

Sewage farm ✕ B Coy

El Manzala Lake

MEDITERRANEAN SEA

Cemetery ✕

Coast Guard barracks

Key
← Movement of British forces
✕ Main centres of Egyptian resistance

Shanty town

Arab town   Port Said

ASSAULT ON PORT SAID 5/6 NOVEMBER

3 Para

2ᵉ RPC

French dropping zone

Raswa bridges

42 Commando

Arab Town

SUEZ CANAL

Port Said

40 Commando

Navy House

Business quarter

42 Commando

40 Commando

French dropping zone   2ᵉ RPC

Port Fuad

C Sqdn 6 RTR

16 Para Bde
Outer basin

45 Commando

Salt pans

Key
← British forces
⇠ French forces

MEDITERRANEAN SEA

319

soldiers disappeared to the mountains to hunt Colonel Grivas and his EOKA terrorists, a small Army/RAF planning cell settled itself at RAF Nicosia to examine the airborne problems. Time was not a factor since lengthy political discussions were still afoot in London, with little danger of quick decisions.

The task allotted to the brigade was to capture El Gamil airfield at Suez. This immediately posed the first problem. A fair inference at the time was that an airfield of that size probably contained at least 2,000 men. For our part we had sufficient aircraft to drop a force of about 800. It was clear therefore, that if we were to succeed, we must achieve complete surprise. From this initial deduction, two decisions emerged: first, to drop directly onto the objective and second, to arrive at an unsocial hour, ie, at dawn.

It was normal practice to employ a small, about 40-man, pathfinder group who dropped some 30 minutes before the main force and, by laying cloth markers, lighting flares and setting up an electronic beacon, not only guided the main force to the drop zone, but indicated precisely where the drop was to begin and end. But this would clearly not be possible on an occupied airfield. Surprise would be lost and the pathfinders mopped up before the main force arrived. Recourse was therefore made to a Canberra pathfinding aircraft of Bomber Command. A cross was marked on a large-scale air photograph of El Gamil. The Canberra crew were confident that they could lay a flare or smoke bomb precisely on that point. This then would become the marker for our drop and the Canberra, by circling the DZ, would guide the main force in.

El Gamil was a long, narrow airfield with beaches and sea on its northern edge and a large inland lake to the south. This predicated an approach on an east/west axis. But a mile or so to the east was a dock area which intelligence indicated to be bristling with anti-aircraft defences. No pilot was willing to fly straight and level at low altitude over this area. On the other hand approach from the west at dawn and in tight formation gave a heading directly into the rays of the bright rising sun. Few pilots fancied this. By courtesy of a local hospital large quantities of gentian violet were procured and aircraft canopies were liberally coated. It worked and was gratefully adopted.

We were anxious to get the whole force on the ground in about four and a half minutes. This meant a very tight formation with following aircraft slightly above the leaders so as not to run down parachutists already in the sky. The meteorologists were adamant that there would be stiff cross-winds. This meant that given the narrowness of the drop zone, unless we restricted dropping heights to 700 feet and below, many soldiers might drift onto the beaches, which were mined, or into the sea. So 700 feet became our ceiling. But this too raised problems. A year or so before the brigade had had several fatal accidents when parachutes had failed to open. Thus reserve chutes had become very much the fashion and a substantial proportion of our soldiers had never jumped without one. But they only worked if the dropping height was above 1,000 feet, since below that height, by the time the soldier realized that his main chute was playing truant, it was too late to deploy the reserve. A firm decision was made – no reserve chute – which was not received with universal enthusiasm. However, when each man was issued with his operational load – food, water, medical gear, digging equipment, ammunition, grenades and many other items – only the strongest would have welcomed any additions.

Most military text books state that the time to attack parachute soldiers is when they land. Inevitably they are a straggling mass, with companies and other sub-units inextricably mixed, so that until they can forgather and sort themselves out into some recognizable military order they are largely ineffective as a fighting force. It takes 30 soldiers a given time to leap out of an aircraft and in that time the plane will fly at least a mile and a half. If the two heavily laden extremities close towards the middle much valuable time is consumed in 'rallying'. And even then some 800 men have to be sorted out on the ground into the respective company and platoon groups in which they are normally organized to fight.

We concentrated our minds on where we wanted them to land, if necessary with the acceptance of gross inconvenience before departure. Thus A Company's 120 men were split in packets of six to each of 20 aircraft. This was unpopular. Soldiers like above all to stay in 'family groups'. But since in each case those six men were the first to leave their particular aircraft and, given that the pilots all, in theory, started dropping their troops as they drew level with the smoke marker, each company landed roughly in its chosen location. Other companies were treated the same way. There was much criticism of this tactical loading plan before the event. I heard none after it. In fact 3 Para took all its objectives very quickly and with mercifully light casualties. The 'unsocial hour' operated markedly in their favour.

There was one problem that we could do nothing about. The airfield was covered with a multitude of anti-landing devices of one sort or another. They showed up in depressing clarity on all the air photographs. The only comfort one could offer at the final briefing was that old and well trusted parachuting adage, 'Keep your feet and your knees close together.' In the event parachuting casualties were agreeably light. However, one was serious. A wireless message to Cyprus after the drop indicated that Sandy Cavanagh, the unit medical officer, had lost an eye. Three local military doctors were immediately summoned. Not one of them was a trained parachutist so they were given the choice of one volunteering or all of them drawing straws. Straws in fact were drawn, but before the reluctant victim could be fitted with a chute, the El Gamil runway was cleared. A much happier officer set off only to find on arrival that his presence was largely superfluous. The indomitable Sandy had patched up his own eye and was busily tending the other casualties.

LIEUTENANT COLONEL PAUL CROOK, 3rd Battalion

I was in Cyprus commanding 3 Para when the Suez Canal business started. We were flown back to England where we did a couple of battalion exercises after which I gave them all leave. Everybody came back on the day including our reservists who had been called back for active service. Not a single chap was absent.

We went back to Cyprus for a very hot September where I made them train, against the doctor's wishes, on a minimum of water. Then the Israelis invaded and I was sent for on a Monday and told to plan for a real operation but not told where or when or how many aeroplanes until the Thursday. Making plans was difficult because I never knew how many aeroplanes we'd got. We had an odd Hastings and some Valettas; others were off dropping grain to the Hungarians. We had a lot of old-fashioned equipment and we had to string our jeeps up underneath the aircraft. I was very limited. In the event I had 660 parachutists and about 200 containers. We all had to live and fight with what we could take with us; I was all right as the CO because all I had was a flask of whisky, a few bullets and a toothbrush, but people like the signallers had probably a 100-pound load to stagger out with. But we had very few accidents on landing.

Frank King and I devised a plan where every plane had a cross-section of the battalion and on the day it worked. We went off at dawn as usual and I remembered at one period in the flight that the latest photos of El Gamil airfield seemed to be covered in little black dots. These had been verified by RAF pictures. The intelligence officer rushed in with these pictures as I was putting on my equipment in my tent before emplaning. He thought that they were anti-personnel mines. So I said, 'Thanks very much, you and I will keep this to ourselves.' He and I sat in that aeroplane wondering if we were going to be blown up as we landed. Anyway we dropped down, and those black dots turned out to be anti-aeroplane, 40-gallon oil drums, which in fact were good to hide behind when people shot at you. One or two people got hit going down, including our doctor, Sandy Cavanagh (who'd stroked the Oxford boat which sank), who was hit in the eye.

Well, we arrived and the airfield was quickly cleared. We then had quite a battle up towards Port Said. It was a bit strange because in that narrow area you had water on either side so you couldn't deploy a mouse. As we advanced, the ground varied from a little bit of desert to a sewage farm which was really like a Malayan swamp; then to a cemetery which had Christian and Moslem gravestones which people could hide behind. This was followed by another bit of open country, then a block of flats which made lovely OPs for the Egyptians to control their guns, so it was a strange couple of miles.

As I was standing talking to B Company commander, Major Stevens, who had been hit in the hand, there was a burst of fire and he was hit in the knee. We got him back and I gave the second-in-command, Karle Beale, the company.

I brought in C Company and planned a deliberate attack with what mortar and machine-gun firepower we had on the cemetery, which was proving a problem. We were also supported by the Fleet Air Arm who attacked the cemetery very accurately two minutes before we went in at 10.30 am. Suddenly from behind a gravestone up popped an Egyptian and pointed his musket at me, but my personal bodyguard, our PTI, Ray Issitt, promptly used his Sten gun and shot him. Great fellow.

By now there was a lot of action going on in the cemetery. We were shooting at the Eygptians, they were shooting at us and settling old feuds by shooting at each other with their new Russian rifles. Scattered around were a number of old and new corpses that had been unearthed by the bombardment. In the middle of this and our not inconsiderable fire-fight came a funeral party all wailing away. It really was a bit surreal. Anyway we finally cleared through the cemetery and the sappers dealt with the mess.

Brigadier 'Tubby' Butler went off by chopper to talk to his French counterpart and the Commander of Port Said, who'd just recently been to Larkhill and so was a properly trained officer. Then we were told there was a ceasefire. Most people got a pretty civilized night's sleep but 2nd Lieutenant Hogg and his men had to spend the night in the sewage farm with millions of mosquitoes. At dawn a Russian Mig fighter strafed us and caused two casualties.

Just after dawn, I found myself standing on the beach watching a combined operations amphibious assault from the enemy's point of view. We were firing machine-guns in support as the landing craft came in with marines. It was an amazing sight. We went on advancing to where the coast road and another road forked, where there was a hospital. My anaesthetist, Captain Malcolm Elliot, was running out of medical supplies so he went up to the hospital to get some but the people were furious and didn't want to help us. Another hospital a little further on the Egyptians had made a strong point and his patrol was fired on, wounding four. Sergeant 'Lofty' Read, whom they left behind for dead, managed to crawl back later that night, to the great joy of the battalion, and Elliot extricated the others, for which he got an MC.

We carried on advancing and we were supposed to link up with the Royal Marines but no marines appeared. Eventually we found ourselves on the edge of a suburban area and put ourselves in a fairly salubrious looking house. It ponged a bit of scent, and later turned out to have been a house of ill-fame. The mattresses were full of creatures which stayed with us for weeks. That was the night I and others were sitting round listening to the radio and thinking that the Russians were sabre-rattling most effectively with threats of retaliation worldwide. But we had to obey orders. So like Cinderella we came to a halt at midnight. The 2nd Battalion came ashore in the afternoon at Port Said and moved down with tanks to the south. I don't think they had much opposition.

We'd been there a week when we embarked on MV *Australia* and went back to Cyprus, where no-one turned out to greet us. Not only that, the Red Caps were there to search us. The French had apparently come in before us and it was alleged they had sold arms to EOKA. Well, after seeing some pasty-faced lance corporal patting the balls of my soldiers I said to the provost major, 'I will tolerate this no longer.' I was disgusted and disappointed with that and our welcome home. But all that aside the tremendous spirit and courage and efficiency of those young parachutists, many of whom had not been to war, was great. People have said it was a failure; it might have been politically, but we captured the place. We did our job. We did it well. It was also the last airborne assault carried out by the Parachute Regiment.

LIEUTENANT SANDY CAVANAGH, 3rd Battalion

I had been out of medical school 18 months, and during that time had done a job on a children's ward, a casualty job and a surgical house job, two of these posts being the absolute minimum necessary to become registered. Then I was called up for National Service and volunteered for three years as a short service regular in the RAMC. I was swept through Crookham, where the corps had its depot, and in a fortnight they put you into uniform and taught you to salute, to march and to carry a swagger cane – that was about it. I then went to Millbank for two weeks to learn the elements of tropical and military medicine, and then on to Mytchett, just outside Aldershot, for a further two weeks to do field hygiene and learn how to dig deep trench latrines. After that they felt you were on your own as an MO in any capacity they chose.

My fate was sealed by a seductive address by Colonel John Kilgour, then CO of 23 Parachute Field Ambulance who warned us that if we didn't volunteer for airborne training we'd be dealing with smelly feet and drains, and little else. I was called off to do 'P' course, which selected you for parachute training, and then caught glandular fever and fell out of things for a few months. I eventually found myself going to Cyprus, having not trained at all, when Nasser nationalized the Canal.

In Cyprus, they suddenly found that I hadn't yet done the Para course, so, three days later, I got on an aircraft and flew back to the UK. It was typical, a microscopic piece of military chaos, but I did have a somewhat bewildering meeting with 3 Para first. I arrived on a Sunday – I didn't realize it was a Sunday – and I thought well, this is a laid-back place; half the chaps were wearing civilian dress, and the officers all seemed to be drinking gin and tonic in the mess. It took some time too before I realized quite what sort of outfit I had joined. I did my Para course in a week – a rushed job – and came back to Cyprus.

We were out on a great co-ordinated sweep of the mountains where Grivas' main hide-out was supposed to be when suddenly the cry went up, 'We're going back to camp.' We'd only just arrived, but the Israelis had issued their ultimatum and we all clattered back. Everything snowballed. In an atmosphere of dust and wind, we got our stuff together. There was counter-order and disorder, and we had less aircraft space than we expected. At the last moment one of the aircraft went out of action altogether, and we had to unpack half our containers. There were the old ones they'd used in World War II, six-foot tiny cylinders, which held about 300 pounds of kit. Finally, we were got together by the CO for briefing. The whole battalion was assembled, and when the RSM got everybody sitting down, silent, the CO unrolled a map; 'There's Port Said, there's the airfield, that's what I want you to capture.' Long pause. A small voice from some wag in the front of the audience, 'Thank you very much.' Roars of fury from the RSM.

After a little more chaos, we finally went on the 5th. Horace McClelland, the padre, and I had a more or less sleepless night since the rights and wrongs of the whole operation were beyond us. And we were worried because we'd lost a sapper who had been injured and taken to hospital in Nicosia. He had been fully briefed on the operation, and everybody was in a panic about what he might say under anaesthetic. (We might as well have saved ourselves the worry since the BBC Overseas Service warned the citizens of Port Said to keep clear of the beaches that night!)

Off we went in the dark. We had some rather miserable breakfast and traipsed out to our three-tonners. I wondered if we'd ever come back to this fly-blown place. We'd had some very chaotic aircraft drill the day before, but we knew we had only 30 seconds over the dropping zone – it was about a mile long and we were going to cross it at 120 mph. We were dropping from 600 feet, lower than we'd ever dropped from before. After I got out the door, the important thing was to get rid of the wretched personal container which hung on hooks on the parachute harness. It weighed 80 pounds and I was delighted when I got the thing free to hang 15 feet below on its cord. But just as it went, I got this incredible smack in the eye. I didn't realize what was happening at all. Suddenly my equipment was ripped away into the air – I was worried about that until I found on the ground that it had been actually burnt through by a splinter from an anti-aircraft shell. It was obvious now what had happened, but I hadn't heard the thing go off. I thought, 'My God, I've been killed.' The eye only registered white fluff and I thought that whatever it was must have gone straight through my head. I had visions of the game, 'Meet Lord Nelson', but when I touched my eye it didn't seem that bad, so the only thing that really mattered was to land properly.

On the ground my faithful corporal was putting his stuff together, and I went over and got mine, which was in a frightful mess, all the bottles broken. We humped it back to the airport buildings where the medical services were going to set up. There was a lot of shooting. When I was getting out of the aircraft, seeing all those things whirling off, I thought, 'My God, we're giving these people hell.' What I didn't realize was that none of our chaps was on the ground yet; it was all being aimed at us. I was so ignorant it wasn't until I had got to the ground that I remembered my father, who had been on the Somme, telling me that when bullets are coming really close, you get this crack like a whip-lash. Suddenly the air was full of whip-lashes, and you could see these things dotting across the sand towards you. Quite ludicrously I got insanely angry. I thought, 'These buggers, they've got me once, they are not going to get me again,' and I pulled out my pistol. I could see there was a small man with a Bren gun shooting at us and I thought, 'Well, I'll let off a few rounds at him.' It was ridiculous, because he was 200 or 300 yards away.

We went round behind the airport buildings where we were meant to be setting up our show in a garage. The first thing was to get in. The doors were shut and I was thinking, 'Oh, my God, it's probably full of Egyptians,' when out came our company sergeant major. He was carrying his pistol, too, and luckily neither of us fired, but it was a painful moment. And quite unethical, too. The medical officer is only meant to use his pistol in defence of his patients. When I was eventually flown back to Nicosia, there was this wretched pistol, still loaded and cocked, with a round up the spout, in my hospital locker.

Anyway, we met up with Norman Kirby, Maurice Fearnley and Malcolm Elliott, who were getting the place ready. It was a very good spot for a RAP and a surgical team – a big garage with a sort of office where they could do their surgery, and plenty of room and a very good roof. Soon the place was half full of wounded, some of whom were in a very bad way. Norman, Malcolm and the surgical team set to to operate on a corporal who had been shot in the chest. While all this was going on, we were simply giving morphia and bandaging up the people who came in. We were alongside the surgical team for the whole of the morning, simply doing first aid. Norman would come out to choose the next for surgery.

Nobody could see a damn thing in my eye; it was just all puffed up. The splinter had gone through the container, and I think it was only the contents of the container that had blasted into my eye. It was a real miracle, but the eye was more or less out of commission for 48 hours. It closed itself and looked as though I'd done a round with Marciano. It ached a bit but it wasn't particularly painful. What I did lose was my stereoscopic vision. Faced with things like giving injections of morphia into veins I'd suddenly find I couldn't manage.

Our building was filling up pretty rapidly with wounded and we hadn't got the back-up which worked so well in the Falklands later. When men are hit they need to get the right surgery very quickly. At least we had taken some blood with us, some plasma and some saline. Luckily, before very long, some naval helicopters arrived. Then we had to decide whom to evacuate and how many they could take. We got rid of a couple of loads; each helicopter took five or six. One of the boys died just as we got him on board. He had a bad head wound and probably couldn't have been saved, but he was one of the best runners in the battalion and looked just like a fair-haired schoolboy. I remember gulping. The men were all friends, as well as patients. The men of 3 Para had become my family really, and that's what made it so upsetting. 'Tubby' Butler and his brigade major, Charles Dunbar, were passing at that moment, and their concern showed – which helped a lot.

Then the next thing that arrived was a French Dakota, which was the only aircraft that made sensible use of this airfield we had taken all the trouble to seize. We were making up another load, and suddenly Norman Kirby said, 'You are going.' I thought, 'Oh, damn it all,' and he said, 'No, you've got to keep this drip going' – this was the corporal with the wound in the chest. It was obvious the drip did have to keep going, and I suppose as the one-eyed person, I was the most dispensable. I thought I'd better go and say goodbye to the sergeant. 'I wouldn't go walking round out there,' said Malcolm Elliot, 'there's a lot of shit flying about.' And I thought, 'Dear old Mac, he is being a bit pessimistic.' But the next day, after I was gone, he set off in one of the jeeps into town. He drove unwittingly through the front line, was met by a hail of bullets and turned round, came back again and reported to the C Company commander, Ron Norman, to say just how far the company had advanced. Then the message came over the radio that several of C Company had been wounded. So Malcolm went straight off in the jeep and, again under heavy fire, found them. He went into the house where they were pinned down and found Corporal Stead with a shattered arm and some others, also wounded. The sergeant, 'Lofty' Read, said, 'You take these away, sir, and I'll give you covering fire while you go.' Mac couldn't put this ruddy jeep into reverse and he had to do an enormous U-turn into full Egyptian view to get them away; no-one thought he had a hope of getting through. The next thing was a message that the sergeant who had covered him had been killed, and he was frightfully demoralized about it. Mac was back with Ron Norman later that evening and suddenly they noticed this figure crawling along the road with a white flag. It was Lofty Read, who had been shot and damn nearly died, but had come round again and was crawling back, about 200 yards, on his belly. Everybody's morale was up again, and Mac, the pessimist who thought there was a lot of shit flying about, was later given a very well-deserved MC.

So off we went, with about ten on board, back to Cyprus, where it was getting dark. We were the first casualties back to Cyprus, back to the BMH where we'd been only the night before, and now we were getting these wretched boys spread around to various wards. I ended up in a ward myself which felt very ignominious. The corporal with the chest wound died, but most of the others survived all right. One or two wounded came the next day – Jack Richardson, who had got a rocket launcher bomb that took the tips of his fingers off as he was climbing the cemetery wall on the outskirts of Port Said. Before he had had his stitches out Jack was going for runs to keep fit. They were an indomitable crowd. My eye healed with virtually no trouble. It was a major escape really, and I felt a frightful fraud being evacuated with a thing like that.

One of the moving things that happened was the service before we went on the Sunday. I saw all these figures standing round, and wondered how many there would still be the next time. Malcolm Elliot was full of gloom and despondency at that first service, wondering 'how the padre could give us God's blessing and the rest of it.' About a fortnight later they had another service, following which Colonel Paul Crook, our CO, said to the assembled battalion, 'Well, here we are, back again; but we've been let off lightly. We did well, and maybe it was all good fun, but remember we did lose 40 chaps wounded and four dead, and ten days of that and we wouldn't have had much of a battalion left.' Which was true.

CHAPTER EIGHTEEN
CYPRUS
1 9 6 4

T HE ESCALATION OF POLITICAL VIOLENCE IN THE NOW independent Cyprus (*see* map, p. 313) in late December 1963 saw the 1st Battalion recalled from leave to arrive in Akrotiri by 4 January 1964. They first took over responsibility for the Western Zone, keeping rival factions apart while based at Episkopi, until moving to Nicosia on 26 February where they remained until early April. They then became the island's mobile reserve. On 21 March when the United Nations Truce Force (UNFICYP) took over the task of keeping Greek from Turk, the battalion then became part of that force.

MAJOR JOE STARLING, 1st Battalion

On New Year's Eve 1963 we were going to a party at which were most of the battalion's officers. I went off to pick up our baby-sitter and when I got back someone said that we'd just had a message from the ministry and we were off to Cyprus tomorrow! I then spent two hours on the telephone calling people back. The code word was 'Guillemont'. I rang the doctor, Alec Black, and said, 'Alec, it's Guillemont – do you know what Guillemont means?' He said, 'I haven't a fucking clue old man!' 'Alec,' I said, 'get your arse back here.' We then went on to the party. The CO, Pat Thursby, was there and I gave him the message. He said, 'Right – O Group.' All the girls went into one corner and the company commanders and specialists went into another, we had our movement buttoned up at five to twelve, drank the New Year in, then went home and packed our kit.

We got nearly everybody back, except for one guy who was a Canadian called Frost, who gave his address as the Playboy Hotel, Amsterdam. He got on a plane with another battalion from Lyneham and talked his way through and popped up when we were in Cyprus.

We went initially to Dhekelia, into a tented camp as the reserve waiting to be deployed. We did a few countryside patrols trying to separate the Greek and Turkish communities which were completely interwoven. In the south we came across one village that had chopped up another – pretty nasty. For a few weeks we had a hairy time separating communities from doing extraordinary things to each other.

In the south there was a lot of community movement. A Greek village surrounded by Turks would want to move and we would try and protect them so you didn't have too many people butchered and the same thing with a Turkish village surrounded by Greeks. We did quite a lot of that. The day after we'd helped one side to leave, the village would be looted to start with and then burnt to the ground. It always seemed that we were a couple of platoons with a bloody great force of Turks on one side and Greeks on the other!

We then moved to Nicosia to relieve the Gloucesters and the Rifle Brigade. At the original ceasefire General Peter Young had drawn a line with a blunt green chinagraph pencil to represent the truce line between the two communities (which is still in force to this day). I had Neapolis; C Company further north had Trakonas, and Support Company had the flour mills in the Turkish sector. We looked after a building, like a bloody skyscraper, called the Cyprus Cold Store, stuffed with food. It stood on the line between the sectors. The Greeks controlled the entrance, but the Turks wanted to get food out of it. The Turks would start things just before midnight by firing bursts into the air. Then the Greeks would fire a burst or two and the whole place would look like a fireworks display. I would rush over to my Greeks and try to calm them down and OC Support Company would similarly rush over to the Turks. Usually a task force of Turks would turn up, drag off the back door by hitching a tow rope to a truck. Once they'd got their fill the Turkish commander would tell me they'd agree to a ceasefire if the Greeks would. Just to save face, they'd both fire a couple more bursts and all go home to bed.

The day we replaced our red beret with the light blue of the United Nations everything changed. With the red beret we could say to either Greek or Turk, you stay on that side and the others stay on the opposite. If they didn't we usually fired a few rounds – not at anyone, but just to show we meant business.

At one point the Greeks reinforced their police station. It was the classic deterrent effect. But of course, when we replaced our red beret with the blue beret of the UN we had to say, 'You stay on that side or we'll report you to U Thant and he's in a big glass building in New York and he won't like it!' Now that is *not* a very effective way of keeping the peace!

After a few weeks we were pulled into reserve to act as an emergency force and the Canadians took over our role. Well, I don't think they really understood the situation because they'd brought beads from the Congo to exchange for things with the local population!

While we were in reserve my company had been stood down and was generally enjoying itself when the bell went. I staggered down to the ops room with my 2 i/c to be told that the Irish had arrived. We said, 'The IRA?' 'No,' the ops officer said, 'The Army of the Irish Republic.' I'd never heard of them. Anyway he said that they were tired and we were to go and unload their kit. This did not please me one jot. When 1 Para arrive anywhere it's one lance corporal and three toms to unload. So I told this ops officer just what I thought about the Irish army but we were told to stop arguing and get down to the airport and unload.

The guys I took were all a bit heavy-headed from the night before, and when we got down to the airfield the Irish were being inspected by an Indian general. We had a Sergeant Spike Delaney, an Ulsterman, with us and when he saw these Irish soldiers lined up he began shouting, 'Fucking rebels. Rebels – give them "The Sash" lads.' So there were the toms all singing 'The Sash'. The Irish soldiers didn't know whether they should continue at the 'present arms' to this general or get in among us! It was chaos. I'd spent six months trying to keep the Greeks and Turks apart and here I was now trying to keep the Irish apart from the paras!

I was leaning against my Land-Rover feeling distinctly the worse for wear when someone with the unmistakable accent of the Shankhill Road said, 'Would you be liking Irish or Scotch whisky in the officers' mess?' Now this needed a bit of investigating, so I took myself off to find that Sergeant Delaney had found the Irish Army's officers' mess supplies and was redistributing them in the time-honoured fashion of, 'One for the Irish, one for the RSM, one for us!' There were complaints of course, but U Thant had his advantages because by the time this had all been sorted out in New York and Cyprus I could say, 'Oh, we've just posted him!'

The sequel to this was that when the Swedes came in next we were very much better prepared and actually volunteered to unload their aircraft. We turned up with bolt cutters, hacksaws, even an oxyacetylene torch. Now the Swedes drink like fish, but I can only think they'd heard about us, because they didn't bring any with them. What they did bring, however, was some rather nice air force-blue, button-down-at-the-collar shirts. So on muster parade the next morning was the whole bloody company with their blue berets and blue button-down shirts; great grins everywhere.

CORPORAL MALCOLM SIMPSON, 1st Battalion

We were in Guillemont Barracks with nowhere to go and nothing was on the cards. We'd heard there were troubles in Cyprus, but the Dhekelia and Episkopi battalions were capable of looking after it. Everybody deployed on leave, and it was New Year's Day that we got the recall by telegram.

We had a sketchy briefing and then we all deployed to Cyprus, but with no real plan as to what we were going to do. We all ended up in a tented location down at Dhekelia. We were there about two weeks, patrolling out to places like Paphos and into Nicosia itself. The situation got quite severe, and so the battalion was deployed onto what was going to be the Green Line, down in Nicosia itself. At the same time my company, C Company, were involved at the Limni Mines, north of Paphos. There was a group of British Nationals working there in a tin mine, but because of the activities around them they couldn't get out, so they were almost in a hostage situation. Our company moved in and took over the mines. We called in Whirlwinds which came and evacuated all the British workmen. We then took the mine over completely, because it was still functioning. The people's cars were there; their personal effects, the whole works. We stayed there about four or five days. In the meantime down in Limni town itself, there was still a lot of shooting going on and we heard that a few atrocities had taken place.

Once that situation was over we were withdrawn to join the battalion on the Green Line in Nicosia itself, based on Ledra Palace, down to the main road that goes up into Kyrenia. We took over Ayios Nicholaos. All the people had moved out so we took over the houses, whether they were Greek or Turkish, and placed ourselves in this buffer line. Every day we were involved in some sort of incident. In fact the day we arrived there was a major shooting incident when all the Turkish and Greek locations came under fire and some of our positions received indirect small arms strikes, but we did not return fire. We then went out to clear the streets and sadly found that most of the casualties were females who had been shopping; a lot of them with gunshots wounds to the head.

In February the Greeks in Limassol carried out a big attack on the Turks using armoured bulldozers. The problem was that there were more than 130 British families in that area. They were living in a battle zone and could not get out – they couldn't go shopping, they couldn't do anything. So again, a rescue situation arose where they had to be recovered. Eventually a truce was declared. Support Company dealt with that, but it only succeeded because they said, 'If you don't stop shooting, we will open fire on you.' But it was two days before they managed to get them out. Most of them were

RAF families. It certainly must have been disturbing for them.

In March the UN took over. One day we learnt that we were to be flanked with the 22nd Princess Patricia's from Canada and would be the first UN force to assume responsibility for the Green Line. In the beginning trucks turned up with masses of blue berets, which initially we argued about wearing. In the end we got a concession, in that we were able to wear a maroon patch behind the UN badge. That was the one and only time it was granted and to this day no other UN force has been able to identify itself in this way.

Nikos Samson who was well known from the previous Para tour of 1956 began to hang out at a small café where our Company HQ used to visit. One particular occasion he was leading a gang from this café and was causing a tremendous amount of aggravation. We felt a great deal of vindictiveness towards him because not only was he stirring up Greeks against Turks, but also against the paras. From our battalion's point of view we were after him, as we were after Grivas, for a long, long time, and there was this bugger walking the streets and we couldn't do a thing about it. Any time there was a problem, he was involved. It came very, very close, on numerous occasions, to a shoot-out. It was only really through people like Mike Heerey, our company commander, being diplomatic, that more didn't happen.

Just outside Ayios Nicholaos there was a little village where we went on patrol with a UN observer and were shown 17 or 18 bodies, females, males and children uncovered in a grave. By the state of the decomposing bodies this atrocity had happened a couple of months earlier. For us it was a case of basically bagging and burning. It was a bit distressing for some of the lads in our company because of the children.

For the last month we were in reserve in the Sovereign Base area. We did have one major fracas at a place called the Romanza Bar. We were sitting there when somehow things got a bit out of hand and someone opened up on us with a 12-bore shot gun. So the boys set about this place and ripped it to pieces. The next morning the whole battalion was paraded in PT shorts. The word of command was given, 'Battalion will drop shorts.' Everybody had to drop them and bend over so the police could inspect us for shot gun pellets!! We all had to pay a levy for the damage to the Romanza Bar, and then not too many days later we were stuck on a civvy aircraft and sent home.

CHAPTER NINETEEN
THE RADFAN
1 9 6 4 – 7

IN THE SPRING OF 1964 THE QUTAIBIS, THE MAIN TRIBE OF THE Radfan, were causing unrest spurred on by Egypt and the Yemenis. The British authorities decided on a punitive expedition and, on 30 April, 45 Royal Marine Commando set out with the Aden Federal Regular Army to dominate the Dhanaba Basin. B Company of the 3rd Battalion secured the forts of El Naqil. This initial success was exploited by the 3rd Battalion which, along with 45 Commando, then secured the seemingly impenetrable Wadi Dhubsan. The battalion withdrew to Aden on 28 May. Further actions against the dissident tribesmen continued until 1967.

LIEUTENANT COLONEL TONY FARRAR-HOCKLEY, 3rd Battalion
The British Army was sent to help the Aden Federal Government in April 1964 to curb the tribal insurrection in the Radfan. I was in Bahrain commanding 3 Para at the time. On 30 April I was warned to have a company available to parachute onto a key feature code-named 'Cap Badge' and to occupy it until 45 Commando had completed a sweep towards it from Wadi Boran. Unfortunately, a troop from 22 SAS, who had been detailed to mark the drop zone, became embroiled in a fight with the Radfanis and had to withdraw, leaving two of their men dead. A Beverley sent over on a navigation run also came under fire and as a result of these two events all sorts of feet went cold and the idea of parachuting evaporated.

I chose Major Peter Walter's company, B Company, with a section of mortars and machine-guns and they went down to Aden and on to the base camp at Thumier. From there they went forward with 45 Commando. They did an extremely tough, long march, arrived plumb on their objective area and had an extremely unpleasant, small battle in which they lost the

THE RADFAN 1964-7

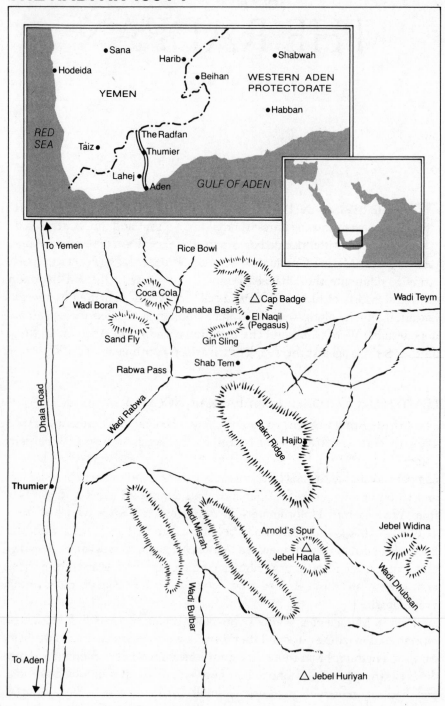

company second-in-command killed and a number of others wounded.

I went down to see them and while I was there I met the land force commander, General John Cubbon, who said, 'I think we may need your battalion down because there are all sorts of problems up in the Radfan and we've got nothing like enough troops.' By problems he meant that the Radfani tribes were trying their muscle to see what they could get away with. They were also very much in league with their clansmen across the frontier in the Yemen and, it was said, had decapitated the two men killed on the SAS patrol to exhibit their heads in the Yemen capital. We did actually find the headless bodies later on. One was Robin Edwards, whose brother, Michael, was in the Parachute Regiment. I went back to Bahrain to be told by the brigade commander, 'You are to take a force down as speedily as possible. But we must leave one company here.' So I decided to bring Peter Walter's company back, leaving as a temporary stop gap, the band of the 3rd Battalion to hold the camp.

The Radfan is mountainous, bare and largely trackless. There were problems about getting the guns into position where they could support us. Some of the attempts to get up into the high country during daylight had resulted in a lot of fighting and sniping so I was determined that we would march by night. I also knew that the Radfanis were not very confident at night. I went out from the deserted village of Shab Tem with two patrols, one commanded by Major Tom Duffy, my MTO (Motor Transport Officer) and the other by Ian McLeod, my intelligence officer. We found a pretty good route which, with a two-night march, would take us up onto the very high ground of the Bakri Ridge. As we were going to have to carry over 120 pounds each on our backs we would need support vehicles. To assist our advance I got the Engineers and part of the battalion to lay a jeep track about another two miles further forward. A section of the Engineers then laid track so that we could tow the guns into a position to cover us. A hell of a rainstorm delayed our move just as everything was ready.

On 18 May I set off with A and C Companies. It was very hot and progress was slow – probably half a mile an hour, but eventually we got to our first intermediate point. The next day the Army Air Corps, with a couple of Scouts, supplied us with all we needed by way of mortar bombs to augment the very few we were carrying; but most important of all, they brought jerrycans of water. When we advanced again late that afternoon I found myself in front of the battalion with two leading company commanders. I had with me my long-standing orderly, Corporal Ted Olive, who is an old and dear friend of mine. I told him to go on to an OP 500 to 600 yards ahead and that I would send somebody up to support him. I saw this lone figure going on ahead and I thought to myself, what am I going to say to his wife, who was just arriving in Bahrain, if he is hit. However, nothing happened.

The march continued in darkness, in all about three or four miles up hill and down dale. It took us to the top of the Hajib escarpment. It was still dark when we arrived. We patrolled, making sure that there was no position for the enemy to hide in. In parallel to our main position was a nasty spur. I told Drill Sergeant Major 'Nobby' Arnold to occupy it with the anti-tank platoon. He surprised a group of Radfanis and captured three. In recognition of this action the feature was named 'Arnold's Spur'.

The advance was resumed on 23 May when C Company, under Tony Ward-Booth, cleared a number of villages but were, for a time, held up at the fortified village of Oudeishi which was situated just below the highest point of the Bakri Ridge. The Radfanis put up considerable resistance here, withdrawing only when RAF Hunters launched a fierce attack, followed by A Company flanking their position, while C Company attacked the village. We now looked down into the Wadi Dhubsan. This area had always been a safe base for the Radfani and was regarded as pretty impregnable. My operations were temporarily halted.

It was thought worthwhile for us to advance right down into this remote valley of the Dhubsan where the Radfanis had all their grain stores and to destroy these stores in order to teach them a lesson. We found an indirect route, one which led us down a 30-foot rock face and along a boulder-strewn gully that ended up in the rear of the village of Bayn Al Gidr. On the night of 25 May, while C Company picqueted the Jebel Haqla to the right and A Company the left, the remainder came down the rock face on ropes. It wasn't a sheer face, but it was steep and we had to get the mortars down as well. By 0600 hours, the upper wadi had been cleared without a shot.

When I got further down the valley I called up a helicopter, and the brigadier also arrived to ask how things were going. While I was talking to him I spoke on the radio to the X Company commander of 45 Commando and asked him where he was; he gave me a grid reference. The brigadier and I realized that it was rather a long way ahead. So I went off by Scout helicopter, with Ian McLeod, to get up behind the Commando to really see what they were up to.

We were flying along, below the tops of the hills, running along the wadi, when I noticed a lot of tribesmen on the valley side firing at us. A bullet hit the feed line and fuel began to flood down over the visor of the chopper. Ian McLeod was also shot through the wrist. I asked the pilot, Major Jake Jackson, if he had control. He said that he had, so I told him to turn round and go straight back. He very coolly and expertly flew back until we could see the Commando elements and a bit of A Company. The Commando, although advancing and clearing out the area, were no further forward than I had expected and had simply slipped up on their grid reference by a mere 10,000 yards! Jake put the chopper down and at last light the AAC brought up a REME corporal and another fitter who worked through the night to repair the damage.

In the meantime I had to disperse the tribesmen with A and C Companies: Mike Walsh and Ted Ashley got forward very quickly. Ian McLeod had to be evacuated along with the RSM who, on seeing us come down, had rushed out with a stretcher party and had been shot himself.

Next morning the fitter said he had done all he could do. Jake climbed in and pressed the self-starter and the blades began to turn. He then tried everything out gently and, amidst much cheering, took off. A great weight was lifted from my mind.

We set light to the grain stores and completed our task. The whole operation was over. The battalion group climbed back to the top of the Bakri Ridge where Wessex helicopters of the Navy were waiting. They lifted us back to Thumier and from there we went back to Aden. We waited there for aircraft to take us back to Bahrain.

MAJOR PETER WALTER, 3rd Battalion

My company, B Company 3 Para, had been selected by Farrar-Hockley along with 45 Royal Marine Commando to seize, on the night of the 30 April, two objectives code-named 'Cap Badge' and 'Rice Bowl'. The plan was for the Marines to march from Thumier and climb and hold Rice Bowl, the most northerly objective, while we would be dropped near the foot of Cap Badge. At the eleventh hour the hierarchy got cold feet. We were just about to board the aircraft when they cancelled it. It was a terrible blow. Had we been sitting on that hillside waiting for the dissidents, instead of them waiting for us, then the boot would have been on the other foot.

We set off and marched all day and all night. There were a number of hiccups in the approach march. We'd been put at the back of the Marine Commando's column and were very late moving off. There seemed to be incessant hold-ups, and I was beginning to lose my patience. There was another hold-up and I got the word back that the commandos were climbing the cliffs with ropes. We simply moved up to a flank, climbed up alongside and past the marines. But then I was on my own and we moved towards Pegasus Village to tackle Cap Badge. We were each carrying about

40 pounds in weight and the company had something like 27,000 rounds of ammo within the group. I decided against mortars because I couldn't see the dissidents getting into concentrations where mortars would have been useful. Also, on balance of weight, I decided we needed as much small arms ammo and hand grenades as possible, rather than mortar bombs.

It wasn't a difficult march through the Wadi Tagan, and the ascent up to Cap Badge was no more than a hill walk. As we moved towards our objective, we saw individuals moving into positions, some carrying lanterns. Ours was the lead platoon and I knew what was going to happen. As dawn broke I warned everyone that they could expect to come under fire. But somehow the young soldiers didn't really take it in. To them it was just another exercise. Only my 2 i/c and company sergeant major had seen action before.

I warned the leading element of Tom Walker's platoon that any second they would be coming under fire. I had sensed it. One lad said, 'If someone were to fire at me now, I think I would lie down and die.' At that moment the first bullet hit the ground between his legs. He took on a new lease of life!

We couldn't go to ground – the normal drill – because we were in open desert. I said we must capture that fort, which was about 300 yards away. So we pepper-potted from bun to bun across these cultivation walls. There was a lot of shooting, but we suffered no casualties. They were firing a Vickers at us and we were firing back with our GPMGs and I think we got a bullet through one of the water jackets and they stopped.

Once inside the compound I could see there was only one entrance to the fort. I chucked a hand grenade inside and we all stood back. There was a big bang and out came a chicken with no feathers on! That broke the ice a bit and so we dashed upstairs, but they'd all flown.

We set up our Company HQ in the fort. The SOO carrying the marker panels had somehow become detached, so I had to send someone back to get them. This was because we had called up the Hunters who were systematically shooting every fort in turn and ours was next. The young lad who'd had the bullet land between his legs volunteered. I could see his little legs going with all these bullets making pock marks around him to get these panels back. But he got them back in the nick of time. He got a Mention in Despatches for that.

About an hour before last light we were ordered onto Cap Badge. It was great to see my company carrying out their drills as they had been taught over the past year. They tackled each pocket of resistance as they saw fit. They went to the village and there was quite a lot of opposition in the wadi.

Barry Jewkes's platoon killed six. He was tail-end Charlie really, picking up the stragglers. They bumped this group of six, and shot the lot. We occupied the village and then there was a lull, while we reorganized ourselves.

Snipers from above the village opened fire fairly accurately. They were in dead ground so the Hunters were again called in. It was here that we suffered casualties including Barry Jewkes, who was killed while helping a badly wounded sergeant.

It was then that those on high insisted we took a resupply of ammunition, which I didn't want. We'd done an ammo check and we were all right. But they insisted on this drop which went wide, way out in the desert. We had to recover it and we lost a man killed doing that. I was extremely annoyed. We then had a problem with the casevac because the RAF wouldn't come in. I regret to say I had to use the second death as a lever. I said we had lost one seriously wounded, which he had been for a few minutes, but they still prevaricated and came in about an hour and a half before last light. They wouldn't take out the dead so we had to bury them, which was not very nice. They then had to be dug up again a few days later – again not very nice. The air support should have been automatic.

Anyway, we climbed up to Cap Badge. Then we stood down and rested for 24 hours and then went back down the wadi. We came under fire a few times going down on the way and took a prisoner who was carrying a flag of surrender. Within a few days we were back in Bahrain.

LIEUTENANT JOHN WINTER, 2nd Battalion

While 2 Para were in Bahrain in 1966 C Company was warned that we were going to the Radfan for nine months or so to continue in a similar role to that which we had been undertaking in Borneo. The company had undergone some changes in personnel and we now had a new commander, Major Alex Young. I was one of the two officers from Borneo. For our time in the Radfan we were based in a tented camp at Habilayn, which used to be called Thumier. This was part of a permanently manned garrison alongside a fairly basic airstrip. From this base for about a week at a time we carried out long-range reconnaissance and strike patrols over the whole of the Radfan.

The countryside was very, very tough and because of the nature of the operations we always moved at night. At last light, we'd be inserted as covertly as possible by road or helicopter and then we'd get eight hours of travelling under our belt. As first light approached we'd set up sangars for each four-man patrol and then we'd lie up for the day. For these seven-day operations you might get four hours sleep in each 24 hours, but it wouldn't be four consecutive hours. You might get a couple of hours or an odd hour here and there which over a period of months became pretty debilitating. You had to watch your soldiers pretty carefully to see no one was affected by lack of sleep. As opposed to Borneo, however, it was much more of a troop or company operation, so we were not as isolated as we had been. But certainly these operations called for you to be mentally and physically robust.

We did have the odd contact with the 'dissies' (the dissidents) and in one contact I lost one of my four-man team seriously wounded. During an ambush one of the enemy casualties was found to be an RSM from the Federal Regular Army. But contact with the dissidents was infrequent as they were fairly fleet of foot and the campaign had really reached a stalemate.

The company had a long operation north of Dahla and was coming down at night from the Jebel to meet up with the helicopters that would take us out at first light. When we got to the rendezvous point, we found one soldier was missing. We went back to look for him, but never found him. Later it transpired that he had fallen off the edge of a cliff, having become separated from his patrol. He had been picked up by some locals and taken over the border into Yemen. Through the local intelligence system we eventually got his body back with his balls cut off and shoved down his throat. A similar type of atrocity befell the SAS patrol in 1964.

The campaign did have its lighter moments. On one occasion we intercepted a camel train coming across the border into the Radfan. We got clearance to search and discovered one man carrying a lot of ammunition, whom we arrested. We were trying to evacuate him for questioning but the only way we could get him out quickly was by helicopter. A Sioux helicopter arrived but no way was our man going to get inside it. He had obviously never flown in his life. The Sioux had a stretcher fitted to the outside for casualty evacuation, so the only way we could get him back was to render him unconscious, using the minimum of force necessary, and strap him into the stretcher which had no cover. The pilot told me later that he'd never laughed so much in his life as he had when this fellow came round at 500 feet.

CHAPTER TWENTY
BORNEO
1965

WHEN IN LATE 1964 INDONESIA THREATENED INVASION of the young Malaysian Federation, the 2nd Battalion were recalled on New Year' Day and flown to Singapore for jungle warfare training. C Company was converted into a special patrol company to assist the SAS on the Borneo/Indonesian border (*see* map of the Far East 1944–1965, p. 306). The rest of the battalion followed on 12 March 1965 and moved straight to the border, at the height of enemy activity. They were immediately involved in intensive patrolling and establishing fortified bases to detect and prevent incursions by units of the Indonesian Army. On 27 April one of the fiercest battles of the campaign took place when an Indonesian battalion attacked B Company at Plaman Mapu. They were finally beaten off with 50 casualties for the company's two killed and seven wounded. Patrols, ambushes and skirmishes continued for the rest of the tour, the last actions being fought on 24 June when ten of the enemy were killed for no loss. This short, but intense, Far East tour ended in July of that year.

LIEUTENANT JOHN WINTER, 2nd Battalion

I joined 2 Para at the beginning of 1964 and in September of that year the battalion was warned that we were going to have to provide an extra squadron to supplement 22 SAS who were involved in the Confrontation campaign against the Indonesians in Borneo. The Guards and Gurkha Parachute Companies were similarly involved. A month later half the battalion underwent SAS selection procedures. Those who passed, supported by specialists such as medics and signallers from 16 Parachute Brigade, became C (Patrol) Company which consisted of about 130 men. C Company's job was to act as a special patrol company to operate in a long-range recce role, organized into four-man patrols. These consisted of a commander, radio operator, medic and demolition man.

This was not the first time the Parachute Regiment had operated in an SAS role because there was a similar squadron in Malaya. In fact two of our instructors in Brunei had been in that squadron. C Company dated back to the Bruneval raid led by John Frost.

Certain officers and NCOs, of whom I was one, were taken out early on and sent to Singapore for two months to learn Malay. C Company went across to Borneo in January 1965 where we all did a training course at the SAS jungle school in Brunei. I think that was the most concentrated month's training I have done in my life. I was learning to live in the jungle which was totally new for me. We were taught by very experienced jungle-trained people and there were no frills – it was the perfect preparation for an operational tour. This was followed by a 'training operation' where we went out into quiet areas with a mentor from the SAS. In my case it was the RSM. We spent two weeks working under his eagle eye, which was a bit intimidating for me. After that we were cleared as a four-man team to go it alone.

My team's main role was one of long-range reconnaissance, and we were to spend the whole six months of the operation monitoring the activities of a small tribe of Poonans whose territory was based in both Sarawak and Kalimantan. We were to see that they did not get too heavily involved with the Indonesians.

We practically lived with the Poonan tribe. They were very small, entirely nomadic and didn't know anything about tilling the land or about farming. They lived entirely by hunting and fishing and what they got from the trees. As a tribe they were dying out because they lived in small groups and were so in-bred that most of the babies were stillborn. Part of our job was 'hearts and minds' and this is where our medic really became the most prominent member of our team.

Our patrols varied in length but were mostly from 14 to 28 days, although on one occasion my patrol did go out for twelve weeks which, for just four of us, was quite interesting. It certainly became tiring, partly because of the climate and the physical strain of moving around in the jungle but also because of the problems associated with being in a small, isolated group working in potentially close proximity to the opposition. The diet of compo, compo and more compo did get to you after a while and you became susceptible to minor bugs and ailments and some of the company got tropical diseases. We never shaved in the jungle because cuts on the face could get infected and the smell of the shaving soap could give us away.

In the beginning I did find it a bit difficult to readjust after my Sandhurst training. I'd been brought up to have a platoon commander or company commander fairly nearby, but in the jungle I found I was over 300 miles from my nearest boss, which was good for me because I grew up quickly. Communication with our company base was entirely by Morse.

After each patrol we would come out for a few days' break to our company base which was fairly comfortable. It had adequate facilities, and you could get a shower and a cold beer, and some decent food. We would re-train in the light of experience that we had in the previous patrol or operational experience from elsewhere. We would concentrate on close-quarter shooting and communications which were vital especially as our patrol covered an area larger than Kent. After our rest we would deploy by longboat up the river to a forward mounting base and then fly by helicopter into our operational area. Each of us would deploy with about 100 pounds in weight, principally made up of ammunition, batteries and food.

Every fortnight while we were out on patrol we'd get resupplied and for the next couple of days we'd have fresh food. We also got a ration of rum which we'd save up. I spent my twenty-second birthday with my team under a tree drinking rum spiced with compo boiled sweets; we never did get the fermentation process right. With the resupply would come our mail which was important to us and we'd send letters back. At one point when we'd been out for weeks we only had one paperback. So as I read a chapter I'd pull it out and pass it around. We also got welfare packs from well-intentioned ladies in England. On one occasion we got a whole bundle of knitting pattern magazines which we read avidly!

Another officer in the company was corresponding with his girlfriend who had a sister who worked in publishing and used to send us magazines. When we got back to the UK two of us decided to repay her kindness and take her out to dinner. She is now my wife.

On one occasion we were running low on food because the resupply hadn't worked, so I shot a gibbon out of a tree. Unbeknown to me she was suckling a baby. We ate mum and I brought up the baby on tubes of condensed milk and he adopted me and used to sit on my rucksack while we were on patrols. When I'd completed my tour in Borneo I had him flown back to England. He finished up in Paignton Zoo. At one point we were on Zoo Quest with Johnny Morris and I had to admit I'd eaten his mother!

Throughout our tour in Borneo we were supported by Fleet Air Arm helicopters, initially 845 and then 848 NACS. They flew superbly in the most difficult conditions and were always most hospitable to our patrols passing through their forward operating base at Nanga Gat, in the Third

Division. Sadly it was near there we suffered our only casualties of the campaign. Two Wessex helicopters of 845 Squadron were returning to their base at last light, having picked up the two patrols commanded by Second Lieutenant Chris Johnson and Sergeant McNeilly. In very poor visibility the two aircraft collided and crashed into a river. All on board were killed instantly.

Back in UK, C Company was reduced in size but we were retained in the battalion in the same role. The following year we went to Bahrain with the battalion, but spent nine months in the Radfan, operating independently again.

COMPANY SERGEANT MAJOR JOHN WILLIAMS, 2nd Battalion

The Indonesians were continuing to try and destabilize the fledgling Federation of Malaysia. So to meet the possible threat of invasion it was decided that 2 Para should be sent to Borneo. Prior to the battalion's departure Lieutenant Colonel Eberhardie decided to send me and a sprinkling of officers and NCOs for a refresher course at the jungle warfare training school in Singapore. About two weeks later the battalion followed me and we trained them up. The battalion was crash-coursed through. One of the platoons that joined B Company, of which I was company sergeant major, hadn't even finished its recruit training at the Depot. It had another three weeks to go, but they decided they would send them out as reinforcements and their final three weeks were to be completed in the jungle instead of Wales. So we had these 19-year-old boys as a platoon.

We really hammered it in the jungle for that period, really did give it stick. Chippy Woods taught them tracking and we all had to learn ten Dyak words a day; like food, water, enemy, tracks, wounds, everything – so that every single soldier had at least 50 words in Dyak. We were tested on them every day. We realized that a hearts and minds campaign was more effective in the long run. So off we went to Borneo. We were choppered in from Balai Ringin to relieve the Jocks (The Argyll and Sutherland Highlanders) at Plaman Mapu. Because we felt we hadn't got down to really showing our soldiers what they should expect, we set up our own little battle school. We pushed each platoon in turn, with all its officers and NCOs, through this mini-battlefield. We made it as realistic as possible and used live ammunition. Unfortunately, two men were killed in separate incidents, which was very sad and everybody was unhappy. But everyone knew that those who'd been killed had done the wrong thing; they hadn't kept their heads down. Their deaths pressed the point home very quickly. It really switched on the young men, young NCOs and officers who had never heard bullets whizzing round their ears. It showed them how to react, which was later to prove an essential factor.

The position we'd taken up was completely unsuitable from a military point of view. For a start it was only 1,000 yards from the border, so that everything we did was overlooked. It was also rat-infested and overgrown. But we steadily began to improve it and started patrolling. Our *modus operandi* was ten days out on patrol then 36 hours in base. During those 36 hours we still had to defend our base. As the CSM I made sure the first thing we did when a patrol came back in was give everyone a tot of rum; then they had a shower, de-loused, got new gear, read their mail, had a couple of big hearty meals, because this was the first cooked food they would have had in the period, then a reasonably good night's sleep. But they still had to do their sentry-go and everything else. The next day they were briefed and got themselves ready for the next ten-day patrol which started that night. So the pressure was very much on. It was killing. Our goal was to get the guys to the peak of physical fitness, maintain it, then ask them not to eat cooked food, drink tea, smoke or speak for ten days. Not only to the young soldiers but across the whole board, it was a new discipline in all sorts of ways.

During this period in the confrontation, Sukarno felt in his dreams that he had to make the one big, bold move, and if he could make it and succeed he reckoned that the emerging Malaysia would come over to his side. All sorts of activity had been reported and we knew something was up; incursions and incidents were happening all over the place. Because we were vulnerable we realized that we were getting more activity in our area than in any other. Subsequently we heard that Sukarno thought that a victory against the Paras would be the coup that would really make headlines. Our patrols brought back reports of enemy preparation for an attack in our area. You know, large bodies of troops in the local kampongs and clearings being cut for mortars. All we could do was stay alert, knowing that something was going to happen. Then of course it hit us. It happened when the young recruits were on their 36-hour changeover. So we had a young recruit platoon, which was below strength, with their platoon commander and sergeant away. But we had a mortar section with two mortars, a company headquarters, the signals, the medic, and an extra officer called Thompson who was standing in for their platoon commander, and we had an artillery FOO (forward observation officer) and that was us. Thirty-five in all. It was normal drill, our circle was split into a 'Y' shape and in each triangle there was a GPMG (general purpose machine-gun). So there were three GPMGs manned right the way through the line.

I'd just got my head down in the CP (command post), when the attack came. No one undressed to go to sleep, you always wore your boots, your trousers and your belt order. The only thing I had done that night was to take my shirt off. They'd opened up with their artillery, mortars, machine-guns and rockets and just blasted it straight into one of the segments. They knew exactly where they wanted to hit and took out one segment of our 'Y'. This was the area they were going to assault. I bounded out of bed. It was pitch black, blinding with rain, it was a monsoon, so it was pissing down. Outside, I was eerily confronted by Kelly, who was the GPMG gunner where the enemy had put the majority of their fire. He had been hit by three bullets down his skull, but was still alive. They'd gone about one-eighth of an inch into his skull so he was completely deranged and thought we'd been overrun. He stuck his SLR (self-loading rifle) in my belly and said, 'I'm going to blow you away.' I took him down to the CP. I came back up to realize that the enemy had taken a whole position out and were advancing. We had to put in a counter-attack, so I called Thompson and said, 'Get your men together, sir, and follow me – you don't know where it is, I'll lead the way and show you where you put a counter-attack in.' 'Right, sergeant major.' He was following me with his men when a mortar bomb landed in the middle of them, wounded him and several others, leaving only two men on their feet. I told one of them, a cook corporal, to put up illuminating rounds to show what was happening. He put about three up and was taken out by mortar fire. I was yelling to see what was happening on the left where Mick Bourne was. He was holding that front, but all the rest were going down so I thought there's only one thing that's going to get them out and that's the GPMG. I ran across, got a hold of it and banged half a dozen belts on, yelling out to Mick that I would give him covering fire if he could launch an assault from his perimeter. The enemy didn't like the GPMG very much so Mick managed to push them out from his side. The enemy now really switched on and realized that we had driven them back down into a gully. They realized where the firing was coming from and launched a platoon attack on me and the gun pit. I was just firing away like billyo but they still kept coming and coming. One of the enemy was only two yards from my gun before he died. He'd been wounded twice in the thigh in the first assault and had tied a tourniquet round it.

They should have massacred us. They really thought they'd win through on their superior fire power. They came straight in firing their Kalashni-kovs. Although the conditions underfoot didn't help us they did more to thwart them because they were coming up a slight incline. Had they had a dry purchase they'd have overrun us on the first assault. But eventually they stopped because Mick had gathered the fire of the other section and was hitting them as well so they fell back down the gully again. I then got someone else on the gun which had been hit four times by bullets. The radio set by my side had been shattered, but I didn't realize then I'd been hit and was blind in one eye. It was still pitch black with mud everywhere. I then raced around, picked up some wounded, took them down to the CP and then took a resupply of ammunition and spread it to the rest of the guys around me. By this time I think there were, on the position, only about 15 of us standing.

The enemy then tried to launch a further attack which we managed to beat off. We'd lost one mortar but the FOO was now firing the remaining one straight up in the air and bombs were landing about 30 yards away on the enemy, which was where we wanted them. I asked for volunteers to take a patrol out and clear the lines and, God bless them, to a man they said they'd go. So I selected three and off we went. We cleared the position around the perimeter and then came back in, by which time the first of the helicopters had arrived with the quick reaction force. Then it all started. There was so much activity it was untrue, people coming in, helicopters, the doctor. They couldn't believe what they were seeing. The lads standing, cuts and wounds, no shirts, just their trousers and boots, with mud everywhere. It must have been a sight.

There was this swathe cut through the jungle, with lots of blood and a trail of equipment, everything discarded by the Indonesians fleeing back to the border. The blood trail was there for three days. Somehow, we had repulsed what was believed to be a full assault by an elite Javanese battalion group on a position 35-strong.

The doctor caught me and stuck a needle in my arm and whacked me on the helicopter and that was the end of that (the battle had lasted about two hours in all). When I got out of this helicopter with the other wounded an old chum of mine, Jack Tapp, saw the state of me, blood pouring down, and he said, 'You can't go to hospital like that – stand against the wall and get your kit off.' So I stripped down to nothing and he turned a hosepipe on me, swooshed me down with this bloody hosepipe! But it was only a holding place really and they couldn't do anything with me because I needed full hospital treatment. Apparently, while I'd been firing the GPMG, the radio set by the left side of my face had been shattered by a mortar and a cloud of shrapnel had gone straight in the side of my head. When they finally finished with me I was deaf in my left ear and blind on the same side.

Of all the young men I remember from that battle McKellar really stands out. His father was an exporter/importer in Scotland and his son had written to him about the prospect of setting up in Malaya when he'd finished with the army. His father had come out to see the area and agreed with him. I found him in my second rush round the positions. A piece of mortar had hit the front of his head and almost taken it right off, but it was still sort of held on by sinew and skin. All I did, in the middle of the mud, was to close it, just like a door. I thought, 'The guy's dead,' but he was still breathing – so I carried him to where Collier was, who had also been wounded. I told him to hold McKellar's hand because he wouldn't last five minutes. When I was put onto the helicopter, McKellar was there as well, still breathing and holding on. When we got to Singapore they put him onto a life support machine and I expected them, at any second, to say, 'McKellar's gone.' But no, he was holding on. Then his mother and father came from Scotland. The doctor made them come and see me, because I didn't think they should see him, particularly the mother. In the end she agreed not to, but his father said he must. Up he went, and put his hand through this sort of envelope window in the machine, and held his son's hand, and as he did so, his son died. I think that boy had been waiting, 'I'm seeing my father in Singapore and I must stay alive until that happens.' His parents said, 'Do you think he'll be happy here?' I said, 'I think he'll be very happy here.' Three days later we buried him.

CHAPTER TWENTY-ONE
ADEN
1 9 6 7

IN JANUARY 1967, THE 1ST BATALLION WAS SENT TO ADEN TO maintain security within the colony. In May they took over 'Area North', the districts of Al Mansura and Sheik Othman. On 1 June civil disorder broke out which lasted for the duration of their stay of six months. They departed on 27 November.

LIEUTENANT COLONEL MIKE WALSH, 1st Battalion

It was shortly after Christmas of 1966 that I was given a warning order to prepare 1 Para for an emergency operational tour in Aden. The Royal Anglians had had a difficult time for some six months, and people were getting through from up-country to reinforce the terrorists who were then operating openly in Crater, in Maalla and also in the area around Khormaksar. I flew out with the advance party. My plan was to actually live in, and occupy Sheik Othman, the key to Aden. This would not be an easy task and would inevitably be subjecting the men on the spot to a lot of incidents and fire, but nevertheless I was not happy to remain isolated in Radfan Camp for the fear of losing control.

The day after I arrived I went with my second-in-command, Major 'Joe' Starling, to ask the Royal Anglians if they would take us on patrol into Sheik Othman. As not many red berets had been seen around, Joe and I dressed up as private soldiers in the Royal Anglians, probably the oldest private soldiers they have ever had! We fell in one morning and to the delight of a company sergeant major were chased along and put in a three-tonner and taken up to Sheik Othman for reconnaissance.

The battalion continued to arrive by air, and by 25 May 1 Para had relieved the Royal Anglians. I said farewell to their commanding officer and as I drove back across the desert to Radfan Camp the radio crackled with a

ADEN 1967

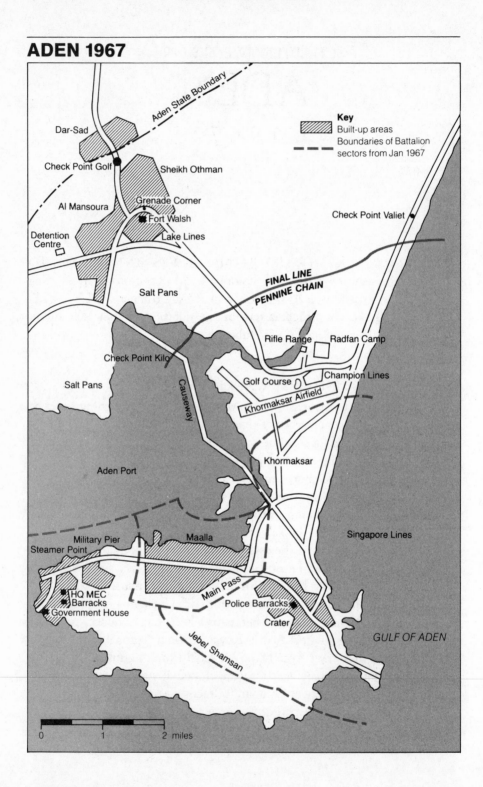

Key
Built-up areas
Boundaries of Battalion sectors from Jan 1967

Dar-Sad

Aden State Boundary

Check Point Golf

Sheikh Othman

Al Mansoura

Grenade Corner

Fort Walsh

Check Point Valiet

Detention Centre

Lake Lines

Salt Pans

FINAL LINE
PENNINE CHAIN

Check Point Kilo

Rifle Range

Radfan Camp

Salt Pans

Golf Course

Champion Lines

Khormaksar Airfield

Causeway

Khormaksar

Aden Port

Singapore Lines

Military Pier

Maalla

Steamer Point

HQ MEC
Barracks
Government House

Main Pass

Police Barracks

Crater

GULF OF ADEN

Jebel Shamsan

0   1   2 miles

message from the adjutant confirming that a general strike was called for the next day. We were in business!

The first test, and possibly the greatest we were to experience came on what the battalion came to call 'The glorious first of June'. On that day a general strike was ordered by a local terrorist organization, the NLF. Their aim was to interrupt the normal services of Aden, bring life to a standstill, and provide an excuse to have a go at us. I knew that I had to move into Sheik Othman and get there quickly. I sent D Company into the police station and eight OPs which we had selected on high buildings and rooftops around the town. These OPs provided good positions from which to dominate the main thoroughfare, and the principal mosque, which, although a religious place, was used by the terrorists as an arms centre. By five o'clock in the morning, just as it was getting light, all was ready for what – in the event – proved to be the most violent strike ever experienced in Aden.

The first incident occurred when a patrol was grenaded outside the main mosque. Immediately fire was returned from one of our OPs, which of course surprised them – they had never known that before – and we killed two men straight away. Throughout the rest of the day until last light we were in action and killed over 16 terrorists for the loss of one of our own men, killed by a grenade.

D Company, commanded by Major Brierley, had to fight it out themselves. It wasn't until last light that I was able to actually see them and order their relief by another rifle company.

At one stage during that day the shortage of ammunition became critical and 'Joe' Starling organized a resupply operation, which was very bravely and successfully carried out by a party under the Intelligence Officer, Lieutenant Ted Loden. Under cover fire from the OPs they ran the ammunition up to the back door of the police station in armoured cars. There's no doubt at all that the terrorists that day were trying to take over Sheik Othman, and to force us to abandon our positions in the town.

On 5 June the brigade commander, Brigadier Dick Jefferies, told me stand by for an outburst of trouble resulting from the Israeli invasion of Sinai – what we now know as the 'Six-Day War'.

C Company took over the disused Scottish Mission Hospital, but the terrorists soon spotted us and a few hours later opened very heavy fire on the hospital from rooftop positions in the town. They also fired upon the OP positions which we had held before, and it became vital for us to reinforce the defences during cover of darkness. Officers and men alike filled sandbags to strengthen our positions and by first light it was three feet six inches high and the men named it Fort Walsh. Every night in 'happy hour', every terrorist who owned a gun would spend an hour just potting at our positions: we could set our watches by it.

At about the same time we occupied a check point at Darsaad, at Byoomi College, which was to be christened 'Check Point Golf'. There were a number of attempts to destroy our positions, including a dam-buster charge, which was rolled one night against the base of the police station tower. To retain the initiative each company took it in turn to man Fort Walsh, the police station and Check Point Golf. We constantly changed our tactics, patrol programmes and *modus operandi*. The armoured cars, a squadron of Queen's Dragoon Guards, played a major part in the operation. During the period that we were in Sheik Othman, we had nearly 800 incidents.

The police station tower took a terrific pounding from small arms fire, and then anti-tank rockets. If this had persisted it would have collapsed. The sappers who did a splendid job, often in very dangerous conditions, strengthened it on the inside with extra breeze blocks but even their efforts really would not stand up to this constant pounding, every day. So Joe Starling got the sappers together and hatched a scheme. They made a protective screen of wire meshing which was to protrude some distance from the top of the tower, and would catch the rockets before they struck the tower. The Army Air Corps practised flying and lowering this difficult underslung load. It wasn't easy because this very cumbersome frame kept swinging with the downblast of the rotor blades and the movement of the helicopter through the air. Also of course there was the threat that some terrorist would blaze away at the helicopters, endangering both the aircraft and the pilot. These difficulties were overcome and one Sunday morning, when it was just getting light, a Scout helicopter took off and lowered this frame on to the tower – it went very well indeed and by nine o'clock that morning the police station tower had been saved.

Besides the Arab/Israeli War there was the growing jealousy and feuds between the two nationalist parties – NLF and FLOSY – both of which wanted to be the ones to whom the British would hand over at the end of our time there. We were starting to feel very lonely and out on a limb, with the only task being to hold on in order for some political settlement to be reached. On the morning of 20 June a rumour spread, very rapidly, that four colonels of the South Arabian Army had been arrested and dismissed. The army in Lake Lines just to the north of Radfan Camp, on the outskirts of Sheik Othman, rioted. The shots were heard in a police barracks, immediately opposite us, in Champion Lines. The police thought that

British troops had fired on the Arabs in Lake Lines, and they in turn mutinied, attacked their armoury in the camp, seized weapons and started to fire indiscriminately across the road into Radfan Camp.

A three-ton vehicle containing 19 soldiers travelling up the road past the two camps was fired on by the Arab police, and nine men were killed. Immediately afterwards two Aden policemen, and a British civilian driving by were shot down. By this stage rounds were coming straight into our camp, and I stood everyone to. We manned the perimeter, and I went round telling people that under no circumstances were they to fire back. There was a great display of discipline by 3 Para and by the Lancashire Regiment, who shared the camp with us. They obeyed their orders although one of the young second lieutenants of the Lancashire Regiment was killed, exhorting his men to hold their fire.

C Company of the King's Own Border Regiment, down from Bahrain to boost my numbers, were, that day, the Internal Security stand-by company. To restore order, and also to protect the lives of the few British personnel still serving with the police who had been isolated in Champion Lines, I quickly called for their company commander, Major David Miller, gave him very short instructions, and told him to get his company across into Champion Lines as fast as he could. It wasn't easy, because they were having to move 300 yards, across open desert, in the face of fire, which we could not return. I knew that they were bound to take some casualties – it was not an easy order to give!

They moved off about 10.45 am. The machine-gunner on their leading vehicle was shot dead, and they had a further eight men wounded before they got through the gate. Once in Champion Lines, they moved quickly, and restored order without much heavy fire or without having to inflict casualties. Major David Miller was awarded a Military Cross for this action. The restraint and discipline of that company was outstanding, and I believe also that both the police and the army were deeply impressed by that action, for it did much to restore their respect for British troops. The final two months of our tour was spent holding a defensive position, which we called the Pennine Chain, much of which was made up of barbed wire. Joe Starling records having to show people how to lay down barbed wire because it had been so long since it had been used.

On the last morning we marched out of Radfan Camp six abreast, with our weapons loaded because we were taking no chances. We cut through the perimeter wire of Khormaksar airfield, marched slap under the watch towers of Champion Lines which had caused so much trouble that terrible day in June, across the sand, wheeled right and down the main runway, finally passing in salute before the General Officer Commanding Aden. I think it did us good to go out that way.

CORPORAL MALCOLM SIMPSON, 1st Battalion

We'd been in Aden before, in 1965, on a short tour. We'd actually done the box formation in the Khormaksar area in a riot. You know, front row kneel, placards up, bugles blowing, the whole shebang. But that was the old riot control – this time it was going to be different.

The length of tour was unknown because the intention was to close Aden, so we were warned off for a twelve-month tour. When we got to Radfan Camp we were briefed on how we were going to deal with the FLOSY/NLF syndrome down in Aden Town, Crater, Sheik Othman, Mansura, those sort of areas. Life elsewhere in Aden was going on as normal. People were still living down town, families were still there and ordinary life existed. Whilst we were out in Radfan Camp, we could hear the explosions and the shootings going on at night time but we got ourselves acclimatized.

In the early hours of 1 June the battalion deployed and my company, D Company, were given the task of going into Sheik Othman and setting up OPs in all the high buildings in and around the main mosque area and also the police station, where the Company HQ would be set up under Major Geoff Brierley. We were seen coming in, but nothing happened during the hours of darkness, and we got ourselves settled in on the rooftops. It was very, very hot and humid. Because we had never really been involved in this sort of situation before, our attempts at defending ourselves really were a little bit primitive. We tended to cut bricks out of the rooftops like a little fort – as in Beau Geste – not appreciating that, although we were reasonably high up, once you stuck your head between the missing bricks, you were shot at.

At first light there wasn't a soul on the streets, not even an animal – nothing at all. So we knew something was about to happen. We saw Barry Andrews' patrol cross from the main bank to the mosque. Then suddenly we heard them shout out, 'Grenade – take cover!' The next thing this bloody grenade goes off. I saw a chap on the other side of the road running into a shop doorway; as he got through the doorway he closed it and must have thought he was safe, but it was a glass door! One of the patrol let fly a round which didn't do the guy's health any good. Within the next five minutes, every single location that we were manning came under heavy automatic small arms and rocket fire. They knew exactly were we were. As a result of this in the next OP young Carver was killed, shot in the head, and we had a few members of our company and C Company wounded in the feet and hands. We had one bloke firing at us and he was good. His shot always seemed louder than anyone else's. I told Ken Yeoman to try and sort this fellow out. Half an hour later Ken came rolling across the roof top covered in blood. He collapsed and we pulled his hands from his head – but he wasn't hit there. We looked at his hands and they were full of metal splinters. Then we looked at his rifle and we realized that the sniper's round had gone down the barrel of Ken's rifle as he was firing his round! There are only two recorded instances of this and the other was in World War I!

Now this firing went on all day, but there was a break just after lunch, when all firing ceased and people came out of their houses and actually went shopping! That lasted about an hour then they all went back into their houses and the firing started again. The Al Mansura picquet on the roundabout certainly got a right old tanning. It got to the stage where they were unable to return fire at all, because they just couldn't get up. That's how intense the fire was. Likewise at our location there was no way you could lift your head at all, because if you did you would get it shot off. You see, they are all born with a rifle in their hands, they are all natural shots. They were also extremely good with the old spigot grenades, they would go whanging across the rooftops, so it was quite a hairy day. Certainly Company HQ in Sheik Othman police station – which at that stage had no protective net round it – was really getting a right old attack.

As a result of the 1 June action we decided to stay in Sheik Othman, dominate the high ground and suppress rebels by vehicle and foot patrols. At last light, as soon as the cinemas had emptied, all hell let loose – we had mortar, rocket and small arms attacks every night, without fail. This was 'happy hour'. The boys used to come out of the old hospital and run with their mess tins into the cookhouse in the outbuildings, grab their food and run back between the mortar fire.

During a reasonably quiet evening at Check Point Golf, just prior to 'happy hour', dinner had been served and the OC and CSM, 'Middile' Campbell, were sitting in the CP having a mug of coffee. At about 1930 hours one round from an RPG 7 scored a direct hit on our CP. Even though we'd sandbagged the outside wall four deep the rocket came through and wounded Middile in the back. He didn't sustain a critical wound, because of the extra sandbagging, but also because as the rocket struck he was leaning forward to pick up his coffee. This became known as the 'Great Escape'!

There were moments of humour amidst all this. We were being persistently sniped at from the area south-west of the Al Mansura picquet.

So Joe Starling decided minimum force was the answer. He brought up a Saladin with a 76-mm cannon, put a round in, fired and this ensured no firing points could be used from those buildings in future! When the gun fired you could hear the boys cheering from Radfan Camp because we knew what Major Joe was going to do.

While we were in Radfan Camp in tents many of the British families were leaving from Steamer Point and places like that. As they were not coming back everything was being shipped off. Lorries would call for the furniture and take it down to the docks. Well, some of our lads decided to join the convoys. They'd call at the houses, explain they'd come for the fridge and air-conditioning and then drive straight back to our tented accommodation and install it. Everyone had a lovely fridge, ice cubes and air-conditioning.

For the last couple of months we built and manned the Pennine Chain between Check Point Kilo and Check Point Juliet and slowly began the withdrawal. We handed over in November, cut the wire at Khormaksar airfield, lined up in sixes and marched out with all our kit. The Royal Navy, never known to miss a trick, flew over in choppers. I suppose we thought they were saluting us, but no, they dropped a few CS canisters and so all the people saw, as we boarded the Beverleys for Bahrain, were these paras crying their eyes out.

CHAPTER TWENTY-TWO
NORTHERN IRELAND
1969 —

THE 1ST BATTALION WERE CALLED UP FOR AN EMERGENCY Operation Banner tour and took over responsibility for the Shankill Road district of Belfast in October 1969. Since that time all the battalions have served innumerable residential and roulement (four-and-a-half months) tours. The Parachute Regiment has been involved in many incidents in the province but two stand out, the riots in January 1972 (Bloody Sunday) and Warrenpoint in 1979.

On Sunday, 30 January 1972 an illegal march began in the Creggan and Bogside area of Londonderry which swelled to some 3,000 strong by the time (15.30 hours) it reached a security forces barrier. The marchers had been joined by some 150 hooligans who stoned and threw CS gas at the security forces with increasing violence as time went on. The 1st Battalion were ordered to mount an operation to arrest and disperse this group in the course of which they came under heavy small arms fire in the vicinity of Rossville Flats. In the ensuing gun battle 13 male civilians were killed. The Widgery Report exonerated the soldiers from the IRA charges of firing indiscriminately at a crowd running away from them and of opening fire before they themselves were fired upon.

At Warrenpoint on 27 August 1979, the 2nd Battalion were caught in a double ambush and lost a company commander and 15 other ranks.

WINNING HEARTS AND MINDS

Corporal, 2nd Battalion
We didn't know what to expect at that time. We hadn't really got a clue

359

BELFAST

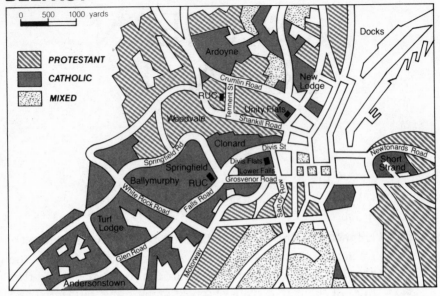

0   500   1000 yards

PROTESTANT

CATHOLIC

MIXED

Docks

Ardoyne

Crumlin Road

New Lodge

RUC

Tennent St

Unity Flats

Woodvale

Shankill Road

Newtonards Road

Clonard

Divis St

Short Strand

Springfield Rd

Springfield

Divis Flats

Lower Falls

Ballymurphy

RUC

Grosvenor Road

White Hock Road

Falls Road

Sandy Row

Turf Lodge

Glen Road

Motorway

Andersonstown

why we were there. The first night, I remember we were all in a little Portakabin and the corporal, he says, 'Right, who's going to go out and get the fish and chips?' I mean, you could just walk out. So a couple of us went into this fish and chip shop, just chatted to everybody, got our fish and chips and went back. Next day we moved into the company location which was Sugarfield Street, at the top end of the Shankill Road. We spent four very happy months there with nothing happening. We had, I think, one demonstration outside the little bakery where we were, and our OC just went outside and politely told the people that if they didn't clear off he would let his blokes loose on them. So they cleared off and came back next day and apologized.

Senior Officer, 1st Battalion

We went to Belfast in the October of '69. I was taken onto the Shankill the night Constable Arbuckle was shot. There was a pool of blood on the road and I remember going and walking round it with a bunch of flowers.

When we arrived, there were so-called no-go areas. Even British troops weren't allowed in. I thought this was absolute nonsense. We were there to try and protect them, and that's what we were going to do. But we had to ignore all the logical military principles because of the political forces and because it was the United Kingdom. It was a frightening thing I found to watch people in the Shankill Road at night in Territorial Army uniforms, carrying Union Jacks, singing 'God Save the Queen', and slinging petrol bombs at us. We'd be standing there with the police in front of us, because we were still sticking to the principles of internal security: police in the front line standing there, no shields – torches, truncheons, we behind with the wire, the armoured vehicles, the guns and everything. But as soon as they started to throw the bottles and things, the police would break up and there'd be blood and we would then have to move in.

Senior Officer, 1st Battalion
We started to develop street-fighting tactics to try and deal with the Shankill mobs. These were the Protestant mobs, and although the Protestant members of the Shankill suggested there were foreigners coming in and stirring it up, usually you could predict when the trouble would happen. After turning-out time and after the fish shops closed they'd all stand on the streets, some drunk would have a go and it would all build up. It usually wasn't necessary to do much. I found that by going over the wire, taking the padre or the RSM in a small group, you could go in amongst them, break up the groups and explain what was going on. You'd find they'd say, 'Ah, all right, sir. I'll be going home now.' And they would disappear and there'd be no problems.

What we had to learn was how to communicate with people and to give them a feeling of security and confidence. So I said to everybody in the battalion, 'Whatever you do, no matter what the situation, smile. Disarm everybody with a smile. Greet them and laugh.' Because there's so much laughter in Northern Ireland and it seemed to me that if we could do that, then we would begin to gain their confidence, providing we maintained the steel of the military presence. Combined with humour, we could perhaps then get some communication. Every Sunday, I detailed everybody in my headquarters to go to church. Everybody had to go. It was all part of the community relations game. The only way to get their confidence was to do what they wanted us to do: tea parties, helping with the chores, playing football with the kids – you name it, we did it. It was part of the integration.

When we went into such things we didn't have the kit, so I had to go down to a local factory and say: 'Look, there's my beret, I wonder if you can make me a number of sweaters that colour, maroon. They've got to be under two pounds each.' They did it, and we had some lovely sweaters made.

The soldiers warmed to the idea. It was a challenge and they thought they were cracking it. But it took a long time to get the locals' confidence.

They were trying desperately to convince us of the philosophy of the Protestant community: we are the people with the right; we look to the Queen; these people are infesting our country from the South; we don't want trouble but there are those who do; their birth rate is higher than ours and they're going to take us over. We slowly began to disillusion them about some of these things.

At that time we were not allowed to talk about either the UVF or the IRA. We were told that there was a sectarian problem, we were not to get involved, all we were to do was keep the peace. Our task was to maintain a balance between the Catholic and Protestant communities and to involve ourselves in community relations while keeping the lid on the violence. We were not in any way to infringe the basic roles that we had been given. The trouble was we were being drawn into the political level because we did not have any Intelligence, and the police seemed even more desperate for knowledge. There was absolutely no information at all on people we wanted to know about. So we decided we had to do it ourselves and set about systematically building up a map of where people lived. We had about 20 patrols out every night and more during the day, and we were able, by talking around, to find out who lived in every house, how many people, where they worked. Slowly we built up a pattern, and as a result we were then able to pick up who was shacking up with whom, whose husband wasn't actually quite as good to his wife as he should be, and so on. We were then able to use those details as levers to get further information later. Because, once a chap was found out by his wife, she'd give him the Belfast kiss, a bottle round his face and all the flesh hanging off. Rather nasty, but slowly we built up a massive dossier.

We thought, naively, we had some solutions to the problems. When we came back seven months later we'd lost our link with the people. Once you get that warmth between people, in any community, in any walk of life, and you put somebody else in, it's all got to start again. It's impossible, that passing on of trust. You can't do it. I think the biggest mistake that was made in the beginning, and it's easy to say this now, was that we had the four-month tour. The battalion changed over after four months with all this knowledge, with all this confidence, and you put in another battalion which had a completely different view. So immediately in this Internal Security situation the thread of confidence was lost and the trouble began again. If we could have kept those battalions there a little longer whilst there was a little more political activity I believe we wouldn't have developed so drastically into the next phase of the operational situation. We could have perhaps avoided some of the bloodshed. But it just wasn't possible.

BRICKS AND GAS

Private, 1st Battalion

The curfew stemmed from the time the Scottish regiment did those searches, and that was probably when the real trouble started – not from 1969, with all the civil rights and the focus of attention on the plight of the Catholics, but 1970. That's when the IRA first emerged. They'd say, 'Look what the soldiers are doing to you. Look how they treat you. We want to protect you.' And the people would think, 'Ah, we need some protection here.' That way the IRA got support for their cause, and still do. The IRA could have lain dormant for years, but they were looking for an excuse and they found it then, during that time when that Scottish regiment did those searches.

Private, 1st Battalion

We went back again to Belfast in September 1970, to Palace Barracks, at Holywood. When we arrived, the commanding officer said that as reserve battalion we would never go on the streets unless the place was running with blood. I remember putting my suitcase down, sorting my locker out, getting an issue with a flak jacket – not that I asked, we had flak jackets given to us anyway – and being called out. We'd just arrived, and we were on the Shankill! The King's Regiment were having a few problems, they'd been turned off the bottom of the Shankill, and it was chaos. They fired the gas and they missed the crowds; it landed amongst us. Our respirators were still packed, we stood behind the Pigs and got gassed quite severely. Gas is not nice, no – you can be in pain. We were out there in an IS situation getting gassed by friendly forces. When we got there they were saying, 'Take your helmets off, put your berets on', so the people could remember who we were from our previous tour. We took our helmets off and put our berets on, and we got bricked even more. We got bricked and gassed, so I was disillusioned with it. The change from when we were last there seven months before was very saddening, disturbing. I must admit I was getting frightened. This shouldn't have been happening. You couldn't put your finger on what had gone wrong: there were lorries burning on the streets, paving stones ripped up – it was different.

Private, 1st Battalion

Belfast then was tremendous. You'd come off the streets from a riot in the Falls and for 2p you could say hello to your wife. You'd have glass in your hair and your beret, and she'd say: 'Everyone's sitting here, we've been watching the television this afternoon.' I thought that was amazing. Whereas before, in Aden and Borneo, you'd be waiting for that letter. The MOD, the generals, the civil servants could visit there as well, take the shuttle. It brought home to people what conditions were like for the soldiers. The gap was much smaller, and so things got done.

THE SHOOTING STARTS

Captain, 1st Battalion

I remember very well the first time I came under fire. It was in early February, the same night that Gunner Curtis, the first British soldier to be killed, was shot in the New Lodge. I was accompanying a TV crew in the Ardoyne, which was a strong Republican area at the top end of the Crumlin Road. There'd been a lot of shooting, and petrol bombs were flying around, and then came the crack and thump, which to the soldier is an unmistakable sound.

Private, 1st Battalion

Most of the trouble we got involved in was when we actually had to go in and physically rip people out. A lot of it was caused by women. Irish women were foul-mouthed and the hardest women you'll ever meet on this earth. They were all Amazons, they really were hard, far harder than the blokes. They were very loyal, for all the wrong reasons. They were passionate, vicious. I mean, I'd never seen women fight, I'd never seen women fight men. You'd come back scratched to blazes, black-eyed, your ears bitten. It woke you up, you started looking at the equality of sexes. You treated them as a different species altogether out there, not a domesticated animal that you keep at home. They were vicious, and if you got attacked or you had to move in amongst them you obviously had to baton them on the ground. They'd cling on until you'd knocked them senseless whereas the blokes would run, the blokes would always run away. It was all part of the strategy of moving the women and kids up front.

Corporal, 1st Battalion

We were parked doing riot control. This woman came up to the company commander and said, 'Mister, mister, one of your soldiers swore at me.' He turned round, quite concerned because she was nice-spoken, and said, 'Which one did it?' And she says, 'That fucking bastard over there.' And you know what he said? 'Go away, madam, go away.'

Corporal, 2nd Battalion

I think the saddest moment of the summer of '71 was when Sergeant Mick Willets got killed down at Springfield Road cop shop in May. Someone threw a suitcase with a bomb into the barracks, and the blast killed him as he stood in a doorway allowing a Catholic family to get to safety. He got the George Cross for that. We were driving around and heard this great big explosion, huge by those days' standards because normally it was just little nail bombs. It was like the last war, we'd never seen pubs and that blown up then. When it went off, there was a great big cheer from the Paddys surrounding the police station. It was a big score for them, that place going up. There was a hit song at the time called 'Where's Your Money Gone?' and all the women and kids were singing 'Where's your barracks gone? Where's your barracks gone?', laughing, joking, dancing, and he was dead on the ground, bubbling, bits of him all over the place. He died saving a kiddie. He should have thought of his own kids rather than that kid, but I know how the bloke felt: he was a father, and you don't want anybody hurt that's not hurting you. I remember the CO telling the sergeant major who was in charge there, 'Get rid of them, those despicable people.' Mick Willets was the first Parachute Regiment soldier to be killed. When a soldier died then, it was headline news. A lot of soldiers were very bitter, including a lot of Irishmen and Southern Irishmen in the battalion.

INTERNMENT

Corporal, 2nd Battalion

It was around 0400 hours and pitch dark. Our faces were totally blacked, the only thing we could really distinguish on each other was the eyes and the parachute wings on the arms of our Denison smocks. Each team had one target house and target person, usually the father or son in that house. One man would position himself round the back of the house leaving the main group at the front. The door would be hammered and as a last resort a four-inch metal picket would be used to gain entry.

We positioned ourselves in the hedge by our target house and waited for the few minutes to zero hour. My adrenalin was up, I felt excited and very impatient to get on with it. We started stealthily approaching the house – six minutes to go. Suddenly there was banging in the next street: the bastards had started too early, so we all broke into a run. I ordered one man round the back through the alley, and then banged loudly with the rifle on the front door – nothing. One of the lads urged me to smash the door down.

I was just about to OK this when I heard the thump-thump of someone coming down the stairs. The door opened and a woman in her fifties stood there scowling with two glittering, hate-filled eyes, saying nothing. I went into the practised routine: 'Does Sean so-and-so live here?', but before I had finished one of my blokes charged up the stairs. She yelled, 'Sean, the fucking Brits are here for ye!' We pushed into the living room, flicked the lights on, and the other man in my group accidentally pulled the rail off the wall as he closed the curtains. 'Why don't ye wreck the friggin place?' she screamed. Her daughter came in and immediately launched into a vituperous attack on us. I pulled out the white card that had been issued to us and read the words out: 'Under the Special Powers Act of 1922 I arrest you. . . .' I was that nervous I fluffed it a couple of times. The mother and daughter were screaming at each other as the old man jammed on his flat cap and looked at us expectantly. We waited until the soldier upstairs had finished his cursory search and began to leave. The missus calmed down, said her goodbyes, and we rushed him to the rendezvous point and threw him in the Rover. There was already an internee on board. They nodded to each other.

Private, 2nd Battalion
It was six o'clock when the shooting started, after the civvies had come home from work: they must have had their tea, and then done the business. I was sent onto the roof of the Henry Taggert, which gave me a very good view of the attack. Our area of responsibility was from the flats at the rear of the base to the open ground at the far side of Springfield Road in the front.

The first shots came from a privet hedge alongside a narrow alleyway behind a row of houses. A gunman was firing from behind a dustbin, and of course the first thing we did was put down fire into it – that bloke ceased firing, he was a sitting duck. There was also a woman there, firing a pistol, and she was taken out too. I know it perhaps sounds callous, but the enemy is the enemy, whether man or woman: if she's got a weapon in her hands and she's going to take me out, do I take her out? Of course I do.

The gunmen started coming across the open land at the front, shooting. A couple would run out, then another, then two more. It wasn't an organized section attack as we would do, with one foot on the ground and the other loose. I don't know what they hoped to achieve. They didn't even reach the dip, the dead ground on the other side of the waste ground. Springfield Road was in full view, and they'd have been taken out for sure as they crossed it. Even if they'd managed to get across, they'd never have cut through the wires surrounding the base. The IRA never made a section attack again.

Corporal, 1st Battalion

On the Wednesday after internment, we came down from Ballymurphy along the Shankill Road and the pavements were lined with Protestants cheering us, throwing us packets of cigarettes, waving Union Jacks. Our driver, a Jock – whether Catholic or Protestant I couldn't tell you, it didn't matter in the regiment – stopped the wagon and shouted at them, 'Don't you start, you bastards. Because it's your turn next. It'll happen to you as well, because you're just as bad.' And it was true, a year later it happened to them. We knew there were stacks of weapons in the Shankill, we knew about the UVF, we knew all about the Protestant bad boys.

'BLOODY SUNDAY'

Captain, 1st Battalion

'Bloody Sunday', as people call it, was, it's fair to say, a high-risk operation. What was intended was very clear. For a number of weekends there had been larger and larger so-called civil rights demonstrations in the Province – this was a good year on from the demise of what I regarded as the genuine civil rights movement, and by then many of the participants were somewhat suspect. All the marches were illegal, all banned. It was known that a very large protest march would take place in Londonderry on 30 January 1972, and the authorities decided that a complete stand was to be made. The aim on our part that afternoon was to make maximum arrests of the hooligan element in the crowd. The arrest operation was to take place within a very limited area, beyond what was then known as the 'containment line', the near side of which the security forces were happy to operate, but on the far side of which they were not. That might seem remarkable now, but that was the policy then. It was our task to make a limited incursion of 200–300 metres beyond the barricade and round up as many hooligans as possible and whistle them off to the local nick.

The gut feeling was that it wouldn't be as simple as the orders in black-and-white suggested. There was no hard intelligence, but it was felt that the opposition would not, and could not, permit such a clear violation of the rules pertaining to the containment line, beyond which they had free rein in the no-go areas of the Bogside and Creggan; that they would be bound to react; and that the problem wouldn't be the hooligan element, but gunmen – two rather different categories of opposition.

Corporal, 1st Battalion

The political side, which is always interesting to a soldier, was obviously human rights. Human rights are great, fine, and there had to be a mediator, but the IRA had infiltrated the organization and were leading a lot of people up the garden path. Manipulating the marchers was a really bitter way of doing it, because those people were decent people. They might have been singing Republican songs, but they weren't the IRA. They were hoodwinked, conned: that was the sad thing.

Captain, 1st Battalion

It was about half past three, quarter to four, when the marchers came off the top of the Creggan Estate and headed down the hill towards the old part of the city centre. The rioting had started against the barricades, missiles were thrown, and the security forces had replied with gas. At about ten to four we were given the order to execute the pre-planned arrest operations. We moved through the troops manning the barricades and passed beyond, three companies on three different axes. The idea was to get beyond the rioters and scoop them up from behind. That was partially achieved, but not completely: a lot of the crowd started running back once they saw what we were doing. Events then took their course.

Corporal, 1st Battalion

We started dealing with the situation exactly as we would have in Belfast. The weapons were never really out of the vehicles. We dispersed the rioters just by using batons – shields we didn't bother with because they were too cumbersome. I captured a few people who were throwing stones. One was an American sailor, United States Navy – he was in a lot of trouble. Then we were fired on. I know in my heart of hearts, and I'll take it to my grave, that we were fired on first. At that, of course, the weapons were given out from the backs of the vehicles.

Sergeant, 1st Battalion

I was crossing the open ground in front of Rossville House, trying to reach the high end of the pram ramp by the shops underneath the flats, when I first heard shooting. A guy on the corner of Rossville House opened up on us with a Thompson; the rounds were way above our heads. I saw him go down, shot by one of our troops over on the right-hand side of the open ground. He also took out a gunman firing from one of the windows in the flats; I think we took two casualties from a machine-gun attack from there. Acid bottle bombs were being thrown from the top of the flats, and two of our blokes were badly burnt.

By that time there were lots of running crowds. It was very busy, very chaotic: panic had struck. People were running in all directions, and screaming everywhere. Innocent people were being bowled over – we were running past women and children, shouting at them to get out of the way. At first they wouldn't believe us, but very soon they were putting up white handkerchiefs, to show they were peaceful, not armed.

Private, 1st Battalion

I was to one side of the open ground, down an alleyway; I'd heard shots but didn't know where they were coming from. The corporal with me had the rifle, and I had the rubber-bullet gun. There were odd little riots in the side streets, so I thought I'd arrest the troublemakers. As I was running towards one, a man came out round the corner 30 metres away with a pistol, probably an old Webley. I fired a rubber bullet at him, and I turned round to the corporal when I heard 'ping' on the wall above. We chased him up the street but lost him. Further along the road somebody else must've got him: by the way he was dressed he was one of the dead picked up later. His tactics were very poor. He didn't really use fieldcraft, or urbancraft: if he'd hidden himself and waited for a target he could probably have shot some of us, but he was just running around firing, which led me to believe he was a novice. The gunmen in the crowds seemed to have pistols that could be hidden, and the riflemen would probably have been firing out of the windows of the buildings.

The shooting seemed to be over in about ten minutes, but perhaps it lasted half an hour. It wasn't continuous – more like a skirmish. When the gunmen realized they'd got the worst of it, they packed up and left. Once the people in the streets started seeing dead bodies, the rioting stopped – they were petrified. It all died down very fast, and we went on a body-collecting patrol. There were three dead by the barricade; the others were round corners, up the alleyways. We loaded the bodies into the back of a Pig and took them to the hospital in the city centre. We carried them up the steps: the nurses were fainting at the blood. The bodies were laid out in the hallway, and when we got to the tenth I thought, 'Bloody hell!' People were starting to worry then: I couldn't see why, but that was the most that had been killed by the Army in one day in Northern Ireland.

Sergeant, 1st Battalion

We thought it a huge success: morale was bouncing off the ceiling. When we got back to our base, a factory at Drunahoe a few miles outside Londonderry, we stepped out of the wagon and were literally put upon soldiers' shoulders and carried in like conquering heroes for the great job we'd done. We were taken to the school across the road and all the village ladies gave us tea. And sitting in the factory that night we had the first real inkling of instant reporting: there was a two-hour programme on the entire history of the Parachute Regiment on television.

They said we killed 13, wounded 16, all the rest of it. There is a distinct possibility that we took out more. All we could count were the bodies we could actually get to. We didn't assume anything: I'd have put the body count at 20, not 13. I believe the extra bodies were whisked across the border. We know, on the grapevine, from friends in other units, that graves were found on the other side. I believe those bodies were taken across because if they had been recovered, forensic tests would have proved without a shadow of a doubt that those people had been firing weapons. Those bodies would have shown that the marchers had been infiltrated, manipulated. Instead, the IRA were able to turn it into a great propaganda exercise, which worked, in my opinion. I think that as a result, the Army had to reconsider its role in Northern Ireland, and its handling of the situation has been different ever since.

Corporal, 1st Battalion

We were stopped that day. We were poised to go further in, into the Bogside, but they pulled us out once they realized the body count had reached 13. We were stopped from high up, because we were ready to carry on. The main tower block just as you enter the Creggan, they reckon it had been set up as a field hospital and clearing station: the IRA were expecting a big confrontation that day. I believe, knowing what I know now, that the Army could have nipped it in the bud then, by going in hard and sharp. In 1972 the IRA were known, they were all known: the Belfast mobs, the Londonderry mobs, even the ones in Dublin.

Private, 1st Battalion

Nobody was ashamed of anything; nobody felt any guilt. We'd done our job, and they'd done theirs; we didn't open fire until the gunmen started. Nobody was about to break down and cry, or feel bad about it. But the next day a TV cameraman came and filmed us individually on parade, on behalf of the Army. I remember I and a few other lads wanted to turn away, but the boss man said to us, 'You've nothing to be scared of.' He was right: we just stood our ground.

Captain, 1st Battalion

It wasn't an easy time, because so-called 'Bloody Sunday' was world news. It was clearly the catalyst for some very important events – the prorogation of Stormont took place some two months after; perhaps it was the single most important event in the history of the British Army in Northern Ireland. And it remains a contentious issue, a subject of enormous controversy. All of a sudden the battalion was being accused of losing its head, running amok – emotional phrases of that nature, which to us didn't make sense, but none the less were being said, and so there was a case to be answered.

To my mind 'Bloody Sunday' was doing the best we could, within the constraints of the game, and within the circumstances presented to us. In other words, we were engaged by fire, and we returned fire. I thought that answer was sufficient, but like any innocent man charged with murder we were worried until acquitted. One could get into an arcane argument as to whether the boys were within the laid-down rules of returning fire, and a far cleverer man than I ruled on that: Lord Justice Widgery was invited to exercise a judicial mind on the factors involved, which he examined in great detail, and his judgement was extremely balanced and carefully thought through. Widgery accepted that on the whole our soldiers were within the prescribed rules; he pointed a finger at one or two soldiers, describing their actions as 'bordering on the reckless', but basically he acquitted the battalion of unprofessional conduct. And, of course, there was relief and pleasure in that decision.

My epitaph might be that the operation was properly executed, but perhaps less surely conceived.

A WAR SITUATION: 1972

Corporal, 1st Battalion

During Operation Motorman I was living at Tennent Street police station. A bunch of young teenagers, Protestants, came in one day, and one of them I recognized as a young kid I had known well in '69. I spoke to him: 'Hello. How's it going? What you doing these days?' He was friendly, shook hands with me, and said, 'I'm fucking trying to kill you bastards.' It was as straightforward as that. He was deadly serious: he wasn't joking.

Corporal, 1st Battalion

No patrols had gone out all day because there'd been trouble the previous night. The Protestants had been threatening to kill British soldiers for alleged brutality on the Shankill Road, and my patrol was told to take a look round. I didn't like it, because there was something in the air: you could sense it. We drove down to the peace line near the Falls Road, and there was not a soul, as if a curfew was on. There were always people in the Shankill, but when we crossed over the Shankill Road at the top end there was nothing in the street. So I stopped our vehicles, got everybody together, and said, 'Right, helmets on. There's something very odd here.' We drove up the Shankill Road again and stopped at a T-junction just above Butler Street. A crowd of maybe 50 UDA guys with batons and little tin shields, all dressed in Belgian camouflage kit, hats, face veils, scarves, came running round the corner and started charging us. Behind them there was another large crowd throwing missiles over their heads. So we deployed and waded into the crowd, totally outnumbered. We were going to be slaughtered and they were trying to slaughter us, but we just went berserk, like Viking warriors. We were slapping people down with batons because we knew that they were going to kill us, that if we didn't fight like hell we would be overwhelmed. They started to withdraw then. They had no bottle, those people: hard pub drinkers, but man to man they were nothing.

The riot was practically over when all of a sudden a Bren gun opened up from Butler Street across the other side of the Shankill Road. A couple of the lads fired back at where they thought the gunman was, which was correct, because he didn't fire again. It just went on from there, lots of silly fire. One fellow in a car would drive across the Shankill firing a Sten gun. I couldn't believe what those people were playing at: of course, the next time he came across we all fired at the car, and he didn't appear again. After that it just escalated.

These were Loyalists, so-called Loyalists firing at British soldiers – great Loyalists, all Union Jacks and spitting in your face.

WARRENPOINT: AUGUST 1979

Lance Corporal, 2nd Battalion

Our platoon was travelling down the dual carriageway from Ballykinler Barracks to Newry in a Land-Rover and two four-tonners. The platoon commander was in the Land-Rover, I was in the first four-tonner, and the second four-tonner was right behind us. As soon as we heard the bang our driver pulled into the central reservation, and I jumped out the cab door on the passenger side, cocking my weapon. As I landed, I turned round and the blokes were already debussing from the back. All I could see of the rear vehicle, well, the impression I got was just an engine block sitting in the road surrounded by hundreds of little fires. The bomb had been packed in straw inside a horsebox parked in a lay-by, and the road was littered with black, burning, smoking straw.

We ran back and the first thing I saw was a bloke on his hands and knees crawling amongst us, still smouldering. I threw my water bottle to another bloke to get some water on him – I was still running on to see if there was anything more. Then my memory becomes hazy. I remember going through the wreckage of the vehicle, and the ammunition started to explode, rounds and magazines going off, so we cordoned off the area and stopped the vehicles coming up from Newry on the dual carriageway. The cars were about ten feet away, and a dozen civilians lined up, arms folded, watching what was happening. One person came forward, a doctor or a fireman I think, and gave first aid to the two survivors from the four-tonner. I started directing the traffic back and over the verge, to keep the outside lane free for any back-up coming from Newry. They arrived within minutes, and I waved them through the traffic. That's the last thing I remember, because I was standing by the road next to some lodge gates, which was where the second bomb was.

Sergeant, 2nd Battalion

What sticks in my mind most wasn't so much the explosion itself, but how everything went black, and this noise: the only thing I can equate it with is thousands of gallons of water rushing, sort of roaring like a waterfall. I must have blacked out for a bit because I then clearly remember sitting in the road feeling bitterly cold – not cold like in cold weather, but like I was encased in a block of ice. It was too cold to imagine: I felt so bitterly cold, it was as though I was entombed. I was sitting holding my left arm, in the road, swaying a bit. Obviously there must have been all sorts of carnage around, but none of it registered, just the bitter cold. Then I must have blacked out again.

Corporal, 2nd Battalion

Lots of people still remember seeing on television a tom sweeping the road afterwards. Everything was put in plastic bags, and my job was to sort through these plastic bags and pick out any personal belongings. Myself and another lad spent a complete week in a Portakabin in Ballykinler going through every bag. I found the remains of a pair of denims, just the back pocket with the guy's wallet completely intact; he'd been blown to kingdom come, just vaporized. The Queen's Own Highlanders phoned up wanting to

NORTHERN IRELAND

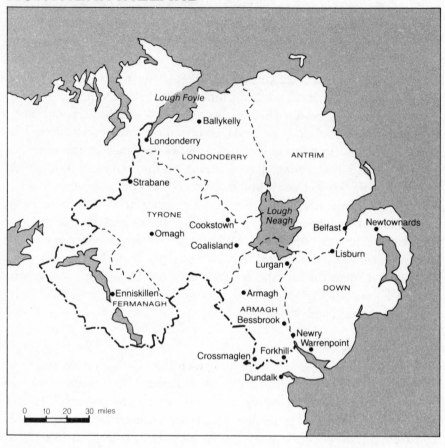

know if we'd found a tam-o'-shanter belonging to their CO. We found it and put it to one side. We were turning up bits of arms, parts of hands. Talk about being sickened: I used to go home at night to the barracks and my wife would say, 'I know what you've been doing, I can smell it. You just smell of death.'

SOUTH ARMAGH

Major, 1st Battalion

South Armagh is unique, it's really an area of its own in terms of the factors which bear on it. It's very beautiful indeed. It's perhaps a little like some

374

areas of Derbyshire or Yorkshire: rolling hills, stone walls, little farm buildings, and when it isn't raining, which isn't often, it's very attractive indeed. The people keep themselves to themselves. I don't think a lot of them give a damn who governs them, provided whoever governs them stays out of the way. I don't think they're very keen on paying taxes or acknowledging authority of any particular nature, whether it be North or South. Very Irish. They enjoy their independence. Of course South Armagh basically is a hard Republican area and the people living there are nearly all Republicans.

The border is totally indistinguishable: it just wanders over fields. It's very easy to cross it by mistake, because nothing marks it whatsoever, except on a metal rail where you've got a yellow paint line across the rail, but in the countryside it might be a small stream, it might be a dry stone wall between two fields. It looks the same on both sides.

It's a totally different problem operating down there from the streets of Belfast. Totally different. In the urban areas you're working in close confines; your ranges, for example, are probably not more than 200 or 300 yards. There are always a lot of people around because you're working in a built-up area. You don't go out probably more than three, four, five hours at a time; it's very close and tight. Reinforcements are always at hand. You can basically drive a military vehicle with, not complete impunity, but getting on that way. In the countryside, particularly in South Armagh, the population is very dispersed and therefore you've got large areas of nothing. Fields, hillsides and the odd wood. You don't have reinforcements easily to hand and driving is a crazy thing to do because you'll get blown up. So either you walk or you fly by helicopter. You've got the consideration of the border, always the border, which is the sanctuary for the terrorist, whereas in Belfast and other urban areas his immediate sanctuary has to be within the town itself. So you might be able to find it and if you can find it you can do something about it. On the border you can do nothing because his sanctuary is off limits to you. I think it's a more dangerous scene of operations than the town. He can hurt you and run across the border and, equally, he can hurt you without even being on your side of the border. If he's got a bomb just outside, he either detonates it by radio or by landline from the other side and there's nothing you can do against it. You have to be very careful to incorporate the Republic's security forces into any operation you may carry out, if they can be of value to you, which very often they can be.

It's very much more a game of lethal chess down there than operating in the streets of Belfast or Derry or wherever. Much slower, much more deliberate and, in terms of intensity, actual frequency of incidents, much less. But in terms of concentration and adrenalin, equally high, if not higher, because you will spend long periods, a long wait and then something will just happen out of the blue, and you've probably got 15 or 30 seconds to make something of it, or not.

Captain, 1st Battalion

Crossmaglen's a one-horse town, there's bugger all there. It's not like Belfast, where there are all the back alleys and ginnels. You know, walk up Newry Street, Newry Road, Dundalk Road, walk round the school and that's it – there's absolutely nothing!

Corporal, 2nd Battalion

We rated the North Louth ASU (active service units) well in 1976 because they'd attacked one of our OPs. They'd sussed it out through various mistakes that we'd made and shot at it and bombed it, luckily after we'd moved out about eight hours before. That was a good attack. About ten people took part in it. Because of attacks like that no VCPs (vehicle check points) were allowed in the border area. But we got clearance from the brigadier to go down and set one up to see if we could attract fire, and find out where it was coming from. So we went down and within about ten minutes we got a couple of rounds. Fairly close shooting as well, passing within a couple of feet of the old Land-Rover, so we skedaddled out. About ten days later we went back but this time we put out three sniper crews to cover that area. We rode down in the two Land-Rovers to do the old VCP and he's watched it. He's watched how we'd done it before and we did the same again. The first Land-Rover pulls into his left and blocks off the road. We pull into the church driveway, and reverse out across the road and block the other side. But 20 pounds of explosive go off as we drive into this gateway! Front wheel's gone, driver's out the back and we've gone down with a dummy that's had its head blown off in the passenger seat. Then, 'wham, wham', about eight or nine rounds come at us. Watching in front of a house was this bloke with a fisherman's hat. We're all scurrying all over the place, but we still haven't picked up where the shooting is coming from. We contact the sniper party, and one of them reckoned he'd seen something, so they'd put down a couple of rounds and said they'd got a kill. We found out later the guy that we saw with the fisherman's hat, 400 metres away, had tipped the wink to a guy who was hiding behind the church, who couldn't see us, and he pressed the button. Very, very good. The same night we went up this great big hill of gorse and found two dead cows that the snipers had shot!

We targeted one of these North Louth ASU guys. We got information coming across from the South as well as our own. He was seen in the scrapyard right on the border. We put in two OPs, and watched for a couple of days. We see the guy is definitely in there and we send a message back to base and wait. To relieve the boredom we leave guys to watch the scrapyard while we do some VCPs on the back roads. About three o'clock in the morning we see this brand new Peugeot, of which there's not a lot around, and decide to stop him. In the back seat he's got about 20 chickens, opens up the boot and there's six piglets. Only the Irish could do this. He didn't want us to open the boot but we thought he might have a kidnapping or something going on and the chickens were a cover. His old man owns two farms in this area and the pigs are some sort of illegal trade. Don't ask me what the EEC rules are between North and South but he's on a winner, so he offers us a pig. So we get back to our OP and tie it up and feed it biscuits for a day. Then we get the call that they've seen the guy we want in the scrapyard and he's got a beard.

We move in slowly, then we charge down through his house into the scrapyard. Out they came, not one guy with a beard, but six of them! I'm saying, 'Which one? Which one?' I haven't got a clue which one it is because the photograph that we have is a blow-up that looks like a bag of sugar. So now it's like something out of *Blazing Saddles*, we're running around this scrapyard, they're trying to hide, we're trying to grab them. Eventually, we get all of them plastic-cuffed under a car. But we have to wait for Pete, the colour sergeant who can identify them, but he's fallen into a swamp on the way down! Eventually he staggers in covered in slimy shit and the other lads are panting behind him. So I say, 'Which one is it?' He goes, 'Oh fuck. I don't know.' Now you've got a ridiculous situation, because the whole yard is erupting. The woman at this farmhouse, she's screaming, the dogs are giving it max, Pete's standing there, not knowing – then he says, 'That's him.' So we cut this guy off the fender and leave the others chained up while we make our getaway – we could hear the Wessex coming. But it turns out we've picked the scrapyard owner's son so now his mother's screaming and kicking us. But Pete's adamant that this is the guy so we drag him off. On the way through we pass my OP and pick up the bergens and the old pig. If you had this on film you wouldn't believe it because you had this great, tough, hairy paratrooper with all his kit dragging this young lad up the hill and his mother clinging on to him, a right frail old dear, and I've got this pig on a lead. Imagine the old loadmaster sitting in the chopper: he kicks the door open, doing his business, looks down and sees this bloody group of paras with this woman throwing punches and kicking and this pig leaping around going spare because of the old rotors – absolute chaos. So we throw the bergens on, the woman's screaming and she's hanging on, so Pete, very gentlemanly, decks her. We jump in with the pig and the guy and take off.

It's only six minutes to Bessbrook, and a couple of minutes from approach the 'loady' flicks the door open in readiness for our exit, the chopper banks, the pig panics, slips his lead. I make a grab at him, miss, and he goes hurtling out! The young guy with the beard, who has obviously never been in a helicopter, thinks he's next – it was outrageous. You wouldn't believe it if it was on telly. We were raging because we'd lost the pig. And the bloke was the wrong one and released that afternoon.

Sergeant, 2nd Battalion

When you prepare an ambush you put the boys in, check all the business and you give 'Ambush Set'. That means nobody moves unless war happens. In front, you've got a killing area. Each man has, say 60 yards, that is his killing area. There we were: cold, wet, lying in a ditch, when two blokes walked into the ambush. We positively identified weapons and we had to open fire. Unfortunately, it was our young lieutenant and his signaller. He'd walked down the road and come back up the wrong side. They were both killed.

Lieutenant, 1st Battalion

In Crossmaglen they had a market on a Saturday. Lots of people about, you know. It's Saturday morning in a village, so I felt perfectly safe about going into the square. I vaguely went through the process of looking at cars, pretending we were alert to our surroundings: reassure the locals, give them visible signs that we are paying attention to what's going on and what's about. I walked up to this car and started to look in it; suddenly the whole thing went up, exploded, and I was covered in fire. I was up shit creek without a paddle. I was screaming, floundering around and I couldn't see a way out. I thought, 'What's going on? What's going on? Oh my God, I'm going to die.' I started heading down the square like a bloody great fireball. One of my platoon had recovered very quickly and shouted to me, I homed into his voice and I ran in his direction. I couldn't see because I was almost blind. I knew my hands, my legs and my head and all the rest of me were on fire but I kept running till I got to him. Whether I rolled myself or whether he rolled me I don't know, whatever happened, I rolled. By now my eyes began to go; the last thing I saw were my hands, huge blisters were forming and just bursting – the stench was pretty awful. I was lying there smelling myself frying. The guy whom I'd run to had whipped off his smock and smothered the flames. It felt strange being underneath that. By then others were around me so I took a deep breath and calmed down and thought, 'It's okay, I'm all right. I'll be okay.' I believe I started asking questions as to how everyone else was, but I can only guess, because I would imagine that severe shock had set in, so whatever I may think is probably a dream of what I thought happened. Once the Toms had the situation under control – and I had a guy talking to me – I don't think I ever panicked after that. I always remember the medic coming up and talking to me and saying something about morphine. I had a hole in my chest and the back of my head, and that was pretty sore. Then the helicopter came and I remember them putting me in a stretcher, and because it was a Scout my feet and head were out of the helicopter so I caught this very cool breeze which was very soothing. At Bessbrook they transferred me to a Wessex. But by then I was as blind as a bat and I thought I was going to be blind for ever. Because there were no recognizable features on my face, the doctor on the Wessex said, 'Well, who are you?' I said, 'You bloody well ought to know who I am. I took you round the square at Crossmaglen two weeks ago!' By all accounts the doctor performed a miracle because in my swollen body he managed to find a vein and pumped two litres of drip into me. After that it's difficult to say, because it was the longest and shortest day of my life.

Private, 1st Battalion

We were coming in from the school to the square and the other section were coming down the bottom of the square and just as we crossed at the top this car exploded. Instead of getting down and looking around, we all went galloping across the square. There was a load of black smoke coming off the motor. When we got there one of the section, who must have been in shock, was just sitting there having a fag. Another was bumbling about. But the lieutenant, I couldn't believe it, he was on fire – from head to foot, totally smothered in fire, just running across, and really screaming. We ran and pulled him down and started putting him out. Paddy did it with a flak jacket on his face, but we told him to stop because a flak jacket's made of a sort of plastic material, and it had started melting on his face. I got my smock off and wrapped it round his legs and someone was using their beret. He was screaming all the time. I couldn't believe that smell, it was terrible. I was sick on him. Looking at him, his face was a mess, like an ashtray. He was black, his nose seemed to have gone, his lips had gone, and his eyes were closed, his hair and his flak jacket had gone. I remember he had his underpants on, and his puttees and boots, and his weapon stock had melted.

But for me there was no way he was going to die. The platoon sergeant was calling the camp, asking for a chopper and a medic. I remember the medic sticking these saline drips into him: he looked more in control than our bunch. I just kept telling the lieutenant he was going to be all right. I'd just got a medical note before we went out there, and I remember it saying: 'In the case of injury, reassure, reassure.' That was coming through straight into my head. I was shocked that he didn't pass out, because he must have been in some pain, but he was awake all the time. I've seen him once since then, but I don't think he recognized me. It's not the sort of thing you say, 'Hello, sir, I put you out once!'

When we got back to the camp they gave us a cup of tea. Then they took us straight out on a confidence patrol – straight back out. We weren't talking much, we were just quiet. Then when we got back in, we didn't stop talking. I slept like a log that night. But I can also remember most of that day seeing the company commander directly after the blast. You know in those black and white cartoon films, where there's an explosion, and there's a bloke standing there with shredded clothes on and his hair all smoking – it was like that. He had a Pye set in his hand and he was talking into it, but it had melted.

Sergeant, 1st Battalion

I was waiting at Bessbrook when we had a call about an incoming casualty. I think they said 40 to 60 per cent burns. We couldn't believe it. Our doctor got his kit out and the rest of the crew were getting to the helipad. I thought, 'Ice. Got to get ice.' The doctor said, 'Where are you going?' and I said, 'Cookhouse. Ice.' He said, 'Ice?' I said, 'Airways, swelling.' You pack the ice onto the throat and neck and try and reduce swelling to stop the airways blocking up. I went to the cookhouse and said, 'I've got a casualty, give me all the ice you've got.' I wasn't stationed there, the cook didn't know me, but he was brilliant, he gave me a big bin liner full. It was ridiculous the amount of ice I had. As the Scout arrived we just ran forward and the lads got the stretcher off. I ran towards the Wessex which was winding up, and tossed in my bag of ice. Then I jumped in to be in the chopper to lift the stretcher on. I thought the medic on the Scout was going to get on, but he didn't. Suddenly, we were off. That was the first time I saw the casualty and, oh dear, what a mess. He was black and his face had gone. I remember distinctly his Northern Ireland watch. The plastic strap had melted away but the watch was embedded in his flesh.

The doctor was busy checking his airways and I was thinking about IVI (intravenous injection) by this time. I'd seen him put an IVI in before and he was a bag of nerves, and I thought, 'Oh please don't fuck up, don't mess this one up.' I cut away the jumper and smock, trying to find his vein. The doctor found it, first go. That was remarkable in a Wessex that's just taken off, shaking and jumping about. Cool as a cucumber. He also put some pain-relieving drug into the IVI. I got down alongside him and his face was dripping plasma. He was in a lot of pain, but the doctor had already given him as much pain relief as possible. He had probably had more pain on his bottom half where the skin was still intact. But I was getting worried about his airways. I just kept talking to him, but he was begging for pain relief. I kept thinking, 'Let's get him there fast,' because I didn't expect him to live. The journey seemed for ever. But we got him to Belfast and I had to leave him there. I never thought I'd ever see him back in the Parachute Regiment – but he is.

CONCLUSIONS

Sergeant, 2nd Battalion
All of Ireland is cold, tired, piss-wet through, and knackered; that is Ireland summed up.

Corporal, 3rd Battalion
Northern Ireland is a good experience for somebody who's young and just come out of the depot. It puts them into reality, puts everything into perspective. The majority of recruits go to Ireland, do a little bit, come back and they're a bit more mature. Instead of having a fight in Aldershot on a Saturday night they have a real fight out there, and when they've done it, they don't have to prove themselves. Ireland is not for everybody, I know that, but it is an experience I wouldn't have missed. I wouldn't join the Army just to go there, but it is something I'm glad I did.

Sergeant, 2nd Battalion
You get 19-year-old lads going to Ireland and in those four months they gain ten years, ten years I'd say.

Sergeant, 3rd Battalion
I'd sooner go back to the Falklands tomorrow morning than Northern Ireland. I suppose I was more likely to be killed in the Falklands because of the amount of ammunition fired, but I feel safer in a conventional war than walking about the streets of Belfast like a figure eleven target. Many times in

the Falklands my life was in my own hands, but in Northern Ireland I'm afraid it isn't, no matter how good your skills are, because without a doubt they're the best terrorists in the world, without a shadow of a doubt. You can be talking to a bloke one minute, and the next minute he can be shooting you.

Major, 1st Battalion
The military campaign will end because politically the Catholics will see that there is light at the end of the tunnel, and the Protestants will have to come to terms with the fact that they could survive pretty well when that light comes. Somebody said that in about 2030 there will be more Catholic voters than Protestant, and they will be able to vote themselves out of the United Kingdom.

Private, 1st Battalion
When the Falklands blew up we were extremely pissed off, because we were stuck patrolling bogs in Fermanagh and not down south amongst it with the rest of the regiment. All we could do was watch the TV, every newscast that came through. We were hanging on every word.

CHAPTER TWENTY-THREE

THE FALKLANDS
Operation Corporate

1982

O N 2 APRIL 1982 ARGENTINA INVADED PORT STANLEY, THE capital of the Falkland Islands Dependencies. With only about 80 marines for defence, the islands and South Georgia were quickly overrun. A British Task Force was rapidly gathered to retake the islands. At this time the 3rd Battalion were the spearhead battalion and they were attached to 3 Commando Brigade Royal Marines, leaving the UK on 9 April on SS *Canberra*. The 2nd Battalion were also stood to and departed on 26 April on MV *Norland*. During the long voyage south, both battalions carried out intensive training.

On the night of 21 May 3 Commando Brigade Royal Marines went ashore at Ajax Bay. The 2nd Battalion established itself on Sussex Mountain, protecting the south of the bridgehead without opposition, and the 3rd Battalion landed in the north near Port San Carlos. On 26 May, the 2nd Battalion were ordered to move south and engage the Argentinians on the Darwin/Goose Green Peninsula. The attack began during the early hours of 28 May with naval and artillery support. At daylight, however, it was held up by strong enemy defensive positions near Darwin and the CO and adjutant were killed trying to take out a machine-gun post. The assault continued and by last light the whole peninsula, less the Goose Green Settlement, was taken. Negotiations with the Argentinians produced their surrender the next day. Over 1,250 prisoners were taken and 256 Argentinians killed.

Mount Longdon was attacked by the 3rd Battalion during the night of 11 June. The enemy were well dug-in and prepared and it was only after ten hours of fighting that the 3rd Battalion secured the objective. They then held it for 48 hours under intense and accurate artillery fire.

GOOSE GREEN: 2 PARA 28/9 MAY 1982

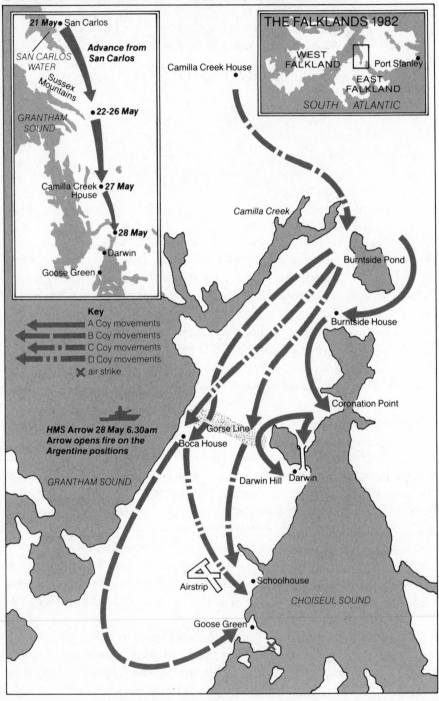

21 May ● San Carlos

SAN CARLOS WATER

Advance from San Carlos

Sussex Mountains

GRANTHAM SOUND

● **22-26 May**

Camilla Creek ● **27 May**
House

● **28 May**

● Darwin

Goose Green ●

THE FALKLANDS 1982

WEST FALKLAND

Port Stanley ●

EAST FALKLAND

SOUTH ATLANTIC

Camilla Creek House ●

Camilla Creek

Burntside Pond ●

Burntside House ●

Key

A Coy movements
B Coy movements
C Coy movements
D Coy movements
✕ air strike

HMS Arrow 28 May 6.30am
Arrow *opens fire on the Argentine positions*

GRANTHAM SOUND

Coronation Point ●

Gorse Line

Boca House ●

Darwin Hill Darwin ●

Airstrip

● Schoolhouse

CHOISEUL SOUND

Goose Green ●

On the night of 13 June the 2nd Battalion passed behind the 3rd Battalion and attacked Wireless Ridge. This again was secured by first light and shortly afterwards the enemy resistance collapsed. Both battalions followed up and were the first troops to enter Port Stanley. In all, the two battalions suffered 40 dead and 93 injured.

MAJOR JOHN CROSLAND, 2nd Battalion

After we had been on the *Norland* for four or five days I got the toms together and told them what my thoughts were, that we were going to war! The reason I felt that was that Margaret, who is a very determined lady, had set the ground rules very early on. She had said she wouldn't negotiate until the Argentinians had left, and having been involved in the Iranian Embassy siege in London in 1980 I knew her thinking because she'd set the ground rules there.

We had about three weeks before landing in which we could concentrate on one solid objective – training for war. We'd never had a period like this since Borneo, which was 14 years ago. I could really concentrate the toms' minds because there were no outside imbuggerancies like duties and guards and everything else.

Fortunately, I'd given a lot of thought to the psychological preparation and battlefield stress, based around Lord Moran's book, *The Anatomy of Courage*. I'd also had previous experience in Northern Ireland and with the SAS in Oman.

Northern Ireland has its very violent periods and some prolonged operations but none with the full orchestration of war. There were shooting engagements but you can't compare those to a full-scale battle. The toms in my company hadn't heard the noise of a sustained battle or felt the intense loneliness and fear that results from such an experience. I was fortunate to have had that experience, so spent a lot of time talking to my company, to the officers and NCOs, taking them through a scenario which was to prove close to the reality of the battles that were to come.

The one thing I had to impress on my soldiers was that the Northern Ireland image of a casualty halting an operation wasn't going to happen in the Falklands. We had an objective to take, so whoever got bowled over had to administer their own first aid and look after themselves. Then once we'd secured our objective, we'd come back and sort out the casualties. So, for ten days, the highly professional medical people in the FSTs (Field Surgical Teams) put the toms through an intensive medical cadre on life-saving, first aid, gunshot wounds, tears, rips, and all the rest of it. At the end of it, they could take blood, put in drips and repair all manner of wounds very efficiently. Because I'd instilled in them that we were going to war, they didn't play at it – they were totally committed. This was going to be the most frightening thing they had ever come across in their lives but they'd have to get over that and get on and do their job. In their training, I'd tried to instil in them the need to be aggressive, because I don't think people understand the amount of violence that's got to be generated to impress your point of view on somebody who's equally keen to impress his view on you.

The opposition would be a regular army with conscripts, so if we made our presence felt initially, they might just crack. This proved correct, because at Goose Green we not only beat them physically but psychologic-ally. So from then on (although there were severe battles in the mountains), they never counter-attacked, yet they had the troops, ammunition and logistics. In the first encounter at Goose Green, we'd given them what's called a classic Parachute Regiment punch-up – a gutter fight – but then our blokes are bloody good at that, probably the best in the world. Some of the rumours about the Argentinians being ill-equipped, underfed and lacking ammunition were just not true. I mean, our blokes were amazed at what we found around the place. With our calibre of blokes in those positions, it would have been Crete all over again and we would have wiped anyone out.

We landed on 21 May, and had five or six days of bad weather until we moved off from Sussex Mountains towards Goose Green. Our first scheduled attack on Goose Green was cancelled. We moved off again on the 26/27th towards Camilla Creek House. On that march down, which was a four- or five-hour trog, we were carrying a lot of weight on our backs, but at least the toms were on the move. There were various shell holes on the way and I remember some of the younger ones asking what they were. I said, 'Well, they're not moles!' I then asked them what they thought they were; artillery or what? What I was trying to get them to do was to look for signs. I'd seen shell holes before and pointed out some that were fresh and had obviously been made that night because there was ice on the others. The blokes then started to become attuned to what to look for and what the signs meant. I also told them to listen carefully so they would tune their ears to the incoming artillery fire. They could hear the guns firing and the whistle and they were all going down a bit bloody quick. So I explained that the shots that they'd just heard were well over to our east, but it was the first time they'd heard it and as it was coming vaguely towards them, they were obviously very wary. So I really had to orchestrate their ears.

The one thing I stressed was, 'You will get artillery and mortar fire against you but you've got to maintain your momentum – I may not be there, you may lose your section commanders or senior soldiers but someone's got to keep it going, that's what it's all about, you may be on your own, isolated and feeling afraid but you must keep thinking, because if you don't think you'll get killed.

We stayed at Camilla Creek House for a while. While we were there a breach of security happened when, for some inexplicable reason, the BBC World Service told the world and his wife where we were. That involved 400 of the enemy flown in and positions being turned round to meet our likely advance. A fairly stressful time, especially as H. (Lieutenant Colonel H. Jones) had already told us that we were going into action against odds of two to one; these were already sporting odds so we didn't need them increased!

We were fairly well forward of our own defensive position and well in range of enemy artillery and their air recce, facing a garrison which was fairly well equipped. H. gave an O Group and I got back to give my orders just after last light. I sat facing my company O Group, three young platoon commanders: the eldest could only have been in the army for a year and a bit, and the youngest had only been with me since January of that year, so for them it was a big occasion. My three platoon sergeants were not that experienced either, so it was not the best time to start giving out orders or talking about hundreds of the enemy. But one had to be fairly blunt about things, and enforce one's own personality on the orders' performance. I told them that the training we had done before was all part of the great maxim that in peace we were training for war. We had trained aggressively and realistically and now we were at war.

I went through our battle plan of what I wanted them to do: how we were going to get on with it; how they would do their job in controlling their platoons and sections; how I would keep the direction with the forward observation officer. I then talked about keeping the supporting fire moving ahead, casualty procedure and prisoners of war. We'd been put on the west side to blockbust down towards Boca House. H.'s plan was for a six-phase day/night or night/day silent/noisy attack. H. knew well that B Company was a fairly aggressive company because that's the way I had trained them and they had confidence in their own ability. I knew that we'd been put on a side that had a fair amount of problems. So we knew we were in for a hard slog and that time was precious. I told them that we must get on, that we were not interested in capturing hundreds of dagos, someone else could do that. What I wanted to do was go through position after position after position and keep battering away at them. Finally, I said to them, 'These people have nicked our islands – we're going to make them wish they had never heard of the Falkland Islands.'

Later we moved to the forming-up point at the neck of the isthmus leading down to Goose Green. A Company had to swing round to the east in order to take out Burntside House before the whole battalion could move straight down. If we hadn't done that we would have been hitting one another with crossfire. So we moved into position and just lay down in our assault formations. The blokes lit cigarettes and we listened to the night noises of HMS *Arrow* which was firing away, but unfortunately a mechanical problem nullified her very impressive fire support which later we were to rue.

A Company started to make their attack and although there were shells coming over, they caused little problems. Slowly my lads started to get attuned, but there was a tension around because we knew from our own patrols that facing us, about 400 or 500 yards away, there was an enemy company defensive position with a machine-gun.

In support for the attack we had three light guns based at Camilla Creek House which were firing ahead of us. We only had very limited helicopter lift to come forward with the small amount of ammunition that we had. The support boys carried forward two mortars with ammunition. A normal battalion would have six or eight, but we only had two. However, we did have six detachments of Milans and we also had six heavy machine-guns. We had, of course, expected HMS *Arrow* to be the main thrust of our artillery attack.

It was such an awful night in terms of the weather that one of our problems was actually being able to see what we were coming into. Although it was dark, raining and even snowing at times, the toms got accustomed to it. At least they'd had some experience of night fighting during the previous November whilst carrying out exercises in Kenya.

The one thing I'd learnt in the Middle East was to keep the momentum going – if you stopped on a position, you got hammered. So all through the night we kept crashing on. Their artillery, which was generally well orchestrated, had a job to find us. When we did stop, because we got disorganized or came across a position we didn't know about, the enemy rearranged their artillery to fire back on us. What saved us in these situations was that the ground was very soft and a lot of shells ploughed in or blew up the peat. If it had been a very hard surface, I think the casualties on both sides would have been far worse.

The company killed its first Argentinian about three minutes after the start. This thing actually arose from a trench, in a helmet and poncho; there was no face, just a helmet and poncho. We challenged him twice and nothing happened. The third time, his hands moved and two of my machine-gunners and two riflemen opened up and, rather naturally, this bloke fell over. So that was a release of tension; we knew our weapons worked. As they say in the vernacular, 'Targets scream when hit.' Like the first punch from a boxer or the first run for a batsman, we'd played it and hit home.

That night, in the aggressive trench-to-trench action, we had them all over the place, and we didn't sustain any casualties in my company. We had to fight at really close quarters for four or five hours which showed our soldiers' durability and stamina; certainly their aggressive, hard training paid off. I think we had, without blowing one's own trumpet, the most problems to overcome, but we kept moving in a classic formation of two platoons up and one platoon back. A Company was on our left and we couldn't link in with them, so it wasn't a classic two-company move which we achieved later at Wireless Ridge. Many of the actions were led by young NCOs, senior soldiers and young soldiers. I think the little black woollen hat that I wore throughout the campaign helped the toms to identify me and I'm sure they thought, 'If that stupid bugger's still running around with that hat on, it can't be that bad.'

Come the dawn we were out of the driving seat. We'd come up against the main defence position which was the ridge of Darwin Hill in the east and we were still about 800 metres short of Boca House which we'd expected to take in one run that night. We'd lost two hours of darkness due to D Company having a punch-up behind us, and we'd also hit another position which had taken 45 minutes to clear. These things happen in battle. The only thing to do was to move forward, so I ordered the two leading platoons, 4 and 6, to move ahead with Company HQ into the gully in front of Boca House. We then started to fight our way down this gully into the bottom and up the other side towards a sort of gorse line which gave some cover from the enemy's fairly dominant position at Boca House. As the light increased, so did the accuracy of their fire. I had two options, either withdraw completely or get forward. I certainly wasn't going to withdraw so I ordered my two forward platoons ahead with my own HQ. I left my reserve, 5 Platoon, on the crest line to protect the whole of the high ground in case we had to beat a hasty retreat; it was that platoon that took a battering. We also got fairly well larded with artillery and mortars. I said to 5 Platoon over the net, 'Right, once we get down into the gully you withdraw onto the hill line and just hold the ridge-line position.' It was during this action we lost young Stephen Illingsworth. He had rescued Private Hall, who had been shot, and then, because we were short of ammunition, had gone back for Hall's kit and while doing this was killed. It was a classic young soldier's act, extremely brave, totally unselfish, and one can only give the highest praise for him.

A little later there was a pause in the action as each side tried to sum up its own situation. During this period the toms were able to see the devastation we'd created through the night because we were not standing in the positions we'd taken out. We could see the effects of artillery fire, mortars, grenades and our own handiwork. In this lull, a mortar bomb came through the air, spinning rather badly, hit the crest line and very seriously wounded my second-in-command, Captain John Young.

We were under increasing pressure because we'd been in action for four hours during the night without resupply. About 400 or 500 yards in front of us, across a totally open field, was a very strong enemy position. They were in the driving seat and could put down artillery, air attack or mortar fire whenever they wanted. Although we were putting down fire onto their positions and hitting their bunkers, we weren't actually killing the blokes inside. So I said, 'Cool the fire.' I just kept one machine-gun going because at the back of my mind was the thought that they could counter-attack. We were in a fairly tenuous position because toms were trying to hide behind gorse bushes which, needless to say, hardly provided adequate cover.

The situation changed when Corporal Margerison managed to clear a bunker and Corporal Robinson's lot flattened another. Robinson had a lucky escape when a bullet just missed his balls. All I could hear him saying was, 'If you've hit me in the balls, the wife'll kill me.' But once he'd ascertained he'd still got a pair, he was all right.

I then took command of directing our guns and mortars onto the positions that were giving us problems. To my simple brain, what's hurting you at the moment has got to be eradicated. You worry about positions at Goose Green once you get to Goose Green. It was during this period that I heard that H. was killed. When the news came over the net, I said to Corporal Russell, my signalman, 'That doesn't go any further. We've got enough problems without letting that out.' I was close to H. – we thought along the same sort of lines. His death certainly stiffened my resolve. I mean, I was always determined that we were going to win, but his death just added a bit more oomph.

Shortly after the news of H.'s death I heard that the Argentinians had landed another 200 people to our south; we were in for trouble. I thought of John Frost's A Bridge Too Far and I said to myself, 'We've gone an island too far.' We needed to strike again. Boca House was our major objective but with the weapons that we had, we couldn't get effective fire onto it, so I called up the Milan team. A Milan is an anti-tank weapon which fires a guided missile with a very substantial warhead over a range of 2,000 metres. I thought, if we can bust them with the Milans, we can probably get round their flank, get down to Darwin, knock that off and then worry about Goose Green. The Milan was an unorthodox choice, but it was the only powerful weapon we had. Much to our relief, the first round fired was a perfect bull's-eye. It went straight through the bunker window and blew it out completely, and the second one did the same. Four more rounds and that was Boca House cleared out. Everyone stood and cheered!

A Company achieved a breakthrough in their own right and cleared Darwin Hill. Chris Keeble had taken over command by then and sent D Company off to start attacking Goose Green. We then started to come under fairly intense fire from Goose Green and the airfield. Their anti-aircraft guns had very good optics so they could see us at about a mile and a half's distance. Chris Keeble had been calling for an air strike all day but weather conditions were bad. However, at last light, the Harriers came and I would say their effect was critical. They came in on a low pass and dropped cluster bombs, inflicting a lot of casualties. It was a surgical strike, very precise, and I think this undermined their will to keep fighting.

Prior to the aerial attack we had continued towards Goose Green with D and C Companies. A Company remained on Darwin Hill. We'd heard that there were 112 civilians being held in Goose Green so our idea of going in and flattening the area was out of the question. I said to Chris Keeble that I would swing down the isthmus itself and come in from the south. I'd been looking at the map and seen there were a couple of streams and realized if we could get round and come in from the south, they would feel they were encircled. So psychologically the whole thing really shifted to our advantage; we'd broken the crust, they had no escape. However, their anti-aircraft guns were still extremely intense. I remember telling the two leading platoon commanders that I wanted to get to where we could see the tracers in the sky. I'm sure one or two of them thought, 'J.C.'s deaf or daft, or both.' I told them that we were going to go underneath the trajectory and, although there was a lot of fire, we had a fairly reasonable passage and got through only to realize later that we had been walking through a minefield!

We had to try and neutralize their anti-aircraft guns; some were forward and some were on the promontory of Goose Green. They had their guns in amongst the buildings and were going to be difficult to shift. When we arrived within 300 or 400 yards to the south of Goose Green, we engaged them with machine-guns and they returned very fierce fire. We then heard that six helicopters had landed to my south with reinforcements but we managed to get a few rounds of mortar ammunition, one of which landed right on top of them and dispersed them. There was still the thought in the back of my mind that there were 100 or 200 blokes who had been landed fresh and could catch us with a possible counter-attack. So, after the Harrier attack, I gathered everyone together and told them to go and scrounge all the ammunition they could find. They went off and plundered everything and carried back about 7,000 or 8,000 Argentinian rounds, which fortunately were the same calibre as ours.

I told the lads to go firm, to get into fours, dig in, and then we'd have to wait and see. I don't think anyone knew quite how far round we were so we withdrew that night and dug in to a tight defensive position around a hill. It was a very long, cold night – it snowed and froze very hard. But the toms were very good indeed considering they'd been on their feet fighting for 24 hours. They'd had a bit of a baptism and they'd come through very well. The news had filtered through during the day that we'd lost H. I gave them a sort of Winston Churchill pull up. I said, 'Look we've done bloody well today. Okay, we've lost some lads; we've lost the CO. Now we've really got to show our mettle. It's not over yet, we haven't got the place. We're about 1,000 metres from D Company; we're on our own and an enemy has landed to our south and there's a considerable force at Goose Green, so we could be in a fairly sticky position.'

While we lay there two guys in a hole received virtually a direct hit but fortunately it had gone into the peat. It hadn't wounded them, but it had blasted them, and they were shaken. I shouted to them to come back to the Company HQ and have a cup of tea. It was just what they needed; to get back into the main body and have a cup of tea and a cigarette. You could see the relief on their faces.

We were really set to go in for the last push but that wasn't necessary because the following morning the surrender negotiations had started – 2 Para had captured two senior Argentinian NCOs. Chris Keeble explained his terms of surrender and sent them off to talk to their garrison commander. Eventually they accepted Chris's terms.

After the surrender we were told to stay firm and dig in where we were on the high ground. Later, I went into Goose Green and was pleased to meet some of the very relieved civilians, who had been released. The casualty-clearing process then started. We swept the battlefield trying to get all the Argentinian casualties in and their bodies tidied up. Their officers appeared to have little interest and an extremely vague knowledge of how many men they had. We just lined the enemy bodies up against a hedge; there was nothing else we could do. Our padre, David Cooper, had the task of attempting to organize some kind of burial for them, with little help from the Argentinians.

We then flew to Ajax Bay for what we'd assumed was a memorial service for H. and the others. When we arrived, there was a hole dug ready to receive 18 burial bags and a lot of people gathered round, saying their last farewells. We'd understood that the bodies of those killed would be repatriated. Yet here we were burying them. We didn't know what the hell was going on and a lot of people were, naturally, very upset. The company commanders acted as bearers for H. and for the adjutant David Wood, Chris Dent and Jim Barry. The toms under Regimental Sergeant Major Simpson, who had flown down with us, were the bearers for the other toms.

The first time I had a moment of quietness, I sat down and wrote to the parents of Stephen Illingsworth and told them of his great gallantry. I also wrote to Sarah Jones about H. I hoped these letters would bring them some comfort. I felt responsible for Illingsworth. I don't mean that in a trite sort of way. I was his boss and basically he'd been killed working for me. I also wrote to Cathy Dent, whose husband Chris had been killed in A Company's action on Darwin Hill. I then asked the NCOs and officers to put down on paper the names of those they thought deserved some kind of award.

Things were good within our little group but I was very keen that now we had finished at Goose Green, the company got some rest.

Having called a nearby farm from a local telephone to ascertain if it was clear of Argentinians, we moved on to Fitzroy. The six days we were there were interesting because there was a slight feeling of 'You've done your bit, 2 Para – you can stand back now', which was very dangerous. My message to my toms was quite simple: 'You can stand down when you get to Ascension Island on the way back because that's when it's finished. Drop your guard now and you will get one straight on the chin.' So we set about improving our positions and making ourselves comfortable.

Naturally, they were tired. After all, we'd been in a fairly major fracas for 36 hours and we'd lost 18 men and had 38 wounded. In *The Anatomy of Courage* Lord Moran talks about the 'bank of courage'. Our reserve had been pretty drained; it needed to be replenished, banked up. The next seven days were going to be a useful recuperation phase. After 24 hours we began preparing for other tasks. This kept the element of tension up sufficiently and didn't allow the toms to think too much about their experiences.

It was a great responsibility and also a great privilege to lead such high-calibre blokes. If you have the privilege of commanding such men, then the battle is half won before you start. So I think it behoves you to try and think things out before, because there's no doubt that they are looking to you. I say this humbly, without meaning to sound pompous, but I think that within the battalion, I was the barometer. People knew that I'd had a lot of experience and therefore they were looking at me to see if there was any shake. If there was, then things could have been serious. We had a very good team led by H. and I think the toms knew that such a team thought conscientiously about problems and wouldn't commit them to something that they had no control over. People have said, 'Well, why the hell did you go to Goose Green?' And the answer to that is that the toms were keen to get at the enemy and attack them. It's a great privilege to have people of that nature ready to follow you.

SERGEANT JOHN MEREDITH, 2nd Battalion

I moved down with D Company from Sussex Mountain to our objective Camilla Creek House. The artillery had fired on the area around the house and there had been no response from the Argies. So 10 and 11 Platoons went in and searched the house and found it empty. As it was the only house around, every company decided that they wanted to get their men in, which caused a bit of chaos. The next day, the World Service told its listeners exactly where we were which obviously upset Colonel Jones and really pissed us off. We were then briefed by our company commander, Major Phil Neame, as to what the plan of attack was on Goose Green. As we began to prepare ourselves for that, from out of nowhere a blue and white Land-Rover carrying four Argentinians came on the horizon. A patrol of C Company opened fire, wounded two of them and brought the rest in. These were the first Argies we'd seen. They were interrogated by Captain Bell of the Marines who spoke Spanish and he got some information from them. We'd been given a piece of paper on the ship with Spanish phrases suitable for Benidorm on it – like 'hands up' – but it was all double-Dutch to me. We worked it out that if we pointed a rifle at them or stabbed them with a bayonet they'd stick their hands up anyway. We moved off that night, but a lot of people weren't happy with the artillery support we were going to get. We could only use two of the battalion's mortars because we didn't have enough ammunition to keep the six of them going. We'd taken a whole artillery battery down there with us but they'd taken them away and given us three guns from another battery as support. So, we had three guns and two mortars instead of a full mortar platoon and a battery of guns.

As we moved off down across the creek, A Company was to go over Burntside House and B Company was to swing forward to the right, and we were in reserve at the rear. There was a navigational error on the way down, so we ended somewhere in front of Colonel Jones which didn't please him. Major Neame realized the mistake and told everybody to come back on to line. When we were in position, ready to go, A Company then went up to Burntside House. They opened up on it; luckily they didn't hit any of the three civilians in there. Then B Company went and did their attack on the right and had trouble from fire coming from their left-hand side as they were advancing. Colonel Jones realized that A Company were having to reorganize so he pushed us through and we cleared a position in the centre. We took out about a dozen trenches in front of us and then went firm. Unfortunately, in this move 10 Platoon ended up with two killed, and 11 Platoon, who should have been on our left, crossed over behind us and went in on the right as well and had one killed and one injured.

One of my sections became split up from us and I had to go back and try and find them but I couldn't. As I was moving back in, coming up a fence line to my right I could see four helmets moving. I asked the second-in-command if we had anybody forward on my right and he said, 'No.' We put a mini-flare up and these four Argentinians stood up so we wallied them. We went firm around the trenches that we'd cleared.

B Company had sorted out their problems so the CO decided to revert to the original plan, which meant that A and B would go forward to carry on the attack, and we had to sit it out. By then it had become daylight. A Company then got caught up at Darwin, and B Company was starting to get caught up at Boca House, so Major Neame decided to move forward. Behind us we could see Argentinians coming out of trenches and moving along the beach, which was a bit worrying, so we just opened up on them with the GPMGs and wiped out quite a few. Again, owing to sniper and artillery fire, Major Neame moved up forward behind the ridge that B Company was on which sheltered us from the shelling. While we were waiting there we had another lad named Mechan killed.

We sat there and the OC passed the word to brew up. It was then we were told that the Colonel was injured. Major Crosland and Major Neame had a confab, because B Company had one of their platoons in a very exposed position. They brought the Milan up and attacked Boca House. Before we started our next move to the beach the Argentinians began to surrender. There were white flags so we started to go in, but were stopped. I think Major Keeble, who'd taken over, had decided that B Company needed a supply of ammunition before we could move.

After waiting a bit we went forward through a shallow valley going towards the Argentinian position that appeared to have surrendered. Ahead of us was a minefield with anti-tank mines below the surface; they had orange cord tied between each mine to act as trip-wires. I told the lads to watch the cord while we were moving through. Then suddenly there was a great bloody bang and the next minute we were lying on the ground with our ears ringing. As I got myself together and looked round there was one of my lads, Spencer, with this cord on his foot saying, 'It wasn't me, it wasn't me!' Somebody came running over and said, 'Get him out.' I said, 'Leave him in the bloody minefield, he tripped it.' He was all right, just bowled over. I wasn't very happy with him at all, and so we left him there. There was another little Irish lad attached to us, who'd also been knocked over and was groaning a bit. One of the other blokes said, 'There's nothing wrong with you,' and he got a boot for his pains! We then moved up towards the Argentinians who had surrendered. We gave first aid to their injured, some of whom were badly hurt. We got them out of the trenches and laid them there but they were obviously going to die. We then dealt with our own casualties and left a section to look after the prisoners.

Major Neame then pushed us straight on towards the schoolhouse at Goose Green and 11 Platoon opened fire on the little house first. The trouble was, they used 66s (anti-tank rockets) and phosphorus grenades which caused a fire, which didn't give them very much cover. Then our C Company came down, ready to go in. My platoon were tasked to go up the track and give covering fire on the schoolhouse and also cover behind it to get anybody that tried to withdraw. The plan was to bottle them in there.

One of the rear sections saw some white flags waving near the airfield and he reported this to our platoon commander, Mr Barry, who said to me, 'I'll go forward and take the surrender, you look after these two sections.' So I moved to where I could control both sections and see what was going on. I told the radio operator so that he could get into contact with the company commander about what was happening.

Mr Barry went over the rise with his men and I watched them move towards two Argentinians who had come forward with their hands in the air. The others were sitting behind them on the floor with their hands up. Because I had to watch my own section I had to keep my eyes in both directions as I was a bit concerned about Mr Barry going forward. I saw him talking to two Argentinians, who seemed to be worried about the firing still going on at the schoolhouse. Then, for some reason, Mr Barry put his rifle against a fence. Suddenly a burst of fire, probably from someone who wasn't aware that a surrender was taking place, came whistling over the top. The Argentinians who'd been sitting there reacted immediately by picking up their weapons and firing. Mr Barry was killed instantly. Knight, the radio operator, killed two with his SMG but Corporal Smith, who was trying to give covering fire with a 66 and Corporal Sullivan were also killed. Shevill was wounded in the shoulder and the hip. There was now an awful lot of firing going on.

As the senior man there I was doing the chasing about. I saw some of my lads hit the deck because of the volume of fire that was coming our way, but I got a grip on them, got them up and firing. I was covering a lot of ground, but that's my job, that's what I'm paid for. I got across another section and picked up a machine-gun and knocked off three Argies with a couple of bursts each. Then, as I moved again, I took out two more. We moved forward and took their position and dealt with Shevill who was badly hurt. He crawled back into cover and so did Roach, who shouted that he thought that he'd been hit. I shouted back that he would know if he'd been hit! But he'd only had the arse shot out of his trousers. Roach, with the help of Wilson, then gave first aid to Shevill while still under heavy fire. Unfortunately we couldn't get him out for five hours.

There were so many sensations at that time that I had to think fast and hard because everything was changing from second to second – there were rounds going everywhere. I didn't have time to be frightened. When Mr Barry was killed there was a lot of anger; the thing was, to kill them. So for each one I knocked down, I thought, 'Well, that's another.' The thing was to kill them as fast as we could, it was just whack, whack, and the more I knocked down the easier it became, the easier the feeling was – I was paying them back. The feeling was anger, a mixture of both anger and sadness – sadness that three good blokes should die that way.

Then as we reorganized we were told that there would be a Harrier strike coming in, three friendly aircraft from the north. But the next minute we got strafed by enemy aircraft coming in from the south! We had to get Shevill back, as he had taken off across a fence as soon as the strafing came to a close, with his trousers down around his knees and a saline drip hanging out of his backside. We obviously wanted to go forward to collect our dead, but we weren't allowed to. So we dug in, and stayed there all night.

They then attacked us with a Pucara that dropped napalm. It just missed the sergeant major's party with the prisoners and wounded. It also missed a big ammunition dump – so we were lucky. However, this napalm attack did the CSM some good as he had his first crap since the *Norland*. We shot the

Pucara down and captured the pilot. (He was one of the ones they sent in for the surrender, which they did the next day.)

We moved into Goose Green the next morning and dug in. I kept the lads working – most of them were all right but one or two were a bit shaken. I had one who was very shaken; it took us about three days to get him really back round. He was usually a cheerful lad, but he'd lost a couple of NCOs who'd looked after him and he'd taken it badly. So I kept him working. After Goose Green I felt that I had to look after those who were alive, rather than worry about people that had been killed. I wanted to get those that were alive performing properly, because we were out on a limb at Goose Green. But I was very pleased with the way the lads had behaved. I had mixed feelings about the battle but it felt good to have won. Then there was the shock of seeing all those hundreds of Argentinians at the surrender, I couldn't believe it. We'd attacked with a battalion, which was about 400 to 500 men, and they'd had 1,200. In the end we sent one platoon of 24 men in to guard them. I felt we'd won a strategic battle – if we'd by-passed Goose Green we'd have left 1,200 men there with a usable airfield, and that could have later been a big thorn in our side. They could have caused a lot of damage from there.

SERGEANT DAVE ABOLS, 2nd Battalion

We went towards Darwin for a dawn attack on Goose Green. As we advanced we stopped by a little inlet and a recce party went forward. It seemed all clear. Ahead of us there was a fence across our path: 2 Platoon got over it, but as my platoon got half way across the Argies opened up. Half of my blokes ran back to a bank and the rest of us ran forward. So I had lost control of my section. Luckily we found cover in a gorse bush area. Very soon 2 Platoon took out about three trenches that were in the area. They didn't have time to get orders, they just ran forward for a place of cover, and as they were running they noticed the trenches so they just took them out straight away; it was just instinct – what they were trained for. When we got to the gorse it was all burning from the phosphorus grenades, burning the cover that we needed. Everything was on fire and it seemed everyone else had lost control because there were men split up all over the place.

I pushed on through and joined up with two other section commanders, so we stuck together, us three. We had one or two toms with us, so we just went on using common sense, trying to find out what was going on, and where the shooting was coming from. We went up the side of the little gully, took cover, and as we did so we could see rounds landing in front of us. There was a sniper after us. We doubled forward to a bank. In front we saw two blokes, Private Elliot and Private Worrall. They were the front part of 2 Platoon which had gone through. We shouted to them to get back – as they did so Worrall was hit in the stomach. So Stevie Prior and I went out to give him first aid. As soon as we got out there this sniper was after us. It was only about 40–50 metres back to the bank, but as we dragged Worrall I could hear the rounds whizzing past my ear. Both of us were saying, 'He's after you, no, shit, he's after me,' because he was so accurate; it took us about 20 minutes to get him back. There wasn't only the sniper, because when we left the bank it was about four feet high and now it was about two. They were firing anti-tank weapons at us, and at the bank because they knew we were getting covering fire from there and that we'd have to get over it.

We got him to about five metres from the bank. We said we'd count to three, drag him and drop him over. We got to three, went to jump, but his webbing got caught on the roots. So I said right, I'll go over, organize someone to give us cover fire and we'll get him off the root. I organized that and went back to tell Steve. But I had forgotten to ask for some sort of signal, so I had to crawl back again and tell them that when I threw the smoke that was their signal to open fire. Throughout all this the sniper was still after us and Steve and Worrall were out there in the open, very exposed. I got back to them and told Steve that we were going to have to move as soon as I threw the smoke. But Worrall's webbing was still stuck, so by the time we got it off the smoke had run out and so had the covering fire. But we were still out there. So we said, 'Bollocks, count to three and we'll go.' We got hold of him, got to three then, bang, the sniper got Steve right in the back of the head. He fell on top of Worrall. One look at him and I knew he was dead. So I jumped back across the bank and told Corporal Hardman and Lance Corporal Gilbert to come up and give me a hand. We got both of them over so fast that I can't even remember how we did it. We gave Worrall some morphine even though he had a stomach wound, just to stop the pain, and got him back down the bottom of the hill. We just needed a rest then and a few ciggies and that.

We then started to organize ourselves. I was with Farrar-Hockley, the 2 i/c and about four others so we made our way to the top of the hill where ahead we could see ten or eleven trenches. We said, no chance, not unless we did a company frontal assault could we take them on. We came back down, reorganized ourselves and went back up again but each time we went up this hill we were losing blokes. I lost Corporal Hardman, shot in the head; we think that was the sniper again. Captain Dent was shot and fell back on his radio. Then another time I lost my number two on the gun. Farrar-Hockley was nearest the gun so I said, 'You'll have to go number two.' He knew the crunch was on and he wasn't going to say no.

When we got back, the CO, H. Jones, came over and started having a go at us. His actual words were, 'Come on A Company, get your skirt off', and I felt like telling him what we'd been through because we must have lost at least five blokes. At one stage there was just me and Corporal Toole up there with two 66s, trying to fire them at the trenches, that's two blokes out of a whole company.

We tried to show the Colonel; this time with the sergeant major and the CO and everyone that was there, we all went up this slow round hill yet again. When we got to the top he went round to the right moving up forward of the gully. We saw the Argentinians open fire on the side which we hadn't seen before. H. went down and the next minute everybody automatically opened up all at once at all the trenches. There must have been about 17 of them. Then there was a sudden lull, and we began to shout to the Argies to come out of the trenches. One of our blokes could speak Spanish, he tried that but they wouldn't come out. They started firing again. Our sergeant major fired a 66 at what he thought was a command trench but it just went above it. So I fired a 66 at the same trench, hit it on the parapet and obviously got the bloke who was inside, because straight after that they stopped firing completely. They jumped out of the trenches and started running towards us, surrendering straight away, so it must have been the command trench.

We got forward and tried to give the CO first aid. He was in a bad way. I left him with the sergeant major and others to deal with the casualties and went to search the prisoners and clear the trenches. The next minute these two fellas were on the skyline coming forward, obviously going to give themselves up. I shouted to them to raise their hands but they couldn't understand me. So I said to my gun controller, Jerry, 'I'll go half-way and then I'll get down and wait for them to come forward; if they move their hands, open up.' I was about a quarter of the way towards them when Jerry noticed them raising their hands or weapons either to shoot or to put their hands in the air. He wasn't sure so he told the gunner to open up and he cut them down. We got up to them and we found that one of them was the sniper. He had an American-made sight on a Chinese weapon with little hand-made silver rounds. When we got back after sending all the prisoners down we heard the Colonel was dead. We reorganized ourselves, cleared up, got fresh stuff and that and then we waited there.

MAJOR CHRISTOPHER KEEBLE, 2nd Battalion

Lieutenant Colonel H. Jones was the inspiration for making it happen in 2 Para. The way the unit was constructed, its morale, the training with the emphasis on speed and the offence stemmed from him. I found my relationship with H. extremely straightforward and, of course, because of the nature of the man, very demanding – as indeed did the company commanders.

We were on leave prior to departure for the jungle in Belize, Central America, as the crisis blew up. Our sister battalion, 3 Para, had been selected to embark with 3 Commando Brigade and it was felt that 2 Para should remain to fill the gap created by their departure. H., of course, was very impatient, as we watched the Task Force depart, and more so when our overseas tour to Belize was cancelled. Despite these developments, we did not stop planning for the possibility of war.

It was clear the Falklands could only be recaptured by attack. We therefore made it our business, in the few days we had, to acquire what additional weapons and equipment we needed to increase our potential for offence. We also spent much time studying the topography, the Argentinian armed forces and even working out how we could launch an airborne assault directly into Stanley; such was our enthusiasm to go! All this effort paid off when we heard we had been tasked to join 3 Commando Brigade at Ascension Island. We were to be the best jungle-trained battalion in the South Atlantic!

As soon as the battalion had been selected, H. left for Ascension Island to link up with the 3 Commando Brigade staff, leaving me in command. He said, 'Chris, train up the battalion and bring it down to me. I'll meet you at Ascension.' We then spent a week training in Aldershot, getting all the equipment we had planned to acquire, embarked the battalion on *Norland* and worked out a training programme for the remaining three weeks afloat. So I spent four weeks commanding 2 Para, a measure of the trust that existed between H. and me.

We had a meeting, as we departed, to plan the training priorities and programmes and devise the seamanship skills required to turn the *Norland* – a commercial ferry – into an amphibious platform. More importantly there were several weaknesses in 2 Para, which I had seen on Salisbury Plain and at a major field exercise in Norfolk in January. These had to be put right.

The first was our ability to deal with casualties. The existing principle was based on patching up the injured and withdrawing them to expert help well behind the battle. We quickly appreciated that movement, other than by helicopter, would be too slow for casualty survival and so we decided to concentrate on battlefield resuscitation, rather than simple first aid. In other words to prevent the onset of shock and sustain the injured for as long as possible at or near the site of wounding. This was put into operation by our young medical officer, Captain Steve Hughes, RAMC, who had researched the medical experiences of various campaigns, particularly those of the Israelis. I discussed with him, before we left, how we would achieve this objective and what additional medical resources we would need. As a result he acquired 1,000 drips for intravenous infusion to cope with blood loss and even bought a dummy forearm, veins and all, on which to practise. The idea was that we would distribute these IVs to each man, along with the more usual morphine, and shell dressings. A soldier would then have his own medical repair kit which either he or a combat medic could administer at the site of wounding. During the journey south, we taught everyone how to set up a drip either intravenously or through the rectum should the former not be possible. As a result of these measures, we were able to reduce the loss of life dramatically and sustain the casualties until evacuation could occur.

The whole point of war is to apply violence to break the enemy's will, not simply to destroy his weapons or his cities, but undermine his will to fight for what he believes in. Now, how do you reinforce that will in a body of people who've never been to war? This is where our padre, David Cooper, was so marvellous. He took each section (nine men), the smallest fighting unit in the battalion, and he sat down in front of them and said, 'Look, when we go on this battlefield, it's going to be bloody awful. Now, I don't know about you, but I'll tell you how I'm going to feel.' He attempted to penetrate that macho façade that soldiers build around themselves in order to reinforce their own inner resistance to fear. By voicing their own fears for them he got them to talk about how they would actually cope with the trauma of war. Being a padre, and to some extent apart from the military structure, he gave them the opportunity to share their emotions with each other which developed a 'spiritual' bond within the sections, which is so essential if people are going to work successfully together and, for the 2 Para team, to die for each other. It was a tremendous contribution.

In that week after the Goose Green battle there was a closeness between everybody – they were fused by fire. Very difficult to describe, but there was this tremendous brotherhood. It's a word used frequently by people who fought in World War II – the Brotherhood of Arnhem – and it is a brotherhood, too. War is a very emotional business, more than people realize. Much more than I'd ever anticipated and appreciated. I was enormously attracted to the Parachute Regiment because of this wonderful feeling of comradeship. We all have to go through a traumatic selection process, which weeds out a great number of people. We are united in our hardship, by what we have done. It is a very good way of preparing for the actual trauma of war. Soldiers do not fight for Queen and country, or even for Maggie – they fight for each other. But they need to know that their comrades would do the same. Selection produces that mutual trust.

I remember parachuting onto the Arnhem drop zone with our sister battalion, 10 Para, on their annual pilgrimage to the battlefield and the war cemetery. After the jump, we visited the Oosterbeek crossroads, the scene of fierce fighting on the outskirts of Arnhem, and we listened to one of the very few survivors of the battalion describing the battle around the junction. Someone in the audience asked the speaker, 'What made you go on fighting when the battalion had been largely destroyed, the cause lost and defeat inevitable?' He paused, looked across to the suburban junction and with tears brimming up in his eyes he said quietly and simply, 'They were my friends.' That's how it was for 2 Para. We had spent our peacetime training fusing the individuals into a team together. The fire of war merely tempered that process. We would never have given up. We would have fought to the last man rather than compromise the trust that existed between us.

When H. died the situation was really very simple. A Company's battle around Darwin in which H. lost his life trying to sort it out sounded a shambles and the ground favoured the defence there. There was little point in reinforcing failure. B Company with Johnny Crosland, on the other hand, was in a reasonable position, despite being part-caught on a forward slope down, and so I told him to assume command until I could get forward with Major Hector Gullan, the ubiquitous brigade liaison officer, who had a direct line to Brigadier Thompson. I also took with me my orderly room clerk, Corporal Kelly, who had been at my side throughout, to man the battalion radio link. As we left, the RSM, Mr Simpson, called me back, much to my irritation. 'What is it?' I asked sharply. He looked me in the eye and said, 'You are going to do fucking well, sir!' I felt a million dollars! A wonderful touch. He did terribly well in the battle, dealing with the whole procedure of accounting for the casualties, normally the adjutant's job. Very sadly, David Wood had also been killed on Darwin Hill with his CO.

The outcome of the battle was really achieved by the skill of Phil Neame's and Johnny Crosland's companies, D and B, reinforced by the Recce Platoon commanded by Roger Jenner. Subsequently, the devastating violence created by the Harriers who attacked the outskirts of the settlement at last light clinched it. It was at that moment, it seemed to me, that the will of the defence began to break. We, on the other hand, were very short of ammunition and so overnight I prepared two plans. I remember sitting in a gorse bush behind Darwin Hill that night and saying to A Company commander Dair Farrar-Hockley and others that the way to crack the problem was to walk down the hill the next day and tell the bloody Argies the game was up and defeat inevitable. Dair looked at me wearily as if I had lost my marbles! If that failed, well, we would reinforce and launch a massive assault with aircraft, artillery and infantry, and destroy the settlement. There was really no other option, since, not only had we little ammunition, we were all exhausted having been on the go for some 40 hours without sleep. In addition, and perhaps the most significant factor of all, there were 112 civilians locked up in the Community Hall in Goose Green! This fact was discovered overnight and re-emphasized the need to use more subtle means than the bayonet! After all, we had not journeyed 8,000 miles merely to destroy the very people we had come to save.

And so, standing in a small tin shed on the airfield next day, with Tony Rice, the battery commander, and our two bewildered journalists, Robert Fox and David Norris, we confronted the Argies with Plan A! It was clear that the three Argentinian commanders we negotiated with (Navy, Army and Air Force) had had enough. It became apparent later that one of the principal causes for this collapse of will was the breakdown of trust between officer and conscripted soldiers.

The surrender was arranged on a sports field outside Goose Green, close to the hidden position of D Company who had closed up on the settlement. It was a straightforward affair requiring the defenders to lay down their arms, which I allowed them to do with a degree of honour, to avoid the humiliation of defeat. About 150 assembled in a hollow square and, after singing their national anthem, the commander, an airman, saluted me and handed over his pistol. We were very concerned that we could not see any Argentine army personnel in the mass of defeated airmen. Some minutes later everything became clear as we watched about 1,000 soldiers marching up in files to surrender in the same way. It was an incredible sight. We held our breath hoping they wouldn't change their minds!

Victory came from H.'s leadership and the way he inspired the team and is a vivid example of Lord Slim's view that, 'Leadership is of the spirit compounded of personality and vision; its practice is an art.'

COMPANY SERGEANT MAJOR JOHN WEEKS, 3rd Battalion

3 Para waited five days before we got our orders for the attack on Mount

Longdon. We were told that there were 70 men on the hill and that ours would be a company silent night attack. I was surprised because the lesson we'd learnt from Goose Green was that no way should we ever do a silent attack. I thought we should stomp everything, but we didn't have artillery on call, because it was being used in the other battles. I got the company together and told them that some of them would not come off this hill. I'd been their company sergeant-major for two years. I'd like to think all of them were pretty close to me and I knew them well, but I knew some of them were going to die. I knew because I had a feeling that there was more on that bloody hill than 70 guys. I told them, 'It's going to be hand-to-hand fighting from trench to trench and it will be very, very slow and, believe you me, you can't visualize, lads, what it's going to be like, because it's going to be so slow and you're going to have things happen that you've never had before when we've been practising. You're going to have live things coming at you and exploding around you and it's going to confuse you. But you will do well. Now, if you have any thoughts, or if any of you believe in Christ, here's the time to sit down and have a little talk to Him. It's not stupid, because I'm certainly going away now to have a little prayer.' I think a load of them probably did pray. I'm not a religious person but having spoken to the guys afterwards, they all said that at some stage during that night they'd said a prayer. After that battle I sincerely believe that there is Someone who listens to us, but if your number's up, your number's up.

Then I went to speak to personal friends like Doc. Murdoch. It was new to him, so I said, 'Well, it's the same for me, Doc., because I've never done anything like this. But all we can do is give of our best.' You don't know how anyone is going to react in battle. You couldn't line up many people you've known for years and say, 'Well, he's going to be all right in battle,' because guys you wouldn't dream of are those that come up and shine, and the guys you thought would be brave are not very brave at all.

The battalion did a sort of follow-my-leader up to the start-line, where we split up to our fighting order. I was with B Company commander, Major Argue, and we were deployed to the rear of 4 and 5 Platoons; 6 Platoon was taking the opposite way up. We crossed the start-line on time. It was a very eerie, very quiet, cold night. We were going quite well towards the hill and were 500 metres short of the rock formation when Corporal Milne trod on a mine. That was the end of our silent night attack. It then became like Guy Fawkes night; I've never seen so many illuminations. I think most of the Argies must have been asleep. But what came at us was bad enough, so if they'd all been awake, they'd have wiped our two platoons off the face of

MOUNT LONGDON: 3 PARA 11/12 JUNE 1982

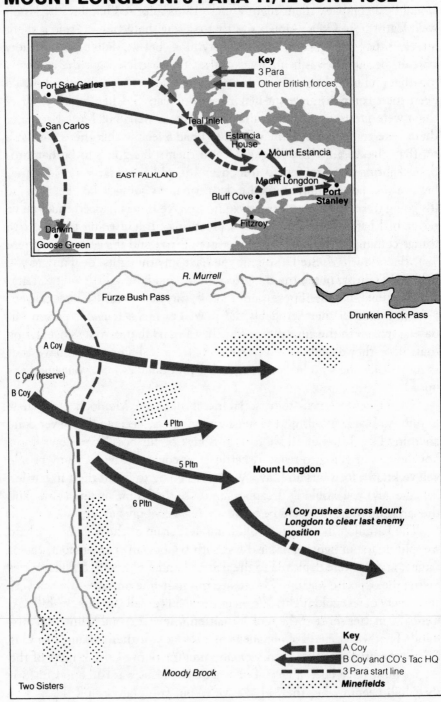

the mountain. For the next eleven hours it was unbelievable non-stop action.

Initially there was confusion. We branched off right and ran into the cover. Myself, Sergeant Pettinger and Captain McCracken, the gunnery officer, all got down into this rock division. The platoon commanders, on the radio, were telling us what was going on up front. You didn't need the brain of an archbishop to realize that 4 Platoon were involved in some considerable fighting, but there were no decisions being made from Company HQ at the time, because we were in limbo. I called to Major Argue, who told me to push forward and clear the way. Sergeant Pettinger and I then went forward rock by rock and cleared the position to make sure there was nobody there. Once we'd cleared it we shouted back to Major Argue, 'Okay, sir, it's clear.' I then started to clear another side with Captain McCracken, but we were stopped and held up by snipers. We couldn't move because we couldn't see them and we didn't have the nightscope with us. But later John Pettinger's sniper came up and – his rifle had a nightsight – took them both out.

We then eventually got up into the rock grooves where they had been. The first thing I heard was John Ross shouting up front and I realized that we were close to the enemy now. As we went forward, we cleared a bunker that someone obviously had gone through before us. There was a body lying with a blanket over it. I stopped the Company HQ moving towards it and said, 'Stay there. You don't find a body on a battlefield with a blanket over it. Something's wrong.' I said to the Engineer corporal, 'Stand at the bottom with my SMG and when I pull this blanket, if his hands move, shoot him.' As I pulled the blanket his hand moved to release a phosphorus grenade. My lad just let loose the magazine.

We had to push forward and from then onwards I was on the net a lot. We'd taken casualties by this time and Sergeant Des Fuller was looking pretty grim about what was going on. So he was dispatched forward to find exactly what had happened to 4 Platoon. He came back a half-hour later and said that 4 Platoon had been virtually wiped out, there were bodies all over the place, the casualties needed to be evacuated and the lads were out of ammunition. They were now using the enemy weapons and ammo. He said that Sergeant McKay had gone forward with a few guys to try and take out gun positions but the rest of the platoon were either injured or without leaders. Fuller was then given the order that he would take over 4 Platoon.

I went forward with Privates Lewis and Clarkson-Kearsley to see what the situation was. When I got down there, there was an officer lying injured and alongside him was Corporal Kelly. Further forward of them there was a number of dead, and to the left Sergeant McKay was in action, although I couldn't see him. I could hear Corporal McLaughlin shouting and a number of other people doing their best to try and fight forward to take these gun positions out. I heard over the net that 6 Platoon had taken some heavy casualties. I then went back to HQ and told them that I needed guys to evacuate casualties. Something had to be done – they were lying there in the battle zone, and they had to be got away from there and have treatment. I didn't have enough guys and because there were so many casualties it meant a number of trips which took a couple of hours. These four or five guys and I were going backwards and forwards under fire, taking guys out. I remember carrying one young lad out, I'll never forget him, he was alive when I carried him out, but he died in my arms – it was terrible. It was his eighteenth birthday.

I only had one medic, so on the net to Major Patton I said that I needed more and I needed stretcher bearers who could carry out my casualties to the RAP. He was trying to reassure me that they were coming, but they were a long time getting there. So I was still going backwards and forwards with the casualties. I didn't move the dead, there was nothing I could do for them. The priority was getting these casualties back. I got hold of Corporal Kelly, who was badly hurt, but he said, 'It's okay, John, I'll walk,' and he did. He was holding on to us, walking; it was unbelievable. The first man I carried out was Lieutenant Bickerdike, who was heavy. I was running with him on my back and he was screaming with pain. We got him out, but the problem was going back for the rest because all the time we were getting sniped at. We couldn't just run in and run out because it took so much time. By this stage I'd got Corporal Proberts, my medic, who did some fantastic jobs. The lads started to cry for ammunition, i.e. grenades and 66-mms, so I had to go forwards and grab the ammunition from the casualties and the dead and then get back and give it to the guys who needed it. But I wasn't the only one doing this.

I then got back and briefed Major Argue about 4 Platoon's situation. There were only a few guys left with Sergeant Fuller out of 20-odd. He'd taken command and just as I got back he'd also come back to brief Major Argue. He'd seen Sergeant McKay killed, and all the other men that had gone in with him were either injured or dead, so it meant we had to go down again to get the casualties out. While I was doing this Sergeant Ross and Mr Cox had lost contact with each other so 5 Platoon had got split. Mr Cox was running in one place and Sergeant Ross in another. It was chaos.

Something needed to be done to regroup and establish what we wanted to do. I got back from looking for the second-in-command to find a platoon commander crying. He'd seen death for the first time and it had shaken him. I gave him a good smack in the mouth because he was hysterical. I said, 'Pick your weapon up and get back and sort your platoon out. They need you.' I'll give him his due, he went back and sorted himself out, and did bloody well. It was sheer inexperience, because he'd never seen anything like it.

I then went back to see the casualties and although Corporal Proberts was still doing a fantastic job, I was still having no joy on the net trying to get somebody to help. I needed people to get the injured down to the RAP because they were losing blood. Corporal Kelly, who knew that if he lost much more blood he would die, also told them in fairly tough terms that he wanted somebody up there to get him out. The second-in-command had his problems, because he'd been ordered to bring ammunition up on the stretchers and the stretchers had got some distance away. So some of my injured guys were there seven to eleven hours, which is a long time. Eventually we got stretcher bearers up and the guy who came up and down that hill the most times was Cook Sergeant Marshall. He was up and down that hill all bloody night long. He was excellent and got a Mention in Despatches.

Other guys throughout the night were bayonet fighting, taking out the enemy trench by trench. I saw Gray and another lad take ground: they threw a grenade into the trench and then as soon as it had gone off they'd go in with bayonets. I jumped in one trench which they had cleared and there was a bloke lying in the bottom. I got the shock of my life when he moved. I nearly shot my toe off with my SMG trying to unload it! The enemy had to be taken out and the only way they could be taken out was by actual bayonet fighting. Dominic Gray and Ben Geoff and another little guy were into it all night long, because they had to be – there was no other way of taking the ground.

We then got A Company coming up and the first person I saw was Sergeant Major Docherty, who was the sergeant major of B Company before I took over. I said to him, 'Sammy, they've done bloody well tonight, but we can't do any more, we're just out of numbers.' Then I saw Major Collet come up and go forward to where he could see what the problem was. It was an anti-aircraft gun and obviously A Company would have to take that out – but that was their problem.

Before A Company arrived some of our company had tried a left-flanking move and four had been killed when they opened up on us. Captain McCracken came forward and fired a 66 straight into where the enemy were which stopped them straight away. He was really switched on, that guy, he was everywhere – he had a great big walrus moustache. We then went in and pulled the casualties out. By this time I'd got another medic, Lance Corporal Lovett, who was helping. Sadly, he was killed by shellfire.

The Argentinian artillery now realized we'd taken their positions so they were stomping us and we were starting to take casualties from this. We moved all platoons to the bottom of Mount Longdon. We stayed there about another 24 hours getting stomped. A Company moved forward and they called in Captain McCracken and asked him if he could bring in artillery fire. He said that he could bring it in within 25 metres. He brought it in brilliantly and without that we would have been bollocksed because we'd never have taken that ground. It was a natural feature for defence. There was everything you could want for a defence and the only thing they didn't have was the bottle, they didn't have the guts to go with it. By the time they had moved off, or surrendered, my lads had given everything, and I mean everything, and some had given their lives.

The next thing we had to do was get the bodies. The following morning when it was light, in between the artillery and the mortar coming down, we had to go and sort out the bodies and do the documentation. Although it sounds stupid, in battle you still have to account for everything and everybody and you have to fill in the bloody paperwork. I went round to the lads who were left and I asked if any of them would come and help me remove the bodies. I didn't particularly want to do it. I found it terribly hard to ask the guys and they found it terribly hard to say 'no' outright. They tried to make an excuse that they were too busy doing other things rather than say they didn't want to go down to their friends and bring their bodies up. Lewis and Clarkson-Kearsley were the only ones who said they'd come. Sammy Docherty also came because it needed four to carry a body on a poncho and get them all down to a central place.

Then Corporal Proberts and myself had the task of doing the documentation, taking off wedding rings and any personal effects and leaving one dog tag on. I then filled in the form to say where they had got the wounds. There was still artillery fire going on all the time we were doing this. Sammy Docherty and I were in tears taking Ian McKay's body, we knew him so well. I've seen dead bodies, loads of dead bodies; bodies don't actually bother me, but when they're people you know and you've got to get them into a body bag, which is a flat polythene thing, it's terrible. Sergeant Brian Faulkner and his crew came up to remove the body bags. Then I went down to the RAP to the padre with the personal effects of the dead.

One of those who died that black night was Corporal McLaughlin. He'd been a tower of strength throughout. Everywhere I looked, there he was; directing blokes, encouraging blokes forward to take these positions out, screaming and shouting, 'We're taking this one, I am now going right.' Telling the guys what to do, then moving back to brief the boss on what was going on. And again, when I went forward some hours later in a similar sort of area, there he was, screaming at blokes, 'We're taking them out – follow me!' He then came back after I got the casualties out and said, 'Is there anything else?' He was one of those guys that, if there was anything going on, he wanted to be amongst it. He was an extremely brave man. He was with Ian McKay when he took out bunkers and came out of that unscathed. People like him and Dominic Gray were the lifestay; they were all over the place, assisting everybody. Gray got two rounds in his head and still carried on fighting until he actually collapsed through lack of blood. Yet he didn't want to be carried back out, he wanted to stay till the bitter end. He was doing things beyond his job as a private soldier.

When there was a lull in battle we had to check equipment. We'd carried 84s (anti-tank rockets) all the way across the Falklands to find that every one we fired, misfired. The lads had carried a weapon weighing 35 pounds plus four shells, weighing six pounds each, only to find the bloody thing didn't work. That made them really angry.

We then moved towards Stanley itself to take the racecourse, but on the way down the surrender went up. Then it was a race between 2 and 3 Para to get into Stanley. The helmets came off for the first time and the red berets went on.

The next two weeks in Stanley gave the lads time to think, and a lot of sad boys there were in my company. They had time to reflect on what had happened. They'd lost friends. One minute their mate had been standing there, and the next he'd been hit by a shell and was just a mass of flesh all over the place. That scars the mind. It took a while to reassure them that they'd not died for nothing. But like us all they understood that we couldn't allow the Argentinians to take over the Falklands. Thank Christ we had Maggie, because she proved that you can't hold this country to ransom.

MAJOR PHILIP NEAME, 2nd Battalion
We began our move to Wireless Ridge with Lieutenant Colonel David Chaundler as our new CO. The move there involved a long night march in the snow. Just before, I had had a dose of the cook's special brew as had most of the company. Every time we stopped I had to step out of line and drop my trousers in the freezing cold for a quick one, much to the amusement of everyone else.

411

We went up into position just north of Longdon and waited for the order to assault Wireless Ridge. Our CO had promised that next time we weren't going anywhere without our full ration of artillery, so we began to feel a little more confident. But there was still a lingering feeling that we had already been through the mangle – my company had picked up eight dead, over half the battalion's total at Goose Green – and we would rather not go through the whole thing again, but if we had to, we had to.

Come the night, things weren't helped by the fact that the plan had changed at least three times. But then we had the reassurance that we'd never known an airborne exercise go off as planned. So when we went ashore at Sussex Mountain and again that night before Wireless Ridge, the toms took the very phlegmatic approach that it was like any other exercise they had ever been on – one big fuck-up! I didn't beat around the bush on this, reckoning it was better to admit things weren't going as planned, but at least keeping them in the picture. That made them feel involved in what was happening, not just pawns, and they were more ready to accept last-minute changes as a result. This helped morale which I think was the difference between us and the Argentinians. They weren't used to all this fucking around, and when it happened, as it always does in war, it got to them. In the case of our toms, it was almost a source of strength.

The main thing about Wireless Ridge was that we were the only company in the whole of that battle that actually had to assault in the face of organized opposition. We actually carried out three separate company attacks in that one night. The initial attack, however, went in with little opposition. We had really leathered it up with artillery before we actually got onto the position. We had also had light tanks from the Blues and Royals, and machine-guns supporting us, so by the time we started moving through it, whatever enemy had been there – anything between a platoon and a company – had already thinned out and all we found was isolated resistance, which was quickly dispatched. So we got onto the position quite pleased with ourselves. The thing about the Argentinians really was that you'd attack positions, and you'd find a large proportion of them completely unready. With all this battle going on around them they would be lying in the bottom of the trenches, or even asleep in their sleeping bags with their hoods up – a sleep of fear really. It's what I call the ostrich factor: they had buried their heads, thinking, 'It's not happening, it won't happen to me, I'm not here . . .'

At Goose Green we never met co-ordinated resistance but here for the first time we did. We were still clearing the first position when we began to get extremely heavy artillery down on us. I had been told to reorganize on the position but there was just no way I was going to do that so we pushed straight through and reorganized about 300 yards further on. The enemy's own artillery completed the job of clearing the position for us!

After A and B Companies had taken their objectives we set off for our next target – the first part of the main ridge line. Again with artillery support and the Blues and Royals providing spot-on response, we met very little opposition. We should have gone straight into an attack on our third and final objective which was known to be very strongly held. I told our FOO (Forward Observation Officer) to fire on the final target but for one reason or another he called for the wrong target number and the next five rounds landed straight on us, which completely broke our momentum. It wounded one section commander and killed another. This lad had already been injured and casevac'd; he'd recovered, returned to us and now, of all things, he'd been killed by our own artillery. It seemed a complete waste. These things happen in war, far worse had happened in the past and far worse will probably happen in the future, but it made me really mad.

We tried again, but the rounds were now landing rather closer to B Company than the enemy. I was getting all ready to assault and then had to call a halt while the artillery went through this long system of adjusting the fire onto the target. We were actually overlooking the enemy position at this time and thank God we had the tanks in support, because they were able, from the flank, to keep firing at the enemy positions and keep them occupied. The enemy remained totally unaware that we were sitting on a bald, open slope just a few hundred yards to their left and above them.

The artillery finally got some rounds on target. 'At last,' I thought. We were literally about to assault when once again the artillery had to stop firing because some rounds had again been landing on B Company. It clearly wasn't B Company's night! I could not advance without fire support and my feelings were, especially having already had 30-odd rounds of our own artillery on my position, that B Company could live with one gun sending the odd round their way while we got on with the war and out of a very nasty situation. But there was no way I could persuade anyone to change their minds. So we then had to go through the farcical rigmarole of firing each gun in turn to try and find out which one needed re-aligning. There we were, literally within spitting distance of the enemy, while this sort of peacetime safety procedure went on – and I got a bollocking for not assaulting earlier! I began to think that it really wasn't my night either, and began to get extremely short-tempered with a number of people.

Eventually we had four out of six guns lined up. I said, 'Sod it, I've had enough. We won't bother with the other two, we'll just go in with what we've got.' I gave the order to attack. The trouble was we'd completely lost our momentum. The toms had almost grown roots waiting in the cold and by this time were very sceptical of our artillery support. I yelled, 'Advance!' and stood up myself, and nothing happened! I thought, 'Shit,' and yelled, 'Advance!' again and the cry was taken up and slowly everyone began to move forward unopposed. We got within about 100 yards of the enemy position when one of the toms put up an illuminating round earlier than he should have done, which attracted the enemy who realized that the assault was coming not from the front but from their flank. So of course everything that they'd got was turned on us. There we were, in the middle of a very exposed, totally bald, little valley with no cover at all, suddenly confronted with this withering hail of small arms fire, accompanied all the time by incoming enemy artillery! Everyone hit the deck. Direct fire at night always is rather more frightening than in daylight.

I thought, 'Fucking hell, what do I do next?' I was almost at a loss, knowing that it was my job to get the assault going but not at all keen on moving myself! I learned a great truth from that moment – if in doubt, start shouting. I'm not normally a great shouter, but I started shouting for all I was worth! Then I heard other people start to shout. I got up and ran a few yards and I could see other people moving and suddenly it all got into its stride again. The blokes started working as they had been trained to do: fire and manoeuvre, moving in pairs, and so on. It suddenly began to happen once more. I lost my signaller in the middle of it all. I thought he had been shot. But as he is as black as the ace of spades there was little chance of finding him that night, so I moved off without him.

Fortunately I had my own personal radio so I was able to talk to the platoon commanders, but there was no way that I could talk back to Battalion HQ. I had also by that stage lost touch with our artillery observation officer. So the only fire I had in support were the tanks which were on the company net. I was able to keep talking to them and they did a great job in chasing the enemy off the ridge in front of us. As we hit the enemy they began to cut and run. If I had gone by the School of Infantry handbook we'd have cleared each position systematically step by step, at a relatively slow and controlled pace, one position at a time. But I remember this distinct feeling that all we had to do was to keep moving very fast and keep the enemy on the run ahead of us. If we went slowly they'd leave one set of positions and reorganize in a further set of positions and we'd have to fight all the way along. So I started to keep the pace moving as briskly as I could, but the platoons on either side of me were trying to conduct things as they'd been trained, in a slightly more measured and controlled way. At one

414

stage, Sergeant Meredith or Sergeant O'Rawe was yelling at some of his guys because the company commander was ahead of them.

We kept on the move so quickly that the enemy didn't have the chance to go firm anywhere until we got to this area called the Telegraph Wires. This was the limit of our exploitation as the SAS were operating further east of that. The ridge line carried on ahead of us, so it was an absurd place to stop, just no obvious feature, but we stopped there as ordered. I guess the Argentinians who were running along ahead of us must have thought we had run out of steam, because from that direction we got this counter-attack. Jon Page, whose platoon I had left up that end, managed to get hold of our artillery by flicking his radio onto their net, as we were still without our FOO. That broke up their attack. I made my way back to Meredith and Page. In the last 30 or 40 yards I had to get across the top of the hillside itself. I became vaguely aware of a lot of shit coming my way. This was confirmed by Meredith who told me to 'fuck off' as I was attracting a lot of shit his way! His platoon was having a very, very rough time indeed. They couldn't move without attracting extremely accurate small arms fire.

There was sporadic artillery fire going on the whole time which one began to live with, but this was really most uncomfortable and the whole platoon was virtually pinned down and couldn't move. A lot of this fire was coming from Tumbledown as 5 Brigade's attack had started late and the Argentinian positions there dominated Wireless Ridge. But I think a lot was coming from snipers on the slope above Moody Brook that we hadn't cleared. There was a lot of shit flying around and it was very hairy for anyone to move about. All this had rather delayed my sorting out exactly what ground I wanted 10 and 11 Platoons to cover. I'd sent my runner, Hanley, back to try and locate the rest of my Company HQ, but he'd not found them as they were further back, still dealing with casualties. So he'd got the two platoon commanders together and started tying up details with them on his own initiative.

Then as daylight broke we got another counter-attack, this time from the Moody Brook side onto Sean Webster's platoon. I wondered what we had got into and thought this was most unlike the Argentinians. For a while they were quite persistent. They got close enough to throw grenades but didn't drive home their attack, a 'Latin' gesture, and we won.

I then met up with Corporal Osborne, my signaller, whom I'd lost at the start of the attack. I thought he'd been hit but he'd actually fallen into an Argentinian shit hole. As I could now get on the battalion net again I called up a fire mission onto the Moody Brook area which quickly discouraged any other counter-attack. Those three hours between starting our final attack and daylight were for me the most harrowing period of the whole war, especially with the cock-ups from the artillery breaking our momentum and losing contact with the CO, and then the counter-attacks. But about half an hour after daylight we saw the Argentinians pulling off Tumbledown. It was an amazing sight. They virtually marched off in single file.

I had been trying to get fire missions down on the retreating closely packed formation of troops but was told that there was no artillery available. I was going quite spare, because I was supposed to have two batteries at my priority call. Here was a golden opportunity being missed. I assumed the enemy were withdrawing to regroup on Sapper Hill and the last thing I wanted was another major battle. Eventually we got the artillery and started blasting away with everything else we had as well. But as soon as we opened up we got very accurate artillery fire back at our own position. I guessed that they were adjusting onto our muzzle flashes so I told the company to stop firing with their small arms. I decided that the only thing was to keep fighting this battle with artillery, otherwise we were just going to have a lot of shit knocked out of ourselves.

The CO then came up and couldn't understand this and I tried to explain what my reservations were but he told me to keep firing with everything I had. Very gingerly I got just two machine-guns to open up to avoid exposing our own position. The machine-guns opened up and nothing came back at us so I felt an absolute idiot! What had of course happened was that during my conversation with the CO the Argentinians had thrown in the towel. We were now able to do anything we liked, so the whole thing turned into a turkey shoot. We were firing away with machine-guns and it was just a slaughter. I think for different reasons David Chaundler told us to stop firing. The change was just so abrupt, within the space of a few minutes, from well-organized opposition to the surrender. We were still on the hilltop when the news of the ceasefire came over.

Everyone stood up and took their helmets off and put their red berets on for the first time in months, just to let everyone know that it was the Parachute Regiment who had won the war. And in much the same way as at the end of an exercise, everyone who had spare ammunition fired it off – smoke grenades, the lot. What really won the day was the quality of the blokes we had, probably the best trained soldiers in the world. We had come through the cauldron and had lost some very brave blokes indeed. Now this fantastic little force one had built up and worked with had done its bit. We marched into Stanley knowing that we were never going to do anything like that again. It was difficult to come to terms with.

What really scored for us was team effort. I think I was lucky, I had some excellent subordinates and it didn't need too much from me to produce results. It was all very effortless and rewarding, very rarely lonely or frightening. As much as I led them they carried me. And though not all of us got back, and I'm sad for their families, I never really mourned them, because for me they're still there, part of the team.

LIEUTENANT COLONEL DAVID CHAUNDLER, 2nd Battalion

We had fought all night amid driving snow flurries and comparatively heavy Argentinian artillery fire which they used effectively to shell each one of our objectives soon after their capture when, standing on the final objective captured by Phil Neame's D Company, we saw a remarkable sight. Off to the east we could see Port Stanley under a pall of smoke, but below us the Moody Brook valley seemed suddenly full of Argentinians as their army broke and, looking like black ants, were pouring out of Moody Brook and off Tumbledown and Sapper Hill across the valley and walking back to Port Stanley – an utterly defeated army. We were of course, firing at them with everything we had. The machine-gun platoon was up, as were the Scorpions and Scimitars of the Blues and Royals and the battery commander was in seventh heaven having asked for, and got, a regimental fire mission. It is difficult to describe the elation we felt when, all of a sudden, I realized we were in danger of crossing that moral threshold where what we were doing was no longer acceptable. I ordered a ceasefire.

It was now evident we must get into Port Stanley before the Argentinians had time to reorganize. John Crosland's B Company moved down through Moody Brook onto the high ground on the other side of the valley, followed by Dair Farrar-Hockley's A Company onto the Port Stanley road. And so at one o'clock, some six hours before the official ceasefire – with D Company, the Troop of the Blues and Royals and C Company of 3 Para, who had come off Mount Longdon, following up – we entered Port Stanley, the first British troops since the Argentinian invasion eleven weeks before. As we walked down that road and the realization began to dawn that it was all over, without orders, steel helmets came off and out of pockets came crumpled red berets as yet another generation came of age proud to wear the beret that has symbolized the airborne soldier from North Africa, through Sicily, Normandy, Arnhem, the Rhine Crossing and the many campaigns since 1945. Like them, we had come through.

Acknowledgements

I would like to thank all serving and former members of the Airborne Forces who told me of their personal experiences and who, throughout the writing of this book, gave me their utmost support and co-operation. Sadly, a place could not be found for every person's story, but all deserved one. I would also like to thank those closely connected with the Airborne Forces, in particular the families and wives whom I met whose stories should also be told and the people of Holland whose hearts have such an affection for those who came to liberate them. As Secretary of the Parachute Regimental Association, Colonel David Mallam was most helpful in introducing me to many members of the Association, and Mrs Pat Black helped me to trace many people. I am most grateful to them both.

I am indebted to Colonel John Waddy not only for writing the Brief History of British Airborne Forces (originally published in *Pegasus*), but for reading through the manuscript and making a number of valuable suggestions. Major Miles Whitelock and Captain Arthur Kellas kindly contributed to the account of the early days of parachuting and the formation of No. 2 Commando.

Sarah Mnatzaganian worked skilfully to restructure a number of the accounts and I thank her. Richard Cohen, as publishing director of Hutchinson, was highly supportive throughout the writing of this book and was ably backed by Robin Cross, Alex McIntosh, and Annelise Evans.

I would also like to express my appreciation of the kind co-operation of all those who supplied photographs for reproduction in the book, viz: the Airborne Forces Museum, Captain H. B. Booty, Camerapress, Cassidy & Leigh, Colonel Bill Corby, the *Daily Express*, Peter Geraghty, Hulton Picture Company, the Imperial War Museum, Marshall Cavendish, Chris Maude, Pacemaker Press Agency, Richard Pohle, the Press Association, Les Prudden, Brigadier Rendell, the Robert Hunt Library, T. Spencer (Orbis), and United Press International.

Finally I thank Carolyn Mallam who transcribed all the taped interviews and typed the many-times-amended accounts in this book.

APPENDIX

A Brief History of British Airborne Forces

In 1940, Britain's darkest hour, when Britain faced invasion, the Prime Minister, Mr Winston Churchill, sought the means to strike back at the enemy. One example was his memo of 22 June, instructing the War Office '. . . we ought to have a corps of at least 5,000 parachute troops . . .' and it is from this date that British airborne forces start their history. Despite a lack of experience and equipment, a small band of resourceful men began at once to create this new force. Events moved fast; the Central Landing School was set up at Ringway, Manchester, by Army and RAF staff: men of No. 2 Commando were selected for training, and the first jumps carried out on 13 July. In September the first Hotspur gliders were ordered.

By the end of 1940, 2 Commando, now 500 strong with a parachute and a glider wing, was renamed 11th Special Air Service Battalion. In February 1941, only nine months after formation, the first airborne operation took place, when 38 men parachuted into Southern Italy to destroy the Tragino Aqueduct.

After these tentative trials, 1941 was a year of development and expansion. The 1st Parachute Brigade was formed in September, and shortly afterwards, an infantry brigade became the 1st Airlanding Brigade, with four airlanding battalions and supporting arms and services, to start training with the gliders now coming off the production line. In India the 50th Indian Parachute Brigade was formed. Major General F. A. M. Browning was appointed Commander Paratroops and Airborne Troops. From his small HQ, the 1st Airborne Division was formed in November. In December, the Glider Pilot Regiment was established, as part of the Army Air Corps, to fly the gliders: initially Hotspurs and Wacos, then Horsas and

Hamilcars. The officer and sergeant pilots, all trained soldiers, fought many gallant actions alongside the airborne troops they had landed. Later in August 1942, all parachute battalions became battalions of The Parachute Regiment in this new corps.

In February 1942, C Company 2nd Parachute Battalion, under Major John Frost, carried out the highly successful parachute raid to capture a vital part of a German radar installation at Bruneval in northern France. During the year, the 1st Airborne Division was built up, based on the original two brigades, with the newly formed 2nd Parachute Brigade, together with a full complement of supporting arms and services, trained to land by parachute or glider. 38 Group RAF was created to work closely with the division. In November, 1st, 2nd and 3rd Battalions carried out three separate battalion parachute operations in North Africa, to support the First Army's advance towards Tunis. During the winter of 1942, the 1st Parachute Brigade fought hard battles in the Tunisian hills, earning a reputation within the Army as high-class infantry: and, from their German opponents, the name 'Red Devils'.

In May 1943, this brigade was joined by the rest of 1st Airborne Division in North Africa, and by the 4th Parachute Brigade from the Middle East. Preparations started for further airborne operations into Southern Europe. In the UK, 6th Airborne Division was created, based on the 3rd Parachute Brigade, and two of the original airlanding battalions. Other elements were converted to form 5th Parachute Brigade and the divisional units. The 1st Canadian Parachute Battalion joined the 6th Airborne Division at this time. On 10 July 1943, British and American airborne troops spearheaded the Allied invasion of Sicily. 1st Airlanding Brigade in their gliders landed first, followed three days later by 1st Parachute Brigade. Landings were scattered and casualties were heavy, especially among the glider-borne troops but the objectives were taken. In September the division operated briefly in Southern Italy, before returning to England, less 2nd Parachute Brigade Group, to prepare for the invasion of Europe.

On 6 June 1944, D-Day, 6th Airborne Division carried out an airborne assault into Normandy to seize important bridges, to destroy the battery at Merville, and to hold the high ground overlooking the left flank of the Allied bridgehead. Using aggressive tactics against strong enemy attacks, the division, with the commandos of the 1st Special Service Brigade, held their ground for the next two months. Meanwhile, in Italy, 2nd Parachute Brigade, after fighting in the line for nearly six months, took part in the Allied invasion of the South of France on 5 August. Two weeks later, the brigade was withdrawn to prepare for the liberation of Greece. Landing near

Athens, they helped the Allied Forces bring peace to the country amidst a bitter civil war.

In September, as the Allies approached Germany, 1st Airborne Division, with 82nd and 101st US Airborne Divisions, mounted Operation Market Garden, an attempt to secure the bridges needed for an advance into Germany. 1st Airborne Division's objective, the bridge at Arnhem, was held for four days, and remnants of the division fought on for another five days until ordered to withdraw.

Just before Christmas 1944, 6th Airborne Division was hurriedly despatched to the Ardennes to help stem the German counter-offensive, which threatened to split the Allied armies. After fighting in the snow-covered forests for two months, the division was withdrawn to prepare for the final airborne operation of the war in Europe. In one huge air armada, 6th British and 17th US Airborne Divisions were landed on the east bank of the River Rhine near Wesel. After a pause, the division fought on across Germany to reach the Baltic first, and to meet the advancing Russian Army.

As the war in Europe ended, the re-formed 1st Airborne Division, after a short spell in Norway, was disbanded, and many of its units amalgamated into the 6th Airborne Division, which was ordered to the Far East for further airborne operations. 5th Parachute Brigade, already there at the time of the Japanese surrender, landed by sea in Malaya and was then sent on to Java to help restore order. In September 1945, 6th Airborne Division was sent to Palestine to be part of the Middle East strategic reserve, but instead became embroiled in the long and thankless task of maintaining peace in that troubled land. With the final withdrawal in 1948 from Palestine the division was disbanded.

British Airborne Forces which in 1944 numbered some 35,000, were now reduced to one brigade, the 2nd Parachute Brigade Group in Germany and this became the nucleus of the post-war Regular Airborne Force. It was re-designated 16th Parachute Brigade Group, and its battalions merged with those returned from Palestine, to be the present 1st, 2nd and 3rd Battalions of The Parachute Regiment, together with supporting Arms and Services. In 1947, a Territorial Airborne Division was formed, also numbered 16 to maintain the numbers of the two original divisions. This formation was recruited through the length and breadth of the UK. In 1956, it was reduced to one brigade group, the 44th.

The immediate post-war internal security operations in Java and Palestine were a distinct change from the more dramatic airborne warfare of the past, but they were, in differing forms, to be the continuing pattern for the next 40 years.

In 1951, 16th Parachute Brigade, starting to regain its airborne capability, was sent to Cyprus at the time of the Anglo-Iranian oil crisis, but soon became involved in maintaining the security of the Suez Canal Zone. This corner of the world became familiar to the brigade, for in 1956 it returned to Cyprus on stand-by to intervene in the Suez Canal situation, but instead it was drawn into the anti-EOKA operations in the mountains of Cyprus, breaking off briefly to carry out the unique parachute assault to capture the airfield at Port Said by the 3rd Battalion, which was followed by the rest of the brigade landing by sea. In 1958, the brigade was again in Cyprus, when there was trouble in Lebanon, but at short notice it was flown into Jordan to protect the sovereignty of that country.

In 1961, the 2nd Battalion, based in Cyprus, flew into Kuwait to deter a threatened Iraqi invasion, and for the next six years a parachute battalion group was stationed in the Arabian Gulf. The 3rd Battalion in 1964 fought an old-fashioned mountain war against dissidents in the Radfan, north of Aden. In 1965, the 2nd Battalion, with D Company 3rd Battalion, were in the jungles of Borneo, defending the borders against Indonesian infiltration. A Parachute Squadron had gained previous experience of jungle warfare in the mid-50s serving with the Special Air Service Regiment in Malaya. Back in Aden again in 1967, the 1st Battalion had to deal with urban terrorists in the last months of that colony.

The Parachute Regiment, in 1969, started the first of its many tours in Northern Ireland, which have continued throughout the past 20 years.

In 1977, as a defence economy measure, a sad decision was taken by the Ministry of Defence to disband the Army's most flexible formation, the 16th Parachute Brigade Group, and to disperse its units under other HQs; a year later, its counterpart in the Territorial Army, the highly effective 44th Parachute Brigade Group, met the same fate.

Nevertheless, in 1982, when the Argentinians invaded the Falkland Islands, and swift, decisive action was demanded, the Parachute Forces, with the Royal Marine Commandos, were to the fore, all operating under command of HQ 3rd Commando Brigade. The actions of the 2nd Battalion at Goose Green and on Wireless Ridge; of the 3rd Battalion in their march across the island to Teal Inlet, and on Mount Longdon, with their affiliated Parachute and Commando Artillery, Engineers, Signals and Medical units, showed that they still maintained the same skill and the same spirit of their forebears, some 40 years before, who fought in the hills of Tunisia, the woods of Normandy and the houses of Arnhem.

Today the same traditions are retained within the new 5th Airborne Brigade, and by the three separate parachute battalions of the Territorial Army.

Index

NOTES: Personnel are indexed under their most senior rank
Page numbers in **bold** type indicate Chapter headings, or contributors' names